A Casebook on Chinese Outbound Investment

China remains one of the top capital exporters in the world, yet there is a paucity of reliable sources through which to assess Chinese corporate decision-making, the implementation of Chinese-financed and Chinese-managed projects, and the socioeconomic effects of those projects. The *Casebook* fills this gap by providing fifteen case studies written by experts and researchers, many from host states and who have firsthand knowledge of the transaction or dispute in question. Case studies are written primarily based on primary source material, including transactional documents, interviews with stakeholders, laws and regulations, and case decisions. Educators in professional schools, including law, policy, and business, will find in the *Casebook* material to supplement class discussions pertaining to Chinese overseas investment, Chinese investment strategies, and the nature of the Chinese firm. This title is also available as Open Access on Cambridge Core.

Matthew S. Erie is an associate professor at the University of Oxford. He practiced law in Beijing and New York City before entering academia. A comparativist and anthropologist by training, he has taught law in the United States, United Kingdom, Singapore, Cambodia, Pakistan, and China.

A Casebook on Chinese Outbound Investment

Law, Policy, and Business

Edited by
MATTHEW S. ERIE
University of Oxford

Shaftesbury Road, Cambridge CB2 8EA, United Kingdom

One Liberty Plaza, 20th Floor, New York, NY 10006, USA

477 Williamstown Road, Port Melbourne, VIC 3207, Australia

314–321, 3rd Floor, Plot 3, Splendor Forum, Jasola District Centre, New Delhi – 110025, India

103 Penang Road, #05–06/07, Visioncrest Commercial, Singapore 238467

Cambridge University Press is part of Cambridge University Press & Assessment, a department of the University of Cambridge.

We share the University's mission to contribute to society through the pursuit of education, learning and research at the highest international levels of excellence.

www.cambridge.org
Information on this title: www.cambridge.org/9781009457866

DOI: 10.1017/9781009457859

© Cambridge University Press & Assessment 2025

This publication is in copyright. Subject to statutory exception and to the provisions of relevant collective licensing agreements, with the exception of the Creative Commons version the link for which is provided below, no reproduction of any part may take place without the written permission of Cambridge University Press & Assessment.

An online version of this work is published at doi.org/10.1017/9781009457859 under a Creative Commons Open Access license CC-BY-NC-ND 4.0 which permits re-use, distribution and reproduction in any medium for non-commercial purposes providing appropriate credit to the original work is given. You may not distribute derivative works without permission. To view a copy of this license, visit https://creativecommons.org/licenses/by-nc-nd/4.0

When citing this work, please include a reference to the DOI 10.1017/9781009457859

First published 2025

A catalogue record for this publication is available from the British Library

Library of Congress Cataloging-in-Publication Data
Names: Erie, Matthew S., editor.
Title: A casebook on Chinese outbound investment : law, policy, and business / edited by Matthew S. Erie, University of Oxford.
Description: Cambridge, United Kingdom ; New York, NY : Cambridge University Press, 2025. | Includes bibliographical references and index.
Identifiers: LCCN 2024047309 | ISBN 9781009457866 (hardback) | ISBN 9781009457811 (paperback) | ISBN 9781009457859 (ebook)
Subjects: LCSH: Investments, Foreign – Law and legislation – China – Case studies. | Corporations, Chinese – Law and legislation – Case studies. | Corporations, Chinese – Finance – Law and legislation – Case studies. | LCGFT: Casebooks (Law)
Classification: LCC KNQ3202 .C37 2025 | DDC 346.51/092–dc23/eng/20241008
LC record available at https://lccn.loc.gov/2024047309

ISBN 978-1-009-45786-6 Hardback
ISBN 978-1-009-45781-1 Paperback

Cambridge University Press & Assessment has no responsibility for the persistence or accuracy of URLs for external or third-party internet websites referred to in this publication and does not guarantee that any content on such websites is, or will remain, accurate or appropriate.

Contents

List of Figures	*page* viii
List of Tables	x
List of Contributors	xi
Acknowledgments	xiv
List of Abbreviations	xv

	Introduction Matthew S. Erie	1

SECTION 1 CORPORATIONS

Case Study 1.1	Alibaba and Ant Group: Developing a Hybrid Chinese-International E-commerce Platform Ecosystem Colin Hawes	27
Case Study 1.2	Chinese M&A in Latin America: Jiangsu Yanghe Distillery's Stake Acquisition in VSPT Wine Group in Chile Ignacio Tornero	48

SECTION 2 COMPLIANCE

Case Study 2.1	Africa's Tech Challenge: A Chinese State-Owned Enterprise's Corporate Social Responsibility Experiment in Kenya Yuan Wang	67
Case Study 2.2	State Grid's Localization Strategies in Belo Monte, Brazil Marco Germanò	88
Case Study 2.3	TikTok versus United States Han Liu and Ji Li	113

SECTION 3 INFRASTRUCTURE

Case Study 3.1 The Colombo Port City Project: How Chinese Investment Interacts with Local Public Law 133
Dilini Pathirana and Dinesha Samararatne

Case Study 3.2 The Lower Sesan II: Human Rights Implications for Chinese Overseas Projects 156
Leigha Crout and Michael Liu

Case Study 3.3 The Special Economic Zone at Duqm, Oman: A Chinese-Invested Strategic Port 172
Otari Kakhidze

SECTION 4 LABOR

Case Study 4.1 Chinese Workers and Forced Labor on the Imperial Pacific Casino Project in Saipan 197
Aaron Halegua

Case Study 4.2 The Impact of Chinese Investments on the Gold Mining Sector in Kyrgyzstan 212
Nuraiym Syrgak kyzy and Robin Lee

SECTION 5 FINANCE

Case Study 5.1 Sovereign Debt Restructuring in Zambia: A Chinese Approach 235
Charles Ho Wang Mak

Case Study 5.2 Exiting International Joint Ventures between Chinese and South African Banks 248
Thembi Madalane

SECTION 6 DISPUTING

Case Study 6.1 Chinese Overseas Investment and Environmental Accountability: A Legal Battle against the Chinese-Financed Coal-Fired Power Plant in Boké, Guinea 267
Jingjing Zhang and Emily Scherr

Case Study 6.2 Micron versus UMC and Fujian Jinhua: The Cross-Border Struggle over Integrated Circuits' Trade Secrets 284
Kai-Shen Huang

Case Study 6.3 The Use of Foreign Investment Treaties in the Protection of Chinese Outbound Investments: *Zhongshan Fucheng Industrial Investment Co. Ltd. v. Federal Republic of Nigeria* 297
Ngozi S. Nwoko and Stanley U. Nweke-Eze

Index 319

Figures

1.1.1	Alibaba Group VIE ownership structure	page 33
1.1.2	Alibaba/Ant ecosystem	38
1.2.1	Evolution of Chinese FDI into Chile	49
1.2.2	Increase in wine exports from Chile to China, 2003–2018 (in US$)	56
1.2.3	Main steps of M&As in Chile	59
1.2.4	Roadmap of the project	60
2.1.1	Kenya's export basket, 2020	71
2.1.2	AVIC INTL-PEC shareholding structure	75
2.2.1	Overview of SGCC's global assets, 2021	90
2.2.2	The Belo Monte dam and its location in Brazil	98
2.2.3	Belo Monte dam's daily average energy production, 26 February 2016 to 30 December 2023 (median megawatts, MWmed)	100
2.2.4	Design of the Xingu-Estreito transmission line highlighting ecological parks, buffer zones, and conservation units	103
2.2.5	Design of the Xingu-Rio transmission line detailing sections handled by EPC contractors	106
2.2.6	SGCC's assets in Brazil via SGBH and CPFL, 2021	107
2.2.7	Market share by nationality in Brazil's generation, transmission, and distribution sectors, 2010–2019 respectively	109
3.3.1	Oman–PRC trade statistics	178
3.3.2	Implemented and planned zones at the SEZAD	191
4.2.1	Tilted view of Ishtamberdy mine	217
4.2.2	Aerial view of Ishtamberdy mine	217
4.2.3	Aerial view of Kulu-Tegerek deposit at Kichi-Chaarat mine	220
4.2.4	Tilted view of Suluu-Tegerek deposit at the Kichi-Chaarat mine	220
5.2.1	Standard Bank and ICBC combined footprint	251
5.2.2	ICBC Standard Bank Group structure	251
5.2.3	ICBCS annual profit/loss, 2015–2021	259
6.1.1	SMB's operations in Guinea: (a) truck transporting bauxite on an SMB mining road in Boké; (b) trucks kicking up dust on an SMB mining road in Boké; (c) mounds of bauxite at SMB headquarters in Boké; (d) front gate of SMB operations in Boké	277

List of Figures

6.1.2	CTEA Executive Director, Jingjing Zhang, meeting with the Wawayiré village in the Boké prefecture	279
6.3.1	Annual flow of foreign direct investments from China to Nigeria between 2011 and 2021 (million US$)	300
6.3.2	Map of Ogun Guangdong free trade zone	301

Tables

1.2.1	Main producers of *baijiu* in China, 2020–2022	page 51
1.2.2	Schedule of tariff reduction in the Chile-China FTA	55
1.2.3	Main risks and challenges faced by Chinese companies in their ODIs	57
1.2.4	Main shareholders of VSPT as of 31 December 2017	61
2.1.1	The seven ATC seasons and coverage	84
3.3.1	Oman facts	175
4.2.1	Information on interview respondents	215
5.2.1	ICBC Standard Bank Plc exit mechanisms	256
6.3.1	List of primary documents	299
6.3.2	Summary table of cases	307

Contributors

Leigha Crout is an associate professor at Syracuse University College of Law. She writes and teaches on the subjects of international law, comparative constitutional law, and human rights.

Matthew S. Erie is an associate professor at the University of Oxford. He practiced law in Beijing and New York City before entering academia. A comparativist and anthropologist by training, he has taught law in the United States, United Kingdom, Singapore, Cambodia, Pakistan, and China.

Marco Germanò is a research associate at the University of Oxford and a research assistant at the Institute of Applied Economic Research, Brazil. He holds a master's degree from Peking University and has held visiting researcher positions at the National Autonomous University of Mexico and the University of California, Berkeley.

Aaron Halegua is a practicing lawyer based in New York City and a research fellow at New York University School of Law and the University of Oxford. He assisted 2,400 Chinese construction workers trafficked to Saipan to recover US$14 million in backpay. Aaron has also written extensively on labor issues with China's Belt and Road Initiative.

Colin Hawes is an associate professor in the Law Faculty, University of Technology Sydney, Australia. He has published widely on Chinese corporations, law, and culture, including three books, the latest being *The Chinese Corporate Ecosystem* (Cambridge University Press, 2022).

Kai-Shen Huang is a research fellow at the Research Institute for Democracy, Society and Emerging Technology under the National Science and Technology Council (Taiwan). He specializes in China's critical technology policies and the application of AI in dispute resolution and public administration.

Otari Kakhidze is a former UNESCO Great Wall fellow at the School of Law of Tsinghua University. His research focuses on the intellectual property, digital, and transport aspects of Chinese development.

Robin Lee is a researcher and writes under a pen name. Their work concerns law and globalization. Robin has a policy background.

Ji Li is the John & Marilyn Long Professor of US-China Business and Law at the University of California, Irvine. His recent book, *Negotiating Legality* (Cambridge University Press, 2024), explores how Chinese multinational companies interact with the intricate US legal system.

Han Liu is an associate professor of law at Tsinghua University specializing in comparative constitutional law and cyber law. He regularly advises on cybersecurity law and cross-border litigations involving leading high-tech firms, with his opinions accepted by administrative agencies and courts in China and other jurisdictions.

Michael Liu is a PhD candidate at the Van Vollenhoven Institute for Law, Governance and Society of Leiden University. Previously, Michael was a victims' counsel at the Extraordinary Chambers in the Courts of Cambodia and taught international law at the Royal University of Law and Economics in Phnom Penh, Cambodia.

Thembi Madalane is a research associate at the University of Oxford. She is appointed to the General Commercial Panel of the Arbitration Foundation of Southern Africa, the principal organization of the China-Africa Joint Arbitration Centre. Her PhD at the University of Szeged, Hungary, involves investment dispute settlement related to China.

Charles Ho Wang Mak is a PhD candidate in law at the University of Glasgow and a lecturer in law at Robert Gordon University.

Stanley U. Nweke-Eze is a legal practitioner and academic, admitted to practice law in Nigeria, New York, and England and Wales. He is finalizing a PhD program in International Investment Law (Hong Kong University) and holds LLM degrees in Commercial Law (University of Cambridge) and International Economic Law (Harvard University).

Ngozi S. Nwoko is a sessional lecturer at the Faculty of Law, University of Victoria, Canada, where he teaches Business Associations and Immigration & Citizenship Law. His research is on the regulation of Chinese investments in the extractive industries in Africa and Canada.

Dilini Pathirana is a senior lecturer in the Department of Commercial Law at the Faculty of Law, University of Colombo, Sri Lanka. Her research interests lie mainly in international investment law, focusing on the legal and (geo)political implications of Chinese investments in Sri Lanka.

List of Contributors

Dinesha Samararatne is a professor at the Department of Public and International Law, Faculty of Law, University of Colombo, Sri Lanka. Her research interests include judicial review, constitutionalism and the Global South, fourth branch institutions, women and constitutions, and the rule of law.

Emily Scherr is an environmental lawyer practicing in the United States and was a former staff attorney with the Center for Transnational Environmental Accountability. She graduated from the University of Maryland School of Law in 2020.

Nuraiym Syrgak kyzy is a researcher at Data Solutions and an executive director of the nonprofit organization Jaratylysh (organizations pseudonymized) based in Kyrgyzstan. She has worked as a research consultant for national and regional organizations on various topics: children and youth development, informal employment, women entrepreneurship, climate change, and religion.

Ignacio Tornero is a lawyer and business professional and the founder and CEO of the business and legal consulting firm East Consulting. He is an adjunct professor at the Pontifical Catholic University of Chile.

Yuan Wang is an assistant professor of international relations at Duke Kunshan University.

Jingjing Zhang is a China-trained environmental lawyer, the executive director of the Center for Transnational Environmental Accountability, and a lecturer at the University of Maryland. She works on transnational environmental and climate lawsuits to ensure Chinese companies comply with environmental laws and international human rights norms for their investments overseas.

Acknowledgments

This book is the result of a collaborative effort that has spanned several years, including early planning during the COVID-19 pandemic, and the help that persons and institutions provided requires acknowledgment.

First and foremost, I am grateful for the support of the University of Oxford, which has served as institutional host for the "China, Law and Development" (CLD) project from 2019 to 2024. The CLD project, which takes as its aim the study of how Chinese parties engage with questions of international law and the legal and regulatory systems of host states that receive Chinese capital, could not have been possible without institutional support from the Faculty of Asian and Middle Eastern Studies, the Law Faculty, the Centre for Socio-Legal Studies, and the China Centre.

I thank the European Research Council (ERC) for funding the CLD project through a Starting Grant under the European Union's Horizon 2020 research and innovation program (Grant Agreement No. 803763). The ERC grant provided essential funding for research, writing, administrative support, and publication costs.

I am incredibly grateful to the contributors of this book, each of whom is either from the country in question, has worked on some aspect of the transaction or dispute they discuss, or is otherwise deeply enmeshed in the questions they explore. In spite of their busy schedules, contributors have devoted considerable time to writing and revising their case study to make sure it accomplishes the goal of providing detailed and objective accounts of Chinese outbound investment in practice.

I owe an enormous debt of gratitude to Vicky Hayman, the project coordinator of the CLD project, who has provided invaluable organizational, administrative, and editorial assistance over the life of this project.

I am grateful to the scholars, experts, and faculty members I consulted in preparation for organizing and drafting this casebook in terms of their needs and requirements. While these colleagues are too numerous to mention, their input was extremely helpful in structuring and presenting the information in the case studies.

Finally, I thank Joe Ng and Gemma Smith of Cambridge University Press, who have supported this book project and expertly guided it through each stage of the publication process.

Abbreviations

ABV	alcohol by volume
AGEE	Guinean Environmental Assessment Agency
AI	artificial intelligence
ANEEL	Agência Nacional de Energia Elétrica/National Electric Energy Agency
ASEAN	Association of Southeast Asian Nations
ATC	Africa Tech Challenge
AVIC	China Aviation Industry Corporation
BCE	Before Common Era
BIT	bilateral investment treaty
BMTE	Belo Monte Transmissora de Energia
BNDES	Banco Nacional de Desenvolvimento Econômico e Social/Brazil's Development Bank
BOI	Board of Investment
BRI	Belt and Road Initiative
BVI	British Virgin Islands
CADE	Conselho Administrativo de Defesa Econômica/Administrative Council for Economic Defense
CCCC	China Communication Construction Company
CCP	Chinese Communist Party
CCU	Compañía de las Cervecerías Unidas
CEA	Central Environmental Authority
CEO	Chief Executive Officer
CFIUS	Committee on Foreign Investment in the United States
CFO	Chief Financial Officer
CFPA	China Foundation for Poverty Alleviation
CHNG	China Huaneng Group
CIB	Corporate and Investment Banking
CIECC	China International Engineering Consulting Corporation
CLA	Casino License Agreement
CNMI	Commonwealth of the Northern Mariana Islands
COIP	Chinese Overseas Industrial Park
CPC	Colombo Port City

CPCEC	Colombo Port City Economic Commission
CPEP	Colombo Port Expansion Project
CPFL	Companhia Paulista de Força e Luz
CPSES	Comités Préfectoraux de Suivi Environnemental et Social/Prefectural Committee for Environmental and Social Monitoring
CSO	civil society organization
CSPC	China State Power Corporation
CSR	corporate social responsibility
CTAE	Comité Technique d'Analyse Environnementale/Technical Committee for Analysis and Assessment
CTEA	Center for Transnational Environmental Accountability
DC	direct current
DRAM	dynamic random-access memory
DSSI	Debt Service Suspension Initiative
EAR	Export Administration Regulations
EHS	environmental, health and safety
EIA	Environmental Impact Assessment
EPC	engineering, procurement, and construction
EPE	Empresa de Pesquisa Energética/Energy Research Office
ESG	environmental, social and governance
ESIA	Environmental and Social Impact Assessment
ESMP	Environmental and Social Management Plan
FBI	Federal Bureau of Investigation
FDI	foreign direct investment
FEZ	free economic zone
FOB	free on board
FOCAC	Forum on China-Africa Cooperation
FTA	free trade agreement
FTZ	free trade zone
GCC	Gulf Cooperation Council
GDP	gross domestic product
GHG	greenhouse gas
GOSL	Government of Sri Lanka
HVDC	high-voltage direct current
IC	integrated circuit
ICBC	Industrial and Commercial Bank of China
ICBCS	ICBC Standard Bank Plc
ICCPR	International Covenant on Civil and Political Rights
ICESCR	International Covenant on Economic, Social and Cultural Rights
ICP	internet content providers
ICSID	International Centre for Settlement of Investment Disputes
ICT	information and communication technology

IEEPA	International Emergency Economic Powers Act
IFC	International Finance Corporation
IMF	International Monetary Fund
IPCC	Intellectual Property and Commercial Court
IPI	Imperial Pacific International
IPIH	Imperial Pacific International Holdings
IPO	initial public offering
JICA	Japan International Cooperation Agency
JSE	Johannesburg Stock Exchange
JV	joint ventures
JVA	Joint Venture Agreement
M&A	mergers and acquisitions
MCC	Metallurgical Corporation of China
MDT	Les Mêmes Droits pour Tous
MEDD	Ministère de l'Environnement et du Développement Durable/Ministry of the Environment and Sustainable Development
MENA	Middle Eastern and North African
MMT	Micron Memory Taiwan
MOEAIC	Investment Commission of the Ministry of Economic Affairs
MOEST	Ministry of Education, Science and Technology
MOFCOM	Ministry of Commerce
MOU	memorandum of understanding
MSR	Maritime Silk Road
NAV	net asset value
NDRC	National Development and Reform Commission
NEPZA	Nigeria Export Processing Zones Authority
NGO	nongovernmental organization
NHAR	Ningxia Hui Autonomous Region
NIS	Nigerian Immigration Service
NPCSC	Standing Committee of the National People's Congress of China
NSG	New South Group
NYS	National Youth Service
NYSE	New York Stock Exchange
ODI	overseas direct investment
OECD	Organisation for Economic Co-operation and Development
OFDI	outbound foreign direct investment
OGFTZ	Ogun Guangdong Free Trade Zone
OPAZ	Public Authority for Special Economic Zones and Free Zones
OSHA	Occupational Safety and Health Administration
PAA	Project Approving Agency
PAO	Public Offer for Acquisition
PBOC	People's Bank of China

List of Abbreviations

PES	Philadelphia Energy Solutions
PF	Patriotic Front
PLAN	People's Liberation Army Navy
PPP	purchasing power parity
PR	public relations
PRC	People's Republic of China
R&D	research and development
RAP	*receita anual permitida*/annual allowed revenue
REIES	Environmental and Social Impact Study Report
RIT	right to information
SAFE	State Administration for Foreign Exchange
SAMR	State Administration for Market Regulation
SB	Standard Bank
SBGL	Standard Bank Group Limited
SBIC	Standard Bank Investment Corporation
SBLH	Standard Bank London Holdings Limited
SCARC	Standing Cabinet Appointed Review Committee
SDG	Sustainable Development Goals
SDP	Strategic Development Projects
SEAI	Supplementary Environmental Impact Assessment
SASAC	State-owned Assets Supervision and Administration Commission
SEZ	special economic zone
SEZAD	Special Economic Zone at Duqm
SGBH	State Grid Brazil Holding
SGBP	State Grid Brazil Power
SGCC	State Grid Corporation of China
SGID	State Grid International Development Limited
SLPA	Sri Lanka Ports Authority
SMB	Société Minière de Boké
SME	small and medium-sized enterprise
SNCPM	Service National de Coordination des Projets Miniers/National Service for the Coordination of Mining Projects
SOE	state-owned enterprise
SPV	Special Purpose Vehicle
TJLP	*taxa de juros de longo prazo*/long-term interest rate
TSA	Transportation Security Administration
TVE	township and village enterprise
TVET	Technical, Vocational and Entrepreneurship Training
TVGI	Top View Grid Investment Limited
UDA	Urban Development Authority
UHVDC	ultra-high-voltage direct current
UMC	United Microelectronics Corporation
UN	United Nations

List of Abbreviations

UNDRIP	United Nations Declaration on the Rights of Indigenous Peoples
UNESCO	United Nations Educational, Scientific and Cultural Organization
UNFCCC	United Nations Framework Convention on Climate Change
UNGPS	United Nations Guiding Principles on Business and Human Rights
UNCITRAL	United Nations Commission on International Trade Law
USAID	United States Agency for International Development
USDOL	United States Department of Labor
USP	unsolicited proposal
USTR	United States Trade Representative
VIE	variable interest entity
WMP	wealth management product

Introduction

Matthew S. Erie[*]

1 Spotlight on the Chinese Firm

Starting in early 2019, US President Donald Trump's administration placed a number of restrictions on the ability of the Chinese company Huawei Technologies Co. Ltd. ("Huawei"), the largest telecommunications equipment producer in the world, to buy US technology. In May of that year, the US Commerce Department placed Huawei on a trade blacklist, and in 2020, the government extended that ban to cover all semiconductors made with US technology and which met Huawei's specifications. A few months later, the Commerce Department further extended the ban to cover all semiconductor chips regardless of whether they matched Huawei's specifications.[1] The US government's efforts to freeze Huawei's supply chain were part of a larger US-China trade war, billed as a new cold war, and one between the two largest economies in the world. The Trump administration justified its acts based on the view that Huawei presented a credible threat to US national security given its ties to the government of the People's Republic of China (PRC). The contest has taken the form of not only tech bans but also economic sanctions, long-arm statutes, anti-suit injunctions, and even hostage-taking by both sides in a regulatory race-to-the-bottom that some have decried as marking the end of globalization.

The US government's concerns about Huawei predate the Trump administration and go back to 2011, when the House Permanent Select Committee on Intelligence investigated Huawei and a second Chinese tech company ZTE. The committee concluded that Huawei failed to cooperate with the investigation and, in particular, failed to explain its relationships with the PRC government,

---

[*] This work is part of the "China, Law and Development" (CLD) project, which has received funding from the European Research Council under the European Union's Horizon 2020 research and innovation program (Grant No. 803763). The author thanks contributors to this volume for reading earlier drafts. All mistakes are the author's.

[1] For an overview of the timeline of the US government's actions regarding Huawei, see C. Scott Brown, 'The Huawei Ban Explained: A Complete Timeline and Everything You Need to Know' (*Android Authority*, 14 August 2022) www.androidauthority.com/huawei-google-android-ban-988382/.

the Chinese Communist Party (CCP), and the People's Liberation Army.[2] Over this period, Huawei has offered its own public relations defense and sought to diversify its supply chains and products. Huawei founder Ren Zhengfei has stated, "Neither Huawei, nor I personally, have ever received any requests from any government to provide improper information," citing that sharing personal data without consent would be bad for business.[3]

One of the persistent questions about Huawei is its ownership structure. Whereas the company claims to be owned by "96,768 shareholding employees,"[4] studies suggest that, in reality, employees hold a "virtual stock" that allows them a share in the profits but provides no voting power and thus fails to qualify as shareholder ownership in the traditional sense.[5] Adaptive ownership structures may exist for a number of reasons, but one consequence is nontransparency, which, in the face of persistent doubt about Chinese firms and their relationship to what is commonly referred to as the "Party-State," only exacerbates suspicion if not hostility.[6]

Private tech companies like Huawei exemplify the intense spotlight placed by concerned publics on Chinese companies and their overseas direct investment (ODI). Concerns about links between Chinese capital and the Party-State are even more palpable in regards to Chinese state-owned enterprises (SOEs), which are believed to "play a leading role in [the Party-State's] economic statecraft abroad."[7] Together, Chinese SOEs and, increasingly, Chinese private companies comprise some of the largest enterprises in the world across a range of vital industries, including not only technology but also electricity, petroleum, construction, commercial lending, insurance, construction, telecommunications, and steel, to name a few.[8] Collectively, these companies have investments

---

[2] US House of Representatives, 'Investigative Report on the U.S. National Security Issues Posed by Chinese Telecommunications Companies Huawei and ZTE' (8 October 2012) iv–v https://stacks.stanford.edu/file/druid:rm226yb7473/Huawei-ZTE%20Investigative%20Report%20%28FINAL%29.pdf.

[3] 'Huawei Founder Says Will Not Share Data with China – CBS News' (*Reuters*, 19 January 2019) www.reuters.com/article/us-usa-china-huawei-tech-idUSKCN1Q81HC/.

[4] ibid.

[5] Christopher Balding and Donald Clarke, 'Who Owns Huawei?' (SSRN, 17 April 2019) 5 https://papers.ssrn.com/sol3/papers.cfm?abstract_id=3372669; see also Colin Hawes, 'Why Is Huawei's Ownership So Strange? A Case Study of the Chinese Corporate and Socio-political Ecosystem' (2020) 21 Journal of Corporate Law Studies 1–38 (finding that while top-down governmental control is too facile a characterization, Huawei's success depends on close relationships with government authorities).

[6] The Party-State refers to the fusion of the PRC government and the Chinese Communist Party (CCP) at each administrative level and in all areas of governance, a fusion that has become even closer under current General Secretary of the CCP, Xi Jinping.

[7] Wendy Leutert, 'Challenges Ahead in China's Reform of State-Owned Enterprises' (2016) 21 Asia Policy 83–99, 87.

[8] Clay Chandler, 'Chinese Corporations Now Dominate the Fortune Global 500 List of Biggest Companies by Revenue – But They Are Far Less Profitable Than Their US Rivals' (*Fortune*, 19 August 2022) https://fortune.com/2022/08/18/fortune-global-500-china-companies-profitable-profitability-us-rivals/.

in most countries worldwide and are increasingly becoming central players in domestic politics and media. Concerns often stem from the view that internationalizing Chinese firms are instrumentalities of the Party-State, an authoritarian regime that has in recent years become increasingly repressive toward not only those on the margins of society – ethnic and religious minorities, public interest lawyers, domestic and foreign NGOs, and LGBTQ and women's rights activists – but also those at the center, entrepreneurs, and even CCP members. More fundamentally even, critics lament the rise of "China Inc." as inherently incompatible with the existing international legal order, which historically (at least nominally) valorized democracy, liberal rights, and free trade.[9]

Yet concerns directed at Chinese firms and their purported links to the Party-State rely on certain assumptions about their nature and governance. These assumptions generate theories – often untested – that have animated regulatory and administrative responses in a number of Western countries, including not just the United States but also the United Kingdom, Canada, Australia, Germany, and elsewhere. These responses and their policies have had deep and widespread impact on not just the regulation of Chinese ODI but also collaboration in research and development, cross-border movement of peoples and immigration, foreign study and intellectual exchange, and cooperation on international problems ranging from pandemics to climate change.

Further complicating the picture, not all countries respond to China uniformly, nor do all would-be host states make the same assumptions about Chinese investment. Some responses are the opposite to the foregoing. China has presented itself as the champion of developing countries and, in stark contrast to the US-China trade war, many low-income and middle-income countries proactively welcome Chinese investment. Instead of investment screening mechanisms, import bans, and immigration blockades, these countries offer preferential policies to facilitate Chinese ODI into their economies. Eager to promote Chinese investment, these countries welcome Chinese expertise, technology transfer, and even security and law enforcement.[10]

Under programs such as the Belt and Road Initiative (BRI) and the Global Development Initiative, China is supplying much-needed infrastructure and energy to emerging markets, connecting economies, facilitating trade, and lowering transaction costs. These programs may further reduce poverty and improve standards of living, and hence add real value to recipient states. These benefits do not mean that negative externalities are absent. Chinese firms may also exploit local labor and damage the environment or violate local law. They may further

---

[9] Ji Li, *The Clash of Capitalisms? Chinese Companies in the United States* (Cambridge University Press 2019); Mark Wu, 'The "China, Inc." Challenge to Global Trade Governance' (2016) 57 Harvard International Law Journal 261.

[10] Dawn C. Murphy, *China's Rise in the Global South: The Middle East, Africa, and Beijing's Alternative World Order* (Stanford University Press 2022); Maria Repnikova, *China's Soft Power* (Cambridge University Press 2022); Lina Benabdallah, *Shaping the Future of Power: Knowledge Production and Network-Building in China-Africa Relations* (University of Michigan Press 2020).

cement dependencies between host states and China that may have additional effects through various channels, including, for example, "pro-China" voting patterns in international organizations. In short, the stakes are high, and in a period of ideological competition, precarity, and even paranoia, fact-based and neutral material on which to base responses is all the more important.

Despite the fact that Chinese ODI is, first, of central importance to global trade and investment, and second, heavily contested, there is, to date, a paucity of readily accessible data with which to assess the claims of Chinese firms and exclusionary governments. Further, as a second and related problem, the lack of reliable material is a problem for policymakers and other decision makers, as well as, and, perhaps more crucially farther "upstream," educators. Students in professional schools – law, policy, business – need to understand how Chinese companies work, their corporate governance, and the operation and effects of their overseas projects on host states. This need applies to students regardless of whether they are from developed or developing countries: Chinese capital is present and, in some cases, actively shaping regulatory fields in both types of economies. Minimally, a greater understanding of Chinese ODI helps curtail misconceptions. Furthermore, a more realistic picture can inform better analysis and response, whether at the legal, commercial, or policy levels. It can assist stakeholders to make informed decisions and to weigh risk and opportunities.

A Casebook on Chinese Outbound Investment: Law, Policy, and Business (hereinafter, the *Casebook*) is designed to meet these needs. Comprised of fifteen case studies, based on primary source materials, and written by experts and researchers, many of whom are either from or have extensive experience in the host state in question, the *Casebook* provides fact-based and neutral teaching material for educators and other concerned parties. Case studies are written with specific overarching objectives in mind: to shed light on the decision-making, policies, and practices of Chinese firms; to understand how Chinese firms adapt to challenging regulatory environments; and to assess what kind of effects Chinese projects have overseas, particularly in developing states where China's footprint may be most pronounced.

The remainder of this Introduction will address the following questions that will help prepare the reader in using the case studies and help lay the groundwork to address the overarching objectives cited above: What are Chinese companies? What are China's international investment strategies? What are the trends in Chinese ODI? What is the relationship between Chinese ODI and the Party-State? What are the effects of Chinese ODI in host states? Lastly, how should the reader use the *Casebook* and how is it organized?

2 What Are Chinese Companies?

Over the last several decades, the rate of growth of Chinese companies has been historic. In recent years, more Chinese companies have occupied the Fortune 500 list than companies from any other country, even if US companies remain more profitable.[11] Chinese companies are active in nearly all major industries in most markets across the world. While the volume of Chinese ODI has decreased in the last few years, nonetheless Chinese ODI remains strong and will likely only continue. This section provides a basic overview of Chinese companies, their corporate forms, the evolution of Chinese corporate law, and the differences between SOEs and private companies.

To understand Chinese companies, it is helpful to have a basic understanding of their corporate forms and how PRC corporate law has changed over time. Starting with the economic reforms after the founding of the PRC in 1949, productive assets in the country were organized as SOEs under "line ministries," which reported to the State Council.[12] It was not until the early 1980s that SOEs were given their own distinct legal personality; before then, they were functional equivalents to extensions of the government and their purpose was less to generate a profit and more to fulfill commands from the central or provincial level governments.[13] With the "opening and reform" (*gaige kaifang*) reforms in the early 1980s, the PRC government sought to raise foreign direct investment (FDI), thus injecting foreign private capital into the state-controlled system, which was soon joined with private capital.[14] During this time, the township and village enterprises (TVEs), a novel form of ownership distinct from both SOEs and private firms, contributed significantly to economic development. This combination or tension between private capital and state direction would come to define the Chinese "socialist market economy."

Concurrent with these efforts, the state began the corporatization and privatization of Chinese assets, through a policy of "holding the big and letting go of the small," establishing stock exchanges in Shanghai and Shenzhen in the early 1990s and also the introduction of the "modern enterprise system," including corporate mechanisms with relevant legal norms.[15] The legal basis for these corporatization efforts was the 1993 Company Law,[16] which has since gone through a number of revisions, including in 2005, a major overhaul that established companies limited by shares.[17] One purpose of the Company Law

---

[11] See Chandler (n 8).
[12] See Nicholas Calcina Howson and Vikramaditya S. Khanna, 'The Development of Modern Corporate Governance in China and India' in Muthucumaraswamy Sornarajah and Jiangyu Wang (eds), *China, India and the International Economic Order* (Cambridge University Press 2016) 532.
[13] ibid 533.   [14] ibid 516.
[15] Nicholas R. Lardy, *Markets over Mao: The Rise of Private Business in China* (Columbia University Press 2014) 18, 45–6; see also Robert C. Art and Minkang Gu, 'China Incorporated: The First Corporation Law of the People's Republic of China' (2021) 20 Yale Journal of International Law 273, 275.
[16] Zhonghua renmin gongheguo gongsifa [The Company Law of the PRC] (adopted by the Fifth Session of the Standing Committee of the Eighth National People's Congress on 29 December 1993).
[17] Zhonghua renmin gongheguo gongsifa [The Company Law of the PRC] (adopted by the Eighteenth Meeting of the Standing Committee of the Tenth National People's Congress of the PRC on 27 October 2005) Ch 4, Sec 1.

has been to allow small, private business ventures more regulatory space for expansion. The role of private business is not to replace state-owned assets but rather to provide a supplement, even if this supplement has grown relative to the state sector over time.[18] The growth of the private sector in the last forty years has been massive. In 1978, more than 99% of the workforce was employed by the state, but by 2017, more than 80% of China's 424 million-strong urban workforce was employed by the private sector.[19] Fueling this massive growth, the Company Law established two separate corporate forms: the limited liability company (for closely held companies) and the joint stock company (for publicly traded corporations). For the latter, the China Securities Regulatory Commission became the main regulator of these companies as it oversees all securities trading for publicly listed companies.

While the corporate forms established by the law roughly correspond to those found in Anglo-American common law, Chinese corporate law has a number of distinct features, some of which stem from China's civil law system but others are a distinct legacy of its socialist law inheritance, which requires state ownership of assets.[20] In particular, China's Company Law includes the following distinct characteristics: a "legal representative" (*faren*) who assumes all liability for misconduct of the company, a "board of supervisors" that oversees the board of directors, an extensive grant of authority for the shareholders that allows in many cases the PRC government to exercise majority stock ownership, and even grounds for workers to shape corporate policy.[21]

In addition, the 2005 Company Law mandates that each company registered in China should have a CCP unit. Specifically, Article 19 specifies that "an organization of the Chinese Communist Party shall be established in a company to carry out party activities according to the Charter of the Communist Party of China and mandates the company to 'provide necessary conditions for the activities of the [CCP organization].'"[22] The influence of the CCP unit on the management of Chinese companies is a black box. Whereas it is possible to overstate the unit's presence in terms of the day-to-day operation of a Chinese company, it is likely that the CCP shapes corporate decision-making externally through its allocation of resources and economic policies that influence the firm's strategic aims, as firms seek to profit from sectors that are supported by the Party-State.

---

[18] Art and Gu (n 15) 286.
[19] Colin Hawes, *The Chinese Corporate Ecosystem* (Cambridge University Press 2022) 137.
[20] Jiangyu Wang, *Company Law in China* (Edward Elgar Publishing 2014) 20.
[21] See Art and Gu (n 15) 307 (discussing China's Company Law's borrowing from German civil law).
[22] See (n 17) Art 19. To be more precise, the Company Law needs to be read in conjunction with the Chinese Communist Party Charter, which states that where three or more CCP members request it, a private enterprise must allow the CCP to establish a branch within the firm. In practice, and perhaps surprisingly, in 2019, only 7.42% of private firms had set up CCP branches, and the number has been decreasing since 2016. See Hawes (n 19) Secs 4.7–4.10.

Over the course of the reform period, the corporate governance of SOEs and private companies has diverged. The general model is for controlling stakes in the SOEs to be owned by a central holding company, which in turn is held by a central government agency, the State-owned Assets Supervision and Administration Commission (SASAC), established in 2003, under the State Council.[23] SASAC exists not only at the central level but also at the provincial and municipal levels and SOEs may fall under the jurisdiction of any of these levels. SOEs generally belong to vertically integrated groups; each company's majority shareholder is the parent company of the group and is itself owned by SASAC.[24] While insiders vary in their views of the extent to which SASAC is successful in reining in some of the largest SOEs, nonetheless it is fair to say that, under SASAC, SOEs are subjected to a different degree of control than private companies. For example, SASAC has the power to select and remove top managers, approve all share transfers, and reap cash flow rights.[25] Such control is amplified through not just SASAC but dense and overlapping networks of both governmental and CCP organizations that may not be the case for private companies.[26]

SOEs and private companies thus have different types of relationships to the Party-State. Historically, SOEs have functioned to perform not just economic but also social and geostrategic aims of the Party-State.[27] Several of the case studies in this *Casebook* concern SOEs and suggest both that SOEs may receive substantial support from the Chinese Party-State and, in turn, that they operate overseas in ways that generally align with the Party-State's interests. However, across a number of areas – market access, state subsidies, proximity to state power, and execution of the government's policy objectives – the distance between large private companies and the Party-State may not be as great as is commonly assumed.[28]

A couple of factors render this assertion more likely in the era of CCP General Secretary Xi Jinping, who has sought to solidify the control of the CCP over all aspects of the PRC government, society, and economy.[29] One, pursuant to Xi's centralization of CCP authority, Chinese firms have more incentives than ever to gravitate toward CCP policies. Two, and related, the costs

---

[23] Not all SOEs are subject to this structure; some large SOEs are held by other government agencies. Further, large central state-owned banks are owned by the Ministry of Finance through its agency. For more on the history of SOEs and their reform, see Ji Li, 'State-Owned Enterprises in the Current Regime of Investor-State Arbitration' in Shaheeza Lalani and Rodrigo Polanco Lazo (eds), *The Role of the State in Investor-State Arbitration* (Brill Nijhoff 2015).
[24] Li-Wen Lin and Curtis J. Milhaupt, 'We Are the (National) Champions: Understand the Mechanisms of State Capitalism in China' (2013) 65 Stanford Law Review 697, 700.
[25] ibid 737, 740, 743, 744.   [26] ibid 707, 723.   [27] See Leutert (n 7).
[28] Curtis J. Milhaupt and Wentong Zheng, 'Beyond Ownership: State Capitalism and the Chinese Firm' (2015) 103 The Georgetown Law Journal 665–722, 668.
[29] Jacques deLisle and Guobin Yang (eds), *The Party Leads All: The Evolving Role of the Chinese Communist Party* (Brookings 2022).

of disobedience may be severe, and both PRC regulators and also CCP organs have penalized errant entrepreneurs and top executives for a number of reasons, including having too much autonomy vis-à-vis the Party-State.[30] Under the omnipresent pressures of the Party-State, Chinese firms have little choice but to align their management practices and business objectives with those of the authorities, even if those authorities do not intervene in the day-to-day affairs of companies.[31] Still, and despite the foregoing, as also demonstrated in this *Casebook*, the relationships between private companies and the Party-State (as well as, it should be mentioned, SOEs and the Party-State) are far from uniform and static; rather, they evolve in the face of changing domestic and international policy environments.

3 What Are China's International Investment Strategies?

A threshold question is, does China have international investment strategies? This question goes to the issues of degrees of centralization and coordination in Chinese firms' outbound activities and the financial institutions that support such activities. The answer depends on the unit or scale of one's analysis. At a 30,000-foot level, there is, broadly, coordination as the Party-State sets out broad parameters, including incentives, for Chinese corporations to invest internationally, yet the closer one gets to the granular level, the more disaggregation one sees.

Generally, starting in the late 1990s, first, the major SOEs and then Chinese private companies began engaging in ODI under the "going out" (*zouchuqu*) policy. In 2004, the PRC government reformed what had previously been an onerous "approval" system, a holdover from central planning, toward an "authorization" system that permitted Chinese companies more freedom to invest overseas.[32] During this period in the early 2000s, the various governmental ministries responsible for outbound investment issued a host of regulations that clarified their respective roles and division of labor. For instance, the Ministry of Commerce (MOFCOM) became responsible for authorizing investment projects. The National Development and Reform Commission (NDRC) became responsible for the majority of resource extraction and large foreign exchange projects, with the State Council authorizing large-scale resource extraction, in excess of US$200 million, and also large foreign

---

[30] Angela Zhang, *Chinese Antitrust Exceptionalism: How the Rise of China Challenges Global Regulation* (Oxford University Press 2021); Ning Cao [曹柠], '民营企业的反腐风暴 [Private Enterprises' Anti-corruption Storm]' (*Nanfengchuang* [*South Reviews*], 21 January 2019) https://baijiahao.baidu.com/s?id=1623231503107555258&wfr=spider&for=pc.
[31] Lin Lin and Dan Puchniak, 'Institutional Investors in China: Corporate Governance and Policy Channelling in the Market within the State' (2022) 35 Columbia Journal of Asian Law 75–159.
[32] 关于投资体制改革的决定 (2004) [Decision on the Reform of the Investment System], issued by the State Council in 2004 (no. 20), perma.cc/8UMB-LFD4.

exchange projects, for more than US$50 million.[33] Around this time, the State Administration for Foreign Exchange (SAFE) also began simplifying its procedures and relaxing controls.[34] Lastly, the PRC government established a number of special funds for overseas investments; the policy banks, namely the Export-Import Bank of China (Exim Bank) and China Development Bank, provided more credit support; and also the tax authorities streamlined taxation policies to avoid dual levying agreements with foreign countries, all of which further stimulated ODI.[35]

In 2009, the ODI regime was further refined. MOFCOM delegated more power to lower-level authorities and the NDRC initially sought more centralization of its authority.[36] For ODI, enterprises have ongoing reporting requirements to MOFCOM, and both MOFCOM and SAFE conduct joint inspections each year to verify information and also ensure compliance with PRC laws and regulations.[37] This system applies to both SOEs and private companies, but central SOEs are further subjected to SASAC's system of supervision, including review of their overseas merger and acquisition activities.[38]

It should be noted that, historically, not only has there been some degree of regulatory competition between MOFCOM and NDRC but, given the delegation of powers, there has also been competition between the central and subnational authorities. The consequence is that different local governments compete and may have different priorities in their ODI strategies. These priorities may not always be aligned with those of the central government.[39] Regulatory discoordination means that in practice it is hard to speak of any one coherent ODI strategy. This incoherence is reflected in the disparate outcomes of cases collected in this *Casebook*.

The BRI commenced a new phase of Chinese ODI and sought to create some measure of coherence for ODI, although the BRI has remained mainly a branding opportunity for companies looking to gain governmental support for their projects abroad. In 2015, three Chinese government ministries jointly issued the "Vision and Actions on Jointly Building Silk Road Economic Belt and the Twenty-First Century Maritime Silk Road," inaugurating the BRI.[40] Since then, China's ODI administration and sectoral legislation have been closely tied to

---

[33] Huang Wenbin and Andreas Wilkes, 'Analysis of China's Overseas Investment Policies', Center for International Forestry Research, Working Paper 79 (2011) 11.
[34] ibid 11–12.   [35] ibid 13–14.
[36] Vivienne Bath, 'The Quandary for Chinese Regulators: Controlling the Flow of Investment into and out of China' in Vivienne Bath and Luke Nottage (eds), *Foreign Investment and Dispute Resolution Law and Practice in Asia* (Routledge 2011) 71.
[37] ibid 72.   [38] ibid.
[39] Lee Jones and Shahar Hameiri, *Fractured China: How State Transformation Is Shaping China's Rise* (Cambridge University Press 2021); Yeling Tan, *Disaggregating China, Inc.: State Strategies in the Liberal Economic Order* (Cornell University Press 2021).
[40] 'Vision and Actions on Jointly Building Silk Road Economic Belt and the Twenty-First Century Maritime Silk Road' issued by the NDRC, Ministry of Foreign Affairs, and MOFCOM in March 2015, perma.cc/Q37M-RYZN.

the BRI and led principally by investment in low-income and middle-income countries in infrastructure, transportation, construction, and energy and natural resources. During this phase, both the NDRC and MOFCOM clarified their guidance for ODI, as ODI was divided into categories of "encouraged," "restricted," and "prohibited."[41]

Starting well before the formation of the contemporary ODI regulatory regime, China aggressively signed on to international investment agreements to provide greater certainty under international investment law. These agreements include bilateral investment treaties (BITs), multilateral investment treaties, and free trade agreements with investment chapters. China's international investment agreement program has bilateral, regional, and global dimensions.

As to its bilateral focus, China has signed on to more BITs than any other country in the world, after Germany. China has undergone multiple generations of BITs, which increasingly align China's BITs with international standards and so in a way that gradually provide more protections for investors as China has transformed, in the reform era, from an FDI-focused country to one that continues to be a major recipient of FDI but also a capital exporter.[42]

As to regional integration, through the BRI, Regional Comprehensive Economic Partnership, Shanghai Cooperation Organization, and other initiatives, China is contributing to the reshaping of regional trade, investment, and security in the Asia-Pacific region. At the global level, China has participated in investment facilitation through such initiatives as the G20 Guiding Principles for Global Investment Policy-Making.[43] Through its international investment agreements as well as its soft law equivalents, namely memoranda of understanding and memoranda of guidance, China is a norm-setter across a range of emerging cross-border legal fields including not only investment frameworks and infrastructure but also fintech, central bank digital currency, and dispute resolution.[44]

---

[41] 关于进一步引导和规范境外投资方向指导意见的通知 (国办发(2017)74 号) [Notice of Guiding Opinions Regarding Further Guidance and Regulation of the Direction of Overseas Investment (State Council issued (2017) No. 74)], issued by the General Office of the State Council, MOFCOM, NDRC, and Ministry of Foreign Affairs on 4 August 2017, perma.cc/C8EW-RVPW.

[42] Vivienne Bath, 'Chinese Investment and Approaches to International Investment Agreements' in Fabio Morosini and Michelle Ratton Sanchez Badin (eds), *Reconceptualizing International Investment Law from the Global South* (Cambridge University Press 2017) 72.

[43] Julien Chaisse, 'Introduction: China's International Investment Law and Policy Regime – Identifying the Three Tracks' in Julien Chaisse (ed), *China's International Investment Strategy: Bilateral, Regional, and Global Law and Policy* (Oxford University Press 2018), 1–22.

[44] Heng Wang, 'Selective Reshaping: China's Paradigm Shift in International Economic Governance' (2020) 23 Journal of International Economic Law 583–606, 585–6; Jiangyu Wang, 'China's Governance Approach to the Belt and Road Initiative (BRI): Partnership, Relations, and Law' (2019) 14 Global Trade and Customs Journal 222–8, 223; Guiguo Wang, 'The Belt and Road Initiative in Quest for a Dispute Resolution Mechanism' (2017) 25 Asia Pacific Law Review 1–16, 1–2.

4 What Are the Trends in Chinese ODI?

Coupled with the improvement of its ODI regime, China's international investment program has resulted in a significant volume of outbound investment. Taking a step back, China's ODI must be considered in the broader context of China's capital export, which includes not just investment but also lending, aid, and finance. China became the world's largest economy by purchasing power parity in 2014. In 2016, China became the second largest outbound investment supplier in the world, and China also became a net capital exporting country.[45] Further, as of 2019, China is the world's largest official creditor, supplying more loans than the International Monetary Fund (IMF) and World Bank.[46] To round out the picture, in addition to populating the Fortune 500 list with Chinese companies, China is the largest trading country in the world and has the world's largest banking system, the second largest stock market, the third largest bond market, and one of the fastest growing digital economies in the world.[47]

Specific to ODI, Chinese capital outflows peaked in 2016 when ODI reached US$196.15 billion.[48] Subsequently, the Chinese government sought greater control over outbound investments to curb speculative investing, particularly in such sectors as luxury real estate, entertainment, and sport teams. By 2019, Chinese ODI had declined to US$136.91 billion,[49] but then increased by 12.3% in 2020 to reach US$153.71 billion, thus making China the largest capital exporting country in the world, by measure of investment flows, for the first time.[50] This is all the more remarkable given that China's achievement occurred during the COVID-19 pandemic, which has generally slowed international trade and investment.

The COVID-19 pandemic has certainly negatively impacted the Chinese economy and its outbound capital, mainly due to the PRC government's own anomalous "zero-COVID" policies, which were extended long beyond policies implemented in most other countries, and thus had a deleterious impact on the domestic economy. The COVID-19 pandemic is one factor among others, including other endogenous constraints such as the anti-corruption campaign

---

[45] See Matthew S. Erie, Chinese Law and Development (2021) 62 Harvard International Law Journal 70.
[46] ibid.   [47] ibid 71.
[48] 中华人民共和国商务部 [Ministry of Commerce of the PRC], 国家统计局 [National Bureau of Statistics], 国家外汇管理局 [State Administration of Foreign Exchange], 2016年度中国对外直接投资统计公报 [*2016 Statistical Bulletin of China's Outward Foreign Direct Investment*] (2017) 3.
[49] 中华人民共和国商务部 [Ministry of Commerce of the PRC], 国家统计局 [National Bureau of Statistics], 国家外汇管理局 [State Administration of Foreign Exchange], 2019年度中国对外直接投资统计公报 [*2019 Statistical Bulletin of China's Outward Foreign Direct Investment*] (2020) 3.
[50] 中华人民共和国商务部 [Ministry of Commerce of the PRC], 国家统计局 [National Bureau of Statistics], 国家外汇管理局 [State Administration of Foreign Exchange], 2020年度中国对外直接投资统计公报 [*2020 Statistical Bulletin of China's Outward Foreign Direct Investment*] (2021) 3, 6.

and "crackdown" on technology firms, as well as exogenous ones, including the US-China trade war and currents of Sinophobia throughout the world that have stymied Chinese ODI.[51]

One effect of these converging factors is a general bifurcation in world opinion on China, Chinese companies, and Chinese ODI, specifically between Western democratic states and low-income and middle-income countries in the Global South.[52] Whereas the United States and its allies have become hardened against Chinese capital, many countries throughout Asia, Africa, and Latin America, and elsewhere, continue to engage in China-related business and have even increased their dependence on China over the course of the COVID-19 pandemic, driving incipient regionalization of the global economy. For instance, cumulative engagement in BRI deals since 2013 has been US$932 billion, and the latest figures suggest that investment in BRI projects remains strong in recent years, despite obstacles, at least according to official numbers.[53] These trends will likely continue in the midterm, which raises challenges for Chinese investment strategies, including acquisition of advanced technologies. The Chinese government intends to address such challenges by domestic reliance, although this strategy remains uncertain.

5 What Is the Relationship between Chinese ODI and the Party-State?

The extent to which Chinese firms, engaged in investing overseas, act on behalf of the Party-State or are beholden to the Party-State's authority is a hotly contested question that has generated extensive debate in academic, policy, and

---

[51] See generally, Matthew S. Erie, 'Civilization on Pause – Introduction to Special Issue on "China's Global Capital and the Coronavirus: Views from Comparative Law and Regulation"' (2023) 18 Asian Journal of Comparative Law 1–17.

[52] Compare Laura Silver, Kat Devlin, and Christine Huang, 'Unfavorable Views of China Reach Historic Highs in Many Countries', Pew Research Center (6 October 2020) www.pewresearch.org/global/2020/10/06/unfavorable-views-of-china-reach-historic-highs-in-many-countries/ (tracking negative evaluations of China in advanced economies mainly due to China's COVID-19 response but also human rights concerns in Xinjiang and Hong Kong) with Josephine Sanny and Edem Selormey, 'AD489: Africans Welcome China's Influence but Maintain Democratic Aspirations' (*Afrobarometer*, 15 November 2021) www.afrobarometer.org/publication/ad489-africans-welcome-chinas-influence-maintain-democratic-aspirations/ (noting that in thirty-four African countries China was perceived to be the most positive external actor).

[53] Christoph Nedopil, 'China Belt and Road Initiative (BRI) Investment Report H1 2022', Green Finance & Development Center, FISF Fudan University, Shanghai (July 2022) 5; see also 中华人民共和国商务部 [Ministry of Commerce of the PRC], 2022年1-5月我对"一带一路"沿线国家投资合作情况 [China's Investment and Cooperation with Countries Along the "Belt and Road" from January to May 2022] (28 June 2022), www.mofcom.gov.cn/article/tongjiziliao/dgzz/202206/20220603322656.shtml; Xinhua (新华) [New China], 2023年我国对外投资合作平稳发展 [In 2023, China's Foreign Investment Cooperation with Develop Steadily], 中国一带一路网 [China's Belt and Road Net] (4 February 2024), www.yidaiyilu.gov.cn/p/0BH2HGGF.html.

business circles. As an empirical matter, the relationship between the corporate sector and the government in China is complex and ad hoc, meaning that there is no "one-size-fits-all" scenario.[54] In other words, on the question of whether commercial or political drivers are most relevant in shaping Chinese ODI, the answer requires a fact-based inquiry that depends on a number of issues, including the nature of transaction, the type of firm, the size of the investment, the investment destination, the industry in question, and relations between home and host state, to name a few.

The Party-State has various ways – sticks and carrots – to influence firms domestically. These include both ownership and control as well as less formal mechanisms, including the role of CCP cells in corporations and the thick networks within which corporate managers and executives are embedded, networks invariably shaped by the Party-State's interests.[55] Politically connected entrepreneurs, state subsidies, and chambers of commerce are all additional ways in which the Party-State influences corporations.[56] PRC regulators further have various tools to influence corporate decision-making.[57]

The nexus between the Party-State and corporations, which is already complex, becomes even more complicated when one focuses on corporations' outbound activities. As a legal requirement, when Chinese investors localize in host states, they assume corporate forms under host state law. Incorporation under local law is required regardless of whether the transaction is a merger and acquisition or a greenfield investment, although the former often receives more regulatory scrutiny in many developed economies than the latter.[58] The key question, then, is whether the various mechanisms for Party-State control or influence that characterize the Chinese domestic economy survive the incorporation of a Chinese firm in a host state.

Studies suggest that contextual factors shape the relationship between a Chinese-invested firm abroad and the Party-State. For example, the most extensive study of Chinese investors in the United States concludes that "long-term commercial interests instead of home-state policies drove most of the Chinese investments in the United States."[59] An ethnographic study of Chinese investment in the mining sector in Zambia confirmed that central SOEs operate not just for profit but also out of the "nation's strategic, lifeline, security

---

[54] See Hawes (n 19) 15. See also Meg Rithmire, *Precarious Ties: Business and the State in Authoritarian Asia* (Oxford University Press 2023).
[55] See Milhaupt and Wentong Zheng (n 28) 683–4. See also 中华人民共和国公司法 [PRC Company Law] (promulgated by the National People's Congress, 26 Octpber 2018, effective 26 October 2018) art. 19 (requiring companies to provide the "necessary conditions" to facilitate the activities of party organizations).
[56] See Milhaupt and Wentong Zheng (n 28) 683–6.   [57] See Zhang (n 30) 23, 68.
[58] Karl P. Sauvant, 'Is the United States Ready for FDI from China? Overview' in Karl P. Sauvant (ed), *Investing in the United States: Is the US Ready for FDI from China?* (Edward Elgar Publishing 2009) 9–10.
[59] See Li (n 9) 5.

interests."[60] A more recent study found that Chinese regulators have generally reduced their control over investment decisions but nonetheless maintain important channels of influence, and such influence is particularly regnant in the case of SOEs.[61] Further, whereas SOE investments are aligned with macro-policy in the form of five-year plans, direct intervention on a day-to-day basis by state or CCP officials is less apparent.[62] Additional studies on Chinese institutional investors confirm this view.[63] Hence, while general trends may be observable, much depends on the context for Chinese ODI. This conclusion has implications for host state policy response to Chinese ODI, specifically in regard to investment screening mechanisms and the nature of their review of transactions.

6 What Are the Effects of Chinese ODI?

Just as in the varied types of relationships between Chinese firms engaging in ODI and the Party-State, so too are the effects of Chinese ODI on the host state and relevant stakeholders and communities nonuniform. On the one hand, the PRC government has sought to prioritize sustainable development across nearly all sectors, including Chinese-invested and Chinese-managed projects overseas. On the other hand, China remains mostly dependent on fossil fuels and is therefore one of the largest carbon emitters in the world. This Janus-faced experience of the Chinese economy is, to some extent, internationalizing along with Chinese ODI.

China's commitments to sustainable development and its performance to date remain impressive and far-reaching. China was one party to adopt the 2030 Agenda for Sustainable Development in 2015 and has since published regular national plans on its implementation of the 2030 Agenda for Sustainable Development. In so doing, China has interpreted sustainable development in light of its own development history and experience, with a focus on poverty alleviation, environmental protection, and sustainable governance, rather than, for example, on universal human rights or rule of law, which are core goals of the 2030 Agenda.[64]

---

[60] Ching Kwan Lee, *The Specter of Global China: Politics, Labor, and Foreign Investment in Africa* (University of Chicago Press 2017) 33.
[61] Xiaohan Gong and Anatole Boute, 'For Profit or Strategic Purpose? Chinese Outbound Energy Investments and the International Economic Regime' (2021) 14 Journal of World Energy Law and Business 345–62, 347.
[62] ibid 353.   [63] See Lin and Puchniak (n 31).
[64] Compare Ministry of Foreign Affairs of PRC, 'China's Position on the Implementation of the 2030 Agenda for Sustainable Development', 22 April 2016, www.fmprc.gov.cn/mfa_eng/wjdt_665385/2649_665393/201604/t20160422_679457.html with Council of Europe, 'UN Agenda 2030', www.coe.int/en/web/programmes/un-2030-agenda#:~:text=The%202030%20 Agenda%20for%20Sustainable,equality%20and%20non%2Ddiscrimination%E2%80%9D ("The UN 2030 Agenda envisages 'a world of universal respect for human rights and human dignity, the rule of law, justice, equality and non-discrimination'").

In the context of Chinese ODI, sustainable development has been linked to the idea of the "green BRI," a concept that the PRC government has advocated particularly since some of its overseas projects have attracted criticism for their failure to safeguard the environment and comply with local law.[65] However, in practice, the environmental and social impact of overseas projects has not been a focus of the PRC government. Consequently, there is no legislation with enforcement effect to screen the environmental and social impact of overseas projects. Institutionally, the Ministry of Ecology and the Environment, which is the central administrative unit in charge of environmental protection in China, does not have any mandate to regulate overseas projects.[66] Notwithstanding the lack of enforceable regulation, the PRC government has issued a number of normative documents that purport to foster sustainable development and environmental protection in overseas investment.[67] The problem with all of these documents, however, is that they are nonbinding.[68] The same issue applies to the regulation of so-called "environmental, social and governance investing" as well as "corporate social responsibility" across Chinese industries.

The lack of teeth in Chinese regulation has not prohibited the growth of sustainable development in Chinese ODI. One study by the NDRC's BRI Center, conducted in 2021, collected 241 overseas projects, including 184 green energy projects, 39 green manufacturing projects, 9 ecological environmental protection projects, 4 green transportation projects, 4 green overseas park projects, and 1 green agriculture and forestry project.[69] In addition to such officially sanctioned accounts, scholars have independently verified China's leadership in green finance and green credit.[70] In short, China has made real strides in ensuring that some of its overseas projects promote sustainable development.

---

[65] See, e.g., 环境保护部 [Ministry for Environmental Protection], 外交部 [Ministry Foreign Affairs], 发展改革委 [Nat'l Dev. Ref. Comm'n.], & 中华人民共和国商务部 [Min. Comm.], 关于推进绿色 "一带一路" 建设的指导意见 [Guiding Opinion on Promoting the Building of the Green BRI] (26 April 2017), www.mee.gov.cn/gkml/hbb/bwj/201705/t20170505_413602.htm.

[66] See Matthew S. Erie and Jingjing Zhang, 'A Comparison of Inbound and Outbound Investment Regulatory Regimes in China: Focus on Environmental Protection' in Henry Gao, Damian Ross, and Ka Zeng (eds), *China and the WTO: 20 Years On* (Cambridge University Press 2023) 443–5.

[67] See, e.g., 对外投资合作环境保护指南 (商合发 [2013] 74 号) [The Environmental Protection Guidelines for Foreign Investment and Cooperation (issued by MOFCOM and cooperating ministries [2013] No. 74)], 18 February 2013, perma.cc/7NST-6VYY.

[68] See Erie and Zhang (n 66).

[69] BRI Center, Nat'l Dev. Ref. Comm'n. 绿色一带一路典型项目案例库建设与应用研究 [Construction and Application of the Green B&R Project Case Library], 31 July 2021, 9.

[70] See, e.g., Virginia Harper-Ho, 'Sustainable Finance and China's Green Credit Reforms: A Test Case for Bank Monitoring of Environmental Risk' (2018) 51 Cornell International Law Journal 609, 609; Lin Lin and Yanrong Hong, 'Developing a Green Bonds Market: Lessons from China' (2022) 23 European Business Organization Law Review 143–85.

The other side of the picture, however, shows Chinese firms violating local laws in their overseas projects, including environmental law, labor law, and other areas of both public and private laws. There is a growing literature that demonstrates that Chinese-invested firms either willfully ignore the protection of local rights or unknowingly fail to uphold their responsibilities under law.[71] Some of this behavior can be attributed to the fact that many Chinese firms going abroad do not have sufficient experience and undergo a learning curve in challenging regulatory environments that differ substantially from the status quo back home.[72]

Another related reason for Chinese-invested firms' problems with host state law is that they have not yet developed cultures of compliance with local authorities. Along these lines, when Chinese firms get into legal trouble abroad, they often seek protection from the PRC embassy in the host state, rather than follow established dispute resolution procedures, including administrative consultation or litigation in local courts.[73] Yet another factor that explains Chinese firm behavior overseas is that Chinese financing is not tied to conditionalities of good governance, human rights, and rule of law as are loans from the IMF or World Bank.[74] As Chinese firms may be more risk-tolerant than Western ones in conducting business in jurisdictions with poor governance standards,[75] the lack of conditionalities may exacerbate those conditions. While international financial institutions as well as foreign investors from Western states may bring their own set of suboptimal practices to host states, nonetheless Chinese capital has been shown to have distinct issues. To summarize, whereas the PRC government has made considerable progress in endorsing sustainable development, projects on the ground do not always reflect such priorities and, instead, may lead to negative externalities in host states. This *Casebook* is designed to help multiple stakeholders understand the nature of Chinese firms and their overseas projects, including their positive and negative effects on host economies.

---

[71] See, e.g., Aaron Halegua, 'Where Is the Belt and Road Initiative Taking International Labour Rights? An Examination of Worker Abuse by Chinese Firms in Saipan' in Maria Adele Carrai and Jan Wouters (eds), *The Belt and Road Initiative and Global Governance* (Edward Elgar Publishing 2020); Miriam Driessen, *Tales of Hope, Tastes of Bitterness: Chinese Road Builders in Ethiopia* (Hong Kong University Press 2019); Yifeng Chen and Ulla Liukkunen, 'Enclave Governance and Transnational Labour Law: A Case Study of Chinese Workers on Strike in Africa' (2019) 88 Nordic Journal of International Law 558–86; Muhammed Azeem, 'Theoretical Challenges to TWAIL with the Rise of China: Labor Conditions under Chinese Investment in Pakistan' (2019) 20 Oregon Review of International Law 395–436; Johanna Coenen et al., 'Environmental Governance of China's Belt and Road Initiative' (2020) 31 Environmental Policy and Governance 3–17; Jingjing Zhang, 'Chinese NGOs Meet with African NGOs on Holding Chinese Companies Accountable' (*NGOChina*, 21 November 2019) https://ngochina.blogspot.com/2019/11/chinese-ngos-meet-with-african-ngos-on.html.
[72] Erie (n 45) 111.   [73] ibid 101.
[74] Scott Morris, Brad Parks, and Alysha Gardner, 'Chinese and World Bank Lending Terms: A Systematic Comparison across 157 Countries and 15 Years', Center for Global Development Policy Paper 170, April 2020, 3.
[75] ibid 53.

7 How to Use This *Casebook*

This *Casebook* is designed to be a resource for those interested to learn how Chinese commercial and financial actors balance their respective duties to their owners and controllers, regulators, and affected communities in their overseas projects. It is one of the first casebooks to feature original case studies that illustrate various types of legal, policy, and business issues that arise in the course of Chinese outbound investment.[76] Case studies were selected based on the significance of the issues they present, from the corporate structure of Chinese firms to interactions between Chinese investors and the legal system of host states to questions of international and transnational law. Each case study provides insights on such pressing issues as technology, corporate governance, compliance, labor and environment, lending practices, business and human rights, and global value chains. Whereas there is much discussion of these topics in the public media, the case studies are in-depth fact-oriented descriptions of cases based on primary source material. The cases studies are current as of the time of publication and some are still in the process of being resolved, as in the case of disputes. These have been included, however, as they present important issues for study and enough information about the case has been collected so as to identify the salient concerns.

To ensure the integrity of each case study, such material includes transactional documents, interviews with stakeholders, internal company reports, regulatory and normative documents, and caselaw and arbitrations. This focus on primary source material is consistent with the aim of providing objective and neutral accounts of Chinese outbound investment that are not driven by ideological bent or argument. Furthermore, a distinguishing characteristic of this *Casebook*, and one that further ensures the integrity of individual case studies, is that many of the case studies are written by experts and researchers who have firsthand knowledge of the topics. Authors include lawyers who advised on transactions, organized litigation strategies on behalf of affected parties, and led advocacy efforts at the local, national, and international levels. Many authors are either from China or from the countries that are the host countries for Chinese capital discussed in the case study. Still others have conducted long-term research on the questions they explore in their case study and have insights on the operation of Chinese firms and host state regulators.

---

[76] For past casebooks and for reference, see Runhui Lin, Jean Jinghan Chen, and Li Xie, *Corporate Governance of Chinese Multinational Corporations: Case Studies* (Palgrave Macmillan 2020); Liu Baocheng and Chandni Patel, *Overseas Investment of Chinese Enterprises: A Casebook on Corporate Social Responsibility* (Globethics 2020); Jan Drakokoupil, *Chinese Investments in Europe: Corporate Strategies and Labor Relations* (European Trade Union Institute 2017); Michael Moser and Chiann Bao, *Managing 'Belt and Road' Business Disputes: A Case Study of Legal Problems and Solutions* (Wolters Kluwer 2021); Permanent Forum of China Construction Law, *Legal Risks and Opportunities Facing Chinese Engineering Contractors Operating Overseas* (Wolters Kluwer 2019).

In addition, the case studies provide concrete examples of Chinese corporations' operations particularly in emerging economies. They cover a wide geography from Latin America to Africa to Central Asia and Southeast Asia. While the focus of the *Casebook* is on low-income and middle-income states, to provide breadth of comparison, it also includes two case studies that take place in the United States or its territories, where Chinese corporations face a different set of regulatory hurdles. While it is impossible to cover every topic in Chinese investment law and to include every jurisdiction, the case studies included in the *Casebook* offer a representative sample of Chinese investment processes, experiences, and challenges.

The case studies are written primarily for teaching in professional schools, including law schools, policy schools, and business schools. While each case study may not equally lend itself to the different needs of educators in such diverse institutions, educators will find in the *Casebook* ample material for designing their courses. The *Casebook* will likely not be the sole textbook for designing a course but rather may function as a supplementary resource, to be used where relevant. Each case is loosely based on the case study method developed by Harvard Business School in terms of its content and form, which provides a standard and well-recognized approach to presenting such material but moves beyond a focus on just managerial or administrative situations. Instead, case studies describe either, on the Chinese firm side, specific policies or practices of Chinese companies toward host state authorities or resources (human or natural), their corporate structure and relationship to regulators from China or host states, use of financial instruments such as debt restructuring, approaches to designing, maintaining, and financing infrastructure projects overseas, or, on the side of the host state, regulators, commercial parties, and concerned public's responses to legal issues raised by Chinese firms, as well as examples of resolving such disputes in the course of Chinese cross-border business.

Law educators will find case studies that illustrate specific legal and regulatory controversies across a range of fields, including business organizations, labor and employment, environmental protection, and the role of judicial review in foreign investment. Several case studies are deliberately designed around specific disputes that either entered litigation or arbitration. They reveal key issues pertaining to international contracts including choice of law concerns. Business educators will be able to identify case studies that show adaptive responses by Chinese firms in such areas as forming or dissolving international joint ventures. The cases reveal the localization strategies of Chinese firms. Along these lines, cases show how Chinese managers respond to challenging or even hostile investment environments. Policy educators will be able to use certain cases to illustrate how both the Chinese government and host states can introduce law and policy reform to foster more inclusive and sustainable investment projects. In addition to these core audiences, the *Casebook* will also be of interest to legal practitioners, businesspeople, policymakers, and members of civil society whose rights and interests are implicated in the course of Chinese-invested projects overseas.

Each case study identifies an issue or controversy, explains its importance, communicates what can be learned from the case, and describes the sources used in its drafting. Cases are primarily descriptive and rely heavily on verified facts. Pursuant to the tradition of case studies for educational purposes, the authors do not posit an argument but rather present the facts in as comprehensive a manner as possible. They have, however, pursuant to the data and materials used, identified the key issues raised by the case study. As such, the educator has guidance in terms of generating discussion in class around the major issues.

In terms of structure, each case study contains an overview, an introduction, the details of the case, as well as a conclusion. Each case study also then includes a section entitled "Discussion Questions and Comments" that is meant to guide the teaching of the case study. This section is often divided into three subsections, including questions for law audiences, policy audiences, and business audiences. The legal discussion entails questions of judicial, legislative, and possibly executive authority and lawmaking. They provide some context and background to the legal issues in the case. The policy discussion draws attention to how China or the host state create policy around investment and trade. The questions may also hint at ways to improve such policy. The business discussion is focused on issues of strategy and decision-making, either at the firm or industry level. The discussion points and questions often demonstrate overlap between the three subsections. Not every case will throw up the three types of discussions and questions. Some case studies may lend themselves to legal questions rather than business or policy ones. The discussion points and questions are certainly nonexhaustive but may help as starting points for analysis and class reflection.

8 Organization of the *Casebook*

The *Casebook* consists of fifteen cases grouped into six sections that cover important legal aspects of Chinese outbound investment. The sections include Corporations, Compliance, Infrastructure, Labor, Finance, and Disputing. Collectively, they represent the lifespan of Chinese ODI, from market entry to resolving disputes that arise in the course of business.

Section 1, "Corporations," lays a foundation by presenting the core unit of analysis: Chinese corporations. This section includes two case studies. The first by Colin Hawes, "Alibaba and Ant Group: Developing a Hybrid Chinese-International E-commerce Platform Ecosystem," takes a deep dive into Alibaba, one of the most consequential tech companies in the world, by showing the constantly evolving relationships between the company, the PRC government, and international investors. Importantly, Colin shows how such companies operate in the gray area of financial regulation, through, for example, variable interest entities that show corporate innovation pursuant to a hands-off approach by regulators. Ignacio Tornero, in his case study, "Chinese M&A in Latin America: Jiangsu Yanghe Distillery's Stake Acquisition in VSPT Wine Group in Chile," moves from China to Chile to show how Chinese joint ventures form in foreign markets. Ignacio demonstrates how Chinese companies enter emerging markets and what kinds of international law tools (e.g., free trade agreements) are helpful to that effect.

Section 2, "Compliance," examines, broadly, the relationship between Chinese corporate behavior and the relevant rules (local, national, and international) in the contexts in which they conduct business. The three cases in this section each show how Chinese corporations have confronted and adapted to challenging regulatory environments using an array of means from employing local counsel and lawyers to political lobbying and community and political risk mitigation to formal litigation. These cases help to understand how Chinese firms adapt to regulatory systems that differ from their own. Yuan Wang's "Africa's Tech Challenge: A Chinese State-Owned Enterprise's Corporate Social Responsibility Experiment in Kenya" shows how a Chinese SOE operating in Kenya adopted a highly successful corporate social responsibility (CSR) initiative through bottom-up rather than top-down initiatives. Yuan's case study thus complicates assumptions that SOEs operate only through central commands; rather, CSR can highlight the creativity between Chinese representatives and local counterparties on the ground. Marco Germanò's "State Grid's Localization Strategies in Belo Monte, Brazil" provides another success story in terms of State Grid's learning curve in entering the hydroelectric market in Brazil. Marco shows show State Grid was able to manage complex regulatory concerns in order to build the world's longest transmission line for hydroelectric power. Lastly, Han Liu and Ji Li present in their case study, "TikTok versus United States," an extreme example of a Chinese company adapting to a hostile host environment. As Han and Ji show, TikTok has had to adopt a number of localization strategies to survive investment screening and other prohibitive measures adopted by the US authorities.

Section 3, "Infrastructure," provides three case studies that show what works – and what doesn't – in the establishment and operation of Chinese-financed and Chinese-managed infrastructure projects throughout the world. Infrastructural development has become the hallmark of China's economic footprint overseas, especially in developing states. These case studies each provide an in-depth and granular account of a particular infrastructure project financed, managed, or designed by Chinese companies. Each case study sheds light on either the establishment of such projects, and the various methods employed by diverse actors to facilitate the project's success in the affected community, or the project's effects, including on the environment or human rights of that community. In "The Colombo Port City Project: How Chinese Investment Interacts with Local Public Law" by Dilini Pathirana and

Dinesha Samararatne, the authors examine the public law consequences of the Chinese-financed port. They draw attention to the problem of regime change and regulatory uncertainty but also the possible violations of public law pursuant to the creation of regulatory carve-outs such as in special economic zones (SEZs). Leigha Crout and Michael Liu, in their case study, "The Lower Sesan II: Human Rights Implications for Chinese Overseas Projects," bring attention to the environmental and human rights issues following the construction of Cambodia's largest hydroelectric dam, of which a Chinese SOE has a controlling stake. Leigha and Michael illustrate what happens when nontransparent Chinese corporate practices operate in opaque host states, and the role of local actors, including NGOs and civil society in mitigating the negative consequences. Otari Kakhidze presents a more sanguine view in his "The Special Economic Zone at Duqm, Oman: A Chinese-Invested Strategic Port." Otari's case study shows how a Chinese SEZ in Oman both illustrates common features found in other Chinese SEZs and has distinct features including, for example, the active participation of subnational Chinese actors (e.g., provincial authorities).

Section 4, "Labor," examines through two case studies one of the most consequential areas for Chinese investment. Both case studies spotlight problems in terms of both the use of Chinese labor overseas and the employment of local workers. Beginning with Aaron Halegua's "Chinese Workers and Forced Labor on the Imperial Pacific Casino Project in Saipan," this case study emphasizes how problems arise in the complex subcontracting arrangements involving the use of Chinese workers in overseas Chinese projects. However, Aaron also demonstrates the response by the workers, including legal and advocacy measures. In "The Impact of Chinese Investments on the Gold Mining Sector in Kyrgyzstan" by Nuraiym Syrgak kyzy and Robin Lee, the authors find that, based on their case study, Chinese companies operating in extractives industries in developing countries may not follow domestic labor law. Local recruiting companies play a prominent role in the labor abuses that follow, but forms of local resistance including civil society can correct some of the violations.

Section 5, "Finance," turns to the commercial, lending, and banking structures that support Chinese overseas projects. China has a distinct system of overseas finance which differs from that of international financial organizations such as the IMF or World Bank. These two case studies thus explore how Chinese commercial and policy banks are critical institutions in Chinese outbound investment, supplying loans and debt restructuring to foreign governments and commercial parties. The case studies exhibit both distinct Chinese practices and how Chinese respond to common occurrences such as joint venture termination. First, Charles Ho Wang Mak, in "Sovereign Debt Restructuring in Zambia: A Chinese Approach," explains how China, the largest creditor in the world, operates to restructure debts in one particular instance, that of Zambia. Charles examines China's debt restructuring practices and provides a comparative perspective in light of multilateral efforts. Second, in her "Exiting International Joint Ventures between Chinese and South African Banks," Thembi Madalane examines how a Chinese bank that entered into a joint venture with a South African one manages changing circumstances in the context of contractual expectations.

Section 6, "Disputing," through three cases, examines explicitly how Chinese corporations and their counterparties, as well as interested third parties, resolve conflicts in the course of cross-border (and cross-straits) business. "Chinese Overseas Investment and Environmental Accountability: A Legal Battle against the Chinese-Financed Coal-Fired Power Plant in Boké, Guinea" by Jingjing Zhang and Emily Scherr examines the practices of a Chinese company in the extractives sector in Guinea. Despite official Chinese pronouncements to end the construction of Chinese coal plants overseas, Jingjing and Emily show that such practices continue but are also contested by a range of NGO entities. Kai-Shen Huang presents a different type of dispute in "Micron versus UMC and Fujian Jinhua: The Cross-Border Struggle over Integrated Circuits' Trade Secrets." Kai-Shen's case examines how a Chinese SOE allegedly stole trade secrets from a US tech company by poaching talent from the US company's Taiwan branch in the hypercompetitive semiconductor industry. Kai-Shen shows the different legal responses by authorities in Taiwan and the United States to alleged Chinese theft. Lastly, in "The Use of Foreign Investment Treaties in the Protection of Chinese Outbound Investments: *Zhongshan Fucheng Industrial Investment Co. Ltd. v. Federal Republic of Nigeria*," Ngozi S. Nwoko and Stanley U. Nweke-Eze present yet another different type of dispute. This one is between a Chinese company as investor and a host government and centers on alleged wrongs committed by that host state, Nigeria. Ngozi and Stanley diagnose the various legal strategies – including litigation and arbitration – used by Zhongshan and its affiliates, ultimately succeeding in one of the first instances of investor–state arbitration initiated by a Chinese corporation.

There is some overlap between the sections, and case studies from different sections may demonstrate common trends or issues. For example, several of the case studies demonstrate the problems when Chinese corporations operate in low-income countries with embryonic regulatory regimes. Such situations often lead to poor outcomes in terms of business operations and their externalities, particularly as encountered by affected communities. Likewise, several case studies show how civil society and NGOs can marshal relevant legal or extralegal resources to protect rights infringed upon. Another cross-cutting theme is the role of intermediaries between Chinese corporations and local regulators. Local lawyers, subcontractors, and related interlocutors often have substantial leeway in shaping outcomes. Lastly, the role of geopolitics looms large across a number of case studies. While the US-China trade war is one cause for the geopolitical uncertainty, it is not limited to the US-China relationship and, for example, affects US allies and other important jurisdictions like Taiwan. Many developing countries are caught in the middle of US-China lawfare. While economic sanctions and the severing of global supply chains affect their markets, they also have some agency in affecting regulatory decisions and market directions. In short, while issues pertaining to Chinese overseas investment are continually evolving against such a backdrop, the *Casebook* provides a set of case studies to examine in depth the operations of Chinese corporations operating overseas and the consequences of their projects.

Section 1
Corporations

Case Study 1.1

Alibaba and Ant Group
Developing a Hybrid Chinese-International E-commerce Platform Ecosystem

Colin Hawes

1 Overview

This case study uses Alibaba/Ant Group as an example to show how the meteoric growth of e-commerce and the platform economy in China has transformed the way that business is done and has made Chinese consumers into some of the world's most active online sellers and purchasers. It focuses especially on the constantly evolving interactions between Alibaba/Ant Group, the Chinese government, and international investors, providing evidence of the complexities of these relationships and pragmatic compromises required on all sides. The case study demonstrates that the expansion of large Chinese corporations within China and overseas, as well as their occasional setbacks, cannot be understood without a broader knowledge of the legal structures underpinning cross-border investment and awareness of the multiple competing political interests in China.

The case also gives insights into the multinational links of Chinese e-commerce firms, such as international buyers purchasing Chinese goods online through Taobao and AliExpress, investors buying Alibaba's shares on the New York Stock Exchange (NYSE), and Alibaba acquiring e-commerce firms overseas, especially in Southeast Asia and developing countries elsewhere.

Finally, the case explains how e-commerce platforms like Alibaba/Ant Group evolved into numerous business sectors, especially online banking and financial services. Their huge size and financial complexity have led to some negative impacts and systemic risks, and this in turn has caused the Chinese government to regulate these e-commerce and fintech firms more tightly.

2 Introduction

This case study explores the meteoric growth of Alibaba/Ant Group, one of the most successful private Chinese e-commerce and financial technology (fintech) platforms. While these online platforms have opened up a whole new channel for small and medium-sized enterprises (SMEs) to do business within and outside China, creating tens of millions of new jobs, the sheer speed and scale of their growth has magnified key defects of the Chinese SME ecosystem, especially endemic fraud, product safety issues, and intellectual property violations. Because Alibaba's e-commerce platforms now extend to more than 190 countries and regions throughout the world, both through overseas direct investment (ODI) and through providing efficient channels for global import/export direct from producers to consumers, these issues clearly create concerns well beyond China's borders.

The case study focuses especially on the constantly evolving interactions between Alibaba/Ant Group, the Chinese government, and international investors, providing evidence of the complexities of these relationships and pragmatic compromises required on all sides. The case study demonstrates that the expansion of large Chinese corporations within China and overseas, as well as their occasional setbacks, cannot be understood without a broader knowledge of the legal structures underpinning cross-border investment and awareness of the multiple competing political interests in China – what I call the "Chinese corporate-political ecosystem."

The case study starts with a brief review of Alibaba/Ant Group's main businesses, demonstrating how they have transformed the Chinese commercial landscape and facilitated the rapid growth of SMEs and the private economy. The growth of Alibaba/Ant and other massive Chinese platform firms, and their expansion overseas, could not have occurred without large-scale capital from international investors. This, in turn, has relied on their ability to establish so-called variable interest entities (VIEs) listed in the United States, tacitly permitted yet technically illegal (under PRC law) hybrid structures that continue down to the present. The case study explains how this structure works, the hands-off regulatory role of the Chinese government, how it has facilitated rapid expansion within China and ODI through acquisitions – especially in Southeast Asia – and its legal and political risks.

Besides enabling e-commerce, Alibaba/Ant Group's platform business has also diversified incredibly rapidly into a wide range of financial services, some providing the essential lifeblood for legitimate businesses while others are highly speculative and risky. The case study shows how Alibaba/Ant Group has benefited from gray areas in financial regulation and used its access to extensive customer data to offer financial and investment products to hundreds of millions of users, in collaboration with more than 100 banks and some 6,000 other financial firms.

While initially adopting a hands-off approach to platform finance, more recently the Chinese government has tightened regulations in response to widespread online fraud, official corruption, and numerous financial and e-commerce scandals. The abrupt suspension of Ant Group's initial public offering (IPO) in 2020 was an integral part of this more interventionist approach.

3 The Case

3.1 Creating a Platform for International Trade and Domestic E-commerce: Alibaba's Initial Growth

Alibaba's first business venture was a simple platform website where small Chinese manufacturers could post information about their products in English, allowing internet users around the world to easily locate potential Chinese suppliers. Jack Ma and seventeen founding partners (including six women) established the business in an apartment in Hangzhou City in February 1999.[1]

Hangzhou is situated in Zhejiang Province, which by the late 1990s had become home base for around ten million private firms – mostly small, efficient manufacturers of light industrial and consumer products, from socks to ball bearings and anything in between. Many had evolved out of so-called township and village enterprises (TVEs), former collective firms that sprung up in their millions after the Chinese Communist Party (CCP) relaxed its rules on state ownership in the early 1980s.[2]

Many businesses were keen to attract international buyers, but their knowledge of computers and access to the internet was still extremely limited. Out of China's population of 1.2 billion in early 1999, only 2 million were internet users, mostly in larger cities like Beijing and Shanghai. Fortunately for Alibaba, these numbers expanded exponentially; by 2009, internet users had already surpassed 300 million, and by 2020, they reached 989 million.[3]

In early 2000, Alibaba managed to raise a combined US$25 million from a Goldman Sachs consortium and Japan's SoftBank in return for 80% of its shares.[4] This vital capital injection allowed Alibaba to ride out the dot.com crash and greatly improve the functionality of its platform website. It also added a Chinese-language site for small businesses to sell wholesale products to traders within China, which is now called 1688.com.[5]

Alibaba expanded very quickly, and it continues to connect both Chinese and international wholesale suppliers with buyers through several sub-platforms in

---

[1] Alibaba Group, 'Our History and Corporate Structure' and 'Business' in *Alibaba Group Holding Ltd. Prospectus* New York Stock Exchange (18 September 2014); Ant Group, 'History and Development' and 'Our Business' in Ant Group, *H Share IPO Prospectus*. For useful accounts of Alibaba's early years and growth, see Porter Erisman, *Alibaba's World: How a Remarkable Company Is Changing the Face of Global Business* (Macmillan 2015); Duncan Clark, *Alibaba: The House That Jack Built* (HarperCollins 2016); Shiying Liu and Martha Avery, *Alibaba: The Inside Story behind Jack Ma and the Creation of the World's Biggest Online Marketplace* (HarperCollins 2009).

[2] For more on TVEs, see Ezra F. Vogel, *Deng Xiaoping and the Transformation of China* (Harvard University Press 2011) chs 14–16.

[3] CNNIC [China Internet Network Information Center], 'Hulianwang Fazhan Yanjiu' [Research on Internet Development] www.cnnic.cn/hlwfzyj/.

[4] Clark (n 1) 97–102, ch 7; Erisman (n 1) 17.

[5] Alibaba Group, 'Our Businesses' www.alibabagroup.com/en/about/businesses; Liu and Avery (n 1) 70–4.

more than 190 countries and regions. Enough clients are willing to pay premium fees to make it a profitable business, accounting for 5% of Alibaba's revenues in 2020.[6]

However, Alibaba's business did not really take off until 2003, when it launched a platform for Chinese businesses and entrepreneurs to sell products online to domestic consumers – a kind of Chinese Amazon. China's bricks-and-mortar retail industry was underdeveloped, especially in smaller cities and towns: products were limited, and prices were high due to inefficient distribution. Alibaba set up Taobao, which allowed individual sellers and small businesses to advertise their products, arranged into easily searchable product categories on the Taobao website.[7] Larger brands soon realized the benefits of e-commerce too, and they paid Alibaba to create virtual storefronts on its Tmall (*Tianmao*) site.[8]

Taobao had initially faced stiff competition from eBay, which had entered China by acquiring a local e-commerce startup called Eachnet in 2003.[9] However, eBay/Eachnet was unable to keep up with Taobao due to various cultural and technical failures, not least its inability to establish a secure and efficient online payment system.[10] Alibaba overcame the payment problem, setting up a fully digitized system called Alipay that allowed customers to make payments for online purchases via their computer (or, from 2012 onward, via mobile phone), and the money was withheld from sellers until delivery was confirmed.[11]

The convenience and sheer volume of online traffic made Alipay highly profitable despite very low transaction fees. Alipay's user numbers have now climbed to more than a billion, including online/mobile payments and "offline" payments made at millions of shops and service outlets throughout China (restaurants, hotels, taxis, ticketing agents, even rural farmers' markets).

In 2011, Alipay was spun off into a separate company, Ant Financial (later renamed Ant Group), but Jack Ma remained its controlling shareholder, and Alibaba currently retains a one-third stake in Ant Group. Ant Group's revenues from Alipay fees in 2019 totaled almost RMB 52 billion (US$8 billion).[12]

If we view the Chinese economy as a highly complex system of circulating capital, goods, and labor, the success of Alibaba/Ant Group has come from identifying the most serious blockages within that circulatory system and using the power of the internet and digital technology to open up the flows. Typical early blockages included (1) the difficulties of small Chinese manufacturers/traders to connect with foreign wholesale buyers and even Chinese buyers outside their local regions; (2) the high prices (or unavailability) of consumer

---

[6] Alibaba Group, *Annual Report 2020*, 120 www.alibabagroup.com/en/ir/reports.
[7] Clark (n 1) ch 9; Erisman (n 1) ch 11.   [8] For Tmall, see Alibaba Group (n 5).
[9] Clark (n 1) 152–5.   [10] Clark (n 1) 163–73.   [11] Clark (n 1) 178–83.
[12] Ant Group (n 1) 'Our Business' and 308.

goods outside the largest urban centers; and (3) the trust deficit with online payment systems.

Alibaba (and Ant Group) refer to themselves as an "ecosystem," and the firm does now consist of a complex network of subsidiaries and affiliated companies in diverse sectors, with more than 250,000 employees.[13] However, the firm's success cannot be divorced from the broader corporate, financial, and regulatory ecosystem within which it operates, and it is more accurate to say that Alibaba/Ant Group provides channels to open up the flow of goods and capital within that broader corporate-financial circulatory ecosystem, both in China and overseas.

Though Jack Ma and Alibaba's other founders were quick to spot the potential of this "online platform" business model, and they worked incredibly hard over two decades to constantly adapt and extend its functions and revenue sources, they could not have succeeded without the coevolution of the Chinese commercial system and technological infrastructure, which was facilitated by Chinese government policy initiatives.

First, from the late 1990s, the Chinese government's "informatization" policy funded a massive expansion of broadband and mobile communication networks.[14] Second, the frenzied expansion of the private sector during the 1990s, which was also encouraged by the government as it downsized the state sector, provided Alibaba with a huge potential customer base of sellers among SMEs and coincided with greater disposable income of Chinese consumers due to rising living standards, not to mention private logistics firms to deliver goods efficiently.[15]

Third, there was also the reform of the Chinese banking system to introduce market competition from the late 1990s onward, including setting up more than 100 local city commercial banks hungry for new sources of revenue. These state-owned banks were highly receptive to collaborating with Alipay because its millions of online transactions gave them access to fees from customers who would otherwise have remained underserved by the banking system.[16]

Fourth, there were supportive government incentives encouraging Chinese manufacturers to export their products overseas, as well as growing awareness among CCP officials that private firms were key drivers of GDP growth. As a crucial "platform" facilitating this growth and an exemplar of Chinese hi-tech innovation, Alibaba received numerous visits and statements of support

---

[13] Full-time employees on 31 March 2021: Alibaba Group, 'Frequently Asked Questions' www.alibabagroup.com/en/about/faqs.
[14] Clark (n 1) 94–5; CNNIC (n 3).
[15] Bin Jiang and Edmund Prater, 'Distribution and Logistics Development in China: The Revolution Has Begun' (2002) 32(9) International Journal of Physical Distribution & Logistics Management; Cynthia Luo, 'One Platform to Rule Them All' (*eCommerceIQ*, 7 December 2016) https://ecommerceiq.asia/cainiao-logistics-southeast-asia/.
[16] Ant Group (n 1) 164–5. For early banking reforms, see He Wei Ping, 'Introduction' in *Banking Regulation in China: The Role of Public and Private Sectors* (Palgrave Macmillan 2014).

from local CCP leaders, including Xi Jinping when he was Party Secretary of Shanghai in 2007.[17]

Finally, inbound foreign investment was pivotal to Alibaba's survival in its first decade, and the government's pragmatic attitude toward partial foreign control of internet technology firms (discussed in Section 3.2) allowed Alibaba and other private tech firms to actively seek overseas capital funding when Chinese state banks and stock markets were still focusing their attention primarily on state-owned enterprises (SOEs).

At the same time, the contradictions and fragmentation within the Chinese political/legal ecosystem, the poorly regulated helter-skelter expansion of e-commerce and online banking, and ruthless competition among Chinese technology firms have harmed Alibaba/Ant Group's reputation and potentially increased financial risks for the Chinese economy. The following sections explore these risks and negative impacts, beginning with Alibaba's mutant hybrid corporate structure.

3.2 Foreign Funding with Chinese Management Control: Alibaba's VIE Structure and Fragmented Authoritarian Politics

Despite extensive economic reforms and relative openness to foreign trade and investment, the CCP continues to strictly censor and control all media content in China, including newspapers, magazines, television, and movies. With the massive expansion of the internet and online news via social media, Chinese government censorship has extended its tentacles to cover all online content and to block politically sensitive foreign websites and social media from being accessed in China.[18]

This government censorship is also exercised through restrictions on foreign ownership of Chinese "value-added telecom services," which includes any "internet content providers" (ICPs).[19] In theory, therefore, no "foreign-controlled" ICP firm should be granted a license to operate its business in China, including e-commerce firms like Alibaba who own video streaming and media businesses.

Despite this, most large "Chinese" private internet technology firms are controlled by foreign corporations listed on American or international stock

---

[17] Clark (n 1) 238–9; Leonard K. Cheng and Zihui Ma, 'China's Outward Foreign Direct Investment' in Robert C. Feenstra and Shang-Jin Wei (eds), *China's Growing Role in World Trade* (University of Chicago Press 2010) ch 14.

[18] Cate Cadell and Pei Li, 'Tea and Tiananmen: Inside China's New Censorship Machine' (*Reuters*, 18 October 2017) www.reuters.com/article/us-china-congress-censorship-insight-idUSKCN1C40LL; Anne-Marie Brady, *Marketing Dictatorship: Propaganda and Thought Work in Contemporary China* (Rowman & Littlefield 2007) chs 5–6.

[19] See NDRC, 'Special Administrative Measures on Access to Foreign Investment (2020 edition)' linked from Qian Zhou, 'China's 2020 New Negative Lists Signal Further Opening-Up' (*China Briefing*, 1 July 2020) www.china-briefing.com/news/chinas-2020-new-negative-lists-signals-further-opening-up/.

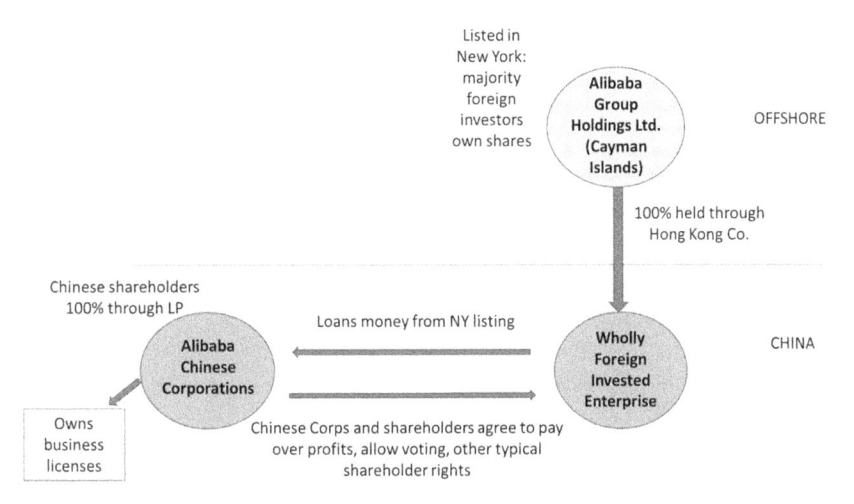

Figure 1.1.1 Alibaba Group VIE ownership structure

exchanges. Yet all of them have managed to obtain Chinese ICP licenses. How did this paradoxical situation arise and why has it persisted for more than two decades?

Alibaba, for example, was first incorporated in 1999 as a Cayman Islands company, Alibaba Group Holdings Ltd., and during the early 2000s the majority of its shares were held by foreign investors, with the rest (around 20%) issued to Alibaba's Chinese founders and employees, including CEO Jack Ma.[20] Even since its IPO in 2014, Alibaba remains majority-controlled by a broad range of international investors.[21] How did Alibaba get around the Chinese restrictions on foreign-controlled ICPs and telecom services?

Like other private tech firms, it used a legal sleight of hand called a variable interest entity (VIE): see Figure 1.1.1.

Cutting through the legal jargon, the VIE structure involves a set of agreements between the Cayman Islands firm Alibaba Group Holdings and several Chinese corporations. These Chinese corporations currently have only five shareholders who are all Chinese citizens, so the corporations are permitted to hold the ICP and telecom licenses.[22]

However, the Chinese corporations and their shareholders have agreed to give all the benefits of their ICP/telecom and other licenses to Alibaba and to allow Alibaba to make all decisions on behalf of the Chinese corporations. In other words, even though Chinese corporations technically own the licenses, a foreign corporation (Alibaba Group Holdings) can oversee every major

---

[20] Alibaba Group (n 1) 250–1, 297; Clark (n 1) 200.
[21] Japanese company SoftBank is still Alibaba's largest single shareholder, with around 25%. See Alibaba Group, *Global Offering*, Hong Kong Stock Exchange (15 November 2019) 169.
[22] For a detailed description of Alibaba's VIE structures, see Alibaba Group (n 1) 87–92; and for the current arrangement, Alibaba Group (n 6) 95.

decision made by the Chinese corporations and receive all financial revenues through a series of contracts, just as if it was a 100% controlling shareholder of the Chinese corporations.[23]

In other words, we see a kind of mutant hybrid corporate structure – a pragmatic compromise – that allows substantial foreign investment in these technology firms through majority shareholding, yet without giving up day-to-day management to non-Chinese shareholders or allowing them to directly own the licenses that are prohibited or restricted from foreign investment.

This VIE structure is purely designed to get around the restrictions on foreign ownership of Chinese licenses, and its legality remains uncertain.[24] Yet it is a very common structure among private Chinese technology firms. By 2010, more than 100 offshore-listed Chinese firms had used this structure to obtain their ICP and telecom services licenses from relevant government ministries.[25]

Several factors will likely perpetuate this pragmatic but unwieldy regulatory fudge. China's security establishment is still unwilling to allow direct foreign control of internet providers, yet the Chinese government relies on these private online platform firms to boost economic growth and provide tens of millions of jobs to Chinese workers and entrepreneurs. The firms are also highly reliant on foreign capital to maintain their rapid expansion.

However, it is not clear whether Chinese courts would enforce the VIE contracts when disputes occur, making investors entirely dependent on the personal integrity and goodwill of the corporations' founders or senior managers.[26] More recently, the Chinese government has launched intrusive "cybersecurity investigations" into several large VIE firms on "data security" grounds, including the ride-hailing firm Didi Chuxing, leading to sudden market delisting, losses, and shareholder lawsuits.[27] It is unnerving to think that hundreds of billions of dollars of foreign investment in Chinese technology firms relies on such shaky legal and regulatory foundations.

A similar lack of regulatory clarity has allowed various online fraud and financial scandals to emerge over the past decade, which we will discuss after tracing the further breakneck expansion of Alibaba/Ant's ecosystem.

---

[23] 'Alibaba Partnership' in Alibaba Group (n 1).   [24] Alibaba Group (n 1) 49, 92.
[25] Thomas Y. Man, 'Policy above Law: VIE and Foreign Investment Regulation in China' (2015) 3 Peking University Transnational Law Review 215–22.
[26] Li Guo, 'Chinese Style VIEs: Continuing to Sneak under Smog?' (2014) 47 Cornell International Law Journal 569–606, part IV.
[27] Coco Feng, Che Pan, and Minghe Hu, 'Didi Chuxing "Forced Its Way" to a New York Listing, Triggering Data Security Review, Sources Say' (*The Star*, 7 July 2021) www.thestar.com.my/tech/tech-news/2021/07/07/didi-chuxing-forced-its-way-to-a-new-york-listing-triggering-data-security-review-sources-say.

3.3 ODI and Alibaba's VIE Structure: Acquisition of Lazada in Southeast Asia

Besides its useful function as a conduit for raising money from international investors, the foreign-listed VIE structure also directly facilitates ODI in the form of overseas acquisitions by Chinese private firms. The Chinese government still imposes capital controls on foreign exchange – in other words, restrictions on Chinese individuals and corporations converting RMB into US dollars or other currencies. Exceptions are made for ODI that is encouraged by the Chinese government, but for private firms that may prefer to invest for their own purely commercial reasons, an overseas listing can give them direct access to US dollars, which can then be channeled into acquisitions without the need for foreign exchange approval.

Alibaba's 2014 IPO provides a clear example, as the company's prospectus stated that the net proceeds raised from the NYSE listing would be used "outside of China, and [we] do not expect to transfer such funds into China."[28] By 2018, Alibaba had invested around US$4 billion of those proceeds to acquire full control of Lazada, which is Southeast Asia's largest e-commerce platform, operating in Indonesia, Malaysia, the Philippines, Singapore, Thailand, and Vietnam.[29] With Alibaba applying its advanced online platform, payment system, and logistical software to improve Lazada's efficiency, not to mention extensive marketing campaigns, this acquisition immediately gave the company a commanding market share in the whole region and significantly increased the use of e-commerce by local consumers for their purchases. Some local intermediary merchants have since complained that Alibaba is using its market power to squeeze out the competition, similar to its alleged monopoly practices in China.[30]

Alibaba also used its IPO funds to acquire local e-commerce companies in several other countries or regions, including Indonesia, Turkey, and South Asia, and to invest in a joint venture with three local firms in Russia. Most of these businesses will be operated under the AliExpress brand, which links international online consumers with commercial sellers in China and dozens of other countries.[31]

The potential benefits for Alibaba from this type of ODI are huge, especially in developing countries: Southeast Asia alone has a population of more than 630 million, with rapidly increasing access to mobile phones and the internet and more room for future expansion than the highly competitive domestic Chinese e-commerce market.[32] At the same time, by creating efficient channels connecting domestic Chinese sellers, many of them SMEs, with international buyers, Alibaba continues to stimulate economic growth in China and (along with other

---

[28] Alibaba Group (n 1) 71.   [29] Alibaba Group (n 20) 203, 236.
[30] Qian Linliang, 'Buying Power: Alibaba in South-east Asia' (*The China Story*, 2018), www.thechinastory.org/yearbooks/yearbook-2018-power/forum-the-power-of-money/buying-power-alibaba-in-south-east-asia/.
[31] Alibaba Group (n 20) 203, 235–6.   [32] Qian (n 30).

large private Chinese firms) solves a perennial headache for the Chinese government of providing employment opportunities for its enormous population.[33]

3.4 Alibaba/Ant Group's Expanding Fintech Ecosystem: "Trust," Credit, and Data

The Alibaba/Ant Group has consistently billed itself as a firm (or "ecosystem") that promotes trust and integrity.[34] To a certain degree this is true, but the broader fragmented political and economic ecosystem within which it operates has facilitated numerous instances of fraud that the company must constantly try to stamp out. In the process of dealing with these trust issues, Alibaba/Ant Group has collected a gargantuan mass of data about its users, which it now employs to identify and target businesses and consumers for each of their new products and to guide their behavior.

In terms of building trust, we noted how Alipay provided a secure online payment system that would not release funds to sellers until buyers had approved the goods received. This system increased user confidence in e-commerce but still left gaps for potential fraudsters. Alibaba/Ant realized that the data it collected on its sellers and their transactions, along with buyer ratings, complaints, and lawsuits, could be used to fill these gaps by calculating a comprehensive "trust score" for each seller (also known as a Sesame Credit Score). Having a high trust score would make a seller more attractive to buyers, whereas a low trust score would lead to warnings and ultimately exclusion from Alibaba's e-commerce platforms.[35]

Alibaba/Ant's most important and financially lucrative insight was that they could then employ this extensive data on hundreds of millions of users to diversify into financial services. To start with, they could offer small business loans to their merchants who had high trust scores and had achieved certain revenue levels and numbers of successful transactions. This kind of short-term finance was crucial for SMEs to survive and expand their operations, but state banks were not interested in lending amounts less than RMB 1 million at a time (around US$200,000) due to high administrative costs and risks of default, whereas SMEs on average only required loans of RMB 36,000.[36]

By June 2020, Ant Group's small business loan program had expanded very rapidly, approving credit for around 20 million SMEs in the previous twelve months, with a loan balance of more than RMB 400 billion (US$61 billion) through its private bank subsidiary MyBank.[37]

---

[33] Vikas Shukla, 'Alibaba Follows Beijing's "One Belt and One Road"' (*Value Walk*, 2 February 2020) www.valuewalk.com/alibaba-follows-one-road-one-belt/.
[34] Alibaba Group (n 6) 4, 220.   [35] Ant Group (n 1) 183; Erisman (n 1) 64–5, 194.
[36] Ant Group (n 1) 197–8; Dong Youying, 'Integrity Capital-Based Finance,' in Ying Lowrey (ed), *The Alibaba Way* (McGraw Hill Education 2016) 178–96.
[37] Ant Group (n 1) 9, 198. For MyBank's five main shareholders, see Wangshang Yinhang, '2020 Niandu Baogao' [2020 Annual Report] 13.

However, Ant Group's largest revenue generator is not SMEs but consumer credit and loans. Since 2014, Ant has used its trademark data-crunching methods to develop a kind of virtual credit card for Alipay/Alibaba users called "Huabei" (which means literally "Why not spend?"). In 2015, Ant also introduced a consumer small loan program called "Jiebei" (literally "Why not borrow?").[38]

These two consumer credit products filled another large gap for the majority of Chinese people who didn't meet the criteria for bank loans or credit cards or wanted a quicker and simpler way to borrow money. Huabei and Jiebei generated an incredible credit balance of more than RMB 1.7 trillion by 2020 (US$262 billion), around four times the amount of Ant Group's SME loan balance.[39]

The other crucial plank in Ant Group's evolving financial services ecosystem is investment and wealth management products (WMPs). Interest rates for depositors at traditional Chinese banks are very low, so Ant developed a low-risk money market fund in 2013 called Yu'ebao (literally "Leftover Treasure") that allowed their Alipay users to deposit their unused e-wallet cash balances and earn interest higher than a bank account, while having instant access to the money via their Alipay mobile phone app. Yu'ebao soon became the largest money market fund in China with more than 600 million users. Ant Group earns money from the spread between deposit rates and its own investment of the funds.[40]

Ant has also promoted a wide range of higher risk mutual funds and other WMPs to online users through its InvestmentTech apps, aimed at China's growing middle classes. For most of these products, Ant acts as an intermediary, first vetting investment firms and working with them to develop online consumer products, then mining Ant's user data to target those in the right income brackets who would be likely to invest in specific funds. Ant receives a "technology services fee" from the fund management firm for locating and recommending the investors. By mid 2020, Ant was already working with around 170 asset management firms, including mutual fund companies, insurers, banks, and securities firms, to offer more than 6,000 products through Ant's platform.[41]

The total amount under investment in Yu'ebao and other investment products offered through Ant's platform by June 2020 was a staggering RMB 4.099 trillion (US$633 billion), and its revenues from InvestmentTech amounted to RMB 16.9 billion (US$2.61 billion) in 2019, or 14.9% of Ant's total revenues. Clearly, Ant has become a major financial services conglomerate in its own right and has developed a huge customer base in the hundreds of millions.[42]

Although Alibaba only owns one-third of Ant Group's shares, one reason that Alibaba and Ant refer to themselves as an "ecosystem" is that their various businesses constantly interact and feed off each other in a kind of symbiotic

---

[38] Ant Group (n 1) 136, 166.   [39] Ant Group (n 1) 13.   [40] Ant Group (n 1) 200–1.   [41] ibid.
[42] For Ant's revenues: Ant Group (n 1) 13; for Alibaba's total revenues: Alibaba Group (n 6) 220.

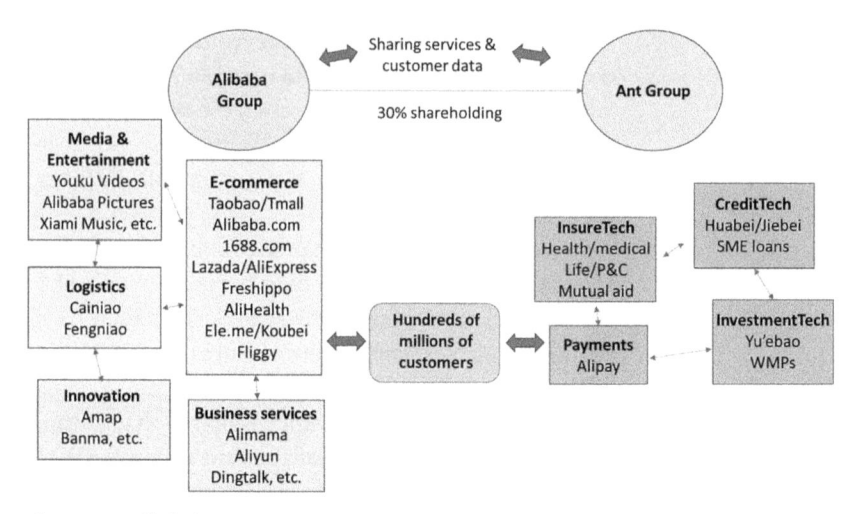

Figure 1.1.2 Alibaba/Ant ecosystem

relationship: see Figure 1.1.2. Ant Group's success has therefore depended to a great extent on Alibaba's ability to develop new lines of business and constantly attract new users previously neglected by traditional business networks.[43]

Other sectors that Alibaba has expanded into include cloud computing services for businesses (Alibaba Cloud, or Aliyun); logistics and product delivery (Cainiao Network); fresh food delivery and smart supermarkets (Freshippo and Fengniao); online restaurant ordering and delivery (Ele.me, literally "Are you hungry?"); as well as travel ticketing and bookings (Fliggy).[44]

Finally, the company has also ventured into pharmaceutical sales and healthcare through AliHealth, mostly focused on online ordering and delivery of safe medical drugs using blockchain and QR codes, to counter the dangers of fake medicine suppliers, which is one of the deepest concerns of Chinese consumers along with tainted food.[45]

These are just some of the key business sectors that Alibaba/Ant has expanded into over the past decade. Their aim is to provide a so-called "seamless" group of business and lifestyle apps that are all integrated and downloaded onto users' mobile phones, so that virtually all their daily life activities will be conducted through an Alibaba or Ant Group platform. As Alibaba put it in a recent Annual Report, "we envision that our customers will meet, work and live at Alibaba."[46]

Like any natural ecosystem, Alibaba/Ant is also continually testing, negotiating, and breaking through the boundaries that separate its own ecosystem from others. Is a small business that sells most of its products online through Taobao/Tmall and distributes them through the Cainiao Network, while

---

[43] Ant Group (n 1) 294, 297–8; Alibaba Group (n 5) 59–60.
[44] Alibaba Group (n 6) 48, 120, 126, 136, 353; Alibaba Group (n 5).
[45] Alibaba Group (n 6) 352.   [46] Alibaba Group (n 6) 3.

paying for promotion by Alimama, storing its data on Aliyun, receiving payments through Alipay, obtaining loans from MyBank, and investing its profits in one of Ant Group's sponsored WMPs really independent, or is it simply a component element of Alibaba/Ant's ecosystem? Has this mutant hybrid (Chinese-foreign) superstructure evolved so quickly and sucked in so many diverse entities that it is now beyond effective control by the supposedly powerful CCP and Chinese government – even, possibly, beyond the control of its own managers? As the next section shows, there is strong evidence that this has already happened, and that the Alibaba/Ant monster cannot be fully tamed. All that government regulators (and Alibaba/Ant itself) can hope to do is act strategically, using market discipline whenever possible, to address its worst abuses and mitigate the potential systemic risks that emerge from all directions.

Of course, Alibaba/Ant is not the only entity seeking to occupy these business niches. It faces fierce competition from other private Chinese firms such as Tencent, JD.com and Meituan. Yet this only increases the urgency of consistently regulating these new corporate ecosystems.

3.5 Alibaba/Ant Group's Scandals and Tussles with Chinese Regulators

The main problem with being primarily a "platform" or channel business "ecosystem" is that when user numbers expand rapidly into the hundreds of millions, it becomes extremely difficult to monitor and control their negative behavior.

Alibaba has long faced criticism for failing to prevent fraudulent activities on its platforms. The US Trade Representative (USTR) has been especially vocal about counterfeit products sold on Alibaba.com and Taobao, especially those that impact consumer safety, such as fake medicines, contaminated pet food, and children's toys. Both platforms have been placed on the USTR's list of "notorious" infringing copyright/trademark markets from 2008 to 2010, and again from 2016 to the present.[47]

The Chinese government has also repeatedly censured Alibaba through its corporate regulator, the State Administration for Market Regulation (SAMR).[48] A 2015 White Paper briefly posted on the regulator's website claimed that only 37% of sample purchases in its investigation of Taobao could be considered

---

[47] For earlier complaints, see *Christine Asia Co., Ltd., et al., against Alibaba Group Holding Limited, et al.*, United States District Court Southern District of New York, No. 15-md-02631 (21 June 2016) 3; for the USTR listings, see Trevor Little and Tim Lince, 'Notorious Markets List 2020: USTR Resists Call to Include US Platforms as Alibaba and Amazon Remain' (*World Trademark Review*, 15 January 2021) www.worldtrademarkreview.com/anti-counterfeiting/notorious-markets-list-2020-ustr-resists-call-include-us-platforms-alibaba-and-amazon-remain.

[48] The earlier action against Alibaba was brought by the State Administration for Industry and Commerce (SAIC), which was merged into the SAMR in 2018.

authentic products.[49] Far from meekly accepting the censure, Alibaba publicly criticized what it called the regulator's flawed and biased investigative methods, and the White Paper was abruptly removed from the regulator's website. The lack of official sanctions demonstrated the company's strength and the government's reluctance to punish the company for fear of impacting China's economic growth.[50]

Several features of the broader Chinese corporate-political ecosystem combine to make Alibaba's task of ensuring "trust" virtually impossible. First, the Chinese government itself is highly fragmented, with local government officials and police frequently turning a blind eye to counterfeit manufacturers in their regions, either because of the employment/tax revenues they provide or because of well-placed bribes aimed in their direction.[51] Second, despite the Chinese government's reputation as an all-seeing force that can track every citizen's online identity, it is still very common for users to create fake internet and social media accounts to engage in fraud.[52] Third, during its incredibly rapid growth phase, more than 100,000 new merchants were signing up to Taobao every day, and it is very difficult to predict which of them will become fraudsters.[53] Fourth, Alibaba and other Chinese e-commerce firms provide indirect employment to millions of honest SME owners and significantly boost China's economic growth, something China's SOEs have failed to do.

In other words, these aspects of the Chinese corporate-political ecosystem have led to a kind of symbiotic codependency of the Chinese government on private firms, limiting its regulatory capacity to situations where firms might endanger the financial or social stability of the whole society or directly threaten the CCP's rule.

The limits of government control are clear from two other major scandals involving Alibaba. The first was its use of market power to engage in monopolistic and anti-competitive practices. Merchants who refused to sign exclusive agreements with Alibaba would be penalized on Tmall/Taobao by adjusting search algorithms to prevent customers from locating their storefronts; or their orders would not be fulfilled efficiently; or their accounts would be temporarily suspended on Alibaba and Ant Group's various sites to disrupt their businesses. These practices had been ongoing since at least 2015, and the firm had repeatedly ignored government warnings, but it was only in April 2021 that the

---

[49] Clark (n 1) 236.
[50] Clark (n 1); Zhang Jinshu, 'Taobao Yu Gongshang: Banzi Gai Da Shei?' [Taobao versus SAIC: Who Deserved a Beating?] (*Caixin*, 31 January 2015) https://opinion.caixin.com/2015-01-31/100780433.html.
[51] Michael Schuman, 'Why Alibaba's Massive Counterfeit Problem Will Never Be Solved' (*Forbes*, 4 November 2015) www.forbes.com/sites/michaelschuman/2015/11/04/alibaba-and-the-40000-thieves/?sh=2475ec629dc7; Daniel C. Fleming, 'Counterfeiting in China' (2014) 10 University of Pennsylvania East Asia Law Review 15–18, 27–8.
[52] Emma Lee, 'Sale of WeChat Accounts Prompts Concern over Fraud' (*TechNode*, 16 January 2019) https://technode.com/2019/01/16/wechat-accounts-sale-online-fraud/.
[53] Schuman (n 51).

SAMR finally fined Alibaba RMB 18 billion (US$2.8 billion) for breaching the PRC Anti-Monopoly Law.[54]

This was the largest financial penalty ever exacted on a corporation in China, but it was only 4% of Alibaba's 2019 sales revenues, so it will not have a major impact on the firm's finances, not least because Alibaba's main competitors like Tencent, JD.com, Didi Chuxing, and Meituan were also penalized.[55]

The SAMR's future ability to control abuses of market power will continue to be limited by its own understaffing as well as resistance by numerous powerful state and private interests who benefit from Alibaba's continuing expansion and profitability.[56]

The other major tussle with the government was the sudden suspension of Ant Group's planned IPO on the Shanghai STAR Market and Hong Kong Stock Exchange. This was a major shock, as the IPO was expected to become the largest ever global public offering, raising around US$34 billion from investors.[57]

Some claimed that this "crackdown" was a first step in the CCP's plan to renationalize private technology firms, but this has not occurred.[58] A more plausible explanation is that Ant Group had consistently neglected warnings about the financial risks of its breakneck expansion. With the increasing liberalization of China's financial services industry, especially since 2010, numerous state banks and other firms (both SOEs and private) have offered a broad range of retail investment products.[59] An increasingly large portion of their business has come from products marketed through Ant Group or Alibaba's platforms. When promoted in this way, it is not clear to investors whether they are investing in an Ant-backed fund or a third-party fund.[60]

The fact that more than 6,000 financial products are now offered on Alibaba/Ant's platforms involving huge numbers of borrowers/investors with

---

[54] SAMR, 'Guojia Shichang Jiandu Guanli Zongju Xingzheng Chufa Juedingshu' [SAMR Administrative Penalty Decision] *Guo shi jian chu (2021) 28 hao*, 10 April 2021, linked from the SAMR's website, www.samr.gov.cn/xw/zj/202104/t20210410_327702.html [hereafter 'SAMR Decision'].

[55] See the SAMR Decision 25. For its 2020 sales and net income, see Alibaba Group (n 6) 106. cf Qian Tong and Denise Jia, 'China Hits More Internet Businesses with Antitrust Fines' (*Caixin*, 1 May 2021) www.caixinglobal.com/2021-05-01/china-hits-more-internet-business-with-antitrust-fines-101704752.html.

[56] See Angela Huyue Zhang, 'Bureaucratic Politics and China's Anti-Monopoly Law' (2014) 47(3) Cornell International Law Journal 672–707.

[57] Karishma Vaswani, 'Jack Ma's Ant Group: World's Biggest Market Debut Suspended' (*BBC News*, 3 November 2020) www.bbc.com/news/business-54798278.

[58] For example, contrast Lingling Wei, 'China Blocked Jack Ma's Ant IPO after Investigation Revealed Likely Beneficiaries' (*Wall Street Journal*, 16 February 2021) with Huo Kan, 'Mayi Xiaojin Huopi Kaiye' [Ant's Consumer Finance Subsidiary Gains Approval to Operate] (*Caixin*, 3 June 2021) https://finance.caixin.com/2021-06-03/101722422.html.

[59] Jinglin Jiang et al., 'Government Affiliation and Peer-to-Peer Lending Platforms in China' (2021) 62 Journal of Empirical Finance 87–90; Emily Perry and Florian Weltewitz, 'Wealth Management Products in China' Reserve Bank of Australia Bulletin (June 2015) 59–68.

[60] Ant Group (n 1) 168, 189, 201.

rudimentary investment knowledge triggers anxiety among regulators about potential social instability. Numerous collapses of large financial firms have occurred in recent years due to corruption and reckless growth. There have also been hundreds of peer-to-peer lending scandals in which millions of ordinary investors lost their savings, with many protesting outside the headquarters of the People's Bank of China (PBOC) in Beijing.[61] And high-risk WMPs have often involved huge amounts of unauthorized local government borrowing and guarantees, which has worsened a massive local government debt crisis.[62]

Ant Group claims that its sophisticated online data analysis can carefully vet investment products to minimize risks.[63] PBOC's officials were not convinced by these assurances, as they had already encountered numerous situations where third-party investment funds had collapsed, leaving investors without their life savings and totally confused about why they could not seek compensation from the platforms that had marketed the funds to them.[64]

This explains the sudden suspension of Ant Group's IPO until it implemented tighter regulations requiring these platform firms to adopt similar risk-control measures as banks.[65] Rather than viewing this as a power grab by the CCP, or an attempt to stifle private enterprise, it is more accurate to see it as a struggle between financial regulators, especially the PBOC, which justifiably fears financial instability, and powerful technology firms working in conjunction with financial service SOEs, who utilize big data to maximize their profits and channel customers' savings into all manner of financial products. To claim that this is a battle between government and private enterprise is to ignore the fact that powerful state interests are involved on both sides of the struggle.[66]

We will conclude with an analysis of this complex codependent relationship that has evolved between Alibaba/Ant Group and the Chinese government/state at many different levels.

---

[61] Bloomberg News, 'Trouble Is Brewing in the Farthest Corner of China's Shadow Banking' (*Business Standard*, 9 October 2019) www.business-standard.com/article/international/trouble-is-brewing-in-the-farthest-corner-of-china-s-shadow-banking-119100900105_1.html; Xie Yu, 'China Regulator Orders Bailout of Peer-to-Peer Lenders by Managers of Distressed Assets' (*South China Morning Post*, 17 August 2018); Jiang (n 59).

[62] He Huifeng, 'China's Provinces Fall Deeper into Local Government Debt Mire, Study Finds' (*South China Morning Post*, 9 May 2021) www.scmp.com/economy/china-economy/article/3132815/chinas-provinces-fall-deeper-local-government-debt-mire-study; Zhuo Chen, Zhiguo He, and Chun Liu, 'The Financing of Local Government in the People's Republic of China: Stimulus Loan Wanes and Shadow Banking Waxes' *Asian Development Bank Institute Working Paper*, No. 800 (January 2018) 1–59 esp. 12.

[63] Ant Group (n 1) 166, 193–203.   [64] Xie (n 61).

[65] For summaries, see Chambers and Partners, 'Fintech 2021: China: Trends and Developments' https://practiceguides.chambers.com/practice-guides/fintech-2021/china/trends-and-developments/O7729; Bloomberg News, 'China Reins in Tech Giants to Curb Push into Financial System' (*Aljazeera*, 30 April 2021) www.aljazeera.com/economy/2021/4/30/bb-china-reins-in-tech-giants-to-curb-push-into-financial-system.

[66] See Zhang (n 56).

4 Conclusion: Alibaba/Ant Group and China's Codependent Corporate-Political Ecosystem

Despite Alibaba/Ant Group's regular run-ins with Chinese regulators, it has become an indispensable private sector partner to the CCP by promoting the Party's policies of economic growth, entrepreneurship, and poverty alleviation among hundreds of millions of lower-income and rural Chinese citizens. Of course, while this approach may indirectly help to guarantee the CCP's hold on power, it also greatly benefits Alibaba/Ant's own bottom line, and makes the CCP (and broad swathes of the Chinese populace) highly dependent on Alibaba/Ant's continuing growth and success.

Like many large private firms, Alibaba set up an in-house CCP branch (in 2008), which had attracted 2,094 members by 2017, around 4% of total employees.[67] However, being a CCP member within a private firm does not necessarily mean prioritizing the Party's interests over the interests of the firm, especially as these CCP members are not paid by the Party but are full-time employees or managers of the firm, with a vested interest in maximizing the firm's profits. For example, Alibaba's CCP Secretary, Shao Xiaofeng, was ranked at number 277 on the *Forbes* 2020 list of richest Chinese people, with an estimated net worth of RMB 14 billion (US$2.16 billion), due to the value of his shares in the company.[68] Former CEO Jack Ma, ranked number one on the *Forbes* 2020 China rich list with a net worth of around US$42 billion, has also been a CCP member since his university days.[69]

Though the firm's profits may come first, these political links and the necessity of maintaining a positive relationship with the CCP mean that the company will frequently assist the CCP to implement its policies and maintain its legitimacy. The most obvious contribution is through opening markets and distribution channels for tens of millions of SMEs, helping them to sell their products and services, and removing many obstacles that blocked the flow of capital, goods, and resources and prevented SMEs from accessing bank loans. This was something the CCP had failed to achieve through its traditional state banks and logistical networks, despite its claims to be the Party of the common people.

Alibaba/Ant is also helping to tackle other social issues that have threatened social stability and the CCP's legitimacy, such as high costs of healthcare

---

[67] Bian Mei, 'Pandian Chengli Dangwei De Hulianwang Gongsi: Qishi Chule BATmen Haiyou Hen Duo' [Inventory of Party Committees Set Up by Internet Corporations: Actually There Are Many Others Besides BAT] (*BiaNews*, 1 July 2017) http://tech.sina.com.cn/i/2017-07-01/doc-ifyhrxtp6420838.shtml.

[68] Forbes, '2020 Fubusi Zhongguo 400 Fuhao Bang' [Forbes 2020 China 400 Rich List]. www.forbeschina.com/lists/1750. For Shao's current position, listed as Secretary-General, see Alibaba Group (n 6) 172.

[69] Liu Xuesong, 'Zai Ma Yun Zhonggong Dangyuan De Jianli Zhong Duchu Zheng Nengliang' [Discerning the Positive Energy in Ma Yun's CCP Member Resume] (*Hunan Ribao*, 3 December 2018) http://theory.people.com.cn/n1/2018/1203/c40531-30438208.html.

(through its cheap insurance products), food safety (through blockchain-secured food supply chains), and rural poverty (through working with hundreds of local governments and telecom SOEs to bring e-commerce supply and distribution networks to remote villages, as well as assisting farmers to market their produce online to customers who would otherwise never see them). Despite its regulatory run-ins, in February 2021 Alibaba still won an award from the CCP for being an "advanced model enterprise" due to its poverty alleviation efforts.[70]

Like other private technology firms, Alibaba/Ant has also assisted with the CCP's attempts to improve governance through technology, especially at the local level. For example, they have codeveloped tax payment and other government apps linked to Alipay and helped to improve enforcement of court judgments by cooperating with local courts to blacklist defaulting judgment debtors on Alibaba/Ant's platforms until they repay their debts, or to prevent them from buying luxury items like plane or high-speed rail tickets.[71]

Behind all these activities is the ever-looming potential risk that these private Chinese firms will fall foul of powerful CCP leaders, or that CCP policies will abruptly change, leaving them without a viable business, as occurred in recent years with many of China's largest private tutoring firms.[72] Even a few unguarded criticisms of government policies in a public speech can lead to a private technology firm's founder being called in for a "chat" with powerful government officials and forced to stay out of the public eye for months, as occurred with Jack Ma in 2021. Large private Chinese firms like Alibaba/Ant must therefore constantly seek to make themselves indispensable to the government to reduce their vulnerability to political risks.

All these evolving interactions point to a highly codependent private firm/government corporate-political ecosystem. Yet to conclude that this is clear evidence of monolithic Chinese government or CCP control over Alibaba/Ant and other private technology firms is too simplistic. While these private firms certainly need to demonstrate their support for the government/CCP by engaging in these kinds of initiatives, in most cases they also benefit greatly through extensive positive promotion of their platforms in the official Chinese media, through setting up e-commerce and physical trading

---

[70] 'Chinese Conglomerates Including Alibaba, Wanda Praised for Poverty Alleviation Efforts' (*Global Times*, 25 February 2021) www.globaltimes.cn/page/202102/1216526.shtml; Alibaba Group, 'Sustainability: Poverty Relief Programs' www.alibabagroup.com/en/about/sustainability.

[71] Yang Yi, 'Chinese Courts Use Technology to Tighten Noose on Debt Defaulters' (*Xinhua*, 3 October 2017) www.xinhuanet.com//english/2017-10/03/c_136657135.htm; Alison (Lu) Xu, 'Chinese Judicial Justice on the Cloud: A Future Call or a Pandora's Box? An Analysis of the "Intelligent Court System" of China' (2017) 26(1) Information & Communications Technology Law 59–71.

[72] Luo Meihan, 'Regulations Forced China's Tutors Out of a Job. Will TikTok Save Them? (*Sixth Tone*, 22 July 2022) www.sixthtone.com/news/1010828.

networks that make local communities highly dependent on their services, and through setting the technological agenda in ways that will make the government more reliant on their products and services, in other words, becoming indispensable.

So far, they have managed to do this without giving up their private ownership. Ant Group, for example, is still controlled by the same group of private shareholders that owned its shares prior to the suspension of its IPO in 2020, even if Jack Ma has now given up his veto power over their collective decisions.[73] In fact, firms like Alibaba/Ant Group have grown so large that even when they get into trouble with regulators, the penalties only act as a temporary brake on their relentless expansion.

It is crucial to understand how Alibaba/Ant operates, and its rapid diversification into financial services, as the firm is already exporting its e-commerce model globally through ODI acquisitions. If Ant Group is able to resolve its restructuring to the satisfaction of Chinese regulators and proceed with its own long-awaited IPO, its plan for the proceeds would involve further global expansion of Ant's online payment services and financial products, technological upgrading through recruitment of top global talent, and further ODI through acquisition of "leading technologies including AI, … machine learning, natural language processing, man-machine interaction, … as well as computing and technology infrastructure."[74]

5 Discussion Questions and Comments

This case study uses Alibaba/Ant Group as an example to show how the meteoric growth of e-commerce and the platform economy in China has transformed the way that business is done and made Chinese consumers into some of the world's most active online sellers and purchasers.

The case also gives insights into the multinational links of Chinese e-commerce firms, such as international buyers purchasing Chinese goods online through Taobao and AliExpress, investors buying Alibaba's shares on the NYSE, and Alibaba acquiring e-commerce firms overseas, especially in Southeast Asia and developing countries elsewhere.

Finally, the case explains how e-commerce platforms evolved into numerous business sectors, and especially focuses on their rapid diversification into financial services. Their huge size and financial complexity have led to some negative impacts and systemic risks, and this in turn has caused the Chinese government to regulate these e-commerce and fintech firms more tightly. The following questions will explore some of these issues in more detail.

---

[73] For details on Ant Group's restructuring and shareholding, see Huo Kan (n 57); Yong Xiong and Laura He, 'Jack Ma to Relinquish Control of Ant Group' (*CNN*, 7 January 2023) www.cnn.com/2023/01/07/intl_business/jack-ma-ant-group-restructuring-intl-hnk/index.html.

[74] Ant Group (n 1) 377.

5.1 For Law School Audiences

1. Briefly summarize how the variable interest entity (VIE) structure works and why it is necessary for Chinese e-commerce and internet firms like Alibaba to use it. How does the structure facilitate ODI by Chinese private firms? What are the key legal risks of the VIE structure?
2. What are the legal risks of Ant Group's online finance businesses, especially in the area of wealth management products (WMPs)? Why was the Chinese government so concerned about those risks that they suspended Ant Group's IPO in 2020? How has Ant Group been required to restructure its financial businesses, and will this help to reduce the risks to consumers and the broader financial system?
3. Why is Alibaba considered to be a Chinese firm when it is actually a Cayman Islands company listed in New York and the majority of its shares are owned by non-Chinese investors? Think about this question in terms of where the legal risks to investors would be resolved if there was a dispute, who actually manages the firm's businesses, and where the firm's core businesses are regulated.

5.2 For Policy School Audiences

1. How did the Chinese government facilitate the rise of platform firms like Alibaba/Ant Group since the late 1990s, either directly through its policies or indirectly through its failure to strictly enforce specific policies? Why was the government willing to allow the growth of these private firms – in other words, how do these firms indirectly benefit the Chinese government?
2. More specifically, why did the Chinese government allow such platform firms to expand so rapidly into online finance (even without banking licenses prior to 2015)? What market demands were they meeting that state-owned banks were unable to meet, and what political risks did this cause from around 2016 onward? Does this explain the government's "crackdown" on these online finance firms in 2020?
3. What political risks are faced by Alibaba/Ant Group due to their status as private firms in China? How can they try to mitigate those risks, and does this create potential problems for them when they try to expand overseas?
4. What is the "symbiotic codependency" of the Chinese government and private Chinese technology/e-commerce firms? Use Alibaba/Ant Group as an example to show how this relationship involves compromises on both sides, and how it has hampered the government's ability to regulate such large firms. Does this case study also reveal competing interests *within* the Chinese government (and SOEs). If so, what are they? Many political scientists have referred to China as a "fragmented authoritarian" political system: How does the case of Alibaba/Ant Group support this characterization?

5.3 For Business School Audiences

1. Alibaba's business growth has been incredibly rapid, from an unknown startup in 1999 to China's largest e-commerce firm by 2014, when it held its IPO on the NYSE. What were the key factors that allowed Alibaba to grow so fast in these initial years? Why were traditional (offline) businesses not able to meet customer and market demand? Which of the key factors were due to Alibaba efficiently filling gaps in the market, and which factors were external, such as technological and policy developments? Could Alibaba have survived as a private e-commerce firm in China if it had started operating in 1990 instead of 1999? Why or why not?
2. Ant Group was initially not an independent corporation but simply the payment service for Alibaba, called Alipay. How did Alipay help Alibaba to win its early competition with eBay in China, and how has it diversified into financial services after being spun off into a separate affiliated corporation called Ant Group since 2011? What gaps in the financial services market did Ant Group fill and who were its main target customers?
3. How do Alibaba and Ant Group work together synergistically to attract more customers and grow their respective businesses? What role does their customer (or user) data play in this, and how is such data shared between the two affiliated firms?
4. What impact has Alibaba/Ant Group had internationally? Think about this in terms of both investment markets (i.e., raising money from international investors) and ODI (i.e., acquisition of businesses overseas). Why does Alibaba's ODI depend so heavily on raising money from international investors? Why do you think those Chinese government restrictions (especially on private businesses and individuals) are in place?
5. Using Alibaba/Ant Group as an example, explain what is a Chinese corporate ecosystem, and how does it interact with the Chinese political ecosystem? Are there some key differences between such Chinese corporate ecosystems and multinational firms in similar business sectors in other jurisdictions, such as Amazon? Think about both the differences in their target markets and the types of "social responsibility" activities they must engage in to remain viable.

Case Study 1.2

Chinese M&A in Latin America

Jiangsu Yanghe Distillery's Stake Acquisition in VSPT Wine Group in Chile

Ignacio Tornero

1 Overview

In 2018, *baijiu* giant Jiangsu Yanghe Distillery Co., Ltd. acquired 12.5% of one of the most well-established and largest global wine conglomerates in Chile, VSPT Wine Group (Viña San Pedro Tarapacá S.A.), for US$65 million. The transaction was the first of its kind in the South American country, in which a Chinese *baijiu* producer purchased a stake in a Chilean wine company listed on the Santiago Stock Exchange. The transaction involved considerable strategic and business planning and the support of experienced legal and financial advisors in both China and Chile. As a window into Chinese companies' strategic entries into emergent markets, this case study first analyzes how a change in alcohol consumption habits in China was a critical factor for Yanghe in deciding to carry out the transaction and the rationale behind choosing a target from the "new wine world" instead of the "old wine world." It then explores how the Chile-China Free Trade Agreement (FTA) has increased the amount of wine exported to China and how Chilean wine is perceived as "value for money" among Chinese consumers. Finally, it discusses how this transaction is an example of how Chinese state-owned enterprises (SOEs) have learned rapidly from their outward foreign direct investments (FDIs) and how Chinese investors are increasingly using experienced advisors to help inform their overseas investments.

2 Introduction

Toward the end of 2016, on a cold winter day in Beijing, I was sitting in my office located in the Central Business District when I received a phone call from an unknown number. On the end of the phone was Mr. Tom Li, who introduced himself as the investment director of Jiangsu Yanghe Distillery Co., Ltd. ("Yanghe").[1] He told me that he had received my contact information from

---

[1] All real names of advisors and executives that worked in the transaction have been replaced by fictitious names for confidentiality reasons. Just the names of the buyer and seller are disclosed in the case. In addition, data and certain information are not limited to that available

Chinese M&A in Latin America: Chilean Wine

Chinese FDI flows to Chile 2012–2023 (million US$)

[Chart showing Chinese FDI flows to Chile from 2012 to 2023, with values ranging from $0 to $8000 million. The line is near zero from 2012-2016, rises sharply to a peak near $6500 in 2017, drops and has a secondary peak around $3000 in 2019, then declines to around $1000 by 2022-2023.]

Figure 1.2.1 Evolution of Chinese FDI into Chile

South Pagoda Law Firm, a leading Chinese law firm that had worked with Yanghe for more than fifteen years. He also mentioned that they knew that I had spent some time at their Beijing office on secondment a few years ago representing Chile Andes Law Firm. Mr. Li told me that there was an urgent matter that they wanted to discuss, and he asked whether I would be able to go to Nanjing in the coming days. He would meet me at the train station so he could drive me to Yanghe's offices and explain the company's idea. He also told me that, as part of the Chinese tradition, they would host a lunch for their guest afterward and that this would be a good chance for me to meet Yanghe's vice president and the wider team.

Initially, I could not believe what had just happened. I had been working hard to attract Chinese investment into Chile for years, investment that had been almost nonexistent prior to 2016, and it seemed that the first transactions were just starting to materialize (see Figure 1.2.1). I also felt that there was a certain degree of coincidence in this invitation, not just considering where the referral was coming from but also because I had spent time at Nanjing University studying Mandarin. I went back to my computer and bought a train ticket to Nanjing for the following week to meet Mr. Li and Yanghe's team.

This case study tells the story of how Chinese *baijiu* company Yanghe planned and executed its entry into the Chilean VSPT Wine Group (Viña San Pedro Tarapacá S.A., hereinafter, "VSPT"), in which it acquired a minority stake of 12.5% for US$65 million. The case covers the early conversations during 2016 to the closing of the transaction in 2018. In doing so, it provides interesting information for a number of reasons. First, it sheds light on how Chinese

---

until the transaction took place. Post-acquisition data is also sometimes included to provide a more complete overview of the industry and trends addressed in this case. For confidentiality reasons, some facts and/or events of the case have been modified.

companies (both private and SOEs) follow consumers' changes in habits and preferences when designing their global strategies (as a business dimension). Second, it provides insights into how policy elements – like the Chile-China FTA – can impact the direction of Chinese outward FDI. Finally, it provides a practical resource for analyzing how Chinese enterprises are increasingly becoming more sophisticated in their outbound investment activities by relying on specialist advisors (i.e., legal services).

The case is structured as follows: (1) an introduction to the *baijiu* market, Yanghe, and VSPT; (2) a description of the change in alcohol consumption habits among Chinese buyers; (3) an overview of the Chile-China FTA and how it has increased the amount of wine sold to China and its competitive position in the Chinese market; (4) a summary of the preliminary conversations of the transaction; (5) an explanation of the execution and closing of the deal; and (6) a general reference to the integration phase and a conclusion.

3 The Case

3.1 What Is *Baijiu*?

Baijiu ("clear or white liquor") is a traditional Chinese alcohol that has been enjoyed throughout China's history. Even though there is no clear date as to when *baijiu* production started in China, some historical records trace it to before the second century BCE.[2] *Baijiu* is usually produced from sorghum, but it can also be made from other grains such as rice. It can be categorized following different criteria (e.g., distillation techniques, fermentation starters, etc.), but it is most commonly classified based on its aroma (e.g., strong aroma, sauce aroma, light aroma, and rice aroma). Even though *baijiu*'s alcohol content has a wide range of 35–60% alcohol by volume (ABV), it is usually above 50% ABV.[3] *Baijiu* has a special significance in Chinese society because it is closely related to its local culture and traditions, and it has been a unique symbol of people's social and business interactions for centuries. *Baijiu* production is localized in different provinces in China by different liquor manufacturers.

3.2 Jiangsu Yanghe: An Iconic *Baijiu* Producer

Yanghe is one of China's largest *baijiu* producers (Table 1.2.1) and, along with Moutai and Wuliangye, it is one of the top *baijiu* brands in China.[4] The official

---

[2] Xiao-Wei Zheng and Bei-Zhong Han, 'Baijiu (白酒), Chinese Liquor: History, Classification and Manufacture' (2016) 3 Journal of Ethnic Foods 19–25 https://doi.org/10.1016/j.jef.2016.03.001.
[3] Tammie Teclemariam, 'Baijiu, the World's Most Popular Spirit You May Never Have Heard Of' (WineEnthusiast, 28 June 2018) www.wineenthusiast.com/culture/chinese-baijiu/.
[4] Jiangsu Yanghe Distillery Co., Ltd., *Annual Reports* (2020–2022) www.chinayanghe.com/article/type/207-1.html.

Table 1.2.1 Main producers of *baijiu* in China, 2020–2022

Company	Year	Production volume (ton)	Operating revenue (CNY)	Net profit (CNY)
Yanghe	2022	197,590	¥ 30,104,896,186	¥ 9,377,832,429
Wuliangye	2022	129,328	¥ 73,968,640,704	¥ 26,690,661,397
Moutai	2022	91,885	¥ 124,099,843,771	¥ 62,716,443,738
Yanghe	2021	204,332	¥ 25,350,178,204	¥ 7,507,682,797
Wuliangye	2021	188,717	¥ 66,209,053,612	¥ 23,377,074,353
Moutai	2021	84,721	¥ 106,190,154,843	¥ 52,460,144,378
Yanghe	2020	161,498	¥ 21,101,051,131	¥ 7,482,228,633
Wuliangye	2020	158,831	¥ 57,321,059,453	¥ 19,954,809,594
Moutai	2020	75,160	¥ 94,915,380,916	¥ 46,697,285,429

US$ to RMB exchange rate (January 2024) 1 US$ = 7.1 RMB.
Source: Prepared by author with data from companies' annual reports for 2020–2022. Ranked by production volume.

origin of the company goes back to 1949 when the group was established; but Yanghe's distillery has been producing *baijiu* for hundreds of years following an ancient recipe. The company is located in Suqian, a prefecture-level city in northern Jiangsu Province that has a long tradition in the production of liquor and is considered to be one of the three most famous wetland liquor-producing areas in the world. This unique location gives Yanghe access to specific qualities of water, soil, and air crucial for *baijiu* production. As such, these conditions produce a beverage that is similar to whisky in Scotland in terms of its quality and popularity.

The Yanghe group has more than 19,500 employees at the parent level and throughout all its subsidiaries. In the "2023 Fortune China 500" it ranked 430,[5] and 53 in the "2023 BrandZ's Top 100 Most Valuable Chinese Brands."[6] Yanghe was listed on the Shenzhen Stock Exchange in 2009 (code 002304).[7]

3.3 VSPT

VSPT has also been a key player in the alcohol industry albeit not for hard alcohol but for wine. The company was established in Chile in 1865 and has since become one of the largest producers and oldest exporters of Chilean wine. It has a presence across several valleys in Chile that have a long tradition of wine production (e.g., the Maipo, Colchagua, and Casablanca valleys) and has an international presence in the Uco Valley, Argentina (Mendoza). The company

---

[5] Fortune China, '2023 Fortune China 500' (25 July 2023) www.fortunechina.com/fortune500/c/2023-07/25/content_436290.html.
[6] Kantar, *BrandZ Most Valuable Global Brands 2023 Report* (2024) www.kantar.com/campaigns/brandz-downloads/kantar-brandz-most-valuable-global-brands-2023.
[7] Shenzhen Stock Exchange, *Jiangsu Yanghe Brewery Joint-Stock Co., Ltd. (002304 洋河股份)* www.szse.cn/certificate/individual/index.html?code=002304.

is considered among the top-twenty world producers of wine. Its portfolio of brands includes Altaïr, Sideral, Cabo de Hornos, Kankana del Elqui, Tierras Moradas, 1865, Castillo de Molina, and GatoNegro 9 Lives. In June 2023, the company announced the strengthening of its international presence – it already had offices in the United States and the United Kingdom – and commitment to the Chinese market through the opening of an international office in Shanghai.[8] Based on the information gathered by the Chilean Customs Office, VSPT ranked second – behind Viña Concha y Toro S.A. – in the total exported volume of bottled wine between January and November 2023: 4,618,838 boxes (of nine liters each) with a total value of US$114,017,736. In relation to the Chinese market – for the same period – VSPT ranked in seventh position with a total volume of 119,665 boxes and a total value of US$4,227,564 (these figures represent an important decline from previous years).[9] The company is listed on the Santiago Stock Exchange.[10]

3.4 *Baijiu* Consumption and New Trends

I arrived at Nanjing South Railway Station early in the morning and was met by Mr. Li. After having exchanged a few words, I quickly realized that my companion was a very experienced executive. His English was great, he had obtained an MBA at a US Ivy League business school, and he had worked in the industry for more than a decade. I felt excited about what was going to happen. Once at the Nanjing offices of South Pagoda Law Firm, Mr. Li introduced to me the managing partner of the law firm, Mr. Fred Wang, and they explained the proposed deal.

Mr. Li started the conversation by introducing Yanghe's history and current position in the Chinese market. He told me that sales for the previous year (2015) had reached more than RMB 16 billion, that the net profit attributable to shareholders was more than RMB 5 billion, and that the company was expected to produce close to 200,000 tons of *baijiu*.[11] He also told me that Yanghe was the market leader in the premium segment (with a market share of more than 20%), the segment that was forecast to experience the highest growth in the coming years (expected to be more than 15%).[12] He also mentioned that

---

[8] Eloise Feilden, 'VSPT Furthers International Expansion with Shanghai Office' (8 June 2023) www.thedrinksbusiness.com/2023/06/vspt-furthers-international-expansion-with-shanghai-office/.

[9] Chilean National Customs Office Data (*Servicio Nacional de Aduanas*) www.aduana.cl/aduana/site/edic/base/port/estadisticas.html.

[10] Santiago Stock Exchange Data (*Bolsa de Comercio de Santiago*). VINA SAN PEDRO TARAPACA S.A. (VSPT ISIN: CL0002209253) www.bolsadesantiago.com/resumen_instrumento/VSPT.

[11] Jiangsu Yanghe Distillery Co., Ltd., *Annual Report 2017* www.chinayanghe.com/article/type/207-1.html.

[12] Anne Ling and Mark Yuan, *Yanghe: Consolidator of Premium Liquor* (2018) Deutsche Bank Research.

Yanghe benefited from a consolidated portfolio of brands. Another comparative advantage of the company was the number of its salespeople and distributors. In the former, it had more than 5,000, compared to less than 600 in Wuliangye and less than 700 in Moutai. Regarding its strong distribution network, it had more than 8,000 distributors, while Moutai had just over 3,000 and Wuliangye just over 1,100. This gave Yanghe access to a wide, flat, and very efficient network of distributors. He also explained that Yanghe, unlike some competitors, offered a diversified portfolio of products and that it was constantly developing new ones to meet changing consumer tastes thus providing a unique corporate culture of continuous innovation.[13]

Mr. Li ended this brief introduction by saying that the aspiration of the company was to become a market leader in the alcohol industry in general and not limit itself to *baijiu*. This would enable the company to maintain sustainable future growth and to keep serving customers' changing preferences. In this regard, he thought that there was considerable room to keep expanding the wine business in China and continue diversifying the company's offering and revenue source, since wine represented less than 2% of the total revenue of Yanghe.[14] He added that Chile and its wine were not new to the company as it had launched its Sidus private label in 2012 through a cooperation with Chilean wineries. If the company already had a wide network of distributors and selling points, the strengthening of the wine category could create strong synergies to the current offer.

Mr. Wang then joined the conversation by saying that he had noticed that Chinese people's alcohol consumption habits have been changing; younger generations were not drinking as much *baijiu* as more senior Chinese people do and they prefer alternatives such as wine, whisky, and vodka. He also referred to how the industry had been affected by the anti-corruption campaign started by President Xi in 2012, a policy that limited the hosting of luxurious banquets in which expensive *baijiu* was regularly drunk. This situation reaffirmed the idea that Yanghe needed to prepare for the future and that wine from the new world (like Chile) could be one solution.

Mr. Li emphasized that the key behind this move was to understand the preference of younger generations, who represented less than 30% of *baijiu* sales – a figure that has been decreasing.[15] One of the reasons that Chinese millennials do not enjoy drinking as much *baijiu* as older generations, he said, is because they associate it with a more banquet/business environment, usually with a government component as well. In those dinners, it is quite common to see people finishing their glasses of *baijiu* at once (*ganbei*) and that situation usually ends up leaving many "in trouble." Millennials, in general, do not like this and often prefer drinking alcohol on other occasions like relaxing at home, during vacations, and at social gatherings. There is also interesting data that shows that many Chinese

---

[13] ibid. [14] ibid.
[15] Daxue Consulting, *China's Wine & Spirit Industry Barometer Report* (2022).

consumers prefer lower-alcohol alternatives and that they tend to see wine as a healthier option and therefore a lifestyle choice. In addition, younger Chinese consumers are more open-minded than before; some of them have traveled or lived overseas while many international brands are now available in China. As a result, Chinese people are increasingly willing to try different products and experiences.[16]

After all this, Mr. Li told me that the intention of Yanghe was to make a minority investment into one of Chile's leading wineries. "What are your thoughts on this idea?" he then asked.

3.5 The Importance of the Chile-China Free Trade Agreement and the Appeal of the New World Wine

When responding to this question, I reminded Mr. Li and Mr. Wang that the strong relationship between Chile and China relied on certain key historical milestones. Chile was the first South American country to establish formal diplomatic relations with China in 1970 and the first Latin American country to support the entry of China into the WTO in 1999. Chile was the first country in the region to recognize China as a market economy in 2004 and the first single economy in the world to sign an FTA with China in 2005. This last point was of critical importance for the matter under discussion.

I then provided additional background of the process to conclude the FTA. I mentioned that before this FTA with Chile, China had just signed a framework agreement with the Association of Southeast Asian Nations (ASEAN) in November 2002,[17] and that China proposed this idea to Chile in the middle of 2002 considering, in part, the important milestones achieved with the South American country in the previous decades.

I then explained that official discussions started in January 2005 in Beijing, and that there were five rounds of discussion that ended in October of that year. One of the reasons for the speed of the negotiation process was the fact it was structured in stages: a first agreement for the trade of goods was signed in November 2005 and entered into force on 1 October 2006; a supplementary agreement regarding the trade of services was signed in April 2008 and entered into force in August 2010; and a final agreement regarding investments was signed in September 2012 and entered into force in February 2014.[18]

---

[16] Ran Guo, 'Why Chinese Millennials Are Saying Bye to Baijiu' (CBBC, 11 June 2022) https://focus.cbbc.org/why-chinese-millennials-are-saying-bye-to-baijiu/; ibid.

[17] Association of Southeast Asian Nations, *ASEAN-China Economic Relation*, www.asean.org/wp-content/uploads/images/2015/October/outreach-document/Edited%20ACFTA.pdf.

[18] Carlos José Villegas Trommer, 'El Tratado de Libre Comercio Chile-China y su Incidencia en las Exportaciones Chilenas' (The Chile-China FTA and its Implications for Chilean Exports), Repositorio Académico Universidad de Chile (December 2015) https://repositorio.uchile.cl/handle/2250/136837.

Table 1.2.2 Schedule of tariff reduction in the Chile-China FTA

Category	No. of items	% of items	Exports to China 2004 (US$ thousands)	% US$ amount
Immediate	2,805	37	2,953,478	92
Year 1	1,947	26	489	0
Year 5	973	13	11,251	0
Year 10	1,611	21	221,300	7
Exclusions	214	3	23,384	1
Total	**7,550**	**100**	**3,209,902**	**100%**

Source: Prepared by author with data from Chilean Congress National Library.

Afterward, I pointed out that one of the critical measures included in the FTA was a progressive elimination of tariffs based on a set schedule (Table 1.2.2). For this purpose, five categories were established and in the case of Chilean exports the category "Immediate" stipulated a zero tariff for 37% of the products exported to China that represented 92% of the total US dollar amount from the date that the FTA entered into force.[19] This was a considerable reduction in the tariff rate in force prior to the FTA when the average tariff in China was 10%.[20] Wine was included in the category "year 10," so in 2015 it started entering the Chinese market tariff-free.

I kept emphasizing the importance of the FTA and the elimination of tariffs in the wine industry for building a more competitive global product. I showed evidence of how Chilean wine exports to China increased after the execution of the FTA (Figure 1.2.2).

Mr. Li agreed that the elimination of tariffs on Chilean wine had been a critical consideration for Chinese consumers when choosing options from an increasing number of choices from different countries. Chilean wine has been consolidating this perception that it is "value for money"; it is as good as more traditional players like French wine but, at the same time, is considerably more affordable. While the average price for a case (9 liters) of Chilean wine is around US$31 (free on board [FOB]) the price for French wine is approximately 50% higher, with an average price of US$47 (FOB).[21] But price isn't everything, he then added. Chilean wineries have also proven to be flexible and creative players by designing private labels pursuant to

---

[19] ibid.
[20] History of Supreme Decree Law No. 317 of Chile (Approves the Free Trade Agreement between the Governments of Chile and the People's Republic of China and Its Annexes) www.bcn.cl/historiadelaley/historia-de-la-ley/vista-expandida/5213/.
[21] Decanter China, 'New China Wine Import Figures: France and Australia Lead the Growth in First Quarter' (5 May 2016) www.decanterchina.com/en/news/china-wine-import-figures-france-and-australia-lead-the-growth-in-first-quarter.

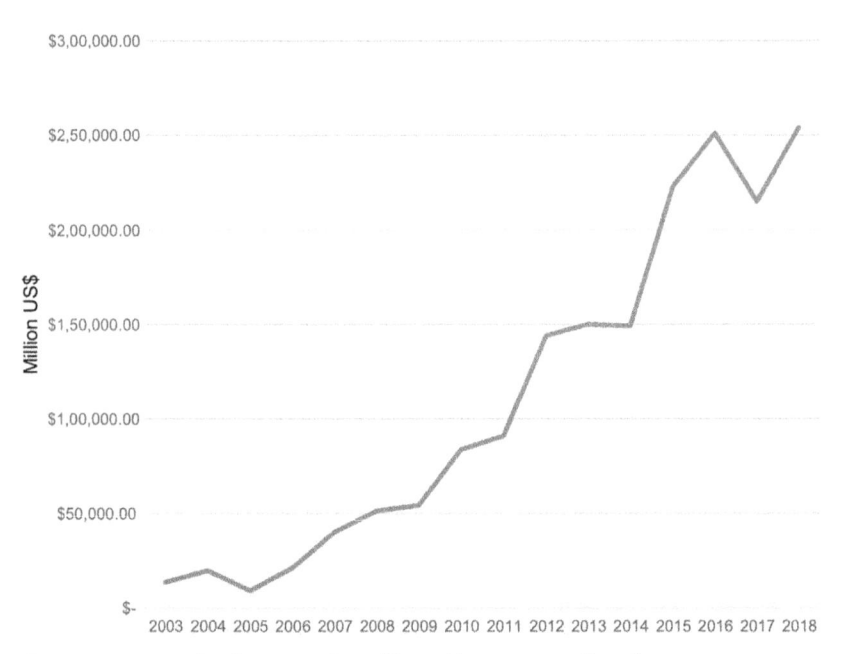

Figure 1.2.2 Increase in wine exports from Chile to China, 2003–2018 (in US$)

clients' requests,[22] and by launching very strong localized marketing campaigns. Another important factor has been good public–private coordination, and the role that the Chilean wine association (Wines of Chile) has played in supporting the image and consistent value proposition of Chilean wine in China and the rest of the world.[23]

"Well, let's find a target for Yanghe then," I said.

3.6 The Transaction

I was aware that this represented a great opportunity for my law firm in terms of a potentially iconic transaction within the wine industry. However, Chinese companies were new players with respect to FDI in Chile and there were considerable risks involved. During my previous research, I had noted that some studies put Chinese M&A failure rate as high as 70%,[24] and that there were several common mistakes made by Chinese companies in their overseas operations (Table 1.2.3), many of which I had witnessed in the past such as the lack of proper and timely use of professional advisors. In order to enable a successful M&A operation, careful planning was required.

---

[22] The Economist, 'Why Chinese Tipplers Like Chilean Wine' (2 January 2021) www.economist.com/the-americas/2021/01/02/why-chinese-tipplers-like-chilean-wine.
[23] Wine of Chiles, www.winesofchile.org/.
[24] Xuedong Ding and Chen Meng, *From World Factory to Global Investor: A Multi-Perspective Analysis on China's Outward Direct Investment* (1st edn, Routledge 2018).

Table 1.2.3 Main risks and challenges faced by Chinese companies in their ODIs

1. Enter the project too late; slow to act.	7. Focus only on targets which are "for sale."	13. Inadequate tax structuring or postponed too late in process.	19. In emerging markets, rely more on government support, not legal documents.
2. Do not have a clear international investment strategy or plan.	8. Reluctant to pay retainer to financial advisor to conduct search.	14. Negotiate MOU without help of external advisors.	20. No decision maker at negotiating table.
3. Unfamiliar with international deal structures.	9. Fail to make persuasive case to seller on buyer's strategic goals.	15. Inadequate due diligence.	21. Long gaps between negotiating sessions with no updates.
4. Do not utilize external advisors effectively.	10. Chinese buy-side introductory materials not up to international standard.	16. Let seller's lawyers draft the deal documents.	22. Inadequate transparency as to internal process and timing.
5. Overreliance on government officials to find targets.	11. Not sufficiently familiar with international business practices.	17. Fail to utilize the protections under the SPA [Sale and Purchase Agreement] fully.	23. Retract concessions made in prior rounds of negotiations.
6. Use inexperienced overseas Chinese "finders."	12. Acquisition funds not in place up front.	18. Sometimes ignore applicable legal requirements on FDI.	24. Significant communication and culture gaps.
			25. Fail to ensure compliance with regulations governing operations.
			26. No post-closing integration plan.
			27. Lower negotiation success rate compared to international standard.
			28. Risk of non-completion results in sell-side demanding a "China premium."
			29. Because slow to act, lose out on good investment opportunities.
			30. Fail to achieve anticipated synergies/incur heavy losses.

Source: Robert Lewis, 'Rules of the Game of Global M&A: Why So Many Chinese Outbound Investments Fail' (China Machine Press 2017). Reproduced with permission.

At this preliminary stage, and after convincing Yanghe to formally retain our law firm, I suggested two actions: (1) find and retain a financial advisor in Chile and (2) start looking for potential suitable targets. Regarding this last point, Yanghe was searching for a top-ten player in Chile with a prestigious brand that could be easily sold to the Chinese market. I was happy to see that Yanghe acknowledged its lack of prior M&A experience in South America and that it was looking for experienced advisors that could help it with the transaction's structure and execution. This was, from my point of view, a good starting point that could bring the required expertise and flexibility to achieve the intended objective.

Mr. Li stated that he was very satisfied with the outcome of this first meeting and that it was time to enjoy a good Chinese lunch and meet the rest of the team. He asked that I brief my firm about the potential work, start preparing a formal proposal, introduce a reputed financial advisor, and also initiate preliminary market research to identify suitable companies in Chile for Yanghe to consider. They agreed to meet in a couple of months to review all this.

After receiving approval from my firm to move on, I proceeded as agreed with Mr. Li. I introduced to Yanghe one of the most respected investment banks in Chile (Chile Patagonia Financial Advisors) so they could also start preliminary conversations with Yanghe. At the same time, our team and I conducted some preliminary research identifying around ten potential targets that may be willing to sell a minority stake to the *baijiu* giant. This was challenging as many of the largest Chilean players with a long tradition in the industry were not for sale or were not listed companies. One senior partner at Chile Andes Law Firm started making a few phone calls to some of his contacts to explore whether there were chances for this project to become a reality.

Contact with Yanghe moved quickly. Both the law firm and Chile Patagonia Financial Advisors were formally engaged by Yanghe, so detailed planning could start. Chile Andes Law Firm explained to the client the general steps involved in an M&A in Chile (Figure 1.2.3) and introduced the list of potential targets available together with the likely chances of acquiring a minority stake in each of them. After a detailed review of the potential targets, Yanghe decided to pursue VSPT after considering its history, brand, and sales. In addition, VSPT was a listed company on the Santiago Stock Exchange, so the chances of entering into partial ownership of the winery by acquiring a certain percentage from minority stakeholders were more feasible than for other alternatives. VSPT was a great target itself; it had become the second largest Chilean wine exporter after the merger of San Pedro Winery and Tarapacá Winery in 2008 and was a leader in premium wine in the domestic Chilean market. Additionally, VSPT was aligned with the definition of China as a "priority market" by Wines of Chile.

The whole deal required close coordination between the work of Chile Andes Law Firm, South Pagoda Law Firm, Chile Patagonia Financial

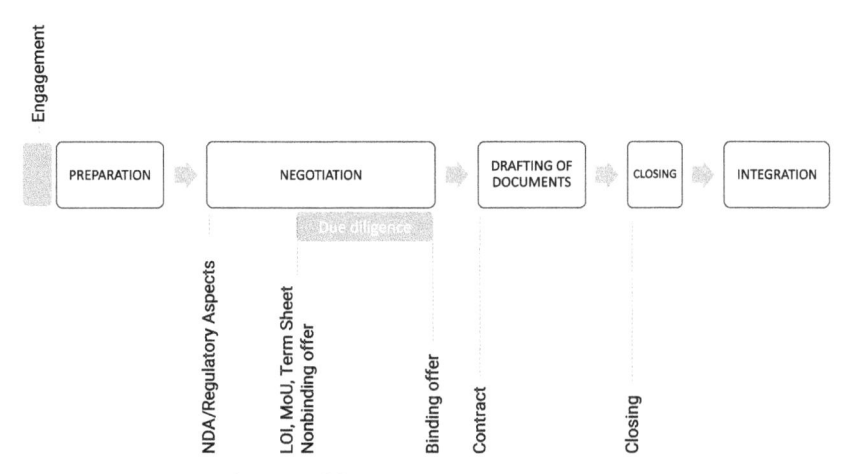

Figure 1.2.3 Main steps of M&As in Chile

Advisors, and the preparation of documents and approvals in China by Yanghe. The advisors prepared a very detailed plan divided into three main parts: pre-acquisition, acquisition, and post-acquisition steps (Figure 1.2.4). This allowed Yanghe to have a very clear roadmap of the transaction, including estimated timelines, areas of responsibility, the required information/documents, and the current status of each stage. As of 31 December 2017, the main shareholders of VSPT and their ownership were the ones listed in Table 1.2.4.

The advisors considered different plans for Yanghe to acquire the required ownership in VSPT in order to obtain a seat on the board and thus have a certain degree of decision-making power inside the company. One alternative was to purchase shares on the Santiago Stock Exchange from minority stakeholders, another was to buy a certain proportion from the main shareholder (Compañía de las Cervecerías Unidas, CCU), and an alternative was to perform a capital increase. The advisors also analyzed the benefits and disadvantages of different financing structures (equity, debt, or equity/debt). They also informed Yanghe about the possibility of a potential mandatory public offer of shares by CCU and the corresponding tender price, which is the scenario that ultimately happened.

On 12 December 2017, CCU acquired 1 million additional shares in VSPT, thus triggering the legal provision that required it to launch a mandatory public offer of shares for the remaining shares (33% approximately) in VSPT not owned by CCU, as a result of owning two-thirds or more of the shares issued by a publicly traded company. CCU carried out the formalities of announcements and the publication of the prospectus, including a tender price of CLP 7.80 per share. VSPT's directors also issued their personal opinions in relation to the tender as required by law. The offer lasted from 28 December 2017 to 26 January 2018 and CCU acquired 6,310,613,119 additional shares in VSPT resulting in an ownership increase to 83.01% interest in the company. In the

Figure 1.2.4 Roadmap of the project

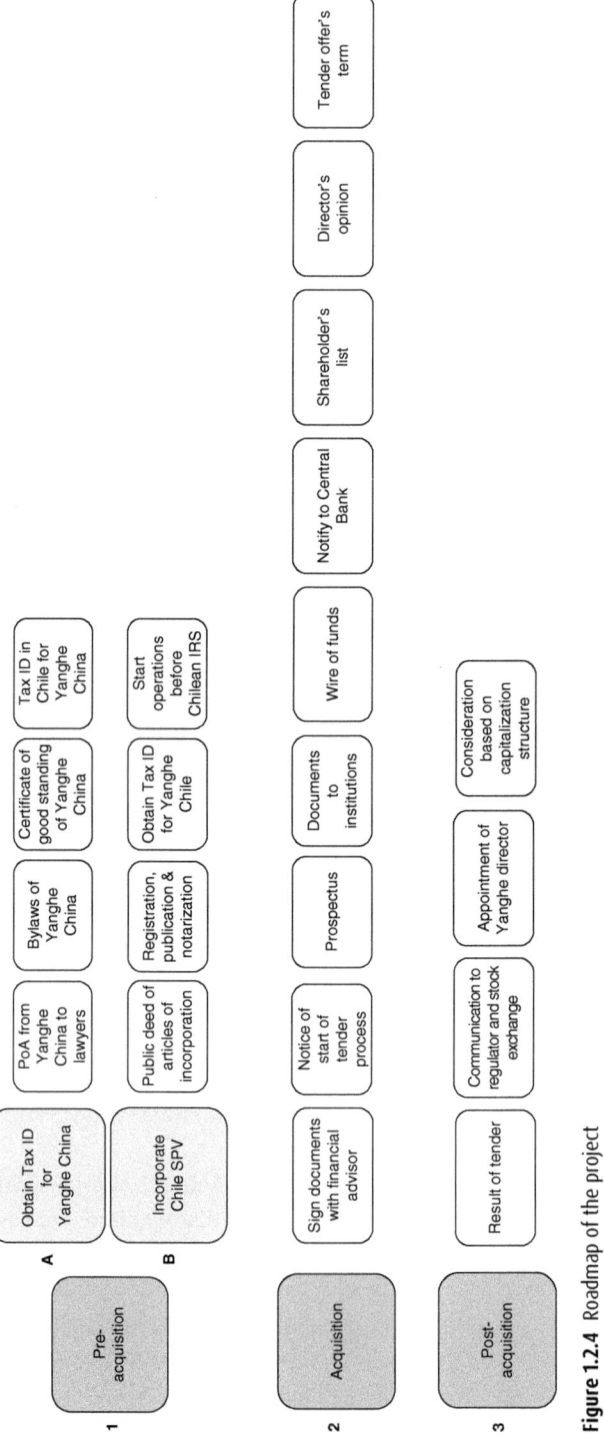

Table 1.2.4 Main shareholders of VSPT as of 31 December 2017

Shareholder name	No. of shares	Ownership (%)
CCU Inversiones S.A.	26,866,493,503	67.22
Compañía Chilena de Fósforos S.A.	2,794,649,759	6.99
Bank of Chile (on behalf of nonresident foreign investors)	1,988,796,991	4.98
Bank Itaú Corpbanca (on behalf of nonresident foreign investors)	1,385,536,989	3.47
Bank Santander (on behalf of nonresident foreign investors)	1,376,502,915	3.44
Compass Small Cap Chile Fondo de Inversión	1,264,834,547	3.16
Siglo XXI Fondo de Inversión	660,769,848	1.65
Fondo de Inversión Santander Small Cap	491,906,385	1.23
Larrain Vial S.A. Corredora de Bolsa	477,368,885	1.19
BCI Small Cap Chile Fondo de Inversión	397,191,944	0.99
BTG Pactual Small Cap Chile Fondo de Inversión (Cuenta Nueva)	260,162,716	0.65
MBI Arbitrage Fondo de Inversión	207,039,548	0.52
Total	**38,171,254,030**	**95.49**

Source: Prepared with data from VSPT Annual Report 2017.

meantime, Yanghe informed the regulators that it had acquired 4,996,212,080 shares (12.5%) of VSPT at CLP 7.90 per share from Compañía Chilena de Fósforos S.A. and other minority shareholders.[25]

4 Conclusion

Yanghe's aim of acquiring an interest in one of Chile's main wineries was ultimately successful. This case study shows how Yanghe used expert market analysis by its Chilean advisors to inform its decisions and how it sought to anticipate changing consumer trends in the *baijiu* business by investing in VSPT. It also provides considerations for a policy discussion on how the Chile-China FTA was a critical factor in allowing Chilean wine to become an appealing product to Chinese consumers. Finally, it highlights the importance of detailed planning and execution and the need to rely on experienced advisors in order to carry out a successful M&A operation.

Can Yanghe claim victory? At least not yet. The last phase of the M&A process is in its initial stage: the integration. This is when partners usually

---

[25] The Chilean Financial Market Commission (*Comisión Para el Mercado Financiero*), VIÑA SAN PEDRO TARAPACA S.A. www.cmfchile.cl/institucional/mercados/entidad.php?mercado =V&rut=91041000&grupo=0&tipoentidad=RVEMI&row=AAAwy2ACTAAABy2AAC&vig= VI&control=svs&pestania=1.

encounter the biggest challenges to building a sustainable approach and where skillful advisors are needed to guarantee a good fit. In addition, the wine sector has been heavily affected by the COVID-19 pandemic, and whether the industry is able to return to pre-COVID levels of sales is an ongoing question.

5 Discussion Questions and Comments

The case "Yanghe – VSPT" provides insights into Chinese approaches to outbound investment from law, policy, and business perspectives. When reading the case, consider the following:

- Exploring how changes in consumer behavior in China may redefine Chinese companies' strategies and their outbound activities.
- Analyzing the importance of bilateral trade agreements as suitable frameworks for increasing international trade.
- Showing how Chinese companies (private and state-owned) have become more sophisticated in their M&A strategies by relying on experienced legal and financial advisors.

In relation to this last point, Chinese companies' familiarity with international transactions has not always been the norm. As shown in Figure 1.2.3, Chinese overseas M&A has not been exempt from challenges, and there is abundant evidence of certain common pitfalls faced by Chinese enterprises in their early outbound activity across different jurisdictions.

For example, in 2012, during one of the first attempts by a Chinese company to acquire a hydropower asset in Chile, the Chinese party was unable to complete the deal due to different mistakes made. In that transaction, the Chilean legal advisor was approached by a well-renowned international financial advisor based in Chile. This advisor had, in turn, been hired by a reputable Chinese financial advisor in order to assist a Chinese SOE in the acquisition of energy assets located in the south of Chile on sale by a Chilean private company. The acquisition process was structured as a private competitive tender process. The potential Chinese buyer was the international arm of a Chinese central SOE that had some previous international experience in other acquisitions worldwide.

Unlike the Chinese financial advisor, who proved to be very familiar with international best practices and standards in the M&A industry, the Chinese client lacked basic skills required for this type of international transaction. For instance, some of the decision makers who attended the negotiation sessions that took place in Chile did not have the required language skills (spoken English), seemed to be unfamiliar with international M&A processes, and had a political background rather than a technical or business one. One of the biggest challenges faced during the acquisition was the poor communication between the team of advisors and the Chinese company. In addition, decision-making inside the potential buyer was considerably slower than for other participants in the tender, and it required multiple regular approvals from the headquarters in Beijing. This circumstance was not duly understood by the Chilean seller and caused miscommunication and even some distrust throughout the sale.

During the final stage of the selling process, it was expected that some assets were going to be awarded to a British company participating in the tender and the other to the Chinese buyer. However, due to circumstances that were never made clear, the Chinese party suddenly "disappeared" from the negotiation table. Therefore, all assets were acquired by the British offeror. This example is just one of many that demonstrates how far Chinese companies have come in their overseas M&A transactions.

5.1 For Law School Audiences

1. How is the approach adopted by Yanghe different from other transactions carried out by Chinese firms overseas that you know of (including, for example, the 2012 case mentioned above)? What are the most common mistakes made by Chinese firms in their overseas transactions?
2. Can you provide any examples of Chinese M&As that have failed due to a lack of proper legal or financial structuring?
3. If you were advising Yanghe and VSPT in their integration strategy, what would your plan be to guarantee that the cooperation is successful in the long term?

5.2 For Policy School Audiences

1. Why has the Chile-China FTA been a critical tool for positioning Chilean wine in China? Can you provide a comparative example in your country that illustrates this?
2. What is the specific competitive advantage granted by the FTA? Did this happen upon its execution or at a later stage?
3. Do you think that FTAs are effective policies to promote international trade? Could the Chile-China FTA be *adversely* affecting the wine industry in Chile?

5.3 For Business School Audiences

1. If *baijiu* is still the most consumed liquor in the world, why did Yanghe decide to acquire a minority stake in a Chilean wine group?
2. What were Yanghe's comparative advantages that placed it in a good position to diversify its business? What were the synergies that the company could benefit from in purchasing a stake in VSPT?
3. Why did Yanghe not acquire a winery from France, considering that French wines are well positioned within the global market, perceived as high quality, and have a higher average price than Chilean wines?

Section 2
Compliance

Case Study 2.1

Africa's Tech Challenge

A Chinese State-Owned Enterprise's Corporate Social Responsibility Experiment in Kenya

Yuan Wang

1 Overview

This case study presents innovative work by a Chinese state-owned enterprise (SOE) to use corporate social responsibility (CSR) as a key component of its business strategy in Kenya. AVIC International's ("AVIC INTL's") core business is exporting Chinese machinery and vocational training curricula to enhance the availability of equipment in host countries and to build the capacity of local technical and vocational training institutions. Through active learning with stakeholders in Kenya, AVIC INTL has developed the "Africa Tech Challenge" (ATC) to host training and competitions for candidates from Kenyan technical and vocational institutes. This CSR project, first initiated in 2014, later became a signature CSR project for the company, one which was repeated annually and received Chinese government awards for companies' overseas brand-building.

The case study shows how CSR can be an effective business strategy for Chinese SOEs operating in African states. Chinese SOEs have started to use CSR projects as a channel for gaining market access, building a positive image both in the host country and in Beijing, and cultivating and deepening ties with host country politicians, industry, civil society, and the (future) labor pool. The study also demonstrates how Chinese SOEs, over the course of overseas operations, have experienced a steep learning curve in host countries with this learning facilitated by SOEs' interactions with stakeholders in the host country. It discusses how, despite structural asymmetry vis-à-vis China, African actors can actively shape the behavior of Chinese SOEs that are financially powerful and technically strong.

2 Introduction

Why do overseas Chinese SOEs engage in CSR initiatives?[1] How do SOEs effectively integrate CSR as part of their business strategy? These questions

---

[1] The term CSR has increasingly been replaced by environmental, social and governance (ESG) and sustainable development, but we keep CSR here as the company under study calls this a CSR project.

are particularly salient for SOEs working in host countries with relatively weak legal and social institutions to regulate corporate behavior. Global engagement by Chinese SOEs exposes them to new sets of local and international norms and practices that are frequently different from those in China. Many SOEs, during years of operations overseas, have experienced a steep learning curve in acquiring practices and norms from host countries, particularly in countries with sociopolitical contexts starkly different from that of China. CSR has become an area where SOEs can experiment with innovative practices that bring their corporate practices closer to the host country's normative frameworks.

This case study examines AVIC INTL's innovative approach of using CSR as a key business strategy in Kenya. It illustrates that in conditions of Sino-African power asymmetry, Chinese SOEs in Kenya learn from their interactions with host country stakeholders and adapt their operations. In 2014, AVIC INTL's Kenya office rejected the standard approach to CSR as advocated by their headquarters in Beijing and instead initiated the ATC that later became a signature CSR project for the company. The ATC was continued annually and received awards from the Chinese government for effective overseas brand-building. What motivates AVIC INTL to allocate large budgets to this CSR project on an annual basis? Why and how did AVIC INTL create such innovative CSR activities in Kenya? And what was the role of Kenyan stakeholders in shaping AVIC INTL's CSR initiative?

This case study draws empirical insights from the author's direct participation in the ATC initiation stage as an early member of the China House, a Kenya-based NGO that participated in ATC's design and implementation, in 2014. Additional empirical evidence was collected through interviews during multiple field trips to Kenya and China in 2017 and 2019 and follow-up telephone interviews in 2021 and 2022. The study also draws on secondary sources such as AVIC INTL's CSR reports, internal documents, and email communications with stakeholders on the ATC projects.

The study is organized as follows. It starts by introducing the sociopolitical context of Kenya and Sino-Kenyan relations. Chinese companies operating in Kenya confront a starkly different sociopolitical landscape from their familiar context in China. The study then briefly discusses the Chinese government's encouragement of Chinese companies, particularly SOEs, to use CSR as a way of overseas operational risk mitigation and it continues by describing AVIC INTL, its shareholding structure, its entry into Kenya, and its core business. The main subsection then elaborates on the initiation and development of ATC from an idea to AVIC INTL's signature annual CSR project covering multiple African countries, and it concludes with a discussion of key points related to institutional learning, African agency, and the identity of Chinese SOEs as for-profit businesses, policy extensions of Beijing's Belt and Road Initiative (BRI), and learning institutions to diffuse innovative overseas practices to China's domestic business community.

3 The Case

3.1 Background on Sino-Kenyan Relations

Kenya is a lower-middle-income country. The country's GDP per capita was US$2,007 in 2021,[2] and GDP per capita growth has averaged 1.3% over the past five years, above the regional average. In 2020, Kenya surpassed Angola to become the third largest economy in sub-Saharan Africa after Nigeria and South Africa, according to the International Monetary Fund (IMF). From 2015 to 2019, Kenya's economy achieved broad-based growth averaging 4.7% per year, significantly reducing poverty (which fell to an estimated 34.4% at the US$1.90/day line in 2019).[3] Tourism in Kenya is the second largest source of foreign exchange revenue following agriculture. In 2020, the COVID-19 shock hit the economy hard, disrupting international trade and transport, tourism, and urban services activity. IMF evaluation shows that Kenya's economic rank in sub-Saharan Africa dropped to seventh in 2021. Russia's invasion of Ukraine in 2022 further exposed Kenya's economy to commodity price shocks, particularly as Kenya's economy is vulnerable to the cost of fuel, fertilizer, wheat, and other food imports.[4]

Kenya has one of the more vibrant media landscapes on the African continent, with professional and usually Western-trained journalists serving as watchdogs. The country's media is highly competitive and diverse, with over 100 FM stations, more than 60 free-to-view TV stations, and numerous newspapers and magazines. Journalists in Kenya, like in many other African countries, have long been trained with Western curricula, which produces a media system that is "an appendage of the Western model" of journalism.[5] Kenya also has an active civil society organization (CSO) sector, and trade unions are active with approximately 57 unions representing 2.6 million workers in 2018.[6] Journalists and CSOs critically assess the operations of domestic and foreign businesses and politics.

In Kenya, like many other African countries, Chinese media reporting tends to be less appealing and less popular than news from Western media sources despite Beijing's emphasis on soft power and discourse power.[7] In 2009, China's central government committed US$6 billion to facilitate Chinese media "going out" and competing with Western media conglomerates.[8] In 2012, CGTN, the

---

[2] World Bank, 'GDP Per Capita – Kenya' https://data.worldbank.org/indicator/NY.GDP.PCAP.CD?Locations=KE 28 November 2022.
[3] World Bank, 'Kenya Overview' www.worldbank.org/en/country/kenya/overview.
[4] World Bank, *Kenya Economic Update* (June 2022) https://documents1.worldbank.org/curated/en/099430006062288934/pdf/p17496106873620ce0a9f1073727d1c7d56.pdf.
[5] Emeka Umejei, *Chinese Media in Africa: Perception, Performance, and Paradox* (Lexington Books 2020) 84.
[6] Freedom House, 'Kenya Profile Page' https://freedomhouse.org/country/kenya/freedom-world/2021.
[7] Herman Wasserman, 'China in South Africa: Media Responses to a Developing Relationship' (2012) 53 Chinese Journal of Communication 336–54; Maria Repnikova, *Chinese Soft Power* (Cambridge University Press 2022).
[8] Zhengrong Hu and Dequiang Ji, 'Ambiguities in Communicating with the World: The "Going-Out" Policy of China's Media and Its Multilayered Contexts' (2012) 5 Chinese Journal of Communication 32–7.

main Chinese global media station, opened its Africa headquarters in Nairobi and China Daily launched its Africa edition. Xinhua News Agency and China Radio International have also been active in their outreach to the continent. China even carried out media training programs for African journalists in China, with the hope that the journalists would portray China in a more favorable light upon returning home but with mixed results.[9] In fact, interviews and surveys with African residents found Chinese media outlets to be unappealing. Local interviewees were largely unaware of CGTN,[10] and a survey of young private sector employees in Nairobi showed that CNN, a US media outlet, was the most watched foreign media channel.[11]

3.2 Kenya–China Relations

China established diplomatic relations with Kenya only two days after Kenya gained independence from the United Kingdom in December 1963. China was the fourth country to open an embassy in Nairobi. Bilateral relations gained momentum when President Daniel arap Moi came to power in 1978 and Deng Xiaoping in China pushed for "Opening and Reform." The Sino-Kenyan relationship gained momentum with high-profile visits and agreements to promote trade, investment, and technology exchange, as well as military exchange.

China is Kenya's largest trading partner and largest source of imports. In 2020, Kenya imported US$5.24 billion's worth of highly diversified products from China, with textiles, chemicals, metals, electronics, and machinery representing the main sectors. In the same year, Kenya exported just US$123 million's worth of products to China, predominantly minerals and agricultural products (see Figure 2.1.1). Kenya's approach of exporting raw materials to China and importing manufactured products from China conforms to China's bilateral trading pattern with many non-resource-rich African countries.[12]

Kenya is the fourth largest destination of Chinese loans in Africa after Angola, Ethiopia, and Zambia. From 2000 to 2020, China extended US$9.3 billion of loans for transport, power, ICT, and other sectors.[13] The largest and

---

[9] Lina Benabdallah, *Shaping the Future of Power: Knowledge Production and Network-Building in China-Africa Relations* (University of Michigan Press 2020) ch 5.

[10] Jacinta Mwende Maweu, 'Journalists' and Public Perceptions of the Politics of China's Soft Power in Kenya under the "Look East" Foreign Policy' in Xiaoling Zhang, Herman Wasserman, and Winston Mano (eds), *China's Media and Soft Power in Africa: Promotion and Perceptions* (Palgrave Macmillan 2016) 123–34.

[11] Yanqiu Zhang and Jane Muthoni Mwangi. 'A Perception Study on China's Media Engagement in Kenya: From Media Presence to Power Influence?' (2016) 9 Chinese Journal of Communication 71–80.

[12] For resource-rich African countries such as Angola, China is in trade deficit with the same trade component: China imports raw materials and exports manufactured products.

[13] BU Global Development Policy Center, 'Chinese Loans to Africa Database' www.bu.edu/gdp/chinese-loans-to-africa-database/. (Note that these are loan commitments and do not equal actual loans provided.)

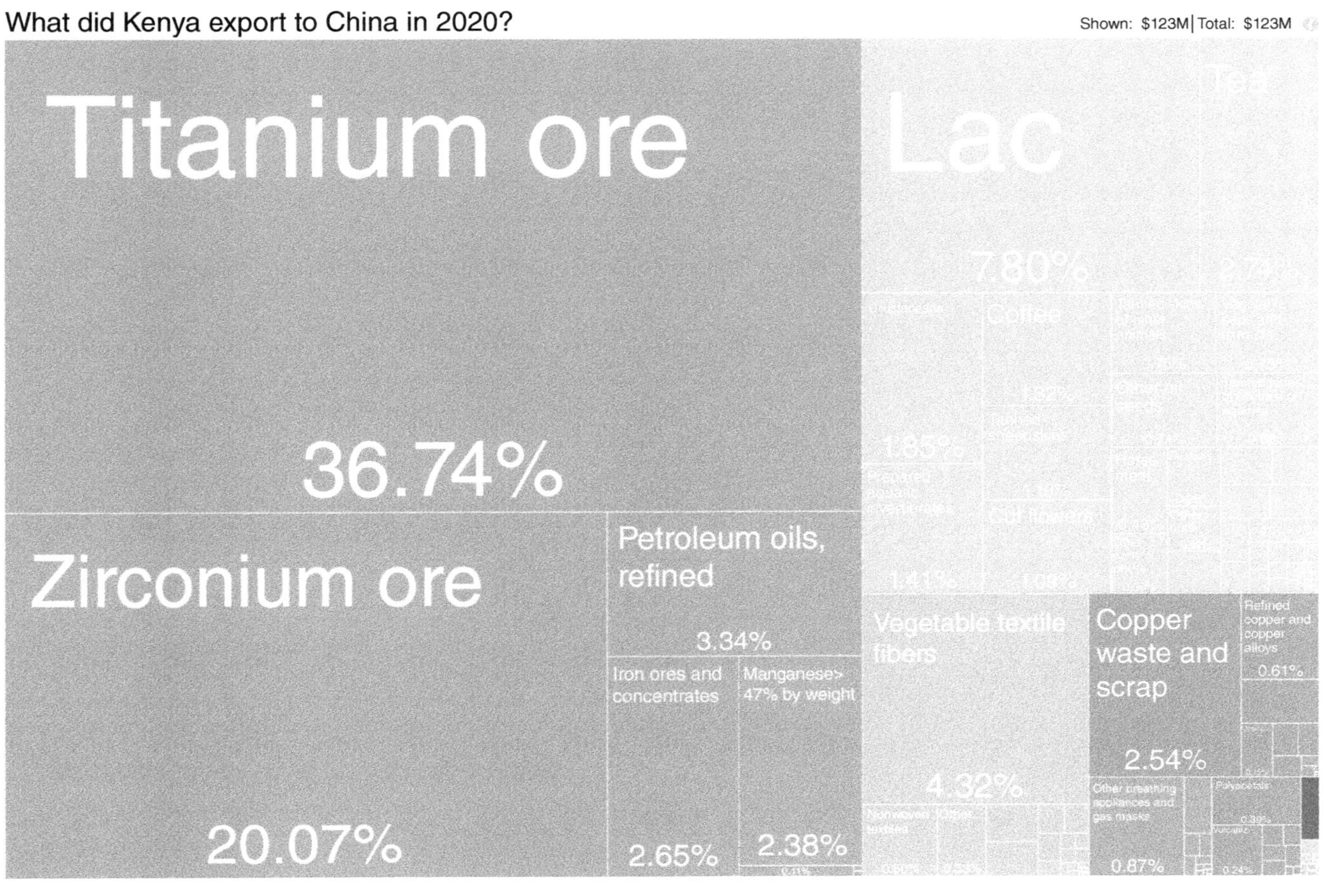

What did Kenya export to China in 2020?
Shown: $123M | Total: $123M
Titanium ore
36.74%
Zirconium ore
20.07%
Petroleum oils, refined
3.34%
Iron ores and concentrates
2.65%
Manganese> 47% by weight
2.38%
Lac
7.80%
Tea
Coffee
1.85%
1.82%
Cut flowers
1.41%
Vegetable textile fibers
4.32%
Copper waste and scrap
2.54%
Refined copper and copper alloys
0.61%
Other breathing appliances and gas masks
0.87%

Figure 2.1.1 Kenya's export basket, 2020

Source: Developed using the 'Atlas of the Economic Complexity' https://atlas.cid.harvard.edu/explore?country=116&product=undefined&year=2020&productClass=HS&target=Partner&partner=43&startYear=undefined.

What did Kenya import from China in 2020?

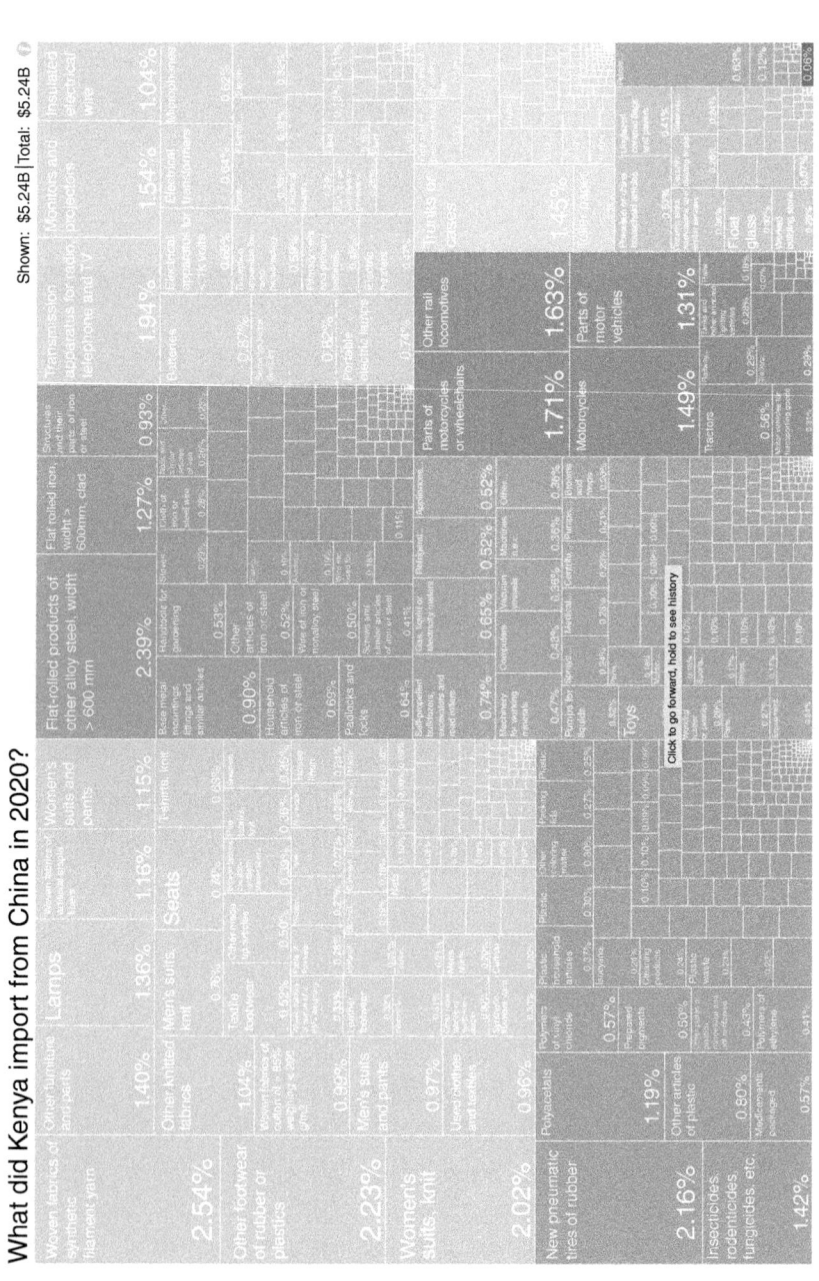

Figure 2.1.1 (cont.)

most expensive project in Kenya supported by Chinese loans is the Standard Gauge Railway Phase I (US$3.6 billion) and Phase 2A (US$1.5 billion). Since 2017, however, concerns over Kenya's debt sustainability and whether China uses debt to seek control over strategic assets such as railways and the Port of Mombasa have generated extensive debate in Kenya and internationally.

The two countries have starkly different sociopolitical systems. China is home to one of the world's most restricted media environments with a sophisticated system of censorship.[14] The publication of the law on foreign nongovernmental organizations in 2017 and the 2016 legislation governing philanthropy significantly reduced CSOs' access to funding from foreign sources and increased supervision and funding from the government. There is only one legal labor union organization, which is controlled by the Chinese government, and which has long been criticized for failing to properly defend workers' rights.[15] Chinese companies operating abroad in highly different sociopolitical contexts such as in Kenya frequently find themselves stepping into unfamiliar situations such as environmental and community welfare activism, labor unions, and media watchdogs. Kenyan employees of Chinese SOEs may resort to strikes to force the management to negotiate on wage and benefits, issues that Chinese managers are ill-equipped to deal with and which are a source of tension that reveal large cultural and management style differences.[16] The sheer size and visibility of the multibillion-dollar projects that Chinese SOEs work on, with frequent visits from high-profile local politicians as well as Chinese and other international political celebrities, draw these projects into the media spotlight. Used to highly controlled media serving as a mouthpiece of the Chinese government, Chinese SOEs find themselves beleaguered by "biased" criticism in local and international newspapers and other outlets. As a result of these challenges, Chinese companies frequently find it challenging to adapt their operation to the Kenyan situation. One response is the defense mechanism of "keeping a distance with respect" (*jing'er yuanzhi*).[17]

3.3 Doing CSR Overseas

The Chinese government has encouraged CSR domestically and published CSR regulations for overseas projects, yet implementation has been slow because these regulations are largely voluntary in nature and have weak

---

[14] Freedom House, 'China Profile Page' https://freedomhouse.org/countries/freedom-world/scores?Sort=desc&order=Country.
[15] ibid.
[16] Uwe Wissenbach and Yuan Wang, 'African Politics Meets Chinese Engineers: The Chinese-Built Standard Gauge Railway Project in Kenya and East Africa', SAIS-CARI Working Paper 2017/13.
[17] Weidi Zheng, 'The Silent China: Toward an Anti-essentialism Approach for South–South Encounters' (2022) 16 International Journal of Communication 20.

implementation monitoring requirements. To coincide with the global expansion of Chinese companies and the ongoing evolution of the BRI, government agencies at both central and provincial levels issued 121 guidelines and regulations between 2000 and 2016, mostly voluntary, requiring Chinese companies overseas to perform CSR or improve environmental, social and governance (ESG) domestically and overseas.[18]

In response to external criticism of Chinese companies' overseas behavior, Beijing recalibrated the BRI and promoted new regulations to oversee its implementation.[19] For instance, in 2016, the Chinese Ministry of Commerce started to publish annual social and political risk assessments and held training programs for Chinese overseas investors. The Industrial and Commercial Bank of China published the first Belt and Road Green Bond at the Summit in 2019. The Environmental Protection Agency committed to training 1,500 officials in BRI countries and establishing technology exchange and diffusion centers along the Belt and Road.[20] However, the majority of these are also nonmandatory, and Beijing's regulatory bodies cannot exercise effective control and oversight of all BRI activities conducted locally or abroad.[21]

3.4 AVIC INTL and the TVET Project in Africa

China Aviation Industry Corporation (AVIC) is a central SOE specializing in aerospace and defense and headquartered in Beijing. It was founded on 6 November 2008 through the restructuring and consolidation of the China Aviation Industry Corporation I (AVIC I) and the China Aviation Industry Corporation II (AVIC II).[22] AVIC's business units cover defense, transport aircraft, helicopters, avionics and systems, general aviation, research and development, flight testing, trade and logistics, assets management, financial services, engineering and construction, automobiles, and more. It is ranked 140th in the Fortune Global 500 list as of 2021,[23] and, as of 2021, has 1,003 subsidiary companies, including 63 second-level subsidiaries, 281 third-level subsidiaries, 340 fourth-level subsidiaries, 261 fifth-level subsidiaries, and 14 seventh-level subsidiaries, with 24 listed companies and 400,000 employees across the globe.[24]

---

[18] UNDP, 改革开放40周年：改变中的中国企业生态与社会可持续发展 [*The 40th Anniversary of Reform and Opening: The Changing Ecology of Chinese Enterprises and Sustainable Social Development*] (2017). The report has an annex with a list of all 121 CSR-related regulations publicized by the Chinese central and provincial governments from 2000 to 2016.

[19] Min Ye, 'Fragmented Motives and Policies: The Belt and Road Initiative in China' (2021) 21 Journal of East Asian Studies 193.

[20] ibid. [21] ibid. [22] AVIC Website, 'About Us' https://en.avic.com/en/aboutus/overview/.

[23] Fortune Global 500, 'Aviation Industry Corp. of China' https://fortune.com/company/aviation-industry-corp-of-china/global500/.

[24] AVIC website (n 22); AVIC 2022 Annual Report 《中国航空工业集团有限公司2021年度报告》 (27 April 2023) www.shclearing.com.cn/xxpl/cwbg/nb/202304/t20230427_1227245.html.

```
                    Aviation Industry Corporation of China (AVIC)
                                    │
                               100% ownership
                                    ↓
                    AVIC International Holding Corporation (AVIC INTL)
                    ┌───────────────┴───────────────┐
                    ↓                               ↓
            14 Domestic Subsidiaries         58 Overseas Offices &
            ┌───────┴───────┐                   Sub-companies
            ↓               ↓
        Regional        Professional
        companies        companies
```

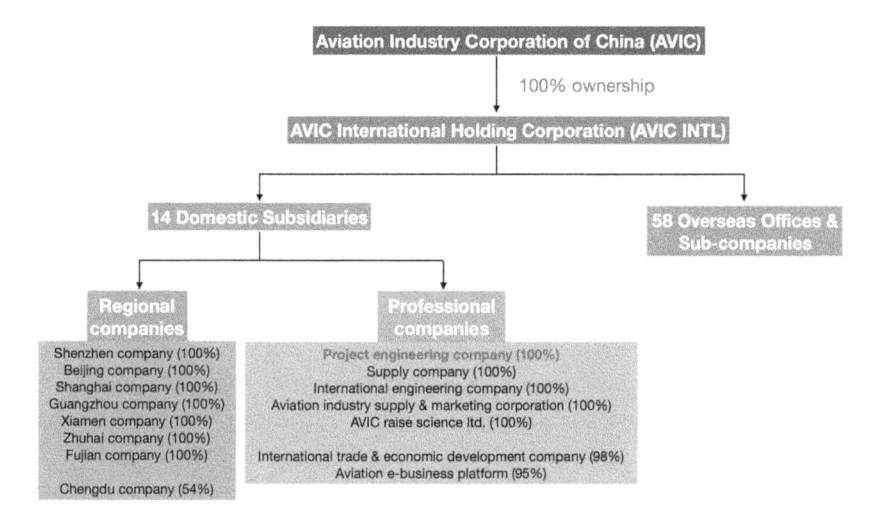

- Regional companies:
  - Shenzhen company (100%)
  - Beijing company (100%)
  - Shanghai company (100%)
  - Guangzhou company (100%)
  - Xiamen company (100%)
  - Zhuhai company (100%)
  - Fujian company (100%)
  - Chengdu company (54%)

- Professional companies:
  - Project engineering company (100%)
  - Supply company (100%)
  - International engineering company (100%)
  - Aviation industry supply & marketing corporation (100%)
  - AVIC raise science ltd. (100%)
  - International trade & economic development company (98%)
  - Aviation e-business platform (95%)

Figure 2.1.2 AVIC INTL-PEC shareholding structure
Source: AVIC INTL Project engineering company's internal document and interview.

AVIC International Holding Corporation ("AVIC INTL") is a global shareholding enterprise affiliated to AVIC. Also headquartered in Beijing, it has six domestic and overseas listed companies and has established branches in sixty countries and regions.[25] In 2008, AVIC INTL became an independent subsidiary company engaging in nonmilitary activities, including project planning, project financing management, export of electromechanical products, general contracting, operation, and maintenance of overseas engineering projects. AVIC INTL Project Engineering Company ("AVIC INTL-PEC") was formally the International Projects Department under AVIC INTL and became a separate company in May 2011, also headquartered in Beijing. The company specializes in four main businesses: (1) people's livelihood projects, including exporting Chinese mobile hospital equipment, vocational training equipment, container inspection system, buses, and so on; (2) energy engineering, procurement, and contracting, notably the Atlas Power Station Project in Turkey; (3) infrastructure construction, such as the rebuilding and expansion of a Kenyan airport project; and (4) industrial facility construction. The shareholding structure of AVIC INTL-PEC is illustrated in Figure 2.1.2.

AVIC entered Kenya in 1995 to export Chinese military aircraft to Kenya and established AVIC INTL Kenya representative office on 2 June 1995. Subsequently, AVIC INTL-PEC, AVIC INTL Beijing (covering businesses including cement engineering, petrochemical engineering, electromechanical engineering, and import and export of heavy equipment), and AVIC INTL Real Estate (newly established in 2014) were established in Kenya. When bidding for projects in Kenya, AVIC INTL-PEC, together with other subsidiaries,

---

[25] AVIC INTL website, www.avic-intl.cn/col_loen?Columnsid=2055.

used the name of the parent company AVIC INTL because it had a bigger branding effect, but in reality these subsidiaries operate relatively separately, having offices in different compounds. AVIC INTL-PEC has engaged in three main projects: the National Youth Service (NYS) Phase I and II,[26] Technical, Vocational and Entrepreneurship Training (TVET) Phase I and II, and the Karimenu dam water supply project.[27]

3.5 TVET Phase I

AVIC INTL's TVET project was developed with the Kenyan Ministry of Education, Science and Technology (MOEST) and involves equipment provision and capacity-building for Kenyan technical and vocational training institutions. In 2008, a MOEST delegation visited China and raised a request to import Chinese machineries and training in support of Kenyan TVET institutions. In 2010, AVIC INTL signed a Memorandum of Understanding with MOEST for US$30 million for Phase I of the TVET project. The following year, the Export-Import Bank of China (Exim Bank) signed an agreement with the Government of Kenya, providing a US$30 million concessional loan in support of this TVET Phase I. The terms of this loan were set at 2% interest rate, twenty-year maturity, and a seven-year grace period. The loan was scheduled for semi-annual repayment between March 2018 and September 2030.

The purpose of the project was to establish ten vocational and technical institutes in Kenya and provide training to 15,000 students.[28] The implementation of the first phase of the project mainly focused on two parts: equipment supplies and course training. This includes providing electronic and electrical goods, mechanical processing, rapid prototyping experimental training equipment, diesel generator sets and corresponding spare parts, supporting facilities for ten affiliated colleges and universities, as well as providing college planning, professional settings, and course packages, including compiling textbooks, laboratory planning, teacher training, assessment and evaluation, integration of production and education, and academic exchanges.[29]

3.6 TVET Phase II

In September 2013, AVIC INTL signed the TVET Phase II contract with MOEST at a cost of US$284 million.[30] This figure was later revised to US$167

---

[26] NYS Phase I started in 2008, US$55 million; Phase II started in 2012, US$70million. AVIC INTL-PEC internal document.
[27] Signed in 2014 and completed in 2022, with a contract amount of US$236 million. AVIC INTL-PEC internal document.
[28] Aid Data, China project information https://china.aiddata.org/projects/46982/.
[29] AVIC INTL 2013, '肯尼亚高教项目2013年6月贷后汇报' [Kenya Higher Education Project Post-Loan Report, June 2013].
[30] The contract value was revised to US$159 million in May 2016 after the Government of Kenya opted to undertake the civil works itself, thereby leaving the supply, installation, and

million via Addendum No. 1 of the contract. The contract value was then further revised to US$159 million via Addendum No. 2 dated 25 May 2016, after the Government of Kenya opted to undertake the civil works itself, while leaving the supply, installation, and commissioning of the equipment as well as human capacity-building to AVIC INTL. According to the contract, AVIC sought to equip a total of 134 educational institutions and provide training across the country. It was stipulated that 1,500 teachers were to be sent to the field and 150,000 students were to be trained by 2020. Exim Bank's approval for financing was pending for three years. It was not until 2017 that Exim Bank signed an agreement to provide an additional US$158 million of commercial loans for TVET project Phase II.

3.7 Challenges during TVET Phase I Implementation

By 2013, however, the imported equipment from TVET Phase I had not been used to its full capacity. A review of the project by Kenya's Auditor General revealed that one university and nine technical training institutes had been supplied with electrical/electronic engineering, mechanical engineering, rapid prototyping manufacturing laboratories, and diesel generators, but a physical verification of the equipment in all of the ten institutes revealed that the equipment had not been utilized to full capacity and the generators had not been put to use.[31] AVIC INTL's progress report to Exim Bank in June 2013 also recognized the limitation of existing infrastructure and the gap between Kenyan and Chinese higher education.[32] AVIC INTL's then project manager Li explained these two points in detail.[33] First, many remote towns in Kenya cannot provide stable electricity, and unstable electric current risks damaging expensive equipment. Second, teachers in TVET institutions, even after weeks of training in China, were still not sufficiently skilled to operate the machines, let alone teach students. For the training, AVIC INTL partnered with Inner Mongolia Technical College of Mechanics & Electrics to design the curriculum and carry out the training, but the language barrier was a key obstacle. Chinese trainers from the college traveled to Kenya and taught through translators but misinterpretation and the need to use technical jargon resulted in misunderstandings.[34] AVIC INTL needed to show that Phase 1 was successful to secure follow-on finance. However, implementation of Phase 1 on the ground was far from successful with some brand-new machines purchased from China laying idle.

---

commissioning of the equipment as well as human capacity-building to AVIC. See Aid Data, https://china.aiddata.org/projects/59494/.
[31] Aid Data (n 28).   [32] AVIC INTL (n 29).
[33] Pseudonym used due to information sensitivity.
[34] Caroline M. Musyimi, Joseph Malechwanzi, and Heng Luo, 'The Belt and Road Initiative and Technical and Vocational Education and Training (TVET) in Kenya: The Kenya-China TVET Project' (2018) 13 Frontiers of Education in China 346–74.

3.8 A CSR Innovation: Africa's Tech Challenge

To secure Exim Bank's funding approval for Phase II, AVIC INTL needed to show that Phase I was a success. An endorsement letter from the Chinese Economic Councilor in Kenya was a crucial step toward securing Exim Bank funding and Liu, the then deputy CEO of AVIC INTL, took a short trip to Kenya in late January 2014. There was a dinner meeting with Han Chunlin, the then Chinese Economic Councilor to Kenya. When Han asked about the progress of AVIC INTL's projects in Kenya, Liu reported on the progress of TVET Phase II and reflected on the experience of implementing Phase I, which had been completed by the end of 2013. He said that, in Phase II, AVIC INTL would further commit, and explore possible solutions, to ongoing issues even beyond the contract framework, such as providing raw materials and manufacturing contracts to schools and ensuring that the products could be used in other AVIC INTL projects in Kenya. By then, the company had already signed a contract with MOEST regarding TVET Phase II and were applying to Exim Bank for a loan thus requiring the endorsement letter from the Economic Councilor.

This was also the time when AVIC INTL-PEC headquarters were considering conducting a CSR project in Kenya. The then AVIC INTL's TVET project manager Li was also at the dinner that evening. Months later, he went on a trip to visit schools in the western provinces of Kenya with Isalambo S. Shikoli Benard, his counterpart from MOEST. On 21 February, on their way to Turkana, Li received an email from AVIC INTL-PEC headquarters in Beijing informing him of the headquarters' interest in developing a CSR project in cooperation with the China Foundation for Poverty Alleviation (CFPA). CFPA approached AVIC INTL headquarters in Beijing and proposed a CSR project featuring the provision of scholarships to African students to continue their study locally or in China. This was relatively easy to prepare and coordinate; CFPA already had rich experience of this type of corporate philanthropy in China. AVIC INTL headquarters allocated RMB 1 million (approx. US$16,000) for the Kenyan office to implement the project in collaboration with CFPA. AVIC INTL's Kenyan office was selected because it was the first office to carry out an education-related program.[35] In the email, AVIC INTL headquarters indicated their plan to form a research team with the Corporate Culture Department and three managers from CFPA for a nine-day field trip to Kenya in March 2014 to carry out a feasibility study of this CSR project. Li was asked to coordinate with local stakeholders to prepare for this fieldtrip but was far from enthusiastic about CFPA's proposal. During the seven-hour drive, Li and Benard discussed this scholarship project and Benard was equally unimpressed.

This prolonged driving trip was an ideal place for Li and Benard to brainstorm CSR project ideas. Benard's team in MOEST had previous experience of hosting the "Robot Contest" and the winner was named "African Tech Idol." The idea

---

[35] Interview with Mr. Li, 19 March 2022.

was to use robot assembly as an entry point to promote engineering and provide a forum for young engineers to display their creative works, exchange ideas, and promote engineering. Sponsored by Samsung, the fourth contest was to be held at TVET institutions.[36] Drawing on MOEST's multiyear experience of successfully hosting the Robot Contest in cooperation with Samsung, Li and Benard borrowed this idea and applied it to AVIC INTL's CSR project to host a technical skills competition using equipment installed by AVIC INTL. When they finally arrived at a village around midnight, Li emailed back to the senior management of AVIC INTL-PEC, copying in Liu, and warned of three difficulties in implementing the scholarship project including the recipient selection criteria, monitoring and evaluation, and most importantly, the corrupt nature of the client ministry:

> The scholarship distribution has to rely on Kenyan Ministry of Education, Science and Technology, and the coordination process may induce corruption. Referencing to previous scholarship programs in cooperation with the Ministry, the scholarship tends to end up [more often] in the hands of some connected individuals than the most needed; or the money was simply divided up within the Ministry before they even reach the students.[37]

In the same email, Li briefly outlined his discussion results with Benard on an alternative "Africa's Tech Idol" project:

- Name: Africa's Tech Idol (tentative)
- Potential candidates for the first season: Kenya Vocational and Technical College (about 30)
- Two rounds of competition for the first season:
  1. The preliminary round: machining competitions are held in five regions in Kenya and the top two in each region will be determined.
  2. The final round: ten teams compete in machining at our workshop at Kensington University. We provide the design, and the team can choose their equipment, including ordinary and numerical control equipment.
- The winning team will be rewarded:
  1. Offered a production and processing contract on the spot.
  2. Will be supported by our technicians in the factory.
  3. We process raw material support.
  4. A certain amount of project funding (in the form of sponsorship or angel funding) or equipment sponsorship, or both.[38]

Sun and Qi (2017) had a subsequent quote from Benard explaining his attitude toward the traditional types of CSR and his enthusiasm toward the skills competition:

> They [the AVIC International staff] were saying, "we could build a hospital..." I said, "All that is good, but it is being done by many people. But where you'll have

---

[36] MOEST 2014, Proposed Tech Idol Contest 2014. AVIC internal document.
[37] Mr. Li's email to AVIC INTL headquarters on 21 February 2014.   [38] ibid.

impetus: you've given us huge equipment, but the equipment is just here. We're not utilizing it. So, if we have a competition to support this equipment, then really, you'll be helping us as a country to build the confidence of our students that they can make things which can actually go out there."[39]

Benard drafted a project proposal for the creation of what eventually became the "Africa Tech Challenge" soon after returning from the Turkana trip.[40] In MOEST, Benard also sought higher administrative support from the Ministry. On AVIC INTL's side, Li's team sent the "Africa Tech Challenge" proposal back to Beijing for approval at the headquarters level. In comparison, the CFPA's scholarship program gradually lost support from the AVIC INTL leadership.

In addition to MOEST's experience in hosting skills competitions, Li also drew from the Japan International Cooperation Agency's (JICA's) extensive support of the Nakawa Vocational Training Institute in Uganda and also the experiences of Japanese companies in conducting CSR and other philanthropic projects – information shared via Li's friend who was working in the Japanese Embassy in Uganda at the time.[41] Li's friend was part of JICA's Nakawa Institute project and, following his friend, he shadowed meetings with the project stakeholders in Uganda. When Li visited the Nakawa Institute, he was impressed to see that JICA's malfunctioning vehicles were sent to Nakawa for maintenance. During the two decades of JICA's cooperation with Nakawa, there was not only education but also a combination of "production and education" (*chanjiao jiehe*) projects in Nakawa, bringing business benefits to the institution in addition to training students. In his proposal to AVIC INTL headquarters, Li also cited the Toyota Academy and Huawei Training Centre in Kenya as successful examples of vocational training.

Upon initial confirmation from AVIC INTL headquarters of the idea of "Africa Tech Challenge," Li and Mwangi, a Kenyan manager of AVIC INTL's TVET project who used to study in China and speaks and writes Chinese fluently, developed the idea into a full concept note in March 2014. Mwangi's family was well-connected in Kenya, and through her family network AVIC INTL managed to mobilize the then vice president (and president since 2023) William Ruto for the "Africa Tech Challenge" ceremony. Through his personal network, Li met the founder and CEO of China House, Huang, a Columbia University graduate and freelancing journalist who had created a Kenya-based CSO to help connect Chinese companies and Kenyan local communities. In his emails with AVIC INTL-PEC headquarters, Li mentioned China House

---

[39] Irene Sun and Lin Qi, 'Creating a Market for Skills Transfer: A Case Study of AVIC International's Skills Transfer Programs in Kenya', SAIS-CARI Working Paper No. 2017/14. This was confirmed in a separate telephone interview with the then TVET project manager Mr. Li, 21 November 2021.
[40] ibid. [41] Phone interview with Mr. Li, 21 November 2021.

and explored the possibility of contracting with China House to help with the development of AVIC INTL's CSR project. Li wrote in his email to AVIC INTL headquarters:

> Huang is very familiar with the media. At the time [of the competition], we will need the help of such talents in media public relations and writing various English reports... China House can recruit excellent summer volunteers to help us solve the labor shortage during the busiest season of AVIC INTL's Kenya office.[42]

Seeking to secure the first project, Huang's friendship with Li led to a service contract between AVIC INTL and China House on the ATC in June 2014. China House recruited two full-time staff for the delivery of AVIC INTL's contract. Among others, China House's main responsibilities included (1) coordinating ATC stakeholders, including MOEST, public relations companies, social media, and the United Nations; (2) publicizing the ATC via China House's own channels; and (3) providing a project evaluation summary report on the ATC's effects to participants and media. Huang brought in his media connections and sensitivity to the ATC's implementation and the involvement of China House was key to the development of the ATC.

Li convinced AVIC INTL headquarters to conduct the ATC as a machining skills competition in cooperation with MOEST. Li, with the help of the Ministry and together with China House, visited twenty-six out of forty-six TVET institutions in Kenya and received twenty-nine team applications, with three members in each team. Each school could nominate one or two teams with one advisor who was responsible for the organization of the participants. In the preliminary round, eighteen teams were selected and the top six then participated in the final competition. After twenty-three days of training, three winning teams were awarded US$100,000 in machine parts contracts and three individual awards with opportunities to continue education in China.[43] AVIC INTL subcontracted with the Inner Mongolia Technical College of Mechanics & Electrics to design the short training curriculum and flew two teachers from Inner Mongolia to Nairobi to train Kenyan candidates and prepare them for the competition. The ATC started in late July 2014 and the final competition was held on 5 September.

AVIC INTL's Kenyan office developed the ATC and media relations strategy not through imposition or borrowing experience from Beijing headquarters but from the company's interaction with stakeholders in Kenya. In addition to China House, AVIC INTL's Kenya office also contracted with a Kenyan public relations (PR) company to run the ATC opening and award ceremonies and media engagement. Invited leaders from AVIC INTL and its parent company, the Chinese Ambassador, the Economic Councilor, the

---

[42] Mr. Li's email communication with AVIC INTL-PEC headquarters.
[43] AVIC INTL, 2014, ATC Assessment Report. AVIC internal document.

Kenyan Minister of Education, Science and Technology, and other government leaders attended the awards ceremony, which attracted wide media coverage. In fact, PR was a key component of ATC from the project design stage onward. PR costs represented 24% of the total ATC budget with expenses including PR company service fees, social media company service fees, and billboard rental and printing fees. AVIC INTL rented a billboard in Nairobi's busy Harambee Avenue for multiple weeks. The ATC project evaluation report conducted by China House showed that the media influence of ATC included fifty-three media items at various stages of the ATC, including the opening and award ceremonies, during training, and the candidates' recruitment. Nine out of the fifty-three pieces were from Chinese media groups in Kenya with the remainder from Kenyan and African media. Western media groups were absent.[44]

The first ATC emphasized entrepreneurship and women's empowerment as key themes beyond general skills training. The theme of entrepreneurship was implemented through ATC Talk, mimicking the format of a TED Talk. This idea emerged from a brainstorming session between Li's team, China House, and the local PR company. The PR company invited successful Kenyan entrepreneurs and young leaders to communicate face-to-face with the students to share their entrepreneurial experiences and growth stories. In August and September 2014, three Kenyan entrepreneurs were invited to give talks to ATC candidates to create opportunities for candidates to interact with local businesses. Invited entrepreneurs shared their thoughts on topics such as "How to become an entrepreneur" by Samuel Kasera, CEO of Mutsimoto Motor Company, and "From student to entrepreneur: dream or reality" by David Muriithi, CEO of the Creative Enterprise Centre. The theme of women's empowerment was addressed by making sure to give at least one female candidate the opportunity to study in China.[45] Charity, the only female winner among three candidates who were awarded a scholarship, continued her study at Beihang University in China and was featured in AVIC INTL's short movie, *A Kenyan Girl's Dream to Become an Engineer*.

The success of ATC resulted in AVIC INTL highlighting it as the company's signature CSR project to be held annually. The ATC was an innovative idea for AVIC INTL, whose existing CSR projects were educational philanthropy, a signature project being a rural teacher training program named "Blue Chalk."[46] It was also AVIC INTL's only overseas CSR project. Each year, the

---

[44] ATC media coverage report.   [45] Interview (n 41).
[46] Blue Chalk Rural Teacher Training Program: Provides training and exchange education for rural primary and secondary school teachers in poverty-stricken areas where education is relatively backward to improve their teaching methods. This is achieved by recruiting outstanding teachers from educationally developed areas such as Beijing and Shenzhen. At present, the training has covered more than 8,000 schools, benefiting more than 20,000 teachers. See AVIC INTL website, 'Blue Chalk Introduction' www.avic-intl.cn/col_lo?columnsId=43.

ATC was featured in AVIC INTL headquarters' annual documentary series, *Glories and Hope*. Although the revenue of the TVET project cannot compete with major construction projects from other AVIC branches, the ATC project was so unique that Li was awarded AVIC INTL "Best Overseas Employee." The success of ATC Season I earned AVIC INTL wide media coverage in Kenya, enhanced client relationship with MOEST, and boosted Chinese domestic recognition.

Publicity for the ATC in China has not been as systematic as overseas in Africa where AVIC and China House's connections were based. In explaining why the ATC's overseas publicity is more important to AVIC INTL than domestic publicity in China, the current TVET project manager Yang explained: "We mainly target the overseas market, so domestic publicity is not very focused. At AVIC level, when they receive notifications from the government, AVIC sometimes requests us to report the ATC case." The ATC project won the "2020 Excellent Case for Chinese Companies Overseas CSR Award," an annual award jointly organized by the State-owned Assets Supervision and Administration Commission of the State Council Information Center, the China Press Office of the China International Publishing Administration, and the International Communication and Culture Center of the China Foreign Publishing Administration.[47] Utilizing its mobilization strength among university students in China, China House has also presented the ATC as a successful activity during policy conferences and student meetings.

Starting in Season III, ATC expanded beyond Kenya with teams invited from Ghana, Uganda, and Zambia. Cooperation with China House, however, finished. Since then, the ATC has become more closely aligned with AVIC INTL's TVET project and women's empowerment and entrepreneurship elements have not been featured.

Since 2014, ATC has been held once a year, and as of 2019, it has successfully held six competitions (see Table 2.1.1). Each year, AVIC INTL allocates approximately RMB 3 million to the event.[48] Due to the global outbreak of the COVID-19 pandemic, the event was temporarily suspended, but in July 2022, after suspension for two years, ATC Season VII launched online. The training was also conducted online through a newly developed app that AVIC INTL developed to use for its TVET projects in response to the pandemic and expanding business globally. The preliminary round of ATC VII has expanded to 42 schools entering 65 teams from six countries, namely Egypt, Ghana, Kenya, Uganda, Zambia, and Zimbabwe, and a total of 259 students.

Yang, the current AVIC INTL's TVET project manager, who was in charge of ATC, explained how this CSR project is being used to develop AVIC INTL's

---

[47] 'The Results of the 2020 Chinese Enterprises Overseas Image Building Case Collection Activity Announced' (*China Report Magazine*, 4 November 2020) http://m.gxfin.com/article/finance/cj/default/2020-11-04/5424099.html.
[48] ATC Project Report 2022, AVIC internal document.

Table 2.1.1 The seven ATC seasons and coverage

	Training and competition majors	Participating countries	Number of teams and participants	Award
ATC-1 (2014)	Machining	Kenya	29 teams from 26 universities and institutions, 116 participants	• AVIC INTL placed products order worth US$100,000s • 3 fully funded scholarships to study at Beihang University • US$3,600 bonus
ATC-2 (2015)	Machining, computer programming, and mobile app development	Kenya	18 teams, 126 participants	• 3 fully funded scholarships to study at Beihang University • US$19,000 bonus
ATC-3 (2016)	Basic and CNC machining	Kenya, Ghana, Uganda, and Zambia	30 teams, 120 participants	• AVIC INTL placed products order worth US$100,000s • 3 fully funded scholarships to study at Beihang University • US$11,200 bonus
ATC-4 (2017)	Construction works		103 participants recruited from society	• AVIC INTL placed products order worth US$100,000s • 25 employment positions at AVIC INTL
ATC-5[49] (2018)	Mechatronics, and CNC lathe	Côte d'Ivoire, Kenya, Gabon, Ghana, and Zambia	26 teams, 124 participants	• AVIC INTL placed products order worth US$100,000s • 3 fully funded scholarships to study at a Chinese TVET institution • US$170,000 bonus
ATC-6[50] (2019)	CNC lathe	Kenya, Uganda, Tanzania, Ethiopia, Gabon, Ghana, Côte d'Ivoire, and Zambia	17 teams, 64 participants	• AVIC INTL placed products order worth US$100,000s • 3 fully funded scholarships to study at a Chinese TVET institution • US$170,000 bonus
ATC-7[51] (2022)	Reading and drafting of construction drawings	Egypt, Ghana, Kenya, Uganda, Zambia, and Zimbabwe	65 teams, 259 participants	To be announced

[49] Edith Mutethya, 'AVIC International Launches ATC Season Five' (*China Daily*, 27 July 2018) www.chinadaily.com.cn/a/201807/27/WS5b59f026a3103la351e90673.html.
[50] Neymar, 'AVIC International, Ministry of Education Launch ATC Season 6' (*KBF*, 2 August 2019) https://kenyanbusinessfeed.com/avic-international-ministry-of-education-launch-atc-season-6/.
[51] AVIC International, '第七届ATC初赛侧写 | 能受训成为建筑师，我们很幸运！' [7th ATC Preliminary Round Profile: We Are Lucky to Be Trained as Architects!] (7 September 2022) https://mp.weixin.qq.com/s/cQQ7B5xlIDaq7oSEABFONA.

main TVET business. ATC's participating countries are usually the ones the company has already had TVET projects in or in which it plans to cultivate TVET cooperation:

> We approached officials from the respective country's Ministry of Education or their Vocational Education Department under the Ministry when we invited them to form teams to participate in the ATC, and for the award ceremony, we invited them over to Nairobi to attend. Similarly, we invite headmasters of TVET institutions in these countries. For each country, we have two official invitation quotas for the ATC award ceremony, and more Kenyan government officials are invited. At the third season of ATC, the current president-elect, William Ruto came.[52]

This quote shows that the SOE smartly connects its CSR project to business development and market expansion. Although business development has not been made directly through the ATC, this platform is used to cultivate and maintain relationships with the leadership from TVET institutions and government officials of the target countries.

4 Conclusion

The ATC, AVIC INTL's signature CSR project, is an example of a multinational company's willingness to adapt to host country situations. First, AVIC INTL's Kenya office demonstrated a learning curve with respect to CSR norms and practices in the host country. Over time, AVIC INTL developed an innovative and successful CSR project with an elevated PR strategy and aspects of gender equality and youth entrepreneurship. Second, the SOE's project manager actively learned through interacting with a variety of stakeholders in Kenya through his personal and professional networks. Project manager Li incorporated expertise from Kenyan counterparts and drew on his knowledge of Japanese corporate practices and JICA projects to come up with tailored solutions appropriate for his project. MOEST's successful multiyear experience of hosting the Robot Contest, in cooperation with Samsung's CSR department and China House's media relations and public engagement expertise, all contributed to the development and implementation of the ATC. Finally, the SOE's internal structure may serve as a channel for the diffusion of good practices from field offices to Beijing headquarters and further spread to other Chinese companies through government promotion. Through AVIC INTL's internal structures, information and experiences from the SOE's field offices in Kenya were applauded by their headquarters in China and shared in internal meetings. The ATC as a case study also received an award from the Chinese government and was promoted to the wider SOE community.

---

[52] Phone interview with Mr. Yang, 25 September 2022.

5 Discussion Questions and Comments

5.1 For Law School Audiences

Upon completion of TVET Phase I, AVIC INTL identified the lack of usage of the machines they provided, which could potentially harm their success of securing Phase II funding from Exim Bank. Mediocre implementation on the host state side is a problem that extends well beyond the TVET case, and thus has broader significance for analyzing China–Africa projects. In the TVET case, substandard implementation was also the motivation for the company to innovate on a CSR project that could "train the trainers" to run the machines. To address the problem, AVIC INTL could have pursued a number of different strategies. For example, instead of initiating the ATC, another approach would have been for AVIC INTL to resort to litigation or other formal dispute resolution means. What are the legal merits for AVIC INTL's claim should it want to sue the Kenyan government for not implementing its part of the contract? What are the potential risks for AVIC INTL if it pursued a legal rather than CSR route to solve the challenge? Do you agree with the company's decision for not resorting to legal procedures?

5.2 For Policy School Audiences

The ATC case raises two main questions with policy relevance. First, are CSR activities instruments of Beijing's global soft power outreach or are Chinese SOEs making genuine progress toward localization and further internationalization? And are these mutually exclusive explanations? Arguably, Chinese SOEs, particularly their CSR activities, are part of Beijing's broader soft power projection in Africa. Indeed, it is frequently perceived that Chinese SOEs, particularly given their state-owned nature, sometimes have broader, noncommercial aims providing a pivotal role in establishing connection between the Chinese government, local media outlets, and universities to promote a positive image of China in Africa. This case study, however, shows a CSR initiative developed by an SOE's Kenyan subsidiary after the Kenyan project manager rejected the original CSR project proposal from the SOE headquarters. Following its success, the CSR project was then promoted by the SOE headquarters and the Chinese government as creating business development opportunities and as an example of corporate stewardship overseas. This case may thus show less a coordinated effort by the Chinese government in Beijing and more a localized learning endeavor by the SOE's Kenyan subsidiary seeking to advance its business through an innovative and targeted CSR project. At the same time, in spite of the fact that the project was driven by local needs and interests, such facts are not to say that the Chinese government in Beijing could not then use the project for its own soft power benefits. Discuss these alternatives.

Second, is ATC an example of African agency or Chinese agency? Is China in Africa more precisely perceived as a global power exercising influence in small states? Or should we see this relationship as an interactive process where both parties have the agency to shape outcomes? We may emphasize the structural asymmetry between global economic and political strengths between smaller African countries and China, the world's second largest economy and a rising power. In dealing with Chinese SOEs, we may perceive Kenyan bureaucrats, media, and CSOs as lacking the agency to shape the behaviors of Chinese SOEs to their benefit. An opposing perspective is to view Chinese SOEs' activities in African countries, and in this case, AVIC INTL's CSR initiatives in Kenya, as jointly shaped by Chinese managers and a variety of Kenyan actors. Discuss these diverging perspectives.

5.3 For Business School Audiences

AVIC INTL's innovation underlines how CSR could help address several operational risks and opportunities for the overseas endeavors of Chinese SOEs and multinational corporations in general, particularly those operating in developing countries. What drives multinational companies' CSR activities? The ATC case shows that in countries with relatively weak social and environmental regulations, CSR could help multinational companies earn the social license to operate and reduce compliance risks. In countries with strong socio-environmental protection laws that are strictly implemented, these legal regulations serve as a guidance for multinationals, particularly those that newly entered a market, to develop amiable community relations and avoid local pushback against their products and operations. In countries where the implementation of socio-environmental regulations is relaxed or even incomplete, how could companies use CSR activities to help them navigate community relations in host countries?

Second, the ATC case also demonstrates an opportunity for companies to strategically connect CSR and business development activities. How specifically did AVIC INTL manage to achieve this connection? In AVIC INTL's case, the ATC's success motivated the company's leadership to further invest in the project and connect it to market expansion opportunities in neighboring African countries. In other words, this is a bottom-up and ad hoc connection between CSR and business development. What are options for companies to cultivate this connection? Could top-down design provide an alternative (or complementary) strategy?

Case Study 2.2

State Grid's Localization Strategies in Belo Monte, Brazil

Marco Germanò

1 Overview

This case study delves into the State Grid Corporation of China's (SGCC's) localization strategies within the Belo Monte hydroelectric project in Brazil, highlighting the challenges and learning experiences of Chinese state-owned enterprises (SOEs) in expanding their reach into Latin America. Over recent decades, Chinese SOEs have emerged as potential collaborators for Latin American countries in need of investment and technology for critical infrastructure projects. SGCC's role in constructing the Xingu-Estreito transmission line for the Belo Monte hydroelectric plant stands as a prime example. This line, among the world's largest and first to implement ±800kV ultra-high-voltage direct current (UHVDC) technology outside China, represents not only an engineering triumph for SGCC but also a significant business and legal accomplishment. The company adeptly navigated the complex Brazilian legal environment, addressing multifaceted regulatory, financial, and environmental challenges. While the Brazilian government has lauded the project for advancing energy security, it has also faced considerable criticism over socio-environmental issues. This case study, drawing on government and corporate documents as well as confidential interviews, examines SGCC's approach to procurement, financial structuring, environmental licensing, and operational management in the context of these grandiose transmission lines.

> Our company is from China, works in Brazil and gives back to the whole world; hence, the better its localization strategies, the more international it becomes.
> Cai Hongxian, Chairman of State Grid Brazil Holding (2010–2020)

> The size of this project is the size of our people. It is grandiose. It is a grandiose power project. The best way to describe Belo Monte is this word: grandiose.
> Dilma Rousseff, President of Brazil (2011–2016)

> Our fish are gone, our village is gone, the blue of the lake we used to care for is gone. They violated our rights and threw us in the trash as if we were disposable.
> Leonardo Batista, a riverside dweller affected by the Belo Monte hydroelectric project

2 Introduction

On 7 February 2014, executives at the SGCC headquarters in Beijing's Xicheng District celebrated their successful bid to construct the Xingu-Estreito transmission line with a toast and smiles. Ten thousand miles away, in Rio de Janeiro, Brazil, the celebration was a bit more boisterous. The victory in the Transmission Auction No. 011/2013 was a watershed moment for SGCC's operations in Latin America. It marked its largest venture in the region and positioned the company as one of the largest foreign players in Brazil's electricity sector. This achievement would be a triumph for any foreign company emerging in a market as competitive as Brazil's. However, this example is particularly remarkable as SGCC had been operating in the country for less than three years – a short time for such a complex economic sector and jurisdiction.

When Cai Hongxian, a 46-year-old senior executive at SGCC, arrived in Brazil in September 2010, he faced the daunting task of leading the company's most significant venture outside China. At that time, SGCC was already the world's largest electricity company, holding assets worth US$3.9 trillion and providing power to more than 1.1 billion people in China (Figure 2.2.1 gives an overview of SGCC's global assets as of 2021). However, the company had little experience investing overseas, having only previously ventured into the nearby Philippine market. Brazil was certainly the company's biggest international challenge at the time – and its greatest economic opportunity. The country had a large consumer market, geographic characteristics similar to China's, and was building stronger political ties with the Chinese government. Furthermore, Brazil was experiencing an economic boom, with a corresponding energy demand increase.

Cai was tasked with a clear goal: to make Brazil a successful case in SGCC's emerging international portfolio, particularly since the board was interested in expanding into new markets. However, the means to achieve this goal were uncertain. When the executive arrived in Brazil, he exemplified SGCC's general lack of knowledge about the country. He did not speak Portuguese, had a limited understanding of the complex regulatory environment surrounding the electricity sector, and was not familiar with the country's business culture. Cai was accompanied by a small team of Chinese colleagues, SGCC's technical expertise, and a blank check from headquarters – the Chinese board pledged to provide financial support for SGCC's activities in Brazil as long as they were sound and profitable.[1] Nonetheless, Cai had to find a way to establish a successful company that could thrive in Brazil's highly complex, competitive, but lucrative electricity market.

---

[1] Cai Hongxian, 'Nove anos de trabalhos duros no Brasil: A história de crescimento da State Grid Corporation no Brasil' in Zhou Zhiwei and Wu Changsheng (eds), *Histórias de Amizade entre China e Brasil* (China Intercontinental Press 2021) 294.

Category	Data
Position on Fortune Global 500 List	2nd
Economic Value Added	US$0.72 billion
Urban Power Supply Reliability	99.955%
Rural Power Supply Reliability	99.815%
National Territory Coverage	88%
Population Served	1.1 billion
Total Assets	US$637 billion
Annual Revenue	US$409 billion
Line Loss	6.25%
Annual Electricity Sales	4,453.6 TWh
Annual Profits	US$11.85 billion
Length of Transmission Lines	1.093 million km
Number of Employees	1.556 million
Fixed Asset Investment	US$70.77 billion
Conversion Capacity (TVA/TW)	4.94

SGCC Assets: Australia, Brazil, Chile, Greece, Italy, Oman, Pakistan, the Philippines, and Portugal.

SGCC Overseas Offices: Brazil, India, Hong Kong, Europe, the Philippines, Russia, and the United States.

Figure 2.2.1 Overview of SGCC's global assets, 2021
Conversion rate: RMB to US$ at 6.5 (Bloomberg, August 2021).
Source: Based on Fortune Global 500 (2021 list); SGCC, 'Corporate Social Responsibility Report 2020' (2020) bit.ly/3VSZJm3.

This case study explores SGCC's foray into Brazil, drawing on a range of sources, including publicly available governmental, corporate, and regulatory documents, along with disclosed and undisclosed interviews with the company's directors and legal advisors. The case study proceeds in five sections: the first provides an overview of the regulatory framework in Brazil that SGCC encountered in 2010; the second outlines the legal and corporate steps taken by SGCC upon entering the country; the third presents the Belo Monte hydroelectric project; the fourth examines the construction of the Xingu-Estreito transmission line; and the fifth evaluates the business aftermath of the line's construction. Finally, the study concludes by highlighting SGCC's successful localization strategies and discussing potential regulatory issues for the local government arising from the company's expanding influence in Brazil.[2]

3 The Case

3.1 Background: The Regulatory Framework of Brazil's Electricity Market

Though SGCC made a swift entry into the Brazilian market, it was nevertheless a latecomer compared to other Western players. When Cai announced SGCC's first investment in Brazil in mid 2010, that country's electricity market was at the apex of a two-decade-long reform period. This era not only revolutionized electricity production and commerce but also led to the establishment of an interconnected grid system under a revamped regulatory structure, known as the National Interconnected System (Sistema Interligado Nacional).

This reform process can be traced back to the early 1990s. Facing a shortage of dollars stemming from a structural balance of payment crisis and an inability to meet foreign commitments, the Brazilian government embarked on a large-scale reform program under the neoliberal auspices of the Washington Consensus. Within the electricity market, the restructuring was grounded in the three principles of the British power grid model: promoting competition through staged segmentation; relinquishing the state's monopoly and encouraging foreign direct investment; and repositioning the government from an active economic participant to a supervisory entity. Accordingly, the Brazilian government first segmented the electricity production chain into four stages: generation, transmission, distribution, and commercialization. Each segment was to be governed by its own set of regulations, standards, and supervisory institutions. Additionally, the government established three platforms for electricity trading: a system of public auctions to allocate concessions for each segment, a wholesale market for facilitating bilateral contracts between agents operating at different stages, and a secondary market for negotiating previously auctioned concessions.

Public and private companies, whether domestic or foreign, were allowed to participate in each segment either by securing new auctions or by acquiring existing concessions in the secondary market. The resulting "4-stages, 3-markets" framework was designed to mitigate risks of market control and supply chain verticalization, while assigning the Brazilian government the responsibility of managing the energy supply in line with its policy objectives.[3]

---

[2] By "localization strategies," I refer to SGCC's specific efforts to indigenize its business decision-making processes within the Brazilian context, as opposed to merely tailoring market strategies to consumer behaviors. This involves SGCC's adaptation to and integration within the local operational and regulatory landscape.
[3] Vertical integration in the electricity supply chain can lead to market distortions. Companies with control over multiple segments might use this influence to sway market dynamics. Such

The liberalization scheme brought about by these reforms significantly reduced public assets and redirected the state's focus toward market regulation. The government created several new bodies to oversee economic activity across all stages, including the National Electric Energy Agency (Agência Nacional de Energia Elétrica, ANEEL), a quasi-independent regulatory agency responsible for supervising all stages and guaranteeing market competition. ANEEL also was tasked with coordinating public auctions for long-term energy concessions, where the bid is awarded to the company that offers the highest discount rate on the annual allowed revenue (*receita anual permitida*, RAP), that is, the lowest annual amount in fees.

The ensuing scenario marked a notable change in the nature of electricity production, transitioning from a predominantly state-owned economic activity to a decentralized, stringently regulated environment with a rising private sector. The market became fragmented, with successful privatizations resulting in the establishment of more than 280 companies in Brazil. Foreign participation became a cornerstone across all stages of the electricity production chain, surging from almost negligible to approximately 21% in the country's installed capacity, 23% in transmission lines, and 52% in energy distribution.[4] In contrast to other Latin American economies such as Mexico and Paraguay, which primarily depend on state-led activities, Brazil boasts one of the most liberalized electricity markets in the region.[5] The majority of these companies are from Europe, North America, and, most recently, China.

Overall, the three reform pillars – competition, regulation, and private/foreign participation – effectively bolstered energy supply and resilience in the country while fostering market competition. From 1990 and 2022, the installed capacity in the country increased markedly from 49,760 MW to 206,451 MW, with the length of transmission lines correspondingly expanding from about 56,000 km to 165,667 km.[6] Brazil now ranks as the sixth-largest electricity producer worldwide, contributing 49.8% to Latin America's total installed capacity.[7]

Despite its progress, Brazil's energy sector still faces critical challenges related to water availability and transmission distances. The heavy reliance on hydropower, accounting for 63% of Brazil's electricity, renders the country vulnerable to climate-induced stresses, as highlighted by the severe 2020

---

control can result in anti-competitive practices, such as favoring their own assets or affiliated companies, leading to distorted energy prices and restricted market access for other producers.

[4] Gesner Oliveira et al., *Análise do ambiente concorrencial do setor elétrico no Brasil* (FGV 2018); 'Centro de Estudos de Infraestrutura e Soluções Ambientai' (*FGV EAESP*, 2019) https://gei-sa.fgv.br/sites/gei-sa.fgv.br/files/u49/go_estudo_concorrencial_energia_fgv.pdf.

[5] Lenin Balza et al., 'Privatization, Institutional Reform, and Performance in the Latin American Electricity Sector', Inter-American Development Bank Technical Note No. 599 (2013) 1–39.

[6] Ministério de Minas e. Energia, 'Anuário Estatístico de Energia Elétrica 2023' https://dashboard.epe.gov.br/apps/anuario-livro/.

[7] US Energy Information Administration, 'International Electric Capacity' www.eia.gov/international/data/world/electricity.

drought.[8] The majority of energy demand, around 48.6%, is in the southeast's urban centers, while approximately 70% of untapped hydropower resources are in the underdeveloped northern region – an area characterized by poor infrastructure, low population density, and a significant distance from consumer centers.[9] Developing projects in this region requires the construction of extensive transmission lines, which incurs efficiency costs and necessitates increased infrastructure investment.

3.2 The Company: SGCC Lands in Brazil

SGCC, a state-owned "profit-driven" utility company headquartered in Beijing, People's Republic of China (PRC), operates under the oversight of the State Council State-owned Assets Supervision and Administration Commission, the body tasked with supervising China's SOEs.[10] Established on 29 December 2002, SGCC emerged from an extensive reform within China's electricity sector, which dismantled the former all-purpose China State Power Corporation (CSPC). This restructuring was driven by the policy of "grasping the large and letting go of the small" (*zhua da fang xiao*), adopted by the 15th Communist Party Congress in September 1997, with the aim of enhancing market competitiveness and fostering innovation through equity segmentation. The subsequent "Plant-Grid" reform led to the fragmentation of CSPC into five smaller generation groups and two grid companies, SGCC – which retained about 80% of CSPC transmission assets and the responsibility for orchestrating the general operations of the grids across the country – and the smaller China Southern Power Grid Company.

In the following years post-reform, SGCC established itself as the dominant force in China's transmission sector, buoyed by public funding, easy credit access, market barriers for new entrants, and a vast consumer market. However, at the turn of the century, SGCC's operations were predominantly confined within China, and few foresaw its venture into overseas investments. This direction shifted with the PRC's "go out" (*zouchuqu*) policy in the early 2000s, encouraging outbound investment. Concurrently, SGCC's business strategy expanded to encompass foreign markets, initially focusing on three objectives: enhancing technology for improved domestic outcomes, securing higher profits compared to the more price-restricted Chinese market, and strengthening its position within China's political landscape.[11]

As a result, in 2007, SGCC embarked on its first international venture in the Philippines. The company secured the operation of the national power grid during a privatization auction of the state-owned National Transmission

---

[8] Sergio Chapa, Gerson Freitas Jr, and Anna Shiryaevskaya, 'Worst Drought in 91 Years Turns Brazil into Hot Spot for LNG' (*Bloomberg*, 3 June 2021) www.bloomberg.com/news/articles/2021-06-02/worst-drought-in-91-years-turns-brazil-into-hot-spot-for-lng.
[9] Empresa de Pesquisa Energética, 'Fontes Hidrelétrica' https://bit.ly/48m3FQy.
[10] See generally, Xu Yi-chong, *Sinews of Power: Politics of the State Grid Corporation of China* (Oxford University Press 2016).
[11] ibid ch 8.

Corporation (TransCo).[12] A consortium comprising SGCC and two Philippine companies, Monte Oro Grid Resources Corporation and Calaca High Power Corporation, clinched the bid with an offer of US$3.95 billion for a twenty-five-year license to operate TransCo. Within the newly formed National Grid Corporation of the Philippines, SGCC held a 40% stake and was able to appoint its chairman. SGCC hired Goldman Sachs to help with the deal.[13]

In the following months, SGCC swiftly enhanced its corporate structure to better manage its emerging international portfolio. The restructured framework included the establishment of various subsidiaries, each tailored to oversee distinct aspects of its global activity.[14] These entities were not limited to but included (1) State Grid International Development Co. Ltd. (SGID Co.), a limited liability company organized under the laws of the PRC; (2) State Grid International Development Limited (SGID), a private company limited by shares organized under the laws of Hong Kong SAR; (3) International Grid Holdings Limited (IGH), a corporation organized under the laws of the British Virgin Islands; and (4) Top View Grid Investment Limited (TVGI), a corporation organized under the laws of the British Virgin Islands (BVI). IGH and TVGI are each direct wholly owned subsidiaries of SGID. SGID is a direct subsidiary of SGID Co., which is a direct wholly owned subsidiary of SGCC.

The Philippines venture highlighted both profits and challenges for SGCC. Initially harmonious, the relationship deteriorated due to events including the 2010 Manila hostage crisis and the 2011 South China Sea dispute. In 2012, the Philippines denied visas to twenty-eight SGCC executives and employees. Diplomatic efforts failed, and SGCC ceased further investments, while Monte Oro sold their shares to a local holding, OneTaipan. By 2015, the Philippines claimed technical self-sufficiency, leading to the exit of remaining SGCC experts. Although SGCC continued to receive dividends, its operational influence ended. Currently, no SGCC executive serves on TransCo's board.

The Philippine experience highlighted the importance of political risk management and stability in international investments for SGCC. It provided valuable lessons that shaped SGCC's more strategic and locally attuned approach to entering the Brazilian market. This new foray into Latin America was also informed by dialogues with the Chinese government, which equipped SGCC's board with insights into global economic opportunities. This advice was crucial in light of the challenges other Chinese SOEs were encountering in their international ventures.[15]

Subsequently, on 28 April 2010, SGCC announced its entry into Brazil by confirming the creation of State Grid Brazil Holding (SGBH), a privately held

---

[12] Karen Lema, 'China State Grid Group Wins Philippine Power Auction' (*Reuters*, 12 December 2007) www.reuters.com/article/us-philippines-privatisation-idUKMAN29202520071212.
[13] Henry M. Paulson Jr, *Dealing with China* (Twelve 2015).
[14] United States Securities and Exchange Commission, SCHEDULE 13D, 2017, www.sec.gov/Archives/edgar/data/1300482/000119312517026721/d337193dsc13d.htm.
[15] Numerous Chinese firms, both state-owned and private, experienced a series of failed investments during the 2000s and early 2010s. See Peter J. Williamson and Anand P. Raman, 'How China Reset Its Global Acquisition Agenda' (2011) 89 Harvard Business Review 109.

company focused on managing local equity interests.[16] SGBH was incorporated in Rio de Janeiro as a subsidiary of TVGI and IGH with a 0.0001% and 99.9999% interest, respectively. The incorporation was soon followed by the announcement of SGBH's first investment in the country.

On 16 May 2010, the newly formed board confirmed the conclusion of negotiations to acquire seven transmission lines from the Spanish consortium Plena Transmissoras, led by Isolux, Cobra, and Elecnor, for US$989 million plus debt assumption. This deal also included a thirty-year license to operate approximately 3,000 km of the consortium's transmission networks in Brazil. The deal involved Brazilian and Anglo-American law firms and was also supported by SGCC's expanding in-house global legal team.[17] While the external firms addressed corporate and transactional legal issues, the internal team spearheaded legal research and played a pivotal role in shaping the investment strategy.

SGBH's investment also coincided with a series of political agreements between Brazil and China. From 2002 to 2010, both governments signed various legal instruments, such as a Joint Plan of Auction and multiple Memoranda of Understanding (MOUs), highlighting economic opportunities and synergies. These documents frequently mentioned energy cooperation, with China expressing interest in Brazil's electricity market.[18]

Thus, when SGBH announced its entry into Brazil, it was celebrated by both presidents, Lula da Silva and Hu Jintao, for fulfilling the pledge of the Chinese government to invest in Brazil's infrastructure gap. For SGCC, the Brazilian market seemed to be the right choice to bolster the company's internationalization drive and it targeted Brazil for several reasons. The 1990s reforms in Brazil had gained international recognition, attracting an increasing number of foreign companies. Post-2008 financial crisis, European utilities, seeking capital, were keen to sell their local assets. Additionally, Brazil was anticipating a 4–5% annual growth in electricity demand from 2001 to 2021, further driven by Rio hosting the 2014 World Cup and the 2016 Olympics. As Cai stated in 2011: "Brazil is a politically stable country and has friendly relations with China … We were attracted to the Brazilian market due to its mature market operations mechanism, transparent decision-making, and orderly sectoral supervision."[19]

The 2010 acquisition proved to be just the beginning of SGCC's plans for Brazil. Over the next few years, SGBH expanded its operations by acquiring other operational Special Purpose Vehicles (SPVs) and participating in public

---

[16] State Grid Brazil SA, 'Demonstrações Financeiras Individuais e Consolidadas em 31 de dezembro de 2022' (1st edn, State Grid Brazil Holding SA 2022) https://stategrid.com.br/wp-content/uploads/2023/05/DFs-State-Grid-Brazil-Holding-S.A.-31.12.2022.pdf.

[17] Interview no. 4 with Former SGBH Director (7 December 2022).

[18] Michelle Sanchez-Badin and Fabio Morosini, 'International Economic Law by Other Means: A Three-Level Matrix of Chinese Investment in Brazil's Electric Power Sector' (2021) 62 (Special Issue) Harvard International Law Journal 105.

[19] República Popular da China, 'Capital chinês no Brasil: oportunidade e não ameaça' (Embaixada da República Popular da China no Brasil, 13 April 2011) http://br.china-embassy.gov.cn/por/zbgx/201104/t20110413_4348974.htm.

auctions conducted by ANEEL. From 2011 to 2013, SGBH acquired five additional transmission lines (covering 1,960 km) from the Spanish group ACS for US$940 million and won four public auctions (covering 1,700 km) to construct new transmission lines in the country.

Despite financial support from the parent company for these operations, the initial phase was challenging for SGCC, as it had no previous experience operating in Brazil. The management team sent to the country, though well-versed in the market's economic prospects, had minimal grasp of the complex regulatory landscape, the rigorous environmental licensing processes, and the robust labor protections involving a unionized workforce. As highlighted by a former SGBH director, the Chinese management, accustomed to a centralized political culture, "did not [initially] understand the regulatory, environmental, and labor intricacies of the country."[20] As a result, the Chinese group employed various strategies to overcome the initial informational asymmetry and cultural gaps.

First, SGBH participated in public auctions as part of consortiums with Brazilian SOEs, a method used in three of the four initial auctions. In Auction No. 006/2011, SGBH secured a 51% majority stake in the Luziânia-Niquelândia substations system concession by forming a consortium with the state-run Furnas, offering a discount rate of 5.2% below the reference value. Similarly, in Auction No. 002/2012, SGBH joined forces with another Brazilian SOE, Copel, to obtain a 51% share in the Tele Pires transmission lines concession, including the Matrinchã and Guaraciaba projects, with substantial discount rates of 43.01% and 28%, respectively. In Auction No. 007/2012, SGBH collaborated with both Furnas and Copel to win a 51% share in the Paranaíba transmission lines project. As the SGBH Investment Director emphasized in 2012, the company's strategy in Brazil at the time was centered on forming alliances with local companies, stating, "Our goal is to seek cooperation rather than competition."[21]

Second, through acquiring Plena Transmissoras and ACS, SGBH gained access to a skilled pool of professionals. Between 2010 and 2013, the company recruited several managers and workers from the acquired companies and the broader market, dramatically expanding its office in Brazil. One notable example was the hiring of Ramon Haddad, a former Plena Transmissoras professional widely recognized as a market expert, who later became the vice president of SGBH. As noted by a former SGBH director, "these acquisitions quickly provided operational infrastructure, but more importantly, valuable knowledge on how to navigate the Brazilian market in terms of regulations and professional networks with authorities."[22]

Over the next few years, the company consistently prioritized local expertise in its board and management roles. While the positions of chairman, CEO, and

---

[20] Interview (n 17).
[21] Rodrigo Polito, 'State Grid busca parceiros para linhas de Belo Monte' (*Instituto Humanitas Unisinos*, 26 October 2012) www.ihu.unisinos.br/noticias/514929-state-grid-busca-parceiros-para-linhas-de-belo-monte.
[22] Interview (n 17).

one vice president were held by long-standing SGCC employees, the other two vice presidents and senior directors were predominantly Brazilian. Of the initial 300 hires within the first three years, nearly all were locally sourced. By 2013, SGBH had also formed a dedicated in-house legal team, even incorporating Brazilian legal professionals who had assisted with the company's initial M&As and public auctions.[23] This team grew over time, taking on most of SGCC's in-house legal responsibilities in Brazil. Currently, they collaborate with local and, occasionally, foreign law firms for complex or specialized legal advice.[24]

This move to localize both the operational and business decisions was a conscious one as Cai explained in 2013:

> Given that we are a Chinese company entering a foreign market, we knew we had to adapt to the local culture and operational environment. We decided right from the beginning to bring twenty Chinese employees to Brazil to give us support through the process of adapting our Chinese culture to the Brazilian way of business. Such first steps are always tentative but we are here to stay and we are ready to do what is necessary to accomplish our targets.[25]

Finally, during the initial period between 2010 and 2013, SGBH focused on strengthening its ties with local economic and political stakeholders, forging its own MOUs independently of the PRC government. A notable collaboration was formed with Brazilian SOE Eletrobras in 2011 during President Dilma Rousseff's visit to China. This MOU facilitated interactions and technical knowledge-sharing between both electricity giants. Shortly thereafter, SGBH and Eletrobras deepened their partnership beyond political engagement, collaborating economically on the Chinese company's most significant overseas investment at the time: constructing the first transmission line of the Belo Monte hydroelectric power plant, a grandiose dam marred by its socio-environmental impact.

3.3 The Project: The Belo Monte Hydroelectric Power Plant

In March 2010, ANEEL released the construction notice for the Belo Monte hydroelectric dam, inviting bids under specific conditions. Accordingly, Brazil was set to build the third largest hydroelectric dam in the world, with an installed capacity of 11,233 MW across eighteen turbines. The proposed power plant, designed as a "diversion" or "run-of-river" facility, differed from traditional Brazilian hydroelectric plants that store river water. This design aimed to minimize the socio-environmental impact of the project.[26]

---

[23] Interview (n 17).   [24] Interview (n 17).
[25] 'Interview with Cai Hongxian, State Grid Brazil Holding S.A.'
(*Energyboardroom*, 17 September 2013) www.energyboardroom.com/interviews/interview-with-cai-hongxian-state-grid-brazil-holding-s-a.
[26] 'Relatório de Impacto Ambiental: Aproveitamento Hidrelétrico Belo Monte' (Ministério de Minas e Energia 2009) http://philip.inpa.gov.br/publ_livres/Dossie/BM/DocsOf/RIMA-09/Rima_AHE%20Belo%20Monte.pdf.

Figure 2.2.2 The Belo Monte dam and its location in Brazil
Source: Bruno Batista, licensed under CC BY 2.0 https://bit.ly/3U6F6BD; NordNordWest, licensed under CC BY-SA 3.0 https://bit.ly/49u6ga6.

The announcement of the Belo Monte dam project was greatly celebrated by then president Lula, whose administration revived the plan, originally conceived by Brazil's military government in 1975. Lula's administration advocated for the dam as crucial for Brazil's energy security. However, civil society and environmental groups raised significant concerns. They criticized the project's potential environmental and social impacts, particularly on Indigenous communities. Despite the design with reduced impacts, issues like water management and economic viability remained contentious.

Additionally, the dam was to be built in the Xingu River in the state of Pará, far from the country's industrial region (Figure 2.2.2 provides an aerial view of the dam and its location). According to the transmission technology available in the country at the time, such long distances would result in significant losses during transmission to Brazil's southeast. The most advanced transmission line in Brazil at the time was the Rio Madeira high-voltage direct current (HVDC) system. It consisted of two bipolar ±600 kV DC transmission lines, each with a capacity of 3,150 MW, and an approximate loss rate of 11%.

Some of the concerns surrounding the project proved to be valid. The dam led to the displacement of several communities and significantly altered the region's environmental conditions.[27] Fluctuations in river flow affected power production, with the dam's guaranteed minimum capacity set at 4,571 MW, approximately 39% of its maximum capacity (Figure 2.2.3 gives annual average production). Furthermore, the consortium that won the bid for the hydroelectric plant, comprising several prominent Brazilian companies, faced numerous corruption allegations and environmental disputes in federal courts. These challenges delayed the dam's completion by fourteen months and doubled its total cost from approximately US$9 billion to US$18 billion.[28] Despite these issues, the initial fears of energy loss did not materialize, as Brazil was on the brink of witnessing the construction of one of the world's largest UHVDC lines.

3.4 The Line: Xingu-Estreito

The construction of the Belo Monte dam started in 2011, but only two years later the auction notice for its transmission lines was made public – a short but crucial period for the lines' design. ANEEL produces feasibility studies before officially launching a project via its Energy Research Office (Empresa de Pesquisa Energética, EPE), which details the expected technicalities required in each project. In 2007, EPE published the first studies for a transmission line connecting the Belo Monte dam to the national grid. These studies proposed using an HVDC of ±600 kV, similar to that seen in Rio Madeira.

---

[27] See Diego Magalhães et al., 'Electrification of Forest Biomes: Xingu-Rio Lines, Chinese Presence, and the Sociotechnological Impact of the Belo Monte Hydroelectric Dam' in Fernando Brancoli et al. (eds), *Tropical Silk Road: The Future of China in South America* (Stanford University Press 2022).

[28] 'Ibama "divulga" licença de Belo Monte' (*O Eco*, 27 January 2011) https://oeco.org.br/salada-verde/24752-ibama-divulga-licenca-de-belo-monte/; Valdo Cruz et al., 'Propina de Belo Monte foi de R$ 150 milhões, diz Andrade Gutierrez' (Folha de São Paulo, 7 April 2016) www1.folha.uol.com.br/poder/2016/04/1758468-propina-de-belo-monte-foi-de-r-150-milhoes-diz-andrade-gutierrez.shtml.

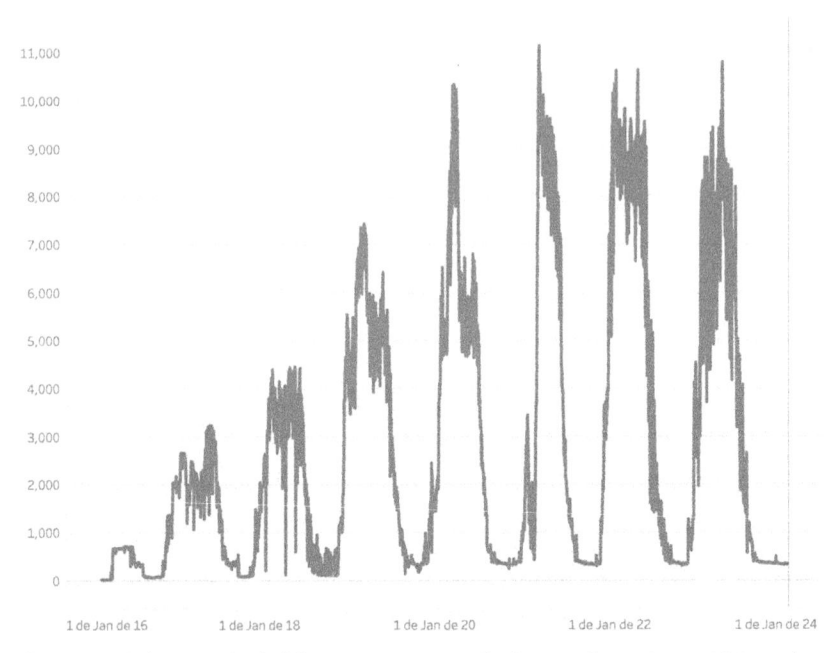

Figure 2.2.3 Belo Monte dam's daily average energy production, 26 February 2016 to 30 December 2023 (median megawatts, MWmed)
Source: Operador Nacional do Sistema Elétrico, 'Resultados da Operação: Geração de Energia' www.ons.org.br/Paginas/resultados-da-operacao/historico-da-operacao/geracao_energia.aspx

In 2011, EPE conducted new feasibility studies. This time it recommended using a UHVDC system consisting of two bipolar ±800 kV DC transmission lines, each with a capacity of 4,000 MW. UHVDC technology offers lower transmission costs and higher efficiency for transmitting very high power over long distances. However, at the time, the technology for this voltage level was not only unavailable in Brazil but only used in one place in the world: China.

On 19 December 2013, the auction notice for the Xingu-Estreito line was then published, confirming the use of UHVDC. When the offers for the construction and thirty-year use concession were opened on 7 February 2014, a consortium composed of SGBH and two Eletrobras subsidiaries, Eletronorte and Furnas, won the bid to Auction No. 011/2013. The three companies offered US$217 million of annual revenues to build and operate the lines, a 38% discount rate to the notice threshold. Chinese officials noted that SGCC's competitive bid was enabled by its ability to source significant equipment from China.[29]

In March 2014, the three companies then established an SPV named Belo Monte Transmissora de Energia (BMTE) in Rio de Janeiro, Brazil. SGBH held a majority stake of 51% in BMTE, with Eletronorte and Furnas splitting the rest equally. The company's governance structure balanced Brazilian and Chinese

---

[29] Xu Yi-chong (n 10) 282.

influences, featuring an evenly shared presidency and board with three members from each country. Senior management roles were jointly held, pairing a director and a deputy for each area, representing both nationalities.

The partnership between SGBH and Eletrobras proved effective for handling the complexities of the Xingu-Estreito project. Despite SGBH's growing familiarity with Brazil, this project posed larger technical, environmental, economic, and political risks. The planned transmission line, traversing sixty-five municipalities, four states, and three biomes in Brazil, presented a challenging terrestrial landscape. The legal complexities were even more daunting, requiring billion-dollar funding, negotiations with numerous landowners, and adherence to strict environmental standards. Collaborating with Eletrobras, Brazil's largest energy player, presented an advantageous opportunity. SGCC brought state-of-the-art technical expertise, while Eletrobras contributed extensive local knowledge of Brazilian regulations and authorities. As an SGBH former director aptly put it, "This was a successful business strategy from SGCC to adapt to Brazil, mitigate risk, and accelerate learning."[30]

Although the companies collaborated, each had a specific role in particular aspects of the venture. SGBH managed the financial side and appointed the Financial Director to BMTE. Eletronorte was in charge of obtaining environmental licenses and naming the Environmental Director. Furnas handled the technical design and appointed the Technical Manager. Furthermore, Eletrobras engaged in shaping public opinion through a media campaign to address ongoing criticisms of the Belo Monte project.

A distinctive feature of this management structure was the implementation of a "shadow management" system. In this arrangement, whenever a Brazilian professional held a managerial role, a Chinese deputy was assigned to work alongside them. This Chinese deputy closely collaborated with the Brazilian manager, providing insights and relaying important information back to the Chinese headquarters. As explained by a former director: "Every senior executive at SGBH had a Chinese shadow at his side. And this Chinese shadow made reports to the Chinese headquarters on the matters dealt with. It was a way that the Chinese found to learn about the Brazilian operation in practice."[31]

In legal matters, the SGBH in-house team led operations for BMTE in conjunction with teams from Eletronorte and Furnas, maintaining close collaboration with the Chinese management, the global SGCC legal team, and external law firms, especially for intricate tasks such as debenture issuance, audits, and labor- and tax-related issues. While ultimate decision-making authority rested with the Chinese management, the Brazilian legal team enjoyed significant autonomy in handling local affairs. As one SGBH lawyer noted, "Brazilians were at the forefront of all legal operations, reporting to Chinese managers. Direct interactions with Chinese executives were rare." A former director further explained, "Cai

---

[30] Interview no. 1 with Former SGBH Director (28 November 2022).
[31] Interview (n 17).

had the final say, but our legal team had substantial independence in determining the best strategies for matters involving concessions, public bids, or landowner negotiations to achieve the company's economic goals."[32]

To finance its investment, BMTE used a combination of loans, private debt, and equity, totaling an estimated US$1.8 billion. The consortium secured 46% of this amount, approximately US$818 million, in loans from Brazil's Development Bank (Banco Nacional de Desenvolvimento Econômico e Social, BNDES). Benefiting from BNDES's special subsidized credit line, BMTE accessed the long-term interest rate (*taxa de juros de longo prazo*, TJLP), enjoying interest rates between 2.98% and 4.10%, notably lower than typical market rates. Additionally, BMTE raised US$600 million in private debt through a debenture issuance, facilitated by local law firms.[33] The consortium also received an equity infusion from its shareholders to support construction costs. Over time, BMTE further diversified its financing by issuing a second debenture and obtaining additional loans from BNDES, thereby spreading out operational costs and risks.

Upon securing local financing, BMTE then faced a significant challenge in acquiring environmental licenses, due to Brazil's extensive and complex regulatory landscape featuring more than 20,000 environmental standards. This framework poses considerable hurdles for foreign entities, as exemplified by China Railway Eryuan Engineering Group's failed attempt to construct the Brazil–Peru Transcontinental Railway.[34] To navigate these complexities, BMTE employed a locally focused approach, engaging an interdisciplinary team of Brazilian experts for conducting Environmental Impact Assessment (EIA) studies.[35] Furthering its strategy to local expertise, BMTE engaged Tracbel, a subsidiary of the French multinational utility company Engie, renowned for its extensive experience in Brazil.

BMTE's EIA outlined eighteen initiatives to mitigate environmental concerns, including route optimization, implementation of forest replenishment programs, and provision of support to affected communities. The final line design stretched over approximately 2,089 km, surpassing the direct distance between stations (about 1,990 km), to navigate around sensitive environmental areas (Figure 2.2.4 gives the line design). On 20 May 2015, Brazilian authorities granted approval to the studies, marking a crucial milestone in the project's progression.

BMTE then enlisted a mix of Brazilian, European, and Chinese contractors. The line was segmented into eight stretches, each around 260 km in length, and corresponding engineering, procurement, and construction (EPC) contracts

---

[32] Interview (n 17).
[33] Interview no. 3 with Local Lawyer Representing SGBH (7 December 2022).
[34] Prioritized by Xi Jinping for Latin America in 2014, the project was eventually abandoned by Brazilian and Peruvian authorities due to unsatisfactory environmental and feasibility assessments. See Leolino Dourado, 'China-Backed Infrastructure in the Global South: Lessons from the Case of the Brazil–Peru Transcontinental Railway Project' (2022) 44 Third World Quarterly http://dx.doi.org/10.1080/01436597.2022.2154204.
[35] JGP Consultoria e Participações Ltda, 'Linha de Transmissão CC ±800 kV Xingu/Estreito e Instalações Associada' (*Belo Monte Transmissora de Energia*, 2014) www.bmte.com.br/wp-content/uploads/2016/06/RIMA.pdf.

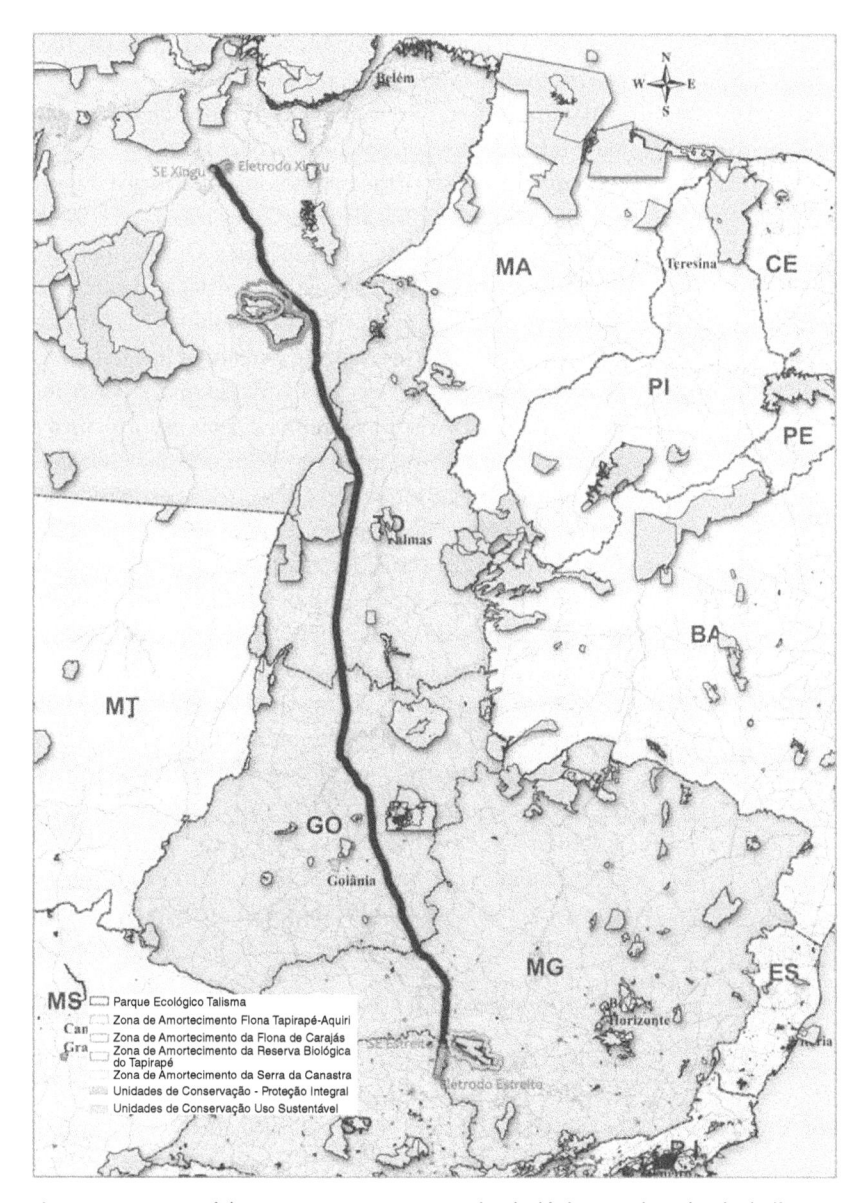

Figure 2.2.4 Design of the Xingu-Estreito transmission line highlighting ecological parks, buffer zones, and conservation units
Source: JGP Consultoria (n 40) 29.

were awarded for these sections. Brazilian firms Tabocas (for sections 3 and 4), São Simão (sections 6 and 7), and Incomisa (section 8) were engaged, while the Chinese company SEPCO 1, a subsidiary of PowerChina, took on sections 1, 2, and 5. In addition, infrastructure components like towers and substations were contracted to other companies, including Brametal, Electrovidro, SAE Towers, and Siemens. While BMTE oversaw the EPC contractors' operations, it did not directly involve itself in the construction process. SGCC's affiliates – such as

NARI, CET Brazil, and Xuji – also played a pivotal role by providing specialized automation and smart metering technologies. Notably, NARI established a manufacturing plant in São Paulo at the time, aiming to emerge as a key supplier for Brazil's grid construction efforts.

The construction of the transmission line involved approximately 8,000 workers, predominantly Brazilian. As Cai noted in 2012, SGCC's approach in Brazil did not rely on importing Chinese labor: "Our strategy involves bringing Chinese executives to Brazil while also employing local workers. We aim to blend the best aspects of Chinese and Brazilian work cultures."[36] To bridge cultural gaps, SGBH even engaged a firm specializing in cultural integration to facilitate interactions between Brazilian workers and Chinese managers. A former SGBH executive reflected, "from their arrival in Brazil, there was a focused effort to enhance company performance by integrating Chinese and Brazilian cultural elements."[37] Nonetheless, linguistic barriers remained a persistent challenge, even during the operational phase of the project, as highlighted by another director: "Language has always remained a challenge, even today with an operational line."[38]

Construction of the line began in June 2016 and finished by December 2017, two months ahead of schedule. Upon completion, SGBH solidified its presence in Brazil, establishing significant operations in Rio de Janeiro with a local workforce of 800 and investing US$60 million in five floors of a 16-story building, which also accommodates other Chinese companies. The project not only deepened SGBH's understanding of the Brazilian market but also strengthened its local team and its relationship with Brazilian partners. This experience would soon prove valuable for the construction of the Belo Monte hydroelectric plant's second line – currently the world's largest transmission line. However, this time, SGBH embarked on the new project alone.

3.5 Aftermath: SGBH Accessing Other Stages of the Production Chain

The successful completion of the Xingu-Estreito transmission line significantly elevated Brazil's status within SGCC's global operations, positioning it as the corporation's second most crucial market after China. The construction and overall operation of the Xingu-Estreito line was also a testing ground for the Chinese in both exploring new markets and experimenting with their UHVDC technology outside of China. These achievements sparked heightened interest from SGCC's headquarters, and over the following years SGCC aimed to broaden its portfolio in Brazil. The aftermath saw two distinct strategies: securing a more robust position in the transmission market through ANEEL auctions and shifting the initial emphasis from transmission lines to other segments of Brazil's electricity production chain.

---

[36] Marcos Todeschini and Carlos Rydlewski, 'A invasão chines' (*Época Negócios*, 2014) https://epocanegocios.globo.com/Informacao/Acao/noticia/2012/04/invasao-chinesa.html.
[37] Interview (n 30).   [38] Interview no. 2 with SGBH Director (1 December 2022).

First, SGBH made significant investments in new public auctions, thereby extending its control over more than 16,000 km of transmission lines, which currently accounts for approximately 10% of Brazil's total high-voltage network. Notably, in 2015, the company won the auction to build and operate the second line of the Belo Monte project, the 2,543 km Xingu-Rio UHVDC transmission line (Figure 2.2.5 showcases the second line's design, detailing the sections handled by EPC contractors).[39] The strategies used in this second venture were inspired by the successes and mistakes of the first operation. In areas such as financing, the same approaches were used, while environmental strategies were refined. In 2023, SGBH secured another major project, constructing 1,463 km of HVDC lines, offering a 40% RAP discount rate, and committing to invest an additional US$3.6 billion. In both instances, SGBH submitted bids independently, marking a departure from its previous strategy of collaborating with local SOEs. The company managed construction on its own, subcontracting for equipment and line construction, while engaging a larger number of Chinese companies in the projects.

Second, SGBH broadened its scope within Brazil's electricity chain, moving beyond transmission to acquire operational assets in other stages. A significant development occurred in August 2016, when SGCC's subsidiary, SGID, invested US$1.8 billion to acquire a 23% stake in Companhia Paulista de Força e Luz (CPFL), the largest private player in the Brazilian electricity sector and a publicly traded company on São Paulo's B3 stock exchange. To manage CPFL's assets, SGID incorporated State Grid Brazil Power (SGBP) as a new holding company based in Campinas, São Paulo. This acquisition was further reinforced by a Public Offer for Acquisition (PAO) in November 2017, valued at US$3.5 billion, which aimed to purchase shares from CPFL's minority shareholders. The successful PAO led to SGCC acquiring a controlling interest of 83.7% in CPFL, along with complete ownership of CPFL Renováveis, a subsidiary specializing in renewable energy. While CPFL's remaining shares continued to be traded freely, its American Depositary Shares were delisted from the New York Stock Exchange, and CPFL Renováveis was fully withdrawn from B3.

The acquisition of CPFL positioned SGCC as Brazil's second largest electricity utility, only behind Eletrobras. By 2021, SGCC had a significant presence in the Brazilian electricity sector, both directly and via its subsidiaries. The company controlled 4.4 GW, or the equivalent to 2.1% of the country's generation capacity, and owned 22,000 km of transmission lines, representing 11% of Brazil's network. Additionally, it managed the electricity distribution for 10 million clients, accounting for 13% of Brazilian consumer units (Figure 2.2.6 provides a comprehensive view of SGCC's assets in Brazil via SGBH and

---

[39] SGBH established a new SPV called Xingu-Rio Transmissora de Energia (XRTE) to facilitate the construction process. Given the requirement in the Brazilian legislation of having two partners for an SPV, SGBH leveraged the broader SGCC corporate structure. XRTE was incorporated in Rio de Janeiro, Brazil, with SGBH holding 99.999% of the shares and TVGI, SGCC's BVI subsidiary, holding the remaining 0.001%.

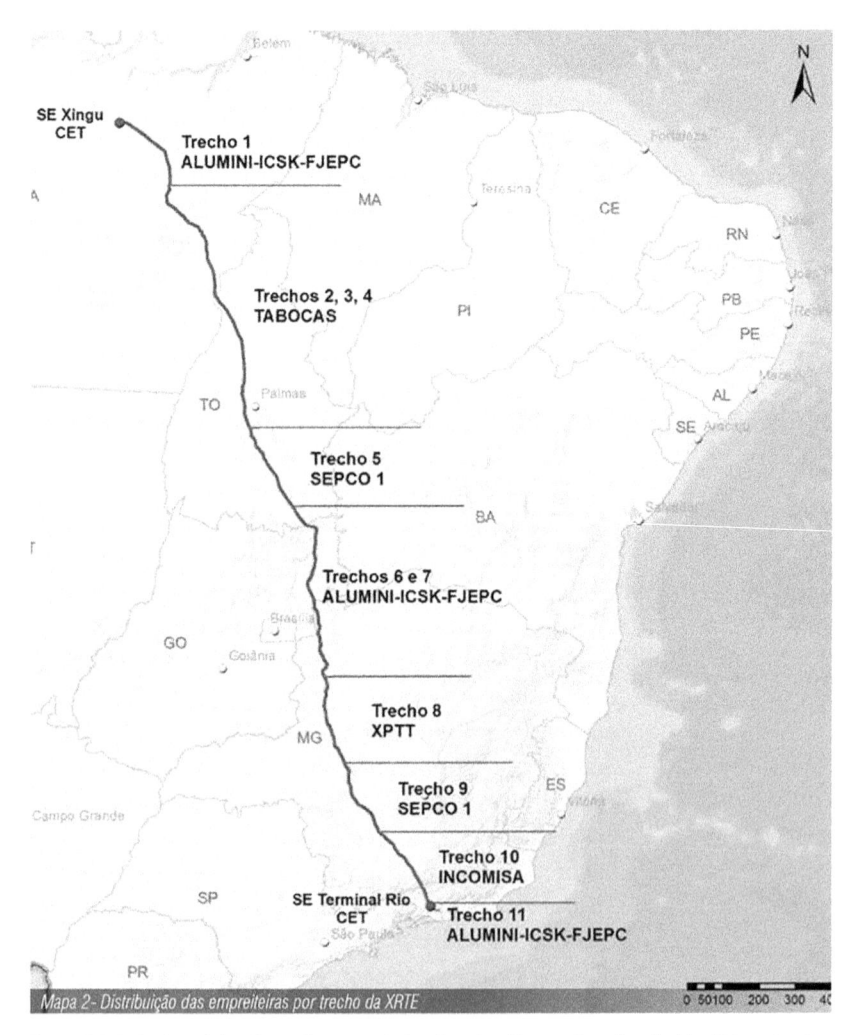

Figure 2.2.5 Design of the Xingu-Rio transmission line detailing sections handled by EPC contractors
Source: Ricardo Abranches Felix Cardoso Júnior and others, 'A XRTE e o Meio Ambiente' (Rio de Janeiro 2020) 12.

CPFL as of 2021). SGCC's operations in Brazil are organized under a holding model, managing more than sixty SPV companies through SGBH, SGBP, and CPFL. As of 2021, SGCC held US$6 billion in Brazilian assets, and its reported revenues and net profit in the country were US$8.4 billion and US$2.2 billion, respectively.[40]

Cai served as the chairman of SGBH until 2020, after which he returned home upon completing his mission in Brazil. In China, he assumed the role of General Manager of State Grid Fujian Electric Power Co., an SGCC subsidiary

---

[40] State Grid Brazil Holding, 'Relatório de Responsabilidade Social Corporativa da SGCC (Brasil) 2021' www.grupocpfl.com.br/sites/default/files/2021-12/CPFL_RelatorioAnual2019_0.pdf.

focused on providing electricity to the province of Fujian. He also became a frequent spokesperson of SGCC success in Brazil. Meanwhile, SGCC went abroad, expanding its activities internationally and becoming the world's fifth largest company by total assets. As of 2023, it has investments in nine countries – Australia, Brazil, Chile, Greece, Italy, Oman, Pakistan, the Philippines, and Portugal – and activities in more than forty countries. Its overseas investments surpass US$21 billion, with approximately 60% of these funds allocated to Brazil. The Belo Monte transmission lines, along with CPFL, are among the crown jewels of SGCC's global portfolio.

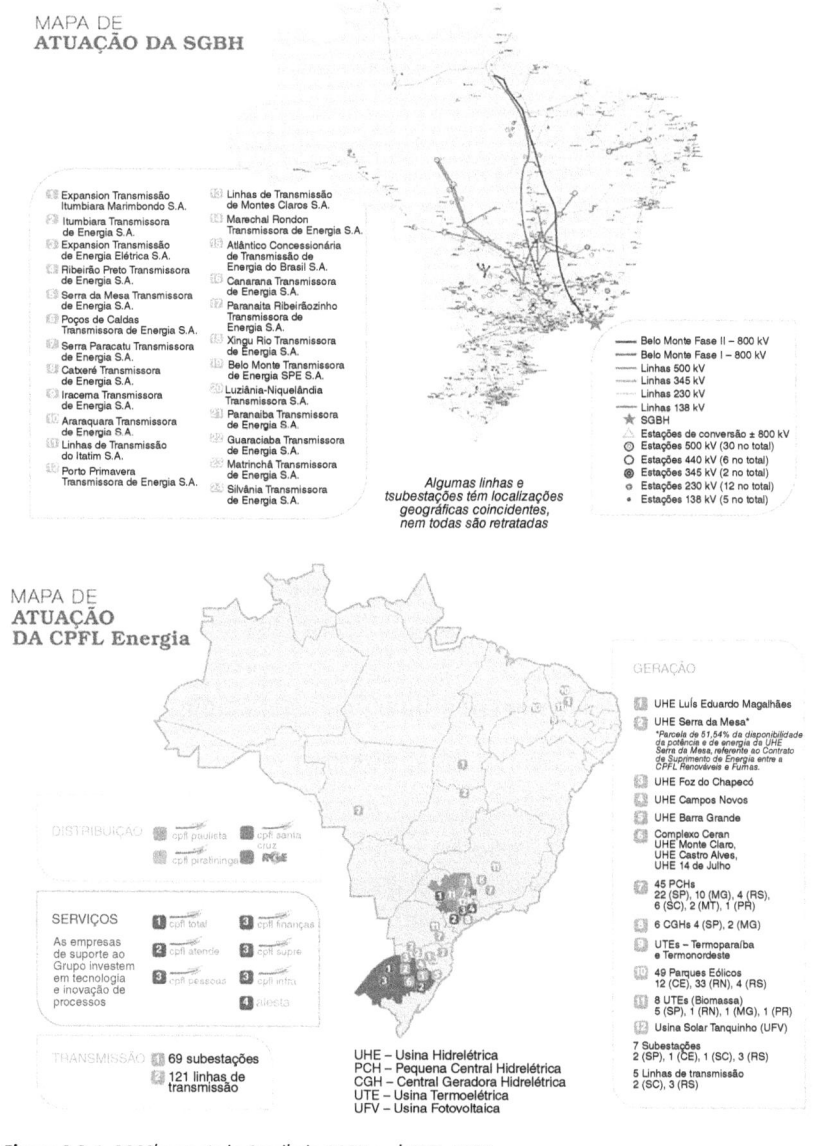

Figure 2.2.6 SGCC's assets in Brazil via SGBH and CPFL, 2021

4 Conclusion

This case study explores SGCC's strategic foray into Brazil, highlighting its effective approach compared to its earlier challenges in the Philippines. Yet it also points to concerns about SGCC's increasing influence in Brazil's electricity sector, especially after diversifying its operations post the Xingu-Estreito transmission line project. Key issues involve potential impacts on market competition and the necessity for regulatory oversight to prevent market dominance (Figure 2.2.7 details market share by nationality in Brazil's generation, transmission, and distribution sectors from 2010 to 2019).

Evaluating the impact of Chinese investments in Brazil's electrical sector requires a nuanced analysis that considers diverse perspectives. While these investments typically comply with Brazilian corporate legislation, their alignment with national policy objectives and the market's design remain a matter of debate. This issue is critical not only for Brazil but also for other developing nations grappling with inadequate infrastructure, economic instability, and reliance on foreign capital. Moreover, despite having regulatory bodies like the Administrative Council for Economic Defense (Conselho Administrativo de Defesa Econômica, CADE) to monitor market concentration, Brazil lacks specific measures for national security considerations, unlike mechanisms such as the Committee on Foreign Investment in the United States.

Reflecting this complexity, two former SGBH directors present differing views. One states, "Regardless of market concentration, a company in the Brazilian market does not have much power such as to dictate prices or take control of an asset. Everything is a concession under a robust regulatory framework."[41] Another counters, "Chinese investments raise many issues, including market concentration. It is not just a matter restricted to Chinese investors, but it is clear that their financial capacity and interest in new investments in Brazil are now relevant. ... We need to think seriously about this."[42]

5 Discussion Questions and Comments

5.1 For Law School Audiences

SGCC's venture in Brazil's Belo Monte project introduces several intricate legal challenges of foreign companies emerging in new jurisdictions. These may include navigating a complex regulatory environment, addressing socio-environmental concerns, and ensuring compliance with both local and international legal frameworks. Given the information provided in the case, discuss the following questions:

1. Regulatory Navigation: How did SGCC successfully navigate the complex regulatory framework in Brazil, particularly in contrast to its Philippine

---

[41] Interview (n 30).   [42] Interview (n 17).

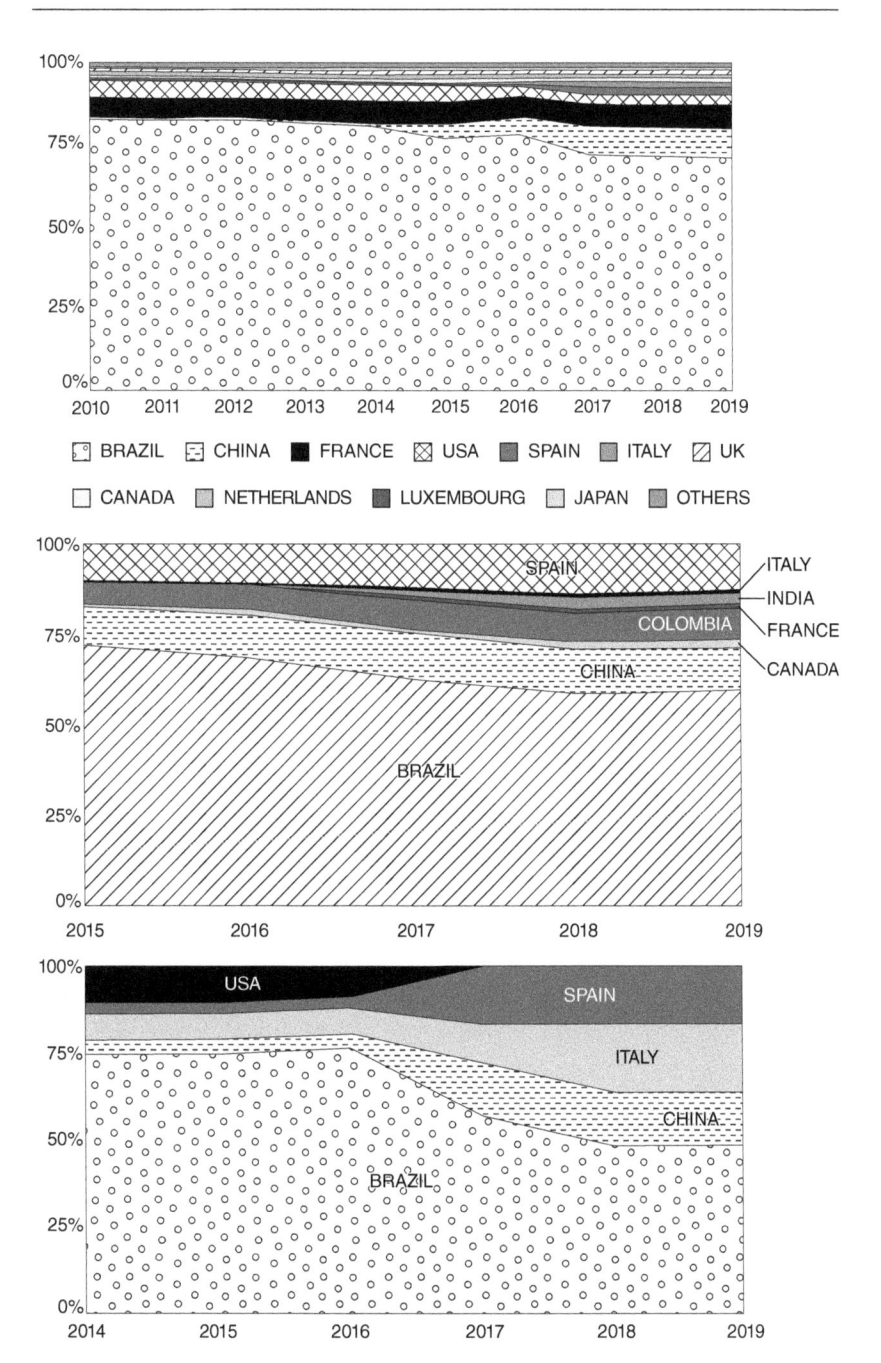

Figure 2.2.7 Market share by nationality in Brazil's generation, transmission, and distribution sectors, 2010–2019 respectively
Source: Pedro Henrique Batista Barbosa, 'New Kids on the Block: China's Arrival in Brazil's Electric Sector' Global Development Policy Center GCI Working Paper No. 012 (December 2020) www.bu.edu/gdp/files/2020/12/GCI_WP_012_Pedro_Henrique_Batista_Barbosa.pdf.

experience? Analyze the specific legal strategies employed by SGCC in Brazil, evaluating their effectiveness in adapting to this market. Further, consider which of these strategies could be feasibly replicated by other multinational companies in similar contexts, and discuss any factors that might limit their viability.
2. Financial Design: Analyze SGCC's legal strategies that supported the financial design for the Xingu-Estreito transmission line project in Brazil. Discuss how these strategies facilitated effective risk management and consider their adaptability to similar projects in other countries. Evaluate the availability of funding options domestically in China or in other countries, locally in Brazil, or transnationally, and assess which approach might be most advantageous for other multinational companies venturing into developing countries.
3. Corporate Governance: Explore the legal consequences of SGCC's decision to delist CPFL from the NYSE and CPFL Renováveis from B3. How does this decision reflect SGCC's corporate governance and market strategy in an international context? If you were part of SGCC's legal team, would you have advised in favor of this move? Discuss the potential benefits and drawbacks of such a decision from a legal and corporate strategy standpoint.
4. Legal Team Localization in Multinational Corporations: To what extent does the localization of a legal team within a multinational corporation, such as SGCC in Brazil, enhance the company's capacity to effectively navigate intricate local regulatory and legal landscapes? Delve into the advantages and potential obstacles associated with this strategy, particularly in regions where legal norms and practices diverge significantly from the corporation's home country.
5. Market Integration and Competition Law: With SGCC's rapid expansion and integration into the Brazilian market, questions regarding competition law and national security have come to the forefront. Delve into the legal implications of SGCC's increasing market influence, including the challenges it poses to the Brazilian market design and potential national security concerns. Consider whether these concerns would be the same if the case involved a company from a different nation and how regulatory bodies should oversee such complex issues.

5.2 For Policy School Audiences

SGCC's involvement in the Belo Monte hydroelectric project in Brazil presents a compelling case for exploring policy implications in international energy projects for developing countries. This case study offers an opportunity to analyze policy decisions related to energy security, environmental sustainability, international cooperation, and developmental policies. The case also aims to scrutinize the interplay between business interests, governmental regulations, and public policy, highlighting the complex dynamics that shape such projects. Given the information provided in the case, discuss the following questions:

1. Regulatory Frameworks, Market Concentration, and Investment Attraction: Discuss the specific regulatory measures in Brazil aimed at preventing market concentration in critical infrastructure sectors. Assess the impact of these regulations on the competitive environment and the flow of foreign investments. Examine if the current design is under constraint by the activity of SGCC. If so, how could regulatory oversight be improved to maintain competition and still be attractive to foreign investment.
2. Energy Security and Environmental Concerns: Policymakers often grapple with complex decisions when dealing with projects like Belo Monte, balancing energy security needs with environmental considerations. Explore Brazil's energy security imperatives and the role of projects like Belo Monte in meeting these requirements. Analyze the environmental consequences of large-scale hydroelectric projects and Brazil's policy choices in mitigating them while pursuing energy security goals. Gain insights from international experiences and compare how other nations have addressed similar policy dilemmas, providing a comprehensive perspective on the topic.
3. Sustainable Energy Transition: Large-scale hydroelectric projects offer a shorter path for countries to align with their sustainable energy transition goals. However, these projects also have significant socio-environmental impacts. Explore strategies and policy options that could reconcile the energy potential of projects like Belo Monte with socio-environmental considerations. Analyze how countries can enhance sustainability in energy projects, ensuring minimal harm to local communities and ecosystems. Additionally, discuss the role of technology and innovation in mitigating environmental impacts while meeting energy security needs.
4. International Cooperation in Collaborative Infrastructure Projects: Analyze the significance of international cooperation in advancing development through collaborative infrastructure initiatives. Delve into the advantages and obstacles associated with global collaboration in achieving development goals, including technology transfer benefits and the potential financial burdens on host nations. Additionally, explore the potential roles of international agencies in facilitating and supporting such collaborative endeavors.

5.3 For Business School Audiences

SGCC's involvement in Brazil's Belo Monte hydroelectric project represents a successful case in international business strategy and operations. As one of the world's largest utility companies, SGCC's expansion into the Brazilian market poses a range of challenges and opportunities. This case study delves into the strategic decision-making processes, risk management techniques, and stakeholder relations in SGCC's venture. Given the information provided in the case, discuss the following questions:

1. International Expansion Strategy: Assess SGCC's approach to entering and expanding in the Brazilian market. Examine the critical factors that shaped their decision-making and the risk management strategies they employed in executing this extensive international project. Explore the limitations and shortcomings of SGCC's strategies. Compare and contrast SGCC's international expansion strategy with those of other multinational companies entering global markets, drawing insights from other relevant case studies.
2. Overcoming Information Asymmetry in a New Market: Delve into the specific strategies that SGCC implemented to tackle the complex issue of information asymmetry when entering the Brazilian market. Explore the intricacies of information gaps, including differences in local knowledge, business practices, and regulatory nuances. Assess the effectiveness of SGCC's chosen strategies in not only facilitating a successful market entry but also sustaining ongoing operations. Additionally, analyze the potential applicability of these strategies for other multinational corporations seeking to enter markets characterized by information asymmetry.
3. Navigating Financial and Operational Challenges: Discuss the landscape of financial and operational challenges that SGCC encountered during its involvement in the Belo Monte project, such as funding constraints, logistical complexities, and regulatory issues. Investigate the strategies and solutions that SGCC employed to effectively address these challenges, whether through innovative financing, project management techniques, or regulatory negotiations. Assess the outcomes and lessons learned, highlighting both successful approaches and areas that presented difficulties. Identify transferable insights and best practices that can serve as valuable guidance for companies venturing into large-scale international projects in the future.
4. Localization Strategies: Explore how SGCC's localization strategies influenced its success in Brazil. Assess whether a more globally centralized approach could have achieved similar results and analyze SGCC's unique decision not to centralize all management decisions, such as funding and financial risk activities. Discuss the implications for multinational corporations operating internationally.

Case Study 2.3

TikTok versus United States

Han Liu and Ji Li

1 Overview

This case study provides a comprehensive analysis of the intricate political risks faced by TikTok, the Chinese social media giant, within the complex US political landscape. Beginning with an exploration of the security concerns articulated by the US government, including during President Trump's administration, the discussion centers on TikTok's data collection practices and their perceived impact on US national security.

The narrative unfolds by elucidating the multifaceted strategies employed by TikTok and its parent company, ByteDance, to address these challenges, including litigation, endeavors toward Americanization, and technological adaptations. It also examines the evolution in the US government's stance as the Biden administration assumes leadership as well as TikTok's adaptive strategies aimed at sustaining and expanding its presence in the US market.

The study depicts the responses of the Chinese government to US policies, unraveling the broader implications of these developments on the global political-economic landscape, exploring the intricate dynamics involved in US-China relations, and providing readers with a deeper understanding of the complexities inherent in such interactions.

Finally, this case study invites readers from the fields of law, business, and policy to engage in contemplation on the broader themes of political risks faced by multinational corporations, the challenges inherent in navigating global legal frontiers, and the intricate nature of US-China relations, understanding how multinational corporations adapt to the complexities of international political environments.

2 Introduction

In August 2020, former US president Donald Trump issued two executive orders to effectively ban TikTok, one of the most popular social media apps owned by a Chinese company ByteDance, from the US market, drawing TikTok into the middle of the US-China geopolitical rivalry. Since then, the Chinese-owned company has been confronting increasing political risk in the United

States, and to mitigate this risk it has taken a variety of coping measures. This case study examines these measures and their institutional contexts, shedding light on how other China-based multinationals with substantial outbound foreign investment react to ever-growing political risks in their host countries.

2.1 ByteDance and TikTok

TikTok's parent company, the Beijing ByteDance Technology Co., Ltd. (hereinafter "ByteDance"), is a privately owned, multinational technology company incorporated in the Cayman Islands and based in Beijing, China. The multinational company has opened offices in the United States, the United Kingdom, Singapore, and other countries. Founded by Chinese entrepreneur Zhang Yiming in March 2012 and owned by Zhang and major global institutional investors, some of which are based in the United States, ByteDance owns a set of popular social media products such as Toutiao (one of the most famous Chinese online news platforms), Douyin (one of the most popular video-sharing apps in China), its overseas version TikTok, and Watermelon Video, among other apps.

ByteDance has achieved great business success within a relatively short period. By 2018, ByteDance's mobile apps had more than 1 billion monthly users and was valued at US$75 billion, surpassing Uber to become the world's most valuable startup.[1] Among Chinese high-tech social media startups, ByteDance is the first one that did not seek commercial protection or financing from one of the few established internet powerhouses such as Alibaba, Tencent, or Baidu. Rather, ByteDance emerged as their fierce competitor. As of March 2020, ByteDance's 2019 revenue was estimated at RMB 104 billion to RMB 140 billion, more than Uber, Snapchat, and Twitter combined.[2]

With success in China, ByteDance began to pursue an expansive global strategy in 2016, when it released TikTok, the overseas version of Douyin. In just a few years, ByteDance has become one of the most successful, internationalized Chinese tech companies, generating vast user bases in the United States, Southeast Asia, Japan, and other places. As of July 2019, ByteDance's products and services have spread across 150 countries and regions in 75 languages and have been ranked at the top of app store lists in more than 40 countries and regions.[3] Notably, ByteDance has been more successful than Alibaba, Baidu,

---

[1] Lulu Yilun Chen and Mark Bergen, 'The Unknown 35-Year-Old behind the World's Most Valuable Startup' *The Sydney Morning Herald* (1 October 2018) www.smh.com.au/business/companies/104b-goliath-the-unknown-35-year-old-behind-the-world-s-most-valuable-startup-20181001-p5072r.html.

[2] 'ByteDance Is Going from Strength to Strength' *The Economist* (18 April 2020) www.economist.com/business/2020/04/18/bytedance-is-going-from-strength-to-strength.

[3] 'About ByteDance' https://web.archive.org/web/20190721021507/www.bytedance.com/zh/about.

and Tencent in terms of overseas businesses. It excels in attracting younger audiences abroad. *The Economist* labeled ByteDance the first global Chinese tech giant.[4]

The most successful app ByteDance owns and operates outside China is TikTok, an application that provides an online platform for users to create and share short-form videos.[5] Like its Chinese version Douyin, TikTok was an immediate business success. In November 2018, it ranked first in the number of app downloads and installs in the US market and topped the overall charts of App Store or Google Play many times in Japan, Thailand, Indonesia, Germany, France, and Russia.[6] By September 2021, TikTok's global monthly active users had reached 1 billion.[7]

As in other countries, TikTok gained popularity in the United States, especially after 2018 when it purchased Musical.ly, a Chinese social media company based in Shanghai with millions of US users. In October 2018, TikTok became the most downloaded and installed app on a monthly basis in the United States,[8] putting a great deal of pressure on established US social media platforms such as YouTube and Instagram.[9] In terms of corporate structure, TikTok is owned and operated by ByteDance's subsidiary TikTok Inc., an American company incorporated in California and headquartered in Los Angeles with a US-based management team. Its key executives responsible for the operation of TikTok in the United States, including its CEO, global chief security officer, and general counsel, were, at one time, all Americans.

3 The Case

3.1 Trump's TikTok Ban: Background and Facts

3.1.1 Background

An old Chinese proverb says, "tall trees catch much wind." The business success of TikTok in the United States has triggered many concerns and controversies. TikTok's overseas expansion largely coincided with the deterioration of US-China relations. And given its investors' Chinese ownership and its business nature, TikTok has been caught in the crossfire of US-China rivalry. Its collection, storage, and use of US user data have been regarded as a threat to US national security. For example, in May 2019, the White House issued an

---

[4] 'ByteDance' (n 2).
[5] TikTok Inc. v Donald J Trump, Case No 20-cv-02658 (CJN) (US Dist Ct for the Dist of Columbia) 'Reply Memorandum in Support of Plaintiffs' Renewed Motion for Preliminary Injunction Against Commerce Department Prohibitions' 2.
[6] 'News: TikTok Becomes Most Downloaded App in US' *Pedaily* ('快讯|TikTok成为美国下载量最高应用' 投资界) (6 November 2018) https://news.pedaily.cn/201811/437459.shtml.
[7] 'TikTok Announces 1 Billion Monthly Active Users Worldwide' *Sina* ('TikTok宣布全球月活跃用户突破10亿'新浪网) (27 September 2021) https://finance.sina.com.cn/tech/2021-09-27/doc-iktzscyx6711337.shtml.
[8] 'News: TikTok' (n 6). [9] 'ByteDance' (n 2).

executive order declaring a national state of emergency related to information and national security: "foreign adversaries are increasingly creating and exploiting vulnerabilities in information and communications technology and services, which store and communicate vast amounts of sensitive information, facilitate the digital economy, and support critical infrastructure and vital emergency services, in order to commit malicious cyber-enabled actions, including economic and industrial espionage against the United States and its people."[10] The first among the "foreign adversaries" was China.[11] Large-scale use of foreign information and communications technology and devices was thought to constitute an "unusual and extraordinary threat to the national security, foreign policy and economy of the United States."[12] Naturally, TikTok caught the spotlight. On 11 January 2019, the Peterson Institute for International Economics issued a report describing TikTok as a major threat to national security in the United States and the West.[13] On 23 October 2019, Republican Senator Tom Cotton and then Democratic Senate Minority Leader Chuck Schumer jointly called on then acting Director of National Intelligence to keep a watchful eye on the potential risks of censorship and data security of TikTok.[14]

TikTok soon responded directly to the allegations. On 25 October 2019, TikTok issued a public statement on its official website, stating: "We store all TikTok US user data in the United States, with backup redundancy in Singapore. Our data centers are located entirely outside of China, and none of our data is subject to Chinese law."[15] Besides, TikTok stated: "TikTok does not remove content based on sensitivities related to China. We have never been asked by the Chinese government to remove any content and we would not do so if asked. Period."[16]

But TikTok's statement failed to ease the national security concerns of the US government. On 17 December 2019, the US Navy banned the use of TikTok on government mobile devices, deeming the app a cybersecurity threat. Users who had installed TikTok software on government mobile devices were not allowed to access the internal network of the US Marine Corps or use TikTok while in

---

[10] See White House, 'Executive Order on Securing the Information and Communications Technology and Services Supply Chain' (15 May 2019) www.whitehouse.gov/presidential-actions/executive-order-securinginformation-communications-technology-services-supply-chain/.
[11] ibid.   [12] ibid.
[13] Claudia Biancotti, 'The Growing Popularity of Chinese Social Media Outside China Poses New Risks in the West' (*PIIE*, 11 January 2019) www.piie.com/blogs/china-economic-watch/growing-popularity-chinese-social-media-outside-china-poses-new-risks archived 12 February 2019.
[14] Haley Samsel, 'Senators Ask U.S. Intelligence to Investigate Potential Security Risks of TikTok and Chinese-Owned Companies' (*Security Today*, 28 October 2019) https://securitytoday.com/articles/2019/10/28/senators-tik-tok-security.aspx archived 18 August 2022.
[15] 'Statement on Tiktok's Content Moderation and Data Security Practices' https://newsroom.tiktok.com/en-us/statement-on-tiktoks-content-moderation-and-data-security-practices.
[16] ibid.

uniform.[17] In January 2020, the US Army also announced it was banning TikTok on government-distributed phones.[18] In February 2020, the US Transportation Security Administration (TSA) barred employees from using TikTok to create videos on their personal devices for use in TSA's social media outreach.[19]

Meanwhile, a more threatening political risk was looming. In October 2019, Senator Marco Rubio asked the Committee on Foreign Investment in the United States (CFIUS) to investigate TikTok and ByteDance for its threat to US national security.[20] In November 2019, CFIUS began to review ByteDance's acquisition of Musical.ly in 2017.[21] In July 2020, the United States Treasury Secretary Steve Mnuchin confirmed that TikTok was under a national security review by CFIUS.[22] If a national security threat is found, the agency has the authority to order a foreign investor to divest its US investment.

As one of the most popular social media apps in the United States, TikTok could not stay away from American politics, especially in the year leading up to the 2020 presidential election. Since mid 2020, TikTok users had amassed millions of posts about American politics. Many videos shared on TikTok mocked and satirized Donald Trump. For example, the comedienne Sarah Cooper used Trump's own words to ridicule him in her videos, which attracted millions of followers. Moreover, many American anti-Trump politicians used TikTok, like Governor Michael DeWine of Ohio, Senator Ed Markey of Massachusetts, and Governor Gavin Newsom of California. This led to President Trump's reelection campaign putting out Facebook advertisements asking his supporters to sign a petition to ban TikTok.[23]

In June 2020, some TikTok users coordinated mass ticket reservations for Trump's reelection campaign rally in Tulsa, which caused a huge embarrassment for the president's campaign, because fewer than expected participants appeared at the Trump rally.[24] On 31 July 2020, a furious Trump declared his

---

[17] M. B. Pell and Echo Wang, 'U.S. Navy Bans TikTok from Government-Issued Mobile Devices' *Reuters* (20 December 2019) www.reuters.com/article/us-usa-tiktok-navy-idUSKBN1YO2HU.

[18] Neil Vigdor, 'U.S. Military Branches Block Access to TikTok App amid Pentagon Warning' *New York Times* (4 January 2020) www.nytimes.com/2020/01/04/us/tiktok-pentagon-military-ban.html.

[19] 'TSA Halts Employees from Using TikTok for Social Media Posts' (*Associated Press*; archived from the original on 26 February 2020) https://apnews.com/tsa-halts-employees-from-using-tiktok-for-social-media-posts-aafc69bc4dfdbff93168df118e30ef8f.

[20] 'Marco Ruvio Seeks U.S. Government Probe of TikTok over Chinese Censorship Concerns' *The Washington Post* (9 October 2019) www.washingtonpost.com/technology/2019/10/09/sen-rubio-us-government-should-probe-tiktok-over-chinese-censorship-concerns/.

[21] 'U.S. Government Investigating TikTok over National Security Concerns' *The Washington Post* (1 November 2019) www.washingtonpost.com/technology/2019/11/01/us-government-investigating-tiktok-over-national-security-concerns/.

[22] 'US Treasury to Make Recommendation on TikTok to Trump This Week: Mnuchin' *Reuters* (29 July 2020) www.reuters.com/article/us-usa-china-tiktok-treasury-idUSKCN24U288/.

[23] TikTok Inc. v Donald J Trump, Case No 20-cv-02658 (CJN) (US Dist Ct for the Dist. of Columbia) 'Reply Memorandum in Support of Plaintiffs' Renewed Motion for Preliminary Injunction Against Commerce Department Prohibitions' 6.

[24] ibid.

intention to ban TikTok: "As far as TikTok is concerned, we're banning them from the United States."[25] Trump's ire, even if not the sole determinative factor, greatly contributed to TikTok's political troubles in the United States.

3.1.2 Trump's TikTok Ban

On 6 August 2020, invoking presidential powers granted by the International Emergency Economic Powers Act (IEEPA) and the National Emergencies Act, Trump issued the Executive Order on Addressing the Threat Posted by TikTok (hereinafter "the first order").[26] The order banned "any transaction by any person, or with respect to any property, subject to the jurisdiction of the United States, with Byte Dance Ltd. … or its subsidiaries," and it would become effective within forty-five days (i.e., 20 September 2020).[27] Although the order did not directly prohibit the use and operation of TikTok in the United States, the ban on any transaction by any company, like Apple and Google, would make the TikTok app effectively dysfunctional in the United States.[28]

The Chinese background of TikTok's parent is the stated cause of the national security concern. According to the first order, "TikTok automatically captures vast swaths of information from its users, including Internet and other network activity information such as location data and browsing and search histories."[29] That would allow the Chinese authorities to gain access to American's personal and proprietary information and potentially track the locations of US employees and contractors. Moreover, the US government argued that TikTok could censor what Chinese authorities deem as sensitive information.[30]

On 14 August 2020, Trump issued a second executive order concerning ByteDance's acquisition of Musical.ly, which closed in 2018.[31] Following CFIUS's national security retroactive review of that acquisition, this second order compelled ByteDance to divest its US investment by selling or spinning off TikTok within ninety days (i.e., before 12 November 2020). Trump stated in

---

[25] Ellen Nakashima, Rachel Lerman, and Jeanne Whalen, 'Trump Says He Plans to Bar TikTok from Operating in the US' *The Washington Post* (31 July 2020) www.washingtonpost.com/technology/2020/07/31/tiktok-trump-divestiture/.

[26] See 'Exec Order No 13942' (6 August 2020) 85 Federal Register 48637.   [27] ibid § 1(a).

[28] 'Commerce Department Prohibits WeChat and TikTok Transactions to Protect the National Security of the United States' US Department of Commerce (18 September 2020) https://2017-2021.commerce.gov/news/press-releases/2020/09/commerce-department-prohibits-wechat-and-tiktok-transactions-protect.html.

[29] 'Executive Order on Addressing the Threat Posed by TikTok' *The White House* (6 August 2020) https://trumpwhitehouse.archives.gov/presidential-actions/executive-order-addressing-threat-posed-tiktok/.

[30] Some countries, like India, have already banned the use of Chinese mobile applications in their domestic country. India's Ministry of Electronics and Information Technology asserted that Chinese mobile application producers stole and transmitted users' data in an unauthorized manner to the servers outside. 'India Bans Nearly 60 Chinese Apps, Including TikTok and WeChat' *New York Times* (29 June 2020) www.nytimes.com/2020/06/29/world/asia/tik-tok-banned-india-china.html.

[31] See 'Presidential Order Regarding the Acquisition of Musical.ly by ByteDance Ltd.' (85 Fed. Reg. 51297, 14 August 2020).

this order that "credible evidence" had made him believe that ByteDance constituted a great threat to US national security.[32] All in all, the message sent to ByteDance was clear: sell TikTok to American companies or be banned.

3.2 TikTok's Coping Strategies

3.2.1 Americanization

On 2 August 2020, shortly after Trump's announcement that he was going to ban TikTok, Microsoft declared in a statement that it was discussing with ByteDance about a potential purchase. While Microsoft initially only considered a minority investment in TikTok, Trump's declaration to ban TikTok encouraged Microsoft to contemplate a total acquisition. As Microsoft announced: "Following a conversation between Microsoft CEO Satya Nadella and President Donald J. Trump, Microsoft is prepared to continue discussions to explore a purchase of TikTok in the United States."[33]

Yet, after the second executive order, Trump announced that Oracle was his acceptable choice of the company acquiring TikTok.[34] Meanwhile, SoftBank, a Japanese company, came up with an acquisition plan with Walmart and Google that would make Walmart a majority shareholder and SoftBank and Alphabet (Google's parent company) minority shareholders.[35] Trump, however, rejected that plan. On 27 August 2020, Walmart declared that it would try to purchase TikTok with Oracle. On 14 September 2020, Oracle confirmed a US Department of Treasury's announcement that Oracle was a party to the proposed transaction involving TikTok.[36] Trump said he was satisfied with that plan.

However, disagreements over the concrete terms of the deal quickly transpired. Reacting to the Oracle plan, ByteDance said it would own 80% of TikTok Global, a new US-based company to be set up to facilitate the transfer of TikTok ownership.[37] That meant ByteDance would continue to own TikTok. However, Oracle responded that ByteDance would not have any stake

---

[32] ibid.
[33] Clare Duffy, 'Microsoft Says It Is Still Talking with Trump About Buying TikTok from Its Chinese Owner' *CNN Business* (3 August 2020) www.cnn.com/2020/08/02/tech/microsoft-tiktok/index.html archived 25 August 2022.
[34] David McCabe, 'Trump Says Oracle Could "Handle" Owning TikTok' *New York Times* (19 August 2020) www.nytimes.com/2020/08/19/technology/trump-oracle-tiktok.html archived 25 August 2022.
[35] See Tyler Sonnemaker, 'Walmart Reportedly Tried to Become TikTok's Majority Owner by Teaming Up with Alphabet and SoftBank before the Trump Administration Nixed the Idea' *Business Insider* (27 August 2020) www.businessinsider.com/walmart-alphabet-softbank-tiktok-deal-talks-before-microsoft-government-rejected-2020-8 archived 25 August 2022.
[36] Stan Choe, 'Trump Backs Proposed Deal to Keep TikTok Operating in US' *The Washington Post* (19 September 2020) www.washingtonpost.com/business/technology/trump-backs-proposed-deal-to-keep-tiktok-operating-in-us/2020/09/19/08cc901a-fadf-11ea-85f7-5941188a98cd_story.html archived 25 August 2022.
[37] Georgia Wells and Alex Leary, 'TikTok and Oracle Spar over Ownership, Threatening Deal' *Wall Street Journal* (21 September 2020) www.wsj.com/articles/tiktok-and-oracle-spar-over-ownership-threatening-deal-11600702185 archived 25 August 2022.

in TikTok Global. ByteDance explained that, despite its continuous ownership, TikTok Global would remain under American control, as ByteDance itself was about 40% owned by US investors.[38]

Yet some politicians opposed that proposed solution. On 14 September 2020, Senator Josh Hawley criticized the deal with Oracle and urged CFIUS to block it. He argued that the plan would fall short of fully implementing the president's second order because it would still allow Chinese forces to influence the United States.[39] Four days later, the US Department of Commerce issued a rule to implement the first TikTok executive order.[40] Under this rule, from 27 September 2020, app stores in the United States would not support or distribute the TikTok app, and, from 12 November 2020, all other transactions vital to TikTok's operation, such as storing data, would be prohibited.[41]

3.2.2 Litigation

The plan to divest TikTok through a sale was met with strong resistance in both the United States and China, so the company soon resorted to legal means. On 24 August 2020, TikTok Inc. filed a complaint in the federal court for the Central District of California, where the company was based, challenging the Trump ban.[42] TikTok argued that the ban was motivated by Trump's personal goal of reelection, and it violated the Fifth Amendment of the US Constitution by denying due process rights of TikTok and other companies. On 20 September 2020, TikTok voluntarily withdrew the case,[43] as it filed lawsuits in other courts. Meanwhile, Patrick Ryan, a TikTok employee, sued Trump as well as the Secretary of Commerce and sought an injunction to prevent the enforcement of the executive orders banning TikTok.[44] Ryan contended that Trump's ban would cause US employees of TikTok to lose their salaries, thus violating the Fifth Amendment by denying their right to due process and taking property without just compensation. He also claimed that the ban was motivated by Trump's personal reasons and anti-China bias.

---

[38] ibid.
[39] 'Senator Hawley Calls for CFIUS to Reject TikTok Partnership, Violates President's Executive Order' (*Josh Hawley*, 14 September 2020) www.hawley.sen-ate.gov/senator-hawley-calls-cfius-reject-tiktok-partnership-violates-presidents-executive-order archived 25 August 2022.
[40] 'Identification of Prohibited Transactions to Implement Executive Order 13942' (85 Fed. Reg. 60061, 24 September 2020) (15 C.F.R. ch VII).
[41] See Satish M. Kini et al., 'U.S. Commerce Department Announces "Prohibited Transactions" Related to Tik-Tok, WeChat Mobile Apps' (*Debevoise & Plimpton*, 24 September 2020) www.debevoise.com/insights/publications/2020/09/us-commerce-department-announces archived 26 August 2022.
[42] Complaint, 'TikTok, Inc. v. U.S. Dep't of Commerce' No. 2:2020-cv-07672 (C.D. Cal., 24 August 2020).
[43] Notice of Voluntary Dismissal, 'TikTok, Inc. v. U.S. Dep't of Commerce' No. 2:2020- cv-07672 (C.D. Cal., 20 September 2020).
[44] Notice of Motion and Motion for Preliminary Injunction, 'Ryan v. Trump & Ross, JR.' No. 3:20-cv-05948(C.D. Cal., 3 September 2020).

On 23 September 2020, a group of US users of WeChat, a China-based "super app" used by many in the United States to communicate with families and friends in China and owned by a separate Chinese company from ByteDance, won a case against Trump's executive ban of WeChat.[45] The WeChat ban parallels the TikTok ban and the two evoke the same set of legal authorities and have similar constitutional implications. Therefore, shortly after the court decision in favor of the WeChat users, TikTok Inc. sued the Trump administration in the federal court for the District of Columbia, seeking to enjoin the enforcement of the order prohibiting US companies from supplying services to TikTok. TikTok contended that the ban went beyond the president's emergency powers under IEEPA because no emergency or grave threat to national security exists in the TikTok case. Moreover, it argued that IEEPA forbids the president from regulating or prohibiting the importation or exportation of "information or informational materials," which qualifies as an exception to the emergency powers.[46]

Four days later, just before the deadline for the TikTok ban, Judge Carl Nichols, a federal judge nominated by Trump, enjoined part of the Department of Commerce's order implementing Trump's executive order. Judge Nichols supported the argument of TikTok that the information and informational materials exception applies to the TikTok case and Trump's executive order was *ultra vires*.[47] On 7 December 2020, Judge Nichols granted a preliminary injunction against the ban on other transactions.[48]

TikTok also mobilized its users to join the litigation efforts.[49] Parallel to TikTok's suit, three TikTok creators, who described themselves as comedians, fashion creators, and musicians with millions of fans on TikTok, sued Trump in the US District Court for the Eastern District of Pennsylvania.[50] Their complaint was that Trump's ban on TikTok violates their right to free speech and deprives them of "professional opportunities afforded by TikTok" since the TikTok platform is unique and irreplaceable; they also argued that the ban was *ultra vires*.[51] On 30 October 2020, Judge Wendy Beetlestone sided with these TikTok creators and ruled that the executive order barring new downloads of

---

[45] 'U.S. WeChat Users All. v. Trump' (2020) 488 F. Supp. 3d 912 (N.D. Cal.).
[46] 50 U.S.C. § 1702(b)(3).
[47] Memorandum Opinion (Signed by Judge Carl J. Nichols on 27 September 2020), 'TikTok Inc. et al v. Trump et al' No. 1:2020cv02658, Document 30 (D.D.C. 2020) https://law.justia.com/cases/federal/district-courts/district-of-columbia/dcdce/1:2020cv02658/222257/30/ archived 27 January 2023.
[48] 'TikTok Inc. v. Trump' (2020) 507 F. Supp. 3d 92, 106 (D.D.C), appeal dismissed sub nom. 'TikTok Inc. v. Biden' No. 20-5381, [2021] WL 3082803 (D.C. Cir.).
[49] "TikTok to Challenge Trump Administration over Executive Order" *New York Times* (22 August 2020) www.nytimes.com/2020/08/22/technology/tiktok-lawsuit-trump-executive-order.html.
[50] Memorandum of Law in Support of Plaintiffs' Motion for Preliminary Injunction at 1, 'Marland v. Trump' 498 F. Supp. 3d 624 (E.D. Pa. 2020) (No. 2:20-cv-04597) [2020] WL 8613435.
[51] Complaint for Injunctive and Declaratory Relief at 18, para 61, 'Marland v. Trump' 498 F. Supp. 3d 624 (E.D. Pa. 2020) (No. 2:20-cv-04597) [2020] WL 8613435.

the TikTok app violated the informational materials exception under IEEPA and would result in the TikTok creators' loss of connections to millions of followers as well as related brand sponsorship.[52] Therefore, a preliminary injunction was granted, blocking the implementation of the TikTok ban by the US Department of Commerce. Notably, Judge Beetlestone did not touch upon the free speech argument, because the plaintiffs' *ultra vires* argument was enough to buttress the preliminary injunction.[53]

Shortly after the above cases, TikTok, as well as ByteDance, began to challenge CFIUS in the federal bench. On 10 November 2020, they sued CFIUS in the US Court of Appeals for the D.C. Circuit.[54] They made four main arguments. First, the CFIUS order was *ultra vires*; second, it violated their due process rights; third, it violated the Administrative Procedure Act since the order was arbitrary; and fourth, the compelled divestment of TikTok to a US government-supported company violated the Fifth Amendment of the US Constitution since it constituted a taking without just compensation.

Before the court issued an injunction against the CFIUS order, the federal government extended the deadline of implementing the order several times as the negotiation of ByteDance's divestiture continued. On 12 November 2020, CFIUS extended the deadline from 12 November 2020 to 27 November 2020.[55] On 25 November 2020, CFIUS granted another one-week extension, that is, from 27 November 2020 to 4 December 2020.[56] As 4 December 2020 approached, the Department of Treasury refused to extend it further, but it also stated it would not compel transaction.[57] CFIUS scrutiny of TikTok survived the Trump administration, and the agency demanded in March 2023 that its Chinese owners sell their shares.[58]

3.2.3 Coping Strategies in the Biden Era

The United States in 2021 under the Biden administration amended its policies on TikTok. On 19 February 2021, Biden moved the D.C. Circuit court to hold the CFIUS case in abeyance, pending a review, and the court subsequently dismissed the case following a joint stipulation of both parties.[59] On 9 June 2021, the US

---

[52] 'Marland v. Trump' (2020) 498 F. Supp. 3d 624, 641 (E.D. Pa.). [53] ibid 642 n.8.
[54] 'TikTok Inc., et al v. Committee on Foreign Investment, et al' Docket No. 20-01444 (D.C. Cir., 10 November 2020).
[55] See Plaintiffs' Notice of Extension in CFIUS Matter at 1, 'TikTok, Inc. v. Trump' No. 20-cv-02658 (D.D.C., 25 November 2020).
[56] 'TikTok Inc. v. Trump' (2020) 507 F. Supp. 3d 92, 101 (D.D.C.).
[57] Jay Greene, 'TikTok Sale Deadline Will Pass, Though Regulators Will Hold Off on Enforcing Divestiture' *The Washington Post* (4 December 2020) www.washingtonpost.com/technology/2020/12/04/tiktok-sale-deadline/ archived 24 August 2022.
[58] Echo Wang and David Shepardson, 'TikTok Says US Threatens Ban If Chinese Owners Don't Sell Stakes' *Reuters* (16 March 2023) www.reuters.com/technology/us-threatens-tiktok-ban-if-chinese-owners-dont-sell-stake-wsj-2023-03-15/.
[59] 'TikTok Inc. v. Committee on Foreign Investment' Docket No. 20-01444 (D.C. Cir., 19 February 2021).

government withdrew the two executive orders of Trump and its appeal of the TikTok case. On 4 July 2021, the D.C. Circuit granted the Biden administration's motion to dismiss the appeal. On 20 July 2021, the case was dismissed.[60]

In place of Trump's two executive orders, the Biden administration issued a new order about TikTok, commanding the Secretary of Commerce to review the TikTok app for national security concerns and emphasizing that the review must be based upon "rigorous, evidence-based analysis" while scrutinizing and addressing the risks of national security, economic interest, and core values of the United States.[61] Notably, the Biden administration did not fully change the CFIUS order. That meant that TikTok still needed to be divested from its Chinese mother company, but the timetable was voided.[62]

Though some consider the Biden administration's approach to have "importantly depoliticized the treatment of TikTok,"[63] the ease of the political pressure proved ephemeral. Given the intensifying US-China rivalry, TikTok's status in the United States remains highly precarious. Legally speaking, it is still under CFIUS review. TikTok also faces spreading bans at the state level and a partial ban at the federal level. On 2 December 2022, Chris Wray, Director of the Federal Bureau of Investigation, raised national security concerns about TikTok, warning that the popular video-sharing app was "in the hands of a government that doesn't share our values, and that has a mission that's very much at odds with what's in the best interests of the United States."[64] Then some Republican-controlled states barred the use of TikTok on government electronic devices.[65] Starting from late 2022, many public universities have restricted or banned the use of TikTok on school computers, mobile phones, and other devices, following the orders of those states,[66] with students questioning those decisions.[67] Congress also passed a law to forbid the use of TikTok on federal devices.[68]

---

[60] See 'TikTok Inc. v. Biden' No. 20-5381, [2021] WL 3082803, at *1 (D.C. Cir., 14 July 2021); 'TikTok Inc. v. Biden' No. 20-5302, [2021] WL 3713550, at *1 (D.C. Cir., 20 July 2021).
[61] Executive Order No. 14,034, 86 Fed. Reg. 31,423 (9 June 2021).
[62] Wang and Shepardson (n 58).
[63] Anupam Chander, 'Trump v. TikTok' (2022) 55 Vanderbilt Journal of Transnational Law 1145, 1173.
[64] 'FBI Director Raises National Security Concerns about TikTok' AP News (2 December 2022) https://apnews.com/article/technology-china-united-states-national-security-government-and-politics-ac5c29cafaa1fc6bee990ed7e1fe5afc.
[65] William Melhado, 'Gov. Greg Abbott Bans TikTok on State Phones and Computers, Citing Cybersecurity Risks' The Texas Tribune (7 December 2022); Shawna Chen, 'Texas Is Latest State Banning TikTok on Government Devices amid National Security Concerns' (Axios, 7 December 2022) www.axios.com/2022/12/07/tiktok-national-security-republican-governors archived 25 August 2022.
[66] 'These Are All the Public Universities That Have Instituted TikTok Bans' NBC News (18 January 2023) www.nbcnews.com/tech/tiktok-bans-public-universities-list-rcna66185.
[67] 'Their Colleges Banned TikTok over Security Fears: These Students Vow It Won't Stop Them from Scrolling' NBC News (28 December 2022) www.nbcnews.com/tech/students-question-tiktok-bans-public-universities-rcna62801.
[68] Clare Foran and Kristin Wilson, 'House Passes $1.7 Trillion Government Spending Bill as Funding Deadline Looms' CNN Politics (23 December 2022).

In 2022, a news wave targeting TikTok for data and national security reasons emerged. In June 2022, the American digital media BuzzFeed News issued a report about TikTok.[69] Citing leaked audios from more than eighty internal meetings of TikTok, it said that ByteDance employees in China could get access to US data, especially the personal information of American users. TikTok responded to the report in an official statement that all the US users' traffic had subsequently been routed to US-based servers of Oracle Cloud and all US users' data was to be deleted from TikTok's own data centers.[70] On 28 January 2023, it was reported that ByteDance's general counsel was no longer overseeing US government relations for TikTok. The change was part of a shake-up to improve TikTok's standing facing stringent national security review in the United States.[71]

3.3 Reactions from ByteDance and the Chinese Government

The Chinese government opposed the US government's ban on TikTok. As soon as Trump issued the two executive orders, the Chinese government denounced his multiple actions against TikTok as a "smash and grab" and "an officially sanctioned 'steal' of Chinese technology."[72] In addition, it made an appeal to the United States that it should "earnestly maintain fair and transparent international rules and order."[73] The Chinese Ministry of Foreign Affairs proposed the Global Initiative on Data Security on 8 September 2020, emphasizing that: "States should handle data security in a comprehensive, objective and evidence-based manner, and maintain an open, secure and stable supply chain of global ICT products and services."[74]

The initiative was a countermeasure to the Clean Network Program of the US government, "which would exclude Chinese telecommunications firms, apps, cloud providers and undersea cables from internet infrastructure used by the US and other countries."[75] On 17 September 2020, during the regular press

---

[69] 'Leaked Audio From 80 Internal TikTok Meetings Shows That US User Data Has Been Repeatedly Accessed from China' *BuzzFeed News* (17 June 2022) www.buzzfeednews.com/article/emilybakerwhite/tiktok-tapes-us-user-data-china-bytedance-access.

[70] Albert Calamug, 'Delivering on Our US Data Governance' TikTok Newsroom (17 June 2022) https://newsroom.tiktok.com/en-us/delivering-on-our-us-data-governance.

[71] 'TikTok General Counsel No Longer Oversees US Relations' *Bloomberg* (27 January 2023) www.bloomberg.com/news/articles/2023-01-27/tiktok-general-counsel-no-longer-oversees-us-relations.

[72] 'US Administration's Smash and Grab of TikTok Will Not Be Taken Lying Down: China Daily Editorial' *China Daily* (3 August 2020) www.chinadaily.com.cn/a/202008/03/WS5f2810e3a31083481725de72.html archived 25 August 2022.

[73] 'China Attacks US "Bullying" over Ban on Tiktok and WeChat' *The Guardian* (19 September 2020) www.theguardian.com/technology/2020/sep/19/stay-calm-us-tik-tok-users-prepare-for-world-without-newly-banned-app archived 25 August 2022.

[74] '全球数据安全倡议（全文）(Full text: Global Initiative on Data Security)' (*China.org.cn*, 15 September 2020) www.china.org.cn/chinese/2020-09/15/content_76704524.htm.

[75] Chun Han Wong, 'China Launches Initiative to Set Global Data-Security Rules' *Wall Street Journal* (8 September 2020) www.wsj.com/articles/china-to-launch-initiative-to-set-global-data-security-rules-11599502974.

conference of the Chinese Ministry of Foreign Affairs, responding to a reporter's question about the TikTok issue, the spokesperson of the Ministry of Foreign Affairs Wang Wenbin said: "We urge the US side to respect the market economy and the principles of fair competition, abide by international economic and trade rules, stop politicizing normal economic and trade cooperation, and provide an open, fair, just and non-discriminatory business environment for foreign enterprises to invest and operate in the US."[76] After Biden issued the new executive order about TikTok, Gao Feng, spokesman for China's Ministry of Commerce, said the reversal of the previous administration's executive order on TikTok and other apps was "a positive step in the right direction."[77]

The Chinese government changed relevant policies in the meantime to respond to Trump's plan of selling TikTok to American companies. On 28 August 2020, the Chinese Ministry of Commerce and the Ministry of Science and Technology expanded restrictions on technology exports, now covering "computing and data-processing technologies as text analysis, content recommendation, speech modeling and voice-recognition."[78] Although not explicitly pointing to the TikTok issue, in effect, under the new rule, if ByteDance sought to transfer its proprietary algorithms to Oracle or other foreign companies, it would need to get approval from the Chinese central government.[79] As noted, this new rule created a high regulatory hurdle that precluded any planned sale of TikTok to a US buyer, which has not been publicly discussed since the amended Chinese export control regulation.

After Trump's ban, China passed a series of laws related to the TikTok issue. First, on 17 October 2020, the Standing Committee of the National People's Congress of China (NPCSC) passed the Export Control Law (formally implemented on 1 December 2020), tightening the export control system and providing an underlying legislative basis for relevant lower-level rules like the restrictions on technology exports.

Second, starting from June 2020, the NPCSC began to review the draft of China's Data Security Law, which was passed on 10 June 2021 and came into force on 1 September 2021. In particular, Article 26 of that law stipulates: "When any country or region adopts discriminatory prohibitions, restrictions,

---

[76] 'The Latest: Bytedance Said the TikTok Deal Needs Approval from China and the US, the Foreign Ministry Responded' *National Business Daily* ('最新！字节跳动称TikTok交易需中美两国批准，外交部回应《每日经济新闻》') (17 September 2020) www.nbd.com.cn/articles/2020-09-17/1507496.html.

[77] 'Biden Administration Reverses Ban on TikTok and WeChat, China Commerce Ministry Responds'('拜登政府撤销对TikTok和微信禁令，中国商务部回应') *Forbes China* (11 June 2021) www.forbeschina.com/billionaires/55793.

[78] 'Announcement No. 38 of 2020 by the Ministry of Science and Technology of the Ministry of Commerce on Adjusting and Publishing the Catalogue of China's Prohibited and Restricted Export Technologies' ('商务部 科技部公告2020年第38号 关于调整发布《中国禁止出口限制出口技术目录》的公告') (28 August 2020) www.mofcom.gov.cn/article/zcfb/zcfwmy/202008/20200802996641.shtml.

[79] 'The Latest: Bytedance' (n 76).

or other similar measures against the PRC relevant to investment, trade, etc., in data, data development and use technology, etc., the PRC may take reciprocal measures against that country or region based on the actual circumstances." This gives the Chinese government another tool to respond to US restrictions or bans on Chinese telecommunications and internet companies operating in America. China has not taken any action against US measures on Chinese companies like Huawei and ZTE during the Trump administration, but after the implementation of the Data Security Law, China can take reciprocal action against American companies in China when the United States takes action against Chinese companies on a case-by-case basis. The Data Security Law poses a threat to any future action that the Biden administration or Congress might take against Chinese companies operating in the United States.

Third, on 10 June 2021, the NPCSC passed the Anti-Foreign Sanctions Law and it came into force on the date of promulgation. Article 3 of the Anti-Foreign Sanctions Law stipulates: "Where foreign nations violate international law and basic norms of international relations to contain or suppress our nation under any kind of pretext or based on the laws of those nations to employ discriminatory restrictive measures against our nation's citizens or organizations or interfere with our nation's internal affairs, our nation has the right to employ corresponding countermeasures." This article, together with others in that law, adds to a toolkit of measures available to the Chinese government when responding to foreign sanctions or restrictions on Chinese companies doing business overseas.

3.4 The Battle Escalates: 2024 House Bill to Ban TikTok

Just as TikTok management thought the darkest moment had passed and they had effectively managed US political risks,[80] the House of Representatives surprised them by passing a bill that would either ban TikTok or compel ByteDance's divestiture.[81] The bill received unanimous support from the Committee on Energy and Commerce (50–0), and the vast majority of the House Representatives (352–65).[82] Moreover, President Biden publicly announced that he would sign it into law if it has passed both chambers of Congress.[83] While it is still uncertain whether the Senate will deliberate on the bill and pass it,

---

[80] Stu Woo, Georgia Wells, and Raffaele Huang, 'How TikTok Was Blindsided by U.S. Bill That Could Ban It' *Wall Street Journal* (12 March 2024) www.wsj.com/tech/how-tiktok-was-blindsided-by-a-u-s-bill-that-could-ban-it-7201ac8b.

[81] Protecting Americans from Foreign Adversary Controlled Applications Act, H.R. 7521 (14 March 2024) www.congress.gov/bill/118th-congress/house-bill/7521/text.

[82] Bill history, H.R.7521 – Protecting Americans from Foreign Adversary Controlled Applications Act118th Congress (2023–2024) www.congress.gov/bill/118th-congress/house-bill/7521/all-actions.

[83] Sapna Maheshwari, David McCabe, and Annie Karni, 'Houses Passes Bill to Force TikTok Sale from Chinese Owner or Ban the App' *New York Times* (13 March 2024) www.nytimes.com/2024/03/13/technology/tiktok-ban-house-vote.html.

especially given the fact that Trump has surprisingly voiced his objection to banning TikTok,[84] the potential risk is material. While powerholders on Wall Street have jumped at this opportunity and started to work on a possible acquisition of TikTok,[85] one can expect other key stakeholders to react in ways similar to what we have described in this case study. First, the Chinese government has "reiterated common criticisms of US policy as unfair to China," and the amended export control regulation requires government approval for any sale of TikTok to a US buyer.[86] Second, TikTok will for sure double down on its lobbying efforts at the Senate level. Third, had the bill passed the Senate and became law, TikTok would most likely challenge its constitutionality in court. Unlike previous cases, however, this time the court will be forced to make the difficult balance between the constitutional mandate for the protection of free speech and due process on the one hand and congressional authority on the other. The saga continues to unfold, and given the complexity of the geopolitical rivalry between China and the United States, only time will tell how it will end.

4 Conclusion

Caught in the US-China geopolitical rivalry, TikTok faces constant political challenges at both the federal and the state level. In response, the firm has adopted an array of coping measures, including litigation, lobbying, and seeking diplomatic assistance. Other Chinese multinationals with substantial US investment have made similar efforts in managing an increasingly hostile host-state regulatory environment.[87] These measures in turn are shaping US-China relations. The story of TikTok in the United States goes on, yet its ending remains unknown.

5 Discussion Questions and Comments

5.1 For Law School Audiences

5.1.1 Navigating Global Legal Frontiers

The political challenges TikTok faces also manifest at the state level, as exemplified by the fact that, as of the time of this writing, more than thirty state governments have prohibited the use of TikTok by government employees on

---

[84] David McCabe and Sapna Maheshwari, 'TikTok Bill's Progress Slows in the Senate' *New York Times* (15 March 2024) www.nytimes.com/2024/03/15/technology/tiktok-ban-bill-senate.html.
[85] Rachel Louise Ensign and Gareth Vipers, 'Steven Mnuchin Says He Is Putting Together A Group to Buy TikTok' *Wall Street Journal* (14 March 2024) www.wsj.com/tech/steven-mnuchin-says-he-is-putting-together-a-group-to-buy-tiktok-3aac4a33.
[86] Meaghan Tobin and Siyi Zhao, 'What China Is Saying About the TikTok Furor in Washington' *New York Times* (15 March 2024) www.nytimes.com/2024/03/15/business/china-tiktok-house-bill.html.
[87] Ji Li, 'In Pursuit of Fairness: How Chinese Multinational Companies React to U.S. Government Bias' (2021) 62 Harvard International Law Journal 375.

government-owned devices. While the federal government ban has been stalled by legal actions, the state government of Montana has taken the lead in excluding TikTok from the state. On 17 May 2023, the governor of Montana, Greg Gianforte, signed a bill banning TikTok in the state. The ban "imposes a 10,000 dollar penalty for each 'discrete violation,' defined as any time an individual in Montana accesses TikTok, is offered the ability to access TikTok, or is offered the ability to download TikTok."

In response to the accusations, TikTok claimed that it does not share user information with the Chinese government and that it stores all US TikTok data with Oracle, a prominent US public company. In addition, TikTok's Community Guidelines restrict nudity, sexual content, and anything else deemed harmful. TikTok uses technology and human moderators to remove any content that violates the Community Guidelines. Additionally, "for U.S. users under thirteen, TikTok provides a different, age-appropriate experience, with stringent safeguards and privacy protections designed specifically for this age group." Parents with children under thirteen can link their accounts to their child's account in order to set specific parental controls. TikTok also does not require users to use their real names when registering and does not collect GPS information from US users.[88]

TikTok sued Montana, arguing that the ban violates the First Amendment of the US Constitution, along with federal preemption, the Commerce Clause, and the bill of attainder. TikTok claims that the ban violates the First Amendment's guarantee of freedom of speech by shutting down a forum for free speech. Moreover, TikTok argues that the Constitution vests the authority for foreign affairs and national security in the federal government rather than in the state governments. Because Montana cites the Chinese government possibly having access to US users' data as one of the reasons for the ban, this is an issue of national security that the federal government should handle. TikTok contends that the ban interferes with the congressional process for addressing national security concerns. Congress is currently considering "the Restricting the Emergence of Security Threats that Risk Information and Technology Act, or 'RESTRICT Act,' which according to the federal Executive Branch would provide the federal government with 'new mechanisms to mitigate the national security risks posed by high-risk technology businesses operating in the United States'"[89] In addition, TikTok and CFIUS had negotiated for three years on how to restructure the app to address national security concerns, and the Montana ban is interfering with this process. Furthermore, TikTok argues that the Commerce Clause does not allow states to interfere with interstate commerce. Since the ban applies to everyone in the state of Montana, regardless of whether they are residents or visitors, it violates the Commerce Clause. Also, TikTok argues that the ban constitutes an unconstitutional bill of attainder, as

---

[88] TikTok Inc. v. Knudsen, 9:23-cv-00061(D. Mont., 22 May 2023).   [89] ibid.

it applies to only one firm.[90] The Montana Tiktok ban was blocked by a federal judge in late 2023 and has subsequently become embroiled in legislation.

Given the above, discuss the following questions:

1. What are the legal merits of these claims? Are there any other claims TikTok could have made?
2. Compare your answers to (1) to the court's decision rendered on 30 November 2023.[91] How will the judicial decision implicate US law in these subject matter areas?
3. What are the main differences between the legal actions and lawsuits at the federal versus state levels?
4. TikTok has been subject to regulatory oversight and lawsuits in a number of other regions and countries around the world, including the EU, India, and Pakistan.[92] To your knowledge, how do these actions (both on the side of the host-state regulator and on TikTok) differ from the US experience? In other words, is the United States an outlier in foreign investment screening?

5.2 For Policy School Audiences

5.2.1 Policymaking Dilemmas in Geopolitical Tensions

The TikTok case underlines multiple policy issues. First, how to balance national security concerns with maintaining an open economy and the rule of law? How should national security be defined? Does it include speculated risk of foreign government influence? When the Trump government issued the executive order to ban WeChat, it cited national security threat as the primary reason. Yet, as the lawsuit against the ban has revealed, the claim was largely based on speculative evidence.[93] Overly broad or arbitrary interpretation of national security threat risks undermining the rule of law and disrupting market order.[94] On the other hand, the rising influence of China does pose legitimate challenges to the US-led global order. What alternative policy frameworks may better guide policymakers in addressing national security concerns in the current global geopolitical context?

Second, the TikTok case demonstrates the dynamic and triadic interactions between multinational firms and the world's two superpowers. Whether and

---

[90] ibid.
[91] TikTok Inc. v. Knudsen, 9:23-cv-00061(D. Mont., 30 November 2023) https://s3.documentcloud.org/documents/24180112/tiktok_injunction.pdf.
[92] On the case of Pakistan, see Matthew S. Erie and Thomas Streinz, 'The Beijing Effect: China's "Digital Silk Road" as Transnational Data Governance' (2021) 54 New York University Journal of International Law and Politics 1–92.
[93] Judy Tzu-Chun Wu and Ji Li, 'Chinese Immigrant Legal Mobilization in the United States: The 2020 Executive Ban on WeChat and Civil Rights in a Digital Age' (2023) 30 Asian American Law Journal 51.
[94] Matthew S. Erie, 'Property as National Security' (2024) 1 Wisconsin Law Review 255; Mark Jia, 'American Law in the New Global Conflict' (2024) 99 NYU Law Review 636.

how should US policymakers factor the preferences and interests of Chinese non-state actors into the making of foreign policies? Where are US-China relations, arguably the most important bilateral relationship in the next decade or two, headed? TikTok represents a large group of China-affiliated actors that constitute what, in Karl Polanyi terms, could be called the "peace interest," constituencies heavily invested in preserving inter-state collaboration in trade and investment. How should US policies address the "peace interest," the power and influence of which arguably will have profound implications on the future of the global economic, legal, and political orders?

5.3 For Business School Audiences

5.3.1 Multinational Companies in the Headwinds of Globalization

The TikTok case reveals two major risks confronting multinational companies, especially those based in countries that are not US allies, in the current global political environment: growing political risk and compliance risk. In coping with political risks, TikTok has actively employed legal strategies, which have proven to be effective so far. Are there other coping measures multinationals may adopt to address host-state political risk? For instance, TikTok has engaged in active lobbying in the United States and mobilized TikTok users to pressure policymakers. Are these better tools than litigation? What are the trade-offs between these different tools? Among all the potential means to mitigate host-state political risk, how should multinational firms make the selection?[95] How may they effectively be used in concert or in parallel?

Additionally, multinational firms also face a compliance dilemma, as evidenced by the TikTok case. To comply with Trump's executive order, TikTok's Chinese owners initially contemplated a sale to US investors. Yet, as the negotiation was ongoing, the Chinese government amended its export regulation to prohibit any sale of proprietary advanced intellectual property to non-Chinese parties without government approval. As the US law and the Chinese law directly conflict, TikTok simply could not comply with both simultaneously. It therefore had to pursue other solutions. Multinational firms increasingly face such a compliance dilemma, as intensified US-China geopolitical rivalry spawns a proliferation of conflicting laws between the two countries. How do firms with extensive exposure to both jurisdictions address the growing compliance risk? What options do they have? Is exiting from one of the markets the optimal solution? How do coping strategies adopted by multinational firms fit in the broader picture of US-China economic decoupling?[96] Can "forum-shopping" in terms of entering other and diverse markets suffice as an alternative strategy?

---

[95] For a recent study about how Chinese multinational firms cope with US political risk, see Li (n 87).

[96] Ji Li, 'Superpower Legal Rivalry and the Global Compliance Dilemma' (2024) 45 University of Pennsylvania Journal of International Law 891.

Section 3
Infrastructure

Case Study 3.1

The Colombo Port City Project

How Chinese Investment Interacts with Local Public Law

Dilini Pathirana and Dinesha Samararatne

1 Overview

The Colombo Port City Project (CPC or "the Project") is the most prominent Chinese direct investment in Sri Lanka. This case study highlights the prospects and resilience of a Belt and Road Initiative (BRI) project in the cyclical process of democratic decay and consolidation in a host state with democratic dispensation and welfare commitments. It is a case study in which geopolitics of the day and dynamics between transnational discourse on human rights and investment manifest. From a Chinese perspective, it is a reminder of the contingencies of each BRI project and the inherent entanglement between the politics of the Chinese state and Chinese corporations involved in the BRI with the sociopolitical realities of a host state. From a Sri Lankan perspective, this case study reveals the different political and legal narratives around the Project, the challenges these generated for the Chinese from a host state, and the resilience of a BRI project.

The case study combines a legal doctrinal approach with a short commentary on the political economy of the Project. The doctrinal analysis focuses on the litigation and legislation concerning the CPC and offers insights into the prospects for dealing with foreign investment-related legal disputes through the public law of a host state. It also sheds light on the interface (or the lack thereof) between public law (e.g., judicial review) and international law. In this way, the case study attempts to capture the methods by which the domestic legal sphere of a host state responds to the BRI.

2 Introduction

Since the adoption of an open and market-based economic policy in 1977, successive governments in Sri Lanka have given political prominence to foreign direct investment (FDI). FDI has been projected as a method that would guarantee rapid economic development. The Sri Lankan Constitution, perhaps uniquely, provides constitutional protection and status for any investment treaty or agreement if it is tabled before the House.[1] Despite the political rhetoric, the substantive legal, institutional, and policy reform required to facilitate foreign investment has been the exception and the highest level of FDI in Sri Lanka was just 2.8% of GDP in 1997.[2] Unsustainable borrowing and excessive spending over a long period of time have brought Sri Lanka's economy to a debt and balance of payment crisis, resulting in a sovereign default in April 2022 and severe human suffering and political unrest.

Sri Lanka is, in many ways, a paradox. On the one hand, it is the oldest democracy in Asia and universal suffrage was introduced in 1931. Strong welfare policies adopted since 1930 have placed Sri Lanka's human development index on a par with developed states. On the other hand, Sri Lanka has also struggled with ethnic violence, two insurrections, and a three-decade-long war due to severe socio-economic inequality as well as the failure to ensure self-determination for its largest ethnic minority. Constitutions and the rule of law have been instrumentalized in these processes by successive governments to undermine democratic governance. An excessive public service, a diverse range of loss-making and underperforming sets of state-owned enterprises (SOEs), and a heavy defense budget have characterized the Sri Lankan state more recently, giving rise to very serious concerns about corruption and poor governance.

The city of Colombo has been a hub for the political and economic life of Sri Lanka particularly since colonial rule.[3] The new Colombo Port City sits at a key geographical, cultural, economic, and political location in Colombo adjacent to the port, facing Sri Lanka's first parliament (which now houses the Presidential Secretariat and Treasury), and in close proximity to the country's financial hub. Providing an eye-level view of the centrality of Colombo Port City, it is within sight of the Galle Face Hotel (one of the most prominent hotels built during British rule) and the Galle Face Green (a promenade dedicated to the women and children of Colombo by the British). It is also within sight of the recently built Shangri-La Hotel. Finally, the main site for the *Aragalaya* (people's struggle) of 2022 was at one end of the Galle Face Green, between the Port City and the Presidential Secretariat.

3 The Case

3.1 China-Funded Infrastructure Projects in Sri Lanka: Background

Over the past decade, the Chinese presence in Sri Lanka's economy has been on the rise, mainly manifested through large-scale infrastructure development

---

[1] Investment treaties that are approved with a two-thirds majority in the Parliament become part of law in Sri Lanka under Art 157 of the Constitution of Sri Lanka (the Constitution).
[2] The World Bank, 'Foreign Direct Investment, net inflows (% of GDP) – Sri Lanka' https://data.worldbank.org/indicator/BX.KLT.DINV.WD.GD.ZS?end=2021&locations=LK&start=1970&view=chart.
[3] Sri Lanka has been impacted by colonization since 1505. The Portuguese and the Dutch colonized the maritime provinces, and the British ruled the entire island from 1815 to 1948.

projects funded by China.[4] For China, establishing critical infrastructure facilities in a country like Sri Lanka, which is strategically located in the Indian Ocean, is crucial for pursuing its ambitious 21st Century Maritime Silk Road. It is one of the main routes for the BRI that cross the Indian Ocean Region. For Sri Lanka, advancing the country's infrastructure facilities was central to realizing the development agenda led by the then Rajapaksa regime (2005–2015), which repeatedly vowed to make Sri Lanka a dynamic commercial hub in South Asia.[5] This regime relied predominantly on commercial borrowings to finance its infrastructure development agenda, which accelerated after the end of the three-decade-long war in 2009.[6]

As will be shown in this case study, several internal and external economic and political factors prevalent in the postwar scenario compelled the Rajapaksa regime to rely increasingly on bilateral sources of financing. Against this backdrop, China became Sri Lanka's main bilateral sovereign lender, surpassing the country's traditional lenders such as the Asian Development Bank.[7] The lion's share of this capital was allocated to develop specific sectors in Sri Lanka's economy: power and energy, transport and telecommunications, port development, and irrigation. Some of the leading development projects in these sectors commenced even before China officially launched the BRI in 2013. Examples include the Norochcholai Coal Power Plant (2006), the Moragahakandha Development Project (2007), the Hambantota Seaport (2007), the Colombo-Katunayake Expressway (2009), the Mattala International Airport (2010), and the Colombo Lotus Tower Project (2012).

Chinese-funded development projects in Sri Lanka are often labeled as "Chinese investments."[8] Although it is possible to characterize transitional loans as "investments,"[9] this characterization does not reflect the fact that most

---

[4] Sri Lanka's contemporary relationship with China is multidimensional and includes political relationships and cultural exchanges in addition to the economic. The two regions and their people have a much longer history as well.

[5] For Mahinda Rajapaksa's political view in this respect, see the three versions of his election manifesto, namely *Mahinda Chintana* (2005) www.mfa.gov.lk/images/stories/pdf/mahinda_chintana_eng.pdf, *Mahinda Chintana: Vision for the Future* (2010) www.preventionweb.net/files/mahinda_chintana_vision_for_the_future_eng%5B1%5D.pdf, and *Mahinda Chintana: Path to Success* (2015) https://groundviews.org/wp-content/uploads/2014/12/mahinda-chinthana-path-to-success-2015.pdf.

[6] The military defeated the separatist movement, the Liberation Tigers of Tamil Eelam (LTTE).

[7] Umesh Moramudali and Thilina Panduwawala, 'From Project Financing to Debt Restructuring: China's Role in Sri Lanka's Debt Situation' (*Daily FT*, 17 June 2022) www.ft.lk/columns/From-project-financing-to-debt-restructuring-China-s-role-in-Sri-Lanka-s-debt-situation/4-736258.

[8] See, e.g., Ganeshan Wignaraja, Dinusha Panditaratne, Pabasara Kannangara, and Divya Hundlani, 'Chinese Investment and the BRI in Sri Lanka' (March 2020) Asia-Pacific Programme Research Paper www.chathamhouse.org/sites/default/files/CHHJ8010-Sri-Lanka-RP-WEB-200324.pdf.

[9] Transnational loans have been characterized as "investments" by investment arbitral tribunals established under the 1965 Washington Convention. See, e.g., *Fedex N.V. v Venezuela*, ICSID Case No. ARB/96/3, Decision of the Tribunal on Objections to Jurisdiction (11 July 1997).

of the capital flows are loans. Many projects have been financed by commercial borrowings from Chinese banks, mainly the China Development Bank and the Export-Import Bank of China.[10] Only a handful of projects have been financed as direct Chinese investments and the CPC is the only infrastructure development project that can be classified as an FDI. Contrary to loans, FDI does not oblige the host country to repay the capital invested in a project since it is a form of equity finance that ensures foreign capital flows into a given country. Consequently, the Chinese capital invested in the Project cannot be included in the debt that Sri Lanka must repay to China, subject to the ongoing debt restructuring program.

3.2 Chinese Interest in the Project

The Project illustrates the way in which a capitalist approach to foreign investment by a one-party state can play out. Even though the investment is carried out by a company, or a legal entity separate from the Chinese government, it is an enterprise owned by the state and therefore presumably also controlled by the state and subject to its politics. As will be explained, the Chinese investor submitted an unsolicited bid to the Government of Sri Lanka (GOSL) at a time when the government was looking for alternative development partners and approaches. This was due to (1) Sri Lanka being designated as a middle-income country and therefore being unable to obtain loans on concessionary terms, (2) isolation by other powerful states due to allegations of human rights and rule of law violations, and (3) the emergence of an intensified conflation between state, party, and family in governance.

At the time, the Chinese approach to foreign investment converged with the prevailing political and economic dispensation in Sri Lanka. The Chinese economic interests were driven by the political priorities of the Chinese government, resulting in arguably poor investment choices. It is also evident today that, in making such an investment, the Chinese did not have a strategy in place for managing potential risks such as political resistance to projects or domestic legal disputes. However, the Project survived a project suspension and renegotiation and, as will be seen, the Chinese approach in this instance was to be flexible, to negotiate and adapt, rather than to rely on their original contractual rights.

3.3 The History of the Project

The Project itself has its own troubled history and includes at least three narratives. First is the narrative of FDI-led development in a carved-out legal and physical location. Second is the political and economic implications of the

---

[10] Moramudali and Panduwawala (n 7).

BRI project. Third is the narrative that the Chinese were flexible in adapting this project to the infrastructure development approach of the first and second Rajapaksa regimes (2006–2015 and 2019–2022) as well as to the seemingly prodemocratic approach of the good governance (*Yahapalanaya*) regime between 2015 and 2019.

The idea of reclaiming land off the Colombo coast adjacent to the Colombo Port to expand the Central Business District has a long history. It was initially proposed in 1991 by the then Minister of Industries, Science and Technology, Ranil Wickremesinghe (who is the current president of Sri Lanka).[11] The main purpose of this endeavor was to release land for real estate development. However, changes in domestic politics resulted in the Project stalling for several years; it regained prominence only in 2001 when Wickremesinghe returned to power as prime minster.[12] CESMA International Pte Ltd., a Singapore-based urban planning consulting company, was assigned to develop the "Western Region Megapolis Plan," which envisioned developing the entire Western province of Sri Lanka as a single megapolis. This development plan was completed in 2004, and a call for expressions of interest from investors to reclaim approximately 145 ha of land from the sea to the south of the proposed Colombo South Port breakwater by 2010 (see later in this section) was issued.[13] However, the Project went unimplemented for the second time due to the political changes in 2004.[14]

In the meantime, in 2009, the 5.14 km South Port breakwater was constructed as part of the Colombo Port Expansion Project (CPEP), partially funded by the Asian Development Bank. The newly built breakwater made it technically and financially feasible to reclaim land to the south, and thus, in April 2010, the Sri Lanka Ports Authority (SLPA) commissioned an "Initial Technical Feasibility" study to that effect.[15] While the SLPA acted as the project proponent in this regard, the reclamation work was supposed to be carried out as a state-funded project. In June 2010, SLPA commissioned an Environmental Impact Assessment (EIA) for the reclamation of 200 ha south of the newly built breakwater.[16] The National Environmental Act makes it mandatory to conduct an EIA for all projects with a significant environmental impact,[17] and for projects

---

[11] Asanga Gunawansa, 'Creation of New Urban Land by Reclaiming the Sea in Colombo Port City, Sri Lanka' in Katherine Cashman and Victoria Quinlan (eds), *Strengthening Environmental Reviews in Urban Development* (UN-Habitat, 2018) 98.
[12] ibid. See further, Supplementary Environmental Impact Assessment (SEIA) Report of the Proposed Colombo Port City Development Project, Colombo, Sri Lanka (December 2015) 2.
[13] Gunawansa (n 11) 98–99; SEIA (n 12) 2.
[14] The cohabitation government fell apart. The election of Mahinda Rajapakse as president signaled a shift including a renewed effort to militarily defeat the LTTE.
[15] SEIA (n 12) 3.
[16] ibid. Moreover, in October 2010, the Urban Development Authority completed a "Master Plan Study" based on the "Initial Technical Feasibility Study."
[17] See generally, Sumudu Atapattu et al. 'Colombo International Financial City' in Sumudu Atapattu et al. (eds), *The Cambridge Handbook of Environmental Justice and Sustainable Development* (Cambridge University Press 2021).

within Sri Lanka's coastal zone, the Department of Coast Conservation and Coastal Resources Management is the Project Approving Agency (PAA).

Meanwhile, in April 2011, SLPA was approached by a Chinese SOE called China Communication Construction Company Ltd. (CCCC), a Chinese SOE with more than sixty wholly owned subsidiaries working on infrastructure-related constructions, operations, and investments, with an unsolicited proposal (USP) to reclaim the seabed between the southern end of the CPEP and the northern part of the Colombo Galle Face Green.[18] In other words, this proposal was initiated by the CCCC itself. The fact that CCCC is a Chinese SOE made this USP distinctive because most unsolicited proposals for developing infrastructure facilities are initiated by private sector entities, not state-affiliated ones. This USP suggested reclaiming a total area of 233 ha as a direct Chinese investment worth US$1.4 billion without any financial commitment from the GOSL.

While this USP was under consideration, in December 2011, the EIA commissioned by the SLPA for land reclamation was approved by the Department of Coast Conservation and Coastal Resources Management.[19] According to the 2014 Annual Performance Report of the Ministry of Highways, Ports and Shipping, the USP was reviewed by the Standing Cabinet Appointed Review Committee (SCARC) according to the Guidelines on Government Tender Procedure – Part II (Revised Edition – January 1998) and Public Finance Circular No. 444 (i) dated 16 May 2011.[20] SCARC was appointed in June 2010, *inter alia*, to assess unsolicited or standalone development proposals and advise relevant line ministries or government agencies on matters related to such proposals.[21] Accordingly, the line ministers were required to submit unsolicited proposals they received to the SCARC for an initial assessment and recommendation.[22] They were required to do so when such proposals were deemed competitive and advantageous to national interests.

The 1998 Guidelines are applicable for private sector infrastructure development projects initiated by both solicited and unsolicited proposals. Concerning unsolicited proposals, the Guidelines explicitly require calling for further proposals by advertisement, while providing the original company a chance to improve on their submission as part of the invitation for bids/offers.[23] Such

---

[18] Gunawansa (n 11) 101.   [19] SEIA (n 12) 4–5.
[20] Ministry of Highways, Ports and Shipping, *Annual Performance Report-2014*, 69 www.parliament.lk/uploads/documents/paperspresented/performance-report-ministry-of-highways-ports-and-shipping-2014.pdf. The Ministry of Highways, Ports and Shipping was responsible for the development of road and port sectors and the SLPA was assigned to it.
[21] Department of Public Finance, 'Supplement – 23 to the Procurement Guidelines, Part II Reference: 237' (12 May 2011) www.treasury.gov.lk/api/file/5c891efb-a1cb-4098-aba5-4d4360a5cedb.
[22] Ministry of Finance and Planning, 'Public Finance Circular No. 444' (4 August 2004) www.treasury.gov.lk/api/file/2a31a18c-c5a6-4095-952c-8d65e00d2a8a.
[23] Ministry of Finance, Economic Stabilization and National Policies, *Guidelines on Government Tender Procedure-Part II* (Revised Edition January 1998) para. 237 www.treasury.gov.lk/api/file/9f9c06c1-59c4-4d7c-b43e-870c3d71803a.

bids/offers should be called once the relevant line ministry determines the need for a development project as suggested by the USP. This procedure was not followed in this case,[24] as, after receiving the SCARC approval for the USP submitted by the CCCC, the Cabinet of Ministers permitted the CCCC to sign a Memorandum of Understanding (MOU) with the SLPA. This MOU was to discuss the key terms of the draft agreement relating to the investment for reclaiming land adjacent to the Colombo Port.

Following the signing of the MOU, CCCC submitted a detailed project proposal to SLPA, while the SCARC recommended to the Cabinet of Ministers that SLPA enter into a Concession Agreement with CCCC to implement the project, subject to approval by the Attorney-General. In January 2014, the Cabinet of Ministers sanctioned the key terms of the Concession Agreement negotiated between the SLPA and CCCC. Nevertheless, as pointed out by the Attorney-General, the SLPA could not be a party to this agreement for two main reasons. Firstly, the SLPA does not have the legal authority to engage in seabed reclamation for commercial projects. Secondly, under Sri Lankan law, only the president of Sri Lanka has the power to reclaim any part of the foreshore or the seabed.[25] Consequently, a cabinet decision was made permitting the Secretary to the Ministry of Highways, Ports and Shipping to enter into an agreement with the Chinese investor.[26] Terms of this agreement, referred to as the GOSL Contract Agreement, were akin to those in the original Concession Agreement, which was integrated into the GOSL Agreement as a binding annex. This Agreement was to remain in effect until SLPA was granted the legal authority to be a part of the Concession Agreement.

The GOSL Agreement included a provision to the effect of amending the SLPA Act within one year.[27] The amendment to the SLPA Act did not take place as planned due to the subsequent political changes and policy adjustments as will be discussed.[28] However, it is striking that the Project was supposed to affect Sri Lanka's domestic law, enabling a state entity to be a part of a commercial activity that did not originally come under its legal competence. At the same time, CHEC Port City Colombo, the locally incorporated subsidiary of CCCC (the Project Company), entered into the investment agreement with the Secretary to the Ministry of Highways, Ports and Shipping. This agreement was signed on 16 September 2014 during the Chinese president's state visit to Sri Lanka and in the presence of both Chinese and Sri Lankan presidents. The reclamation work began on the same day, making one of Sri Lanka's long-held development proposals a reality. Meanwhile, government borrowings began to increase, and other

---

[24] See generally, Gunawansa (n 11); SEIA (n 12).   [25] Section 60 of the State Land Ordinance.
[26] See generally, Gunawansa (n 11).   [27] ibid. See further Clause 2 of the GOSL Agreement.
[28] Instead, the Cabinet of Ministers decided to extend the GOSL Agreement for a further period of six months from 15 March 2016.

controversial large-scale infrastructure development projects were underway, including the Hambantota Seaport and the Mattala Airport.[29]

3.4 The 2014 Concession Agreement for the Project

An investment contract is the beginning of the "life" of most foreign investments.[30] There are different types of investment contracts, and a Concession Agreement is used to finance large-scale projects such as the development of infrastructure facilities. Some scholars describe Concession Agreements as the "heart of any infrastructure investment."[31] This is firstly because they provide the contractual or legal framework for a project. Secondly, they cover almost all aspects of the project, including the rights and obligations of the parties to the agreement. Thirdly and importantly, it is a manifestation of the bargaining power of the parties to the agreement.

In terms of rights, the 2014 Concession Agreement granted the Project Company an array of entitlements, including land ownership. For context, the Project Company was given the right to hold 108 ha of "Marketable Lands" from the reclaimed landmass.[32] Accordingly, the investor was entitled to hold 20 ha of "Marketable Lands" on a freehold basis with the remaining 88 ha held by the Project Company or its nominee on a leasehold basis. The Project Company was further entitled to select an engineering procurement construction (EPC) contractor without adhering to public procurement guidelines and procedures.[33] Consequently, the Project Company designated another wholly owned subsidiary of the CCCC as the EPC responsible for designing and building the CPC.[34]

The Project Company was given a set of "Development Rights."[35] This set of rights included the right to study, investigate, design, engineer, finance, and carry out the first phase of the Project, that is, land reclamation. In addition, they entitled the Project Company to benefit from and generate revenue from all Project Land in which it has a freehold or leasehold interest and from all other activities.[36] However, "Development Rights" were not absolute since they were subject to restrictions by the SLPA, or any other governmental authority, based on the grounds stipulated in the agreement itself.[37] These grounds for

---

[29] Both located in Sri Lanka's Southern Province, home to the Rajapaksa family.
[30] C. L. Lim, Jean Ho, and Martins Paparinskis, *International Investment Law and Arbitration: Commentary, Awards and Other Materials* (2nd edn, Cambridge University Press 2021) 37.
[31] Jeswald W. Salacuse, *The Three Laws of International Investment: National, Contractual, and International Frameworks for Foreign Capital* (Oxford University Press 2013) 228.
[32] Clause 24.1 of the 2014 Concession Agreement.   [33] Gunawansa (n 11) 102.
[34] The designated wholly owned subsidiary was China Harbour Engineering Company Ltd. (CHEC).
[35] Clause 2 of the 2014 Concession Agreement.
[36] The definition of Project Land includes both freehold and leasehold lands. See Schedule I Part I of the 2014 Concession Agreement.
[37] Clause 2.4 of the 2014 Concession Agreement.

restriction included (1) the development had to protect public health and the safety or the environment; (2) it had to protect national security; and (3) any breach of the Concession Agreement or any applicable permits by the Project Company would also terminate the Project.

Where the impact of any such restrictions by the GOSL is greater than twenty-four hours for any single event or an aggregate of seventy-two hours in any six-month period, the Concession Agreement designates said impact as a "Compensation Event" under the provision of Clause 33. This clause, *inter alia*, identifies any action by any third party in a court of law resulting in a "material delay" in carrying out the reclamation work, or preventing or delaying the Project Company in its work, as events that warrant compensation.[38] The 2014 Concession Agreement moreover barred the GOSL, including the courts of law, from directly or indirectly interfering with the Project Company, its assets located in Sri Lanka dedicated to the Project, its shareholders' interests in the Project Company, or its interest in the Project Land by way of nationalization, expropriation, confiscation, or compulsory acquisition.[39]

Concerning dispute resolution, the 2014 Concession Agreement provided several methods including amicable settlement, mediation, expert resolution, adjudication, or arbitration.[40] Sri Lankan law was chosen as the governing law of the Agreement.[41] Notably, under the Agreement, the SLPA was responsible for conducting environmental studies related to the reclamation work and sand extraction, as well as for obtaining required permits.[42] This responsibility was applicable even during the period leading to the signing of the agreement. As mentioned, the SLPA had successfully completed the EIA up to reclaiming the land, yet it covered an area of only 200 ha, not the 233 ha as specified in the Agreement. Additionally, the SLPA had unsuccessfully commissioned the National Aquatic Resources Research and Development Agency to undertake two Initial Environmental Examination studies to secure permits for sand extraction before signing the Agreement.[43]

3.5 Controversies Surrounding the Project

The rosy picture of the Project began to fade in the months following its commencement. Controversies over the Project revolved around four main

---

[38] However, legal proceedings that arise as a result of any breach of the agreement or applicable law by the Project Company were excluded from the purview of this clause.
[39] Clause 38 of the 2014 Concession Agreement. It should be read alongside the definition of the term "expropriation" included in Schedule I Part I of the same agreement.
[40] Clause 39 of the 2014 Concession Agreement.
[41] Clause 57 of the 2014 Concession Agreement.
[42] Clause 3 of the GOSL Contract and Clause 12 of the 2014 Concession Agreement. See further, SEIA (n 12) 3–6.
[43] SEIA (n 12) 4–5.

concerns. These include the following: first, adverse socioeconomic and environmental impacts of reclaiming the land; second, failure to adhere to Sri Lanka's environmental laws applicable to a development project with significant environmental impacts; third, procedural flaws associated with awarding contracts; and fourth, possible security-related risks posed by an investment driven by a Chinese SOE.

The Project garnered strong opposition. Opposing civil society groups included affected fisherfolk living along the western coast of Sri Lanka from Moratuwa to Negombo.[44] In their opinion, the Project was an undemocratic, illegal, and catastrophic venture that should be abandoned.[45] While arguing that its socioeconomic and environmental impacts have not been adequately studied, opponents underscored the adverse impact of land reclamation and sand dredging which included damaging fish breeding areas and coral reefs and increasing coastal erosion. However, given the nature of these consequences, correlation, not causation, was established. Nevertheless, the fisherfolk claim that they have suffered from a loss of income and that their livelihoods have been affected.[46]

Concerns raised by the affected communities were further reinforced by environmentalists who opposed the Project on the basis that it violated applicable environmental laws in Sri Lanka.[47] First, environmentalists challenged the adequacy of the EIA done by the SLPA in 2011 because it focused predominantly on the impact of land reclamation of 200 ha. It did not address the impact of the sand extraction and quarrying of stones required for the reclamation. Second, they challenged the credibility of the Addendum Report to the 2011 EIA prepared to assess the impact of the proposal to reclaim an additional 33 ha (233 ha in total). In September 2013, the SLPA had submitted this Addendum Report to the PAA without public scrutiny. Public scrutiny is required by Sri Lanka's environmental law and has been consistently emphasized by the Supreme Court.

Thirdly, environmentalists raised concerns over the fact that reclamation work commenced without obtaining required permits for sand excavation. They pointed out that the Development Activity Permit issued by the PAA, following the submission of the Addendum Report to the 2011 EIA, required the SLPA to obtain approval separately for extraction of sand from the Central

---

[44] Environmental Justice Atlas, 'Fisher Folks, Environmentalists and Religious Leaders against the Colombo Port City, Sri Lanka' (*EJatlas*, 30 July 2023) https://ejatlas.org/print/fisherwomens-mobilization-against-the-port-city-sri-lanka.

[45] See generally, People's Movement Against Port City, පෝර්ට් සිටියේ ඇත්ත නැත්ත [*Truth and Myth of the Port City*] (Akura Publications July 2018).

[46] According to local news reports, Rs. 550 million was allocated as livelihood support to be distributed among fishermen. See Sheain Fernandopulle, 'Negombo Fishermen Hit by Port City Project' (*Daily Mirror*, 23 February 2020) www.dailymirror.lk/print/plus/Negombo-fishermen-hit-by-Port-City-Project/352-183623.

[47] See generally, Atapattu et al. (n 17); SEIA (n 12).

Environmental Authority (CEA).[48] Even though the permit for dredging sand should have been sought before the commencement of the Project, it was not obtained before signing the 2014 Concession Agreement as the SLPA had failed to secure the consent for the compensation program for the fisherfolk. This consent was necessary for the CEA to grant the required sand extraction permits.

Some politicians also resisted the Project. Opposing politicians argued that it was necessary to call for bids/offers from other interested parties in the Project.[49] The opacity of awarding the contract was central to the heated political debates over the growing Chinese-funded infrastructure development projects under the Rajapaksa regime. They challenged the decision to give the Chinese investor 20 ha of land on a freehold basis. They further questioned the jurisdiction over this plot of land given its possible threats to national security. Similar security-related concerns were raised by several other regional and global superpowers premised on the concerns that China was using the Project to consolidate its regional presence through numerous additional BRI investments along the 21st Century Maritime Silk Road.[50]

3.6 Suspension and the Resumption of the Project

All the controversies surrounding the Project and other Chinese-funded infrastructure development projects in Sri Lanka gradually culminated in a massive public outcry against the allegedly pro-Chinese Rajapaksa regime. Such projects provoked concerns over the impact on the country's constitutional governance, democratic processes, and the possibility of supporting an authoritarian regime. These concerns were successfully capitalized on by the opposition to discredit the Rajapaksa regime: First, for entangling Sri Lanka in a Chinese "debt trap" by excessive commercial borrowings from China to finance economically unviable infrastructure development projects such as the Hambantota Seaport and Mattala Airport. The myth about the Chinese debt trap has prevailed all the way into the 2022 economic crisis in Sri Lanka.[51] However, analysts have pointed out that the

---

[48] SEIA (n 12) 4–5.   [49] See generally, Gunawansa (n 11).
[50] See, e.g., Teshu Singh, 'The Geopolitics of Chinese Investments in Sri Lanka' (*Institute of Peace and Conflict Studies*, 13 April 2015) www.ipcs.org/comm_select.php?articleNo=4862; Asanga Abeyagoonasekera, 'Before the Phoenix Nest: Questions Surrounding the Port City of Colombo' (*LSE*, 8 July 2021) https://blogs.lse.ac.uk/cff/2021/07/08/before-the-phoenix-nest-questions-surrounding-the-port-city-of-colombo/.
[51] Bart Klem and Dinesha Samararatne, 'Sri Lanka in 2021: Vistas on the Brink' (2022) 62 Asian Survey 201. For a dispelling of this myth, see Moramudali and Panduwawala (n 7) 11. See further Umesh Moramudali and Thilina Panduwawala, 'From Project Financing to Debt Restructuring: China's Role in Sri Lanka's Debt Situation' (*Panda Paw Dragon Claw*, 13 June 2022) https://pandapawdragonclaw.blog/2022/06/13/from-project-financing-to-debt-restructuring-chinas-role-in-sri-lankas-debt-situation/.

debt owed to China is only 20% of Sri Lanka's external debt stock. The bulk of Sri Lanka's debt is owed to international sovereign bond holders. Second, for endangering Sri Lanka's neutral foreign policy for which the country has often been praised. Third, for placing Sri Lanka's sovereignty and national security at risk due to allowing unprecedented Chinese presence in the country's economy, notably through strategic industries and critical infrastructure facilities.

Against this background, Chinese-funded infrastructure development projects became politically sensitive.[52] Consequently, reviewing the Project became one of the popular election pledges of the 2015 presidential and parliamentary elections. These elections brought the opposition led by Maithripala Sirisena and Ranil Wickremesinghe into power under the slogan of "good governance." In complying with its election pledge, the good governance administration appointed an evaluation committee to review the CRC Project soon after the presidential election. Based on this Committee's conclusion, the Cabinet of Ministers decided to suspend the reclamation work unilaterally. Civil society groups who had been demanding that the Project be canceled welcomed this suspension. They further credited the newly elected good governance administration for fulfilling its election promise at the cost of Sino-Sri Lanka relations which were at their peak at that time.

Nevertheless, it would be a mistake to perceive this suspension as a move toward complete cancellation of the Project. During its suspension, the good governance administration took several steps, in consultation with the Project Company, to ensure its revival after addressing concerns regarding the Project. First, it was decided to commission a Supplementary EIA (2015 SEIA) taking the alterations made to the Project since the completion of 2011 EIA into account. This also addressed the concern that the Addendum Report to the 2011 EIA was not subject to public scrutiny. Accordingly, the 2015 SIEA was intended to cover a total land area of 269 ha (as opposed to the originally contracted total land area of 233 ha) and address the environmental impact of the sand and quarry material extraction.[53] Second, it was decided to replace the SLPA with the Urban Development Authority (UDA) and thus the Ministry of Urban Development, Water Supply and Drainage became the project proponent for the 2015 SEIA.[54] Although the UDA was assigned to the Ministry of Urban Development, Water Supply and Drainage, it was subsequently brought under the purview of the Ministry of Megapolis and Western Development.

From the Chinese perspective, resuming the Project was essential for safeguarding its economic interest as an investor and China's policy preference to

---

[52] See generally, Dilini Pathirana, 'The Paradox of Chinese Investments in Sri Lanka: Between Investment Treaty Protection and Commercial Diplomacy' (2020) 10 Asian Journal of International Law, 375–408.
[53] SEIA (n 12) 1.   [54] ibid.

support the BRI at large. Therefore, commercial diplomacy between Beijing and Colombo played a significant role in ensuring the Project's revival contrary to Wickremasinghe's promise to scrap the Project in its entirety.[55] For context, high-level diplomatic engagements took place immediately before the suspension of the Project, including the visit by China's Assistant Foreign Minister in February 2015 who met with then Sri Lankan prime minister Wickremasinghe. This was followed by then Sri Lankan president Maithripala's visit to China in March 2015 soon after the suspension of the Project, signifying Sri Lanka's continued commitment to work with China despite the political changes and policy adjustments that were supposed to be undertaken under the newly elected good governance administration. In the end, after almost one year of suspension, on 9 March 2016 the Cabinet of Ministers permitted the Project Company to recommence the reclamation work.

Understandably, the decision to resume the Project was not welcomed by its opponents. The People's Movement against the Port City (a self-identified social pressure group) continued to protest, underscoring its adverse socio-economic and ecological impact, including the impact on the livelihood of the affected fisherfolk community.[56] Environmentalists continued to dispute the credibility of the 2015 SEIA, highlighting the Project's negative impact on social justice and equity and, therefore, sustainable development.[57] The decision to resume the Project damaged the good governance administration whose domestic reputation and confidence had already been weakened due to perceptions about the tensions within a fragile coalition government.[58] The situation was intensified by the massive public outcry against the leasing of the loss-making Hambantota Seaport to a Chinese enterprise for ninety-nine years. As this port was also to be associated with the establishment of an adjacent industrial zone,[59] the deal gave rise to concerns over potential land grab, particularly in urban and agricultural areas. All these controversies enabled the defeated Rajapaksas, who were seeking reelection, to claim that the good governance administration was selling the country's strategic national properties to China.[60]

---

[55] Pathirana (n 52). See further 'Colombo Port City Will Be Scrapped: Ranil' (*Daily Mirror*, 16 December 2014) www.dailymirror.lk/59031/colombo-port-city-will-be-scrapped-ranil.

[56] Environmental Justice Atlas (n 44). See further, Sheridan Prasso, 'A Chinese Company Reshaping the World Leaves a Troubled Trail' (*Bloomberg*, 19 September 2018) www.bloomberg.com/news/features/2018-09-19/a-chinese-company-reshaping-the-world-leaves-a-troubled-trail?leadSource=uverify%20wall.

[57] See, e.g., Atapattu et al. (n 17).

[58] Jonathan Goodhand and Oliver Walton, 'The Tangled Politics of Postwar Justice in Sri Lanka' (2017) 116 Current History 135.

[59] 'Protest over Hambantota Port Deal Turns Violent' (*Aljazeera*, 7 January 2017) www.aljazeera.com/economy/2017/1/7/protest-over-hambantota-port-deal-turns-violent.

[60] Kinling Lo, 'Sri Lanka Wants Its "Debt Trap" Hambantota Port Back: But will China Listen?' (*South China Morning Post*, 7 December 2019) www.scmp.com/news/china/diplomacy/article/3040982/sri-lanka-wants-its-debt-trap-hambantota-port-back-will-china.

3.7 Access to Investment-Related Information: The 2016 Tripartite Agreement

The decision to resume the Project was followed by the signing of a new investment contract that repealed and replaced the much-disputed 2014 Concession Agreement.[61] From Sri Lanka's perspective, it was essential to remove the controversial contractual terms included in the binding investment agreement. From China's perspective, agreeing to sign a new investment agreement proved its flexibility in adjusting the legal frameworks applicable to BRI investments and showed its willingness to adapt to political changes and policy adjustments in host states. Notably, the Project Company conceded its contractual rights under the 2014 Concession Agreement to receive 20 ha of freehold land.[62] Further, it withdrew claims for compensation arising from the unilateral suspension of the project. There is no publicly known international arbitration brought by the Chinese investor based on the 2014 Concession Agreement or the China-Sri Lanka bilateral investment treaty (BIT) of 1987. (The BIT provides Chinese investors recourse to investor–state arbitration to resolve limited investment disputes such as the amount of compensation payable in an event of expropriation.[63])

A new Tripartite Agreement was signed on 12 September 2016 (the 2016 Agreement). As mentioned, the SLPA was replaced with the UDA, which was subsequently transferred to the Ministry of Megapolis and Western Development. To date, this agreement has not been made publicly available, giving rise to serious concerns over transparency in investment agreements and the people's access to investment-related information. The lack of access to investment agreements is not limited to Chinese investments in Sri Lanka; agreements relating to other disputed ventures have also not been made publicly available. In doing so, parties invoke confidentiality clauses and commercial confidence. For example, the agreement between the US-based energy company New Fortress Energy Inc. and the GOSL (September 2021) relating to the former's investment in Sri Lanka's energy sector and based on a USP, has not been released to the public.[64]

However, civil society activists and environmentalists continued to demand access to the 2016 Agreement through the legal mechanism established by the Right to Information (RTI) Act. The Act aims to promote transparency and accountability of public authorities, guaranteeing the right of access to information as provided for in Article 14A of the Constitution. During such attempts, UDA and other relevant public authorities have refused to release the agreement for several reasons.[65] They invoked the confidentiality clause in

---

[61] See generally, Gunawansa (n 11); SEIA (n 12).   [62] Gunawansa (n 11) 111.
[63] For a detailed discussion on the China-Sri Lanka BIT of 1987 see Pathirana (n 52).
[64] Newswire, 'CEB Explains Why Contents of Yugadanavi Power Plant Agreement Cannot Be Disclosed' (*Newswire*, 4 November 2021) www.newswire.lk/2021/11/04/ceb-explains-why-yugadanavi-us-power-plant-agreement-cannot/.
[65] See generally, *M. F. A. Mansoor v Ministry of Urban Development, Water Supply and Housing Facilities (Ministry of Megapolis and Western Development)* RTIC Appeal (in Person)/1108/2019. (Hereinafter, *Mansoor v Ministry of Urban Development*).

the 2016 Agreement and Section 5(1)(d) of the RTI Act, which permits denial of access to information based on several grounds including commercial confidentiality. Moreover, the Project Company has also raised an objection as a third party against the release of the agreement on the basis that it contains confidential and price-sensitive information.

Nevertheless, in the case of *Mansoor v Ministry of Urban Development*, the Commission decided that the general confidentiality clause in an agreement does not preclude the right to access to the entire agreement. In its Interim Order in 2022, the Commission emphasized the ability to release an agreement "subject to redaction of commercially sensitive information" as provided in the RTI Act. The Commission further decided that the clauses in the 2016 Agreement that are of public interest should be made public. While comparing the 2016 and 2014 Agreements, the Commission determined that many clauses in the former are identical or similar to those included in the latter, which is already in the public domain. In its final Order dated April 2023, the Commission directed the relevant public authorities, including the Ministry of Investment Promotions, to release the 2016 Agreement before 4 May 2023.[66] However, the Project Company has filed an appeal against this Order before the Court of Appeal.[67]

3.8 Litigation before Domestic Courts

The Project was challenged before Sri Lanka's domestic courts in two cases. The first case was the Fundamental Rights Petition filed by the All Ceylon Fisherfolk Trade Union.[68] The petitioners argued that the Project would affect their right to engage in a lawful occupation. The Supreme Court dismissed the petition on the basis that the complaints were vague and lacking in scientific evidence.[69] The second lawsuit was a writ petition filed before the Court of Appeal by a local nongovernmental organization, the Centre for Environmental Justice.[70] It sought a writ of certiorari to quash the 2011 EIA and 2015 SEIA, the 2014 Concession Agreement between the SLPA and the Project Company, and the Development Permit issued by the Director General of the Coast Conservation to the SLPA. It also sought a writ of mandamus to compel the Project Company to conduct a new "comprehensive

---

[66] This decision was premised on several grounds including the failure of the relevant public authorities to discharge its burden in terms of Section 32(4) of the Act, while the public interest has been satisfactorily established by the Appellants.
[67] Interview with a lawyer involved in the litigation against the CPC as well as the right to information request (online, 19 May 2023).
[68] SC (FR)151/2015. This Petition was filed under Art 126 of the Constitution.
[69] 'Supreme Court Terminates Proceedings in the Case against Colombo Port City Project' (*The Sunday Times*, 17 July 2016) www.sundaytimes.lk/160717/business-times/supreme-court-terminates-proceedings-in-the-case-against-colombo-port-city-project-200940.html.
[70] Art 140 of the Constitution.

EIA."[71] This petition was dismissed although the judgment on the writ petition has not yet been issued by the Court. This then resulted in difficulties for the petitioner in appealing against the dismissal. However, an appeal has been filed and the matter is pending before the Supreme Court.[72]

In the fundamental rights matter, the petitioners invoked the Public Trust Doctrine (PTD) recognized by the judiciary in Sri Lanka under the right to equality clause in making a complaint against the violation of their fundamental rights.[73] As with the writ petition, they complained that the required approvals had not been obtained as per the applicable law and that the SLPA had no authority to enter into an agreement on land reclamation. Proceedings in this matter were discontinued in July 2016 on the basis that the petitioners were "free to come back" to Court if they had "any further concerns" regarding any legal or constitutional violations. The Court noted that the Directive Principles of State Policy required the state to "protect, preserve, and improve the environment for the benefit of the community" and noted "[i]n the same breadth, the Court is concerned about the rapid development of the whole country."[74] The Court further noted that "[t]he organs of the States are guardians to whom the people have committed the case of preservation of the resources of the people. The Court is mindful in upholding the cause of environment as an independent right of both the present and future generations."[75]

The Court then commented on two developments. First, it commented that the 2015 SEIA had proposed to the government the payment of compensation to "meet the requirement of the Fisher community, their income support and benefits." It further opined that any concerns that the community may have over the compensation could be taken up with the relevant ministries. Second, the Court noted that if petitioners require any documents "by which approvals were granted," then they could be obtained through the Attorney-General's Department from the Secretary of the Ministry.

In both petitions, a key issue was the challenge faced by petitioners in establishing causation between the environmental impact of the proposed project and the actual harm to the environment. In both cases, it appears that the Court was not convinced that the evidentiary burden was satisfied by the petitioners. However, the judicial responses in these two petitions contrast with the approach adopted by the Supreme Court in the *Chunnakam* case where the Court recognized and enforced the precautionary principle in affirming

---

[71] *Centre for Environmental Justice v Sri Lanka Ports Authority* CA(Writ) 112/2015. The relevant legislation is the Coast Conservation Act 57 of 1981 (as amended) and the Sri Lanka Ports Authority Act 51 of 1979 (as amended).
[72] Interview with one of the lawyers representing a petitioner (online, 19 May 2023).
[73] Art 12 of the Constitution.
[74] SC (FR) 151/2015, order Supreme Court Minutes 7 July 2016.
[75] SC (FR) 151/2015, order Supreme Court Minutes 7 July 2016.

the duty of the state to protect the environment.[76] Moreover, the Sri Lankan judiciary has in the past declared government transactions that have violated applicable procedures to be null and void. In these cases, the Court invoked the PTD to hold that public power can only be used in trust and for the benefit of the people.[77] In the litigation involving the CPC, however, the petitions have been dismissed and the reasons for the dismissals are not yet available in the public domain.

3.9 Establishing the Colombo Port City SEZ

In January 2019, the first phase of the Project – the reclamation of 269 ha – was complete. Parliament then passed a resolution under the Administrative Districts Act to annex the reclaimed land known as "Port City Colombo" to the Divisional Secretary's Division of Colombo in the Administrative District of Colombo and to alter the limits of the Administrative District of Colombo to reflect the same. Under the same Act, on 5 August 2019, the Minster of Internal and Home Affairs and Provincial Councils and Local Government published an Extraordinary Gazette No. 2135/13 notifying the inclusion of Colombo Port City Land as a part of the Colombo Administrative District. Meanwhile, on 18 November 2019, the Rajapaksa regime returned to power under the leadership of Gotabaya Rajapaksa. President Gotabaya continued with the Project and, marking the inception of its second stage, Parliament published a bill on 19 March 2019 to establish a special economic zone (SEZ) called "Colombo Port City SEZ" and a body corporate called the "Colombo Port City Economic Commission" (CPCEC) for the purpose of its administration.[78]

This bill became the subject of an unprecedented public outcry against the establishment of the CPC SEZ and the CPCEC based on several grounds. First, opponents, mainly civil society groups, argued that these legal and institutional establishments could transform this artificial landmass into a "Chinese colony" that would not be subject to Sri Lanka's sovereignty.[79] Second, they disputed several provisions of the bill in advancing the idea that CPC will become a satellite Chinese province. They drew attention to the provisions that exempt (or limit) certain Sri Lankan laws from applying to the "Area of Authority"

---

[76] *Kariyawasam v CEA* [SCFR 141/2015, SC Minutes 04 April 2019]; Dinesha Samararatne, 'Chunnakam Power Plant Case: Court Recognises the Right to Be Free from "Degradation of the Environment"' (*Daily Financial Times*, 29 July 2019) www.ft.lk/columns/Chunnakam-Power-Plant-case--Court-recognises-right-to-be-free-from--degradation-of-the-environment-/4-682834.

[77] *Nanayakkara v Choksy (John Keels case)* [2008] 1 Sri LR 134; *Sugathapala Mendis v Kumaratunga (Water's Edge case)* [2008] 2 Sri LR 339.

[78] Colombo Port City Economic Commission Bill Gazetted 24 March 2021, http://documents.gov.lk/files/bill/2021/4/51-2021_E.pdf.

[79] Dinesha Samararatne, 'The Port City Bill: Legislative Carving Out from a Constitutional Democracy?' (*Groundviews*, 4 April 2021) https://groundviews.org/2021/04/18/the-port-city-bill-legislative-carving-out-from-a-constitutional-democracy/.

of the CPC SEZ.[80] Thirdly, opponent politicians argued that carving out an SEZ to which the normal regulatory regime of the country will not apply contradicts the signature political slogan of President Gotabaya: "one country, one law."[81] This allegation damaged the credibility of the Rajapaksa regime and President Gotabaya; in his presidential election campaign sternly criticizing the Hambantota Port lease, he had vowed to protect Sri Lanka's strategic national resources from foreign powers.

At the regional level too, this bill gained much attention among the regional and global superpowers who were already troubled by China's increased presence in the Indian Ocean Region largely through Chinese-funded infrastructure development projects in Sri Lanka. According to some, the proposed CPC SEZ will be the "Chinese colony in India's backyard," enabling China to find its way to the Indian subcontinent amid the intensified geopolitical rivalry in the region.[82] At the domestic level, the bill's constitutionality was challenged. In its Special Determination, the Supreme Court held that the bill as it was originally proposed undermined the supremacy of Parliament over legislative matters as well as over public finance. For instance, the bill did not provide for parliamentary approval of "Community Rules and Development Control Regulations" issued by the Commission.[83] Similarly, the bill did not provide for parliamentary approval for decisions of the Commission in granting individual tax exemptions or financial incentives. In certain other instances, the bill proposed authorizing the Cabinet of Ministers to exempt the application of laws specified in Schedule II of the bill to "Business of Strategic Importance." Those clauses were deemed inconsistent with the Constitution by the Supreme Court in its Special Determination.[84]

In designating the Port City as an SEZ, the bill sought to authorize the CPCEC to regulate entry and exit to the territory, but the Court held that these provisions were inconsistent with the Constitution as they amounted to a violation of the freedom of movement.[85] The bill vested broad discretionary powers with the CPCEC. In fact, the bill proposed to mandate that other administrative agencies "concur" with the decisions of the CPCEC. This proposed provision

---

[80] Saman Indrajith, 'Proposed Law Will Turn Port City into a Province of China – JVP' (*The Island*, 13 April 2021) https://island.lk/proposed-law-will-turn-port-city-into-a-province-of-china-jvp/.

[81] Amali Mallawaarachchi, 'Port City Bill Contradicts One Country, One Law Concept – Sajith' (*Daily News*, 17 April 2021) www.dailynews.lk/2021/04/17/local/246819/port-city-bill-contradicts-one-country-one-law-concept-sajith.

[82] Mohamed Nalir Mohamed Faslan, 'Regional Security Challenges and Chinese Port City Project in Sri Lanka' (*Instytut Nowej Europy*, 15 November 2021) https://ine.org.pl/wp-content/uploads/2021/11/Regional-Security-Challenges-and-Chinese-Port-City-Project-in-Sri-Lanka-1.pdf.

[83] Parliamentary Deb 18 May 2021, vol 283(3), cols 373–374 www.parliament.lk/uploads/documents/hansard/1621505793027313.pdf. (Special Determinations are published by Parliament.)

[84] Art 148 of the Constitution. ibid cols 385–386.   [85] Art 14(1)(h) of the Constitution.

clearly disregarded an entire body of the common law that has long established several principles on the limits to the exercise of administrative discretion. It cannot be under dictation, even by prevailing policies of the government of the day. The Court noted that the proposed clauses would amount to a violation of the right to equality as interpreted by the Sri Lankan judiciary.[86]

The Court also noted that "the regulatory structure set out in the Bill lacks clarity and provides for the exercise of arbitrary power by the CPCEC" and is therefore inconsistent with the right to equality. The Attorney-General's Department responded with proposals for a further set of amendments to the bill. In addition, the Court further determined that the CPCEC "should always obtain the concurrence of the respective Regulatory Authorities" and that those institutions will continue to exercise their powers "unimpeded" in the Port City.[87]

In the Special Determination of the Port City Bill, the Supreme Court departed from its previous view on the question of consulting provincial councils.[88] Previously, the Court had held that where a bill relates to a devolved subject and where one of the provincial councils cannot be consulted because it has not been constituted, the bill can only be passed with a special majority. In the Determination on the Port City, however, the Court took the view that the consultation of provincial council is a "procedural step in the legislative process."[89] The Court argued that where a provincial council has not been constituted, the principle *lex non cogit ad impossibilia* applies and that it was "not necessary" for the Court to determine whether the bill impacted on devolved subjects.[90] This is a significant inroad into the already weak recognition of devolution in the Sri Lankan Constitution and its implementation.

The bill also required that ordinary courts give priority to legal proceedings arising from the Port City. The Court noted that the objective of establishing the Port City is to create a "conducive environment" for new investments and that the speedy resolutions of disputes is of "critical concern" in this regard. On that basis, the Court determined that this was "a permissible classification."[91] The bill sought to restrict judicial discretion by providing that where a lawyer is unable to be present in the Court, it "shall not be a ground for postponement of commencement or continuation of the trial" or considered as "an exceptional ground" justifying postponement. During the hearing, the Attorney-General's Department proposed to revise this clause to require that courts prioritize legal proceedings emanating from the Port City and that those cases be heard daily except where, in the opinion of the Court, exceptional circumstances warrant postponement.[92]

In the Port City, disputes have to be referred to arbitration. The Supreme Court did not consider this as a contravention of the Constitution. The Court relied on the fact that any person within the Port City is "put on notice that

---

[86] Parliamentary Deb (n 83) cols 365–366. [87] ibid cols 369–370.
[88] Divineguma Bill Vol X (September 2013) SCDPB 69.
[89] Parliamentary Deb (n 83) cols 353–354. [90] ibid cols 357–358.
[91] ibid cols 413–414. [92] Colombo Port City Economic Commission Bill (n 78), Clause 63.

arbitration is mandatory in given circumstances." On that basis, the Court concluded that this provision was consistent with the Constitution.[93]

After making the necessary adjustments to ensure that the bill was consistent with the Supreme Court Determination, it was passed by Parliament on 20 May 2021. With the enactment of the Colombo Port City Economic Commission Act (the Port City Act), a distinctive legal regime was established to deal with matters exclusive to the CPC SEZ. This new legal regime coexists with the general legislative framework for facilitating inward foreign investments in Sri Lanka under the Board of Investment of Sri Lanka Law, 1978 (BOI Act). As mentioned in Schedule III to the Port City Act, which should be read with Section 73 of the same Act, the BOI Act does not apply within the "Area of Authority" of the Port City.[94] Understandably, this is because the Port City Act provides an alternative institutional arrangement for facilitating investors who wish to do business in or from the Area of Authority of the Port City.

The Project itself, notably its first phase, was fostered under the BOI Act and provided with incentives under the Strategic Development Projects Act (SDP Act) No. 14 of 2008. This Act aims to grant special concessions to special projects identified as "Strategic Development Projects."[95] This identification is done by the BOI in consultation with the relevant line ministries. The Port City is exempted from the SDP Act because Part IX of the Port City Act provides its own mechanism to grant incentives and exceptions to ventures designated as "Business of Strategic Importance." This designation should be done by the CPCEC in consultation with the Sri Lankan president.[96] In addition, the CPCEC is vested with competence to administer, regulate, and control "all matters connected with businesses and other operations, in and from the Area of Authority of the Colombo Port City" while acting as a Single Window Investment Facilitator.[97]

According to the Port City Act, the CPCEC consists of five to seven members appointed by the Sri Lankan president.[98] However, the president is expressly required to ensure that the majority of commission members, including the chairperson, are Sri Lankans. One of the main objectives of the CPCEC is to make the Port City an "attractive investment destination" and a prominent SEZ in the region.[99] The CPC SEZ is expected to facilitate the diversification of Sri Lanka's service economy, promote foreign investment, and generate new employment opportunities within the zone.[100] It is further expected to be an international business and service hub that promotes and facilitates an array of economic activities such as international trade, tourism,

---

[93] Parliamentary Deb (n 83) cols 411–412.
[94] The boundaries of the Area of Authority of Colombo Port City have been set out in Schedule I to the Port City Act.
[95] Section 2 and 3 of the SDP Act, No. 14 of 2008.
[96] Section 52 (2) of the Port City Act, No. 11 of 2021. However, in an event of the subject of Port City is assigned to a minister, the CPCEC should consult the relevant minister.
[97] ibid section 3 and 6 (g) Port City Act.   [98] ibid section 7 (1).
[99] ibid section 5 (a) and (b).   [100] Preamble to the Port City Act.

offshore banking and financial services, and shipping logistic operations. In order to achieve these objectives, the first set of regulations have recently been gazetted under the Act, specifying the fees payable to an "Authorized Person" to whom the CPCEC has issued or granted registration, licensing, and authorization as required by the Port City Act.[101] In addition, the CPCEC has issued regulations relating to the incentives and tax exemptions that will be afforded to ventures identified as Business of Strategic Importance as provided in Part IX of the Act.[102] Concerning dispute resolution, the CPCEC has appointed the International ADR Center, Sri Lanka as the designated international Commercial Dispute Resolution Centre required to be established under Section 62 of the Act.[103]

4 Conclusion

This case study provides insights into the contested nature of BRI partnerships in a given domestic host state context and raises many issues. In Sri Lanka, the political aspirations for economic development through FDI intersect with anxieties in the public domain about the China debt trap and loss of sovereignty. These political considerations have a broad effect on domestic politics, including on how charismatic leaders and political parties perform during presidential and parliamentary elections. In the legal domain, doctrinal questions about sovereignty emerge. They span international investment law, law of the sea, environmental law, constitutional law, administrative law, zoning law, and labor law. With respect to the Project, concerns of each of these aspects of law and the different legal doctrines have given rise to multiple legal contestations. Over time, these political and legal contestations have evolved and will no doubt continue to develop.

5 Discussion Questions and Comments

5.1 For Law School Audiences

1. The Port City Act is a law enacted by a sovereign state. On the one hand, this Act falls under the authority of a written constitution and is part of a domestic legal system. On the other hand, it establishes a statutory body, the CPCEC, which has the power to enter into contracts with foreign investors. In this context, what is the relevance (if any) of the Port City Act

---

[101] Gazette (Extraordinary) 28 September 2022 (2299/47). These regulations are made by the Minister of Finance, Economic Stabilization and National Policies in consultation with the CPEC as required by the Port City Act.
[102] Government (Extraordinary) Gazettes 2023 August (2343/60). These regulations are made by the Minister of Investment Promotion in consultation with the CPEC.
[103] Colombo Port City ADR Center (*International ADR Center, Sri Lanka*) www.iadrc.lk/index.php?option=com_content&view=article&id=74&Itemid=194.

and regulations enacted under the Act to the interpretation of any such contracts?
2. What are the significant contractual obligations of the Project on the government and the investor parties? Access the Act and its regulations and consider whether these obligations can be fulfilled within the Port City Act.
3. In Sri Lanka, the common law as interpreted within its Constitution applies to the judicial review of executive and administrative action. Judicial review of these actions is available under the writ and fundamental rights jurisdictions of Sri Lanka's appellate courts. How should these remedies apply to acts or omissions by executive or administrative actions within and in relation to the Port City?
4. What is your assessment of the approach to judicial review in the litigation related to the Port City discussed in the case study? How will the availability of judicial review compare and contrast with arbitration provided for through the International Arbitration Centre, as set out in the Port City Act for disputes arising in the course of business therein?

5.2 For Policy School Audiences

1. How should the Project be situated in the broader context of BRI as an example of how projects may affect the public law of host states?
2. What lessons can be learned from this case study about the impact of social movements (relating to labor, environment, etc.) on infrastructure development projects driven by FDI?
3. In examining the role played by different actors in this case study, what are the different approaches to development that can be identified? What do these different approaches suggest about the effectiveness of FDI on development?
4. How should policy and governance mechanisms and institutions innovate to deal effectively with the different challenges that are raised through projects such as the Port City?

5.3 For Business School Audiences

1. The Colombo Port City has been established as an SEZ with the purpose of accelerating Sri Lanka's economic growth. What role is the Port City Economic Commission expected to play in achieving the fundamental objective of establishing the Port SEZ?
2. There are different political and legal narratives about the Project. How do they impact the investors' confidence in selecting the Port City SEZ as a destination for their investment. The Colombo Port City Act permits the CPCEC to provide selected ventures doing business in and from the Port City SEZ with generous tax incentives and exemptions. The relevant

regulations have been already published. What is the role of such incentives and exemptions in promoting the Colombo SEZ as a business hub and how they would impact Sri Lanka's economy at large? The Port City Act identified alternative dispute resolution, notably commercial arbitration, as the predominant method of resolving disputes. Would such a method contribute to facilitating business to the Colombo SEZ, including fostering and attracting foreign investment?

Case Study 3.2

The Lower Sesan II
Human Rights Implications for Chinese Overseas Projects

Leigha Crout and Michael Liu

1 Overview

This case study examines the human rights implications arising from the construction of the Lower Sesan II dam, Cambodia's largest hydroelectric dam, and one seated at a tributary of the Mekong River. As a long-standing initiative first proposed by the Asian Development Bank in the 1990s, the Lower Sesan II was later adopted by and labeled a "key project" of China's Belt and Road Initiative (BRI). The dam was intended to dramatically expand access to reliable energy sources within Cambodia. As energy demand is expected to increase rapidly by 6–7% each year through 2025 in the Lower Mekong River Basin, the Lower Sesan II provides a valuable alternative to nonrenewable energy sources.

However, project developers and contractors face significant criticism as the construction efforts have displaced Indigenous communities and failed to address environmental reports that projected a substantial disruption to local biodiversity, adverse effects that were later documented by local groups and nongovernmental organizations (NGOs). Drawing from international, transnational, and domestic sources of law, and interviews with various community stakeholders, this study illustrates how Chinese parties building BRI projects engage with applicable human rights obligations through the example of the Lower Sesan II and discusses the consequences of noncompliance.

2 Introduction

The construction of the Lower Sesan II dam in 2018 represents the conclusion of a long-standing and international joint venture intended to address the large-scale energy demand in Cambodia.[1] Coordinated by China Huaneng Group (CHNG), a Chinese state-owned enterprise (SOE) owning a controlling stake in the project, Cambodia's Royal Group, and Electricity of Vietnam, it

---

[1] Asian Development Bank Regional Technical Assistance Team 6367, *Sesan, Sre Pok and Sekong River Basins Development Study in Kingdom of Cambodia, Lao People's Democratic Republic, and Socialist Republic of Viet Nam* (ADB 2010) www.adb.org/sites/default/files/project-document/74950/40082-012-reg-tacr.pdf.

has been designated by PRC officials as a "key project" of the BRI.[2] Investors committed the project to "ensuring the energy security, lowering the price of electricity, and reducing poverty in Cambodia."[3] With 400 MW power, the Lower Sesan II stands as the nation's largest hydropower dam and is projected to contribute to a regional initiative to provide clean energy beyond Cambodia to surrounding states in the region, thus decreasing the need for reliance on fossil fuels.[4] In light of the 2022 UN Resolution on the Right to a Clean, Healthy and Sustainable Environment's formal declaration that the "right to a clean environment" is a human right, this timely project might also contribute to global aspirations to cut carbon emissions for years to come.[5]

However, concerns about the dam's short- and long-term community impact were raised as early as 2008, when a corporate Environmental Impact Assessment (EIA) predicted substantial harm to local groups that would be displaced as a result of the construction.[6] A 2012 study published in *Proceedings of the National Academy of Sciences* echoed the initial report and added that the dam would significantly harm biodiversity, for example, projecting approximately a 10% loss of fish across the Mekong Basin.[7] Today, allegations of involuntary resettlement, deforestation, and significant negative impacts to water quality have all been reported as local communities and Indigenous peoples struggle with the loss of more than 34,000 ha of land.[8]

Drawing from bilateral investment treaties (BITs), corporate regulations and sustainability reports, impact statements, legal complaints, interviews with a range of stakeholders, and national and international human rights laws, this case study provides an in-depth analysis of the major human rights impacts

---

[2] 'Cambodia's Lower Sesan II Hydropower Dam Fully Operational' (*PowerChina*, 23 October 2018) www.chinadaily.com.cn/m/powerchina/2018-10/23/content_37174891.htm (state-sponsored media outlet).

[3] 'Cambodia Hydro Project Powers Up' (*China Daily*, 19 December 2018) https://global.chinadaily.com.cn/a/201812/19/WS5c19a94aa3107d4c3a00195c.html (state-sponsored media outlet).

[4] Royal Group, 'HydroPower Lower Sesan 2' www.royalgroup.com.kh/business-portfolio/energy-division/hydropower-lower-sesan-2; Asian Development Bank, *Building a Sustainable Future: The Greater Mekong Subregion* (2009) www.adb.org/sites/default/files/publication/29307/building-sustainable-energy-future.pdf.

[5] The Human Right to a Clean, Healthy and Sustainable Environment (26 July 2022) UN Doc A/76/L/75.

[6] '[Draft] Environmental Impact Assessment for Feasibility Study of Lower Sesan 2 Hydropower Project, Stung Treng Province, Cambodia – Executive Summary – OD Mekong Datahub' (*OpenDevelopmentCambodia*, 2008) https://data.opendevelopmentcambodia.net/agreement/draft-environmental-impact-assessment-for-feasibility-study-of-lower-sesan-2-hydropower-project-stu/resource/a4d6cd73-4ada-4436-88a2-e19325971255.

[7] Guy Ziv, Eric Baron et al., 'Trading-Off Fish Biodiversity, Food Security, and Hydropower in the Mekong River Basin' (2012) 109 Proceedings of the National Academy of Sciences 5609–5614.

[8] Stephanie Jensen-Cormier, 'Watered Down: How Do Big Hydropower Companies Adhere to Social and Environmental Policies and Best Practices?' (*International Rivers*, 2019) https://3waryu2g9363hdviilci666p-wpengine.netdna-ssl.com/wp-content/uploads/sites/86/2020/10/watered-down-full-report-english-compressed.pdf.

arising from the construction of the Lower Sesan II. It begins with an introduction of the relevant legal standards, including domestic legislation, regional agreements, and international human rights treaties. It then analyses the compliance measures undertaken by CHNG, its corporate partners, and the state and assesses whether human rights obligations were met by the relevant parties. The case study concludes with a summary of the above findings and suggests that further measures are needed to ensure alignment with human rights standards.

3 The Case

3.1 Background on Human Rights Obligations and the BRI

When undertaking BRI projects, both Chinese companies and the project's host country (in this case, Cambodia) are subject to three general categories of human rights standards that govern their conduct: international, transnational, and domestic. At the international level, states have agreed to respect, protect, and fulfill fundamental human rights through a series of treaties drafted by the United Nations (UN).[9] Nonbinding documents such as declarations and guiding principles also influence state and private actions taken by corporations, although they are not legally enforceable.

The transnational level includes binding standards and principles arising from bilateral agreements and regional treaties. BITs are included in this category,[10] and they typically govern the specifics of state-to-state investment projects. These agreements can have provisions governing human rights standards, transparency, and dispute resolution procedures, among other regulations. Finally, domestic rules refer to legislation governing the conduct of the state and private organizations. This includes constitutions, legislation regarding business practices and human rights, and any administrative regulations that might be applicable.

At each level, this framework demands substantive protections for human rights and high levels of transparency. However, multiple BRI projects have been under scrutiny in recent years for failing to meet the obligations imposed by human rights laws.[11] Legal complaints and international resolutions have been levied against Chinese SOEs and private corporations operating in several

---

[9] OHCHR, 'The Core International Human Rights Instruments and Their Monitoring Bodies' www.ohchr.org/en/core-international-human-rights-instruments-and-their-monitoring-bodies.

[10] BITS are included in transnational legal instruments given their often explicit commitment to "facilitate transnational investment flows." Kenneth J. Vandevelde, 'The Economics of Bilateral Investment Treaties' (2000) 41 Harvard International Law Journal 469, 472 (citations omitted).

[11] Between the years of 2013 and 2020, the Business and Human Rights Resource Centre "recorded 679 human rights abuse allegations linked to Chinese business conduct abroad." '"Going out" Responsibly: The Human Rights Impact of China's Global Investments' (Business and Human Rights Resource Centre, August 2021) www.business-humanrights.org/en/from-us/briefings/going-out-responsibly-the-human-rights-impact-of-chinas-global-investments/.

BRI countries, alleging systematic violations of human rights. Notable examples include withheld wages, unlawful deprivations of liberty, human trafficking, and failing to implement safety measures in hazardous working environments.[12] Other harms such as violations to the right of a clean environment have also been reported, although legal cases vindicating this right are rarer.

The case of the Lower Sesan II illustrates the challenges of ensuring transparency and compliance in multilateral projects like those within the BRI. The discussion below articulates the relevant legal standards governing the parties in this case, beginning with international human rights obligations.

3.2 International Human Rights Law

The international human rights instruments relevant to this analysis include the International Covenant on Civil and Political Rights (ICCPR) and the International Covenant on Economic, Social and Cultural Rights (ICESCR). These binding texts will be discussed in the context of Cambodia, as China is not subject to liability for violations of these instruments outside its territory. Under these treaties, it is Cambodia that bears the responsibility to protect and fulfill the rights of its citizens.

Relevant nonbinding texts with broader application include the UN Declaration on the Rights of Indigenous Peoples (UNDRIP), the UN Guiding Principles on Business and Human Rights (UNGPS), and the UN Resolution on the Right to a Clean Environment. China and Cambodia are party to these agreements.

The ICCPR has been signed and ratified by Cambodia, meaning that the state is legally bound to enforce the rights protections in its text.[13] Two rights are most relevant to this discussion. First, Cambodia is obligated to respect and protect the rights of subsistence, which holds that a people or group can freely dispose of their natural wealth and resources without interference by the state.[14] Second, minority groups are entitled to "enjoy their own culture, to profess and practise their own religion."[15] In General Comment 23, the Committee of the ICESCR discussed the latter and suggested that this right required the adoption of legal protections for traditional aspects of minority culture, such as hunting or fishing.[16]

---

[12] See, e.g., European Parliament RC-B9-0600/2021 (15 December 2021), which is a 'Joint Resolution on Forced Labour in the Linglong Factory and Environmental Protests in Serbia'. See also 'U.S. Department of Labor Secures $3.3 Million Judgment against Saipan Casino Developer for Systemic Wage Violations by Contractors' (*DOL*, 25 April 2019) www.dol.gov/newsroom/releases/whd/whd20190425-1.

[13] Cambodia acceded to the ICCPR with no reservations. See generally, International Covenant on Civil and Political Rights (adopted 16 December 1966, entered into force 23 March 1976) 999 UNTS 171 (ICCPR).

[14] ibid art 1 (2).   [15] ibid art 27.

[16] UN Human Rights Committee, CCPR General Comment No. 23: Article 27 (Rights of Minorities) (8 April 1994) UN Doc CCPR/C/21/Rev.1/Add.5.

The ICESCR has also been ratified by Cambodia, and requires the state to provide an adequate standard of living, "including adequate food, clothing and housing, and ... continuous improvement of living conditions."[17] States are further obligated "to ensure the realization of this right, recognizing to this effect the essential importance of international co-operation based on free consent."[18] General Comment 21 introduces a secondary obligation for states to respect the land rights of Indigenous persons.[19]

While the UNDRIP and UNGPS are nonbinding, their standards reflect broad international consensus on these matters. The UNDRIP has been signed by all recognized countries that are party to the UN, and the UNGPS has received widespread endorsement, including from China and Cambodia.[20] The UNDRIP mandates that governments consult with Indigenous peoples to receive their "free and informed consent" prior to making use of their lands.[21] Actions that displace Indigenous peoples from their lands are prohibited under this declaration.[22]

The UNGPS imposes obligations on states and corporate actors and defines potential avenues for remedies. Its core tenets mandate that the state protect its citizens from human rights abuses committed by third parties (including corporations); that corporations conduct human rights due diligence prior to and during its operations; and that states should enforce their human rights laws, with the cooperation of corporations.[23]

Unlike the other measures discussed here, the standards upheld by the UNGPS do apply to China and its domestic corporations. It holds states to account for human rights violations committed by its own organizations and imposes basic regulations on corporate conduct.[24] States moreover have a special responsibility to "take additional steps to protect against human rights abuses by business enterprises that are owned or controlled by the State," which here implicates SOEs like the Huaneng Group.[25]

Finally, the 2022 UN Resolution on the Right to a Clean, Healthy and Sustainable Environment grants the right to a healthy environment the status of a universally recognized human right.[26] While it has not yet been included within binding human rights treaties, a separate regime of international

---

[17] International Covenant on Economic, Social and Cultural Rights (adopted 16 December 1966, entered into force 3 January 1976) 999 UNTS 171 (ICESCR).
[18] ibid art 11.
[19] UN Committee on Economic, Social and Cultural Rights (CESCR), General comment no. 21, Right of everyone to take part in cultural life (art. 15, para. 1a of the Covenant on Economic, Social and Cultural Rights), (21 December 2009) UN Doc E/C.12/GC/21.
[20] United Nations Declaration on the Rights of Indigenous Peoples, UNGA Res. 61/295 (2 October 2007); UN Doc A/RES/61/295 (UNDRIP); UNSC Res 1373 (28 September 2001); UN Doc S/RES/1373 (UNGPS); The Coca-Cola Company, 'Human Rights Principles' www.coca-colacompany.com/policies-and-practices/human-rights-principles.
[21] UNDRIP (n 20) art 32. [22] ibid art 8. [23] UNGPS (n 20) I(A)(1), II(A)(15) II(B)(17).
[24] ibid. [25] ibid art 4. [26] UN Doc A/76/L/75 (n 5).

environmental law is dedicated to the protection of the environment and the promotion of sustainable societies.

3.3 Regional and Transnational Legal Standards

Transnational legal standards govern the business or diplomatic relationships between two or more state parties. They are contextual and can articulate specific procedures for investment, guidelines for private parties, and methods of recourse in the case of legal disputes. In the case of China and Cambodia, two instruments are relevant to human rights obligations: the 1995 Mekong Agreement and the Association of Southeast Asian Nations (ASEAN) Human Rights Declaration.

The 1995 Mekong Agreement is a regional directive concluded between Cambodia, Laos, Thailand, and Vietnam.[27] It governs "sustainable development, utilization, conservation and management of the Mekong River Basin water and related resources."[28] While the Agreement is nonbinding, it established the independent Mekong River Commission that is tasked with supervising the party states and their compliance with the text.[29] The main premises of the Agreement that relate to the right to a clean environment include the obligation to conduct a regional consultation prior to commencing major projects that would impact the Mekong, to protect the environment and cease actions that have a negative impact on the Mekong region, and to ensure adequate reparations are administered for violations of the Agreement.[30]

Like the international human rights declarations discussed in Section 3.2, the ASEAN Human Rights Declaration is similarly nonbinding. It requires that states provide an "adequate standard of living," which includes a number of guarantees; food, housing, clean drinking water, and a "safe, clean and sustainable environment" all fall within this right.[31] While inclusive, ASEAN rights are limited by important caveats. The text recognizes that the realization of rights can be limited by "political, economic, legal, social, cultural, historical and religious" factors, and that rights are subject to domestic laws that govern "national security, public order, public health, public safety, public morality, as well as the general welfare of the peoples in a democratic society."[32]

While additional transnational frameworks exist that govern transnational investment projects, they make limited references to the rights of

---

[27] Mekong River Commission, 'Agreement on the Cooperation for the Sustainable Development of the Mekong River Basin' (5 April 1995) www.mrcmekong.org/assets/Publications/policies/agreement-Apr95.pdf.
[28] ibid.   [29] ibid ch 4.   [30] ibid ch 5(B)(1)(b); art 7; art 8.
[31] Association of Southeast Asian Nations, 'ASEAN Human Rights Declaration' (18 November 2012) https://asean.org/asean-human-rights-declaration/.
[32] ibid art 8.

natural persons. The 1996 China-Cambodia BIT,[33] the ASEAN Comprehensive Investment Agreement,[34] and the 2009 ASEAN China Investment Agreement[35] do not refer to human rights or sustainable development, nor do they suggest that these texts be interpreted in line with applicable domestic or international laws on either subject. Although this is not uncommon, model or draft BITs have increasingly begun to explicitly recognize these obligations in recent years.[36]

3.4 Domestic Legislation and Regulations

Human rights protections found in domestic laws and administrative regulations may have significant bearing on foreign investments and can require strict coordination between the parties to ensure compliance. In the case of Cambodia, the state's Constitution, the 2001 Land Law, the 1996 Law on Environmental Protection and Natural Resource Management, and the 1999 Sub-Decree on Environmental Impact Assessment Process are relevant.[37]

While Cambodia's Sub-Decree No. 11 on Build-Operate-Transfer Contracts,[38] the PRC Administrative Measures for Outbound Investment by State-Owned Enterprises,[39] and PRC Administrative Measures for Overseas Investment[40] are informative, none contain provisions related to human rights.

Cambodia's Constitution codifies legal protections for the ownership of private property,[41] stipulating that "Legal private ownership shall be protected

---

[33] Agreement between the Government of the Kingdom of Cambodia and the Government of the People's Republic of China for the Promotion and Protection of Investment (19 July 1996) https://investmentpolicy.unctad.org/international-investment-agreements/treaty-files/571/download.

[34] ASEAN Comprehensive Investment Agreement (26 February 2009) https://investmentpolicy.unctad.org/international-investment-agreements/treaty-files/3095/download.

[35] ASEAN China Investment Agreement (15 August 2009) https://investmentpolicy.unctad.org/international-investment-agreements/treaty-files/2596/download.

[36] See, e.g., Netherlands Model Investment Agreement (22 March 2019) https://investmentpolicy.unctad.org/international-investment-agreements/treaty-files/5832/download; Accord entre le royaume du Maroc et ____ pour la promotion et la protection réciproques des investissements [Agreement entered between the Kingdom of Morocco and ____ for the promotion and protection of reciprocal investments] (June 2019) https://investmentpolicy.unctad.org/international-investment-agreements/treaty-files/5895/download (hereinafter Draft Model BIT Agreements).

[37] Other domestic regulations can be applied here but cover similar obligations. See also Royal Decree on National Protected Areas (1999); Sub-Decree on Water Pollution Control (1999); Sub-Decree on Solid Waste Management (1999); Forestry Law (2002); Law of Water Resources Management (2007); and Natural Water Resources Policy (2004).

[38] Sub-Decree No. 11 on Build-Operate-Transfer (BOT) Contracts (1997).

[39] 中央企业境外投资监督管理办法 [Measures for the Supervision and Administration of Overseas Investment by State-Owned Enterprises] (2017).

[40] 境外投资管理办法 [Administrative Measures for Overseas Investment] (2014).

[41] Constitution of the Kingdom of Cambodia (2018).

by law. The right to confiscate properties from any person shall be exercised only in the public interest as provided for under the law and shall require fair and just compensation in advance."[42] Similar to the ASEAN Charter, however, constitutional rights in Cambodia can be subsequently limited by other laws.[43] The legal rights to property within the Constitution have not been abrogated by other instruments at the time of this writing.

The 2001 Land Law specifically reserves several articles describing the inviolability of the lands of Indigenous peoples. In relevant part:

> The exercise of all ownership rights related to immovable properties of a community and the specific conditions of the land use shall be subject to the responsibility of the traditional authorities and mechanisms for decision-making of the community, according to their customs, and shall be subject to the laws of general enforcement related to immovable properties, such as the law on environmental protection.[44]

Two exceptions can apply to these provisions, including the government's "acting in the public interest" or in states of emergency.[45] Neither exception was defined within the law.

Finally, the 1996 Law on Environmental Protection and Natural Resource Management and the 1999 Sub-Decree on Environmental Impact Assessment Process require corporations to work in tandem with the Ministry of Energy both prior to and during construction to preserve the environment and promote sustainable development. The former requires that EIAs be conducted prior to any project, "private or public," without exception.[46] The EIA must then be reviewed by the Ministry of Environment and the Royal Government for approval.[47] The 1999 Sub-Decree on EIAs includes the specific procedures for these reports and requires a "Project Owner" to conduct their assessments in consultation with the Cambodian Ministry of Energy.[48]

In sum, there are significant human rights obligations governing Cambodia's and China's efforts during the construction of the Lower Sesan II. While most restrictions applied directly to Cambodia, Chinese corporations operating in Cambodia were nevertheless obligated to comply with Cambodian laws and the mandatory measures for the protection of human rights. Declarations signed by China also informed the state of best corporate practices that would meet desirable human rights standards. The remainder of this case study assesses whether the above obligations have been met through a review of relevant

---

[42] The right to own property is limited to citizens of Cambodia. ibid art 44. [43] ibid art 31.
[44] Land Law (2001) art 26. [45] ibid.
[46] Law on Environmental Protection and Natural Resource Management (1996) art 6. A new law on environmental protection is being considered but currently remains under discussion. 'In Cambodia, a Sweeping New Environment Code Languishes in Legal Limbo' (*Mongabay Environmental News*, 26 August 2020) https://news.mongabay.com/2020/08/in-cambodia-a-sweeping-new-environment-code-languishes-in-legal-limbo/.
[47] Law on Environmental Protection and Natural Resource Management (1996) art 6.
[48] Sub-Decree on Environmental Impact Assessment Process (1999) art 3.

parties' conduct. The analysis begins with the preparatory measures taken in advance of construction, moves on to the construction of the Lower Sesan II, and concludes with ongoing human rights implications.

3.5 Preparatory Measures

Under the above instruments, Cambodia and corporations involved in the project were obliged to undertake or enforce the following measures prior to constructing the Lower Sesan II: conducting an EIA to determine potential harms to the Mekong tributary, submitting an EIA to the Ministry of Environment, providing notification to parties of the 1995 Mekong Agreement, and consulting with Indigenous communities that might be impacted by the project.

Regarding the EIA, one of the corporations party to the Lower Sesan II project (Electricity of Vietnam) did commission such a report in 2008. Prepared by Key Consultants Cambodia, the report predicted exceptionally high damage to the Mekong region. By their estimation, approximately 5,000 people would face involuntary resettlement, 66% of local varieties of fish would be significantly impacted through the destruction of their migration roots, and 30,000 ha of forest would need to be flooded.[49] Reports from NGOs and academic publications further speculated that the authors or commissioners of the 2008 EIA reduced its initial predictions to project a less severe outlook.[50]

In response to this initial report, CHNG, an SOE, which has the controlling stake in the project, commissioned a second internal EIA that has not been shared with the public or its corporate partners.[51] As a result, it is not clear to what extent corporations operating on the Lower Sesan II project worked with Cambodia's Ministry of Energy to minimize anticipated environmental impacts. While the Ministry of Energy is required to disclose its work related to EIAs upon request under the 1996 Law on Environmental Protection and Natural Resource Management, this information has not been released.

The Mekong River Commission, tasked with gathering information on party compliance with the Mekong Agreement, produced a report on an "informal donor meeting" in 2013 during which the Lower Sesan II was the subject of controversy.[52] It suggested that other members of the Mekong Agreement appealed to Cambodia to provide more information on the project,[53] which was not provided. While the specifications of a project like the Lower Sesan

---

[49] '[Draft] Environmental Impact Assessment for Feasibility Study of Lower Sesan 2 Hydropower Project, Stung Treng Province, Cambodia – Executive Summary – OD Mekong Datahub' (n 6).
[50] W. Nathan Green and Ian G. Baird, 'The Contentious Politics of Hydropower Dam Impact Assessments in the Mekong River Basin' (2020) 83 Political Geography 102, 272.
[51] Human Rights Watch, 'Underwater' (10 August 2021) www.hrw.org/report/2021/08/10/underwater/human-rights-impacts-china-belt-and-road-project-cambodia.
[52] Mekong River Commission, 'Report: Informal Donor Meeting' (27–28 June 2013) www.mrcmekong.org/assets/Publications/governance/Report-IDM-2013-Complete-set-final.pdf.
[53] ibid C(7).

II would only technically require Cambodia to merely grant notice to other parties, the gravity of the project's anticipated impacts suggested that it might fall under the Agreement's prohibition against negative impacts on the region.

Finally, consultations with Indigenous communities prior to the construction of the Lower Sesan II did occur but were regarded as insufficient by the impacted parties and civil society groups.[54] Approximately 200 community representatives from the Sesan, Srepok, and Sekong areas adjacent to the project drafted a Joint Statement in 2008 protesting its construction.[55] They anticipated that the Lower Sesan II would destroy farmland, pollute the water sources and alter its flow, induce the extinction of certain types of fish within the area, and fundamentally disrupt the existing social infrastructure.[56] The government did not provide a response and formally approved the dam's construction in 2012.[57]

A second Joint Statement was then submitted to Chinese Ambassador Bu Jianguo in 2013 by the Sesan, Srepok and Sekong Rivers Protection Network requesting that China withdraw its involvement in the project. Affirming that the local communities were in fact experiencing significant environmental disruptions, the representatives noted that "no stakeholders have taken responsibility for addressing the impacts we face or [are] finding a solution to remedy the problem."[58] The Chinese government did not respond. A subsequent 2014 letter to Ambassador Bu and other Chinese officials likewise did not receive a response.[59]

Finally, in 2018, communities impacted by the Lower Sesan II project filed a Complaint with the World Bank Office of the Compliance Advisor Ombudsman. The Complaint indicated "concerns related to community resettlement, impacts on livelihoods, threats against community members opposing the project, damage to sociocultural significant sites such as ancestral graves and spiritual forests, and impacts on the fish population of the Mekong, Sesan, and Srepok Basins."[60] The Complaint has passed the initial Eligibility and Assessment stages and is now under investigation for compliance measures undertaken during the dam's construction.[61]

---

[54] Human Rights Watch (n 51).
[55] 'Joint Statement by the Sesan, Srepok, Sekong Community Network' (*International Rivers*, 11 June 2008) https://archive.internationalrivers.org/resources/joint-statement-by-the-sesan-srepok-sekong-community-network-4306.
[56] ibid.   [57] Human Rights Watch (n 51).
[58] Sesan, Srepok and Sekong Rivers Protection Network, 'The Joint Statement of the Communities along Sesan, Srepok and Sekong River to Madam Bu Jianguo Ambassador of the People's Republic of China in Kingdom of Cambodia' (*Mekong Watch*, 12 December 2013) 1 www.mekongwatch.org/PDF/LS2_statement_20131212_Eng.pdf.
[59] Sesan, Srepok and Sekong Rivers Protection Network, 'Urgent Request to Reconsider China's Investment in the Lower Sesan 2 Dam, Stung Treng Province, Cambodia' (26 May 2014) https://archive.internationalrivers.org/sites/default/files/attached-files/140512_cso_follow_up_letter_to_chinese_ambassador_-_final_-_english.pdf.
[60] 'Cambodia: Financial Intermediaries 01-03 | Office of the Compliance Advisor Ombudsman' www.cao-ombudsman.org/cases/cambodia-financial-intermediaries-01-03.
[61] ibid.

3.6 Construction of the Lower Sesan II

Several protected rights were implicated during the construction of the Lower Sesan II. One major event concerned compensation for displaced persons and families. The right to own property is protected by all three levels of human rights instruments, and special rights are reserved for Indigenous persons or communities and their traditional lands. This right is intrinsically linked to the right to culture. In recognition of the historic and cultural significance of these regions, international law and Cambodia's domestic regulations have created substantive legal barriers to the displacement of Indigenous peoples.[62] In the event that individuals do become displaced from their homes, the state or an agreed party is required to offer adequate compensation in advance.[63]

Although Indigenous communities actively protested the taking of their ancestral lands, few adjustments were made to the project's initial plan to flood culturally significant areas, such as burial grounds and traditional areas for hunting and fishing.[64] Civil society organizations produced reports that the level of compensation provided to the families by CHNG were insufficient and did not accurately reflect the cultural or economic value of the lands; as many as 180 families refused to accept the amount or leave their homes.[65] A submission to the UN Special Rapporteur on Human Rights in Cambodia suggested that residents within the impacted zones were pressured and intimidated into taking the compensation offered by the corporation.[66]

The right to an adequate standard of living, which includes housing, clean water, and the continuous improvement of living standards, was also compromised through limited rehousing efforts. CHNG and other corporations working on the site did not publish their resettlement plan, but Human Rights Watch determined through interviews that a parcel of land was given to affected persons, as well as a choice between a pre-built home or US$6,000.[67] The parcels were located on unfavorable ground for farming and cut off from the river. As further construction compromised the peoples' access to clean water, most were isolated from basic means of subsistence.[68]

Other concerns related to transparency have also been revealed through interviews with various human rights NGOs and other stakeholders. The

---

[62] See, e.g., Land Law (n 44) art 26.
[63] Constitution of the Kingdom of Cambodia (n 41) art 44.   [64] 'Underwater' (n 51).
[65] ibid.
[66] 'Submission to UN Special Rapporteur on the Situation of Human Rights in Cambodia Hydropower Dam Development in Cambodia: Lower Sesan 2 and Stung Cheay Areng Hydropower Projects' (13 January 2015) https://earthrights.org/wp-content/uploads/submission_to_special_rapporteur_on_hydropower.pdf.
[67] 'Underwater' (n 51).
[68] 'Lower Sesan 2 Dam Compensation and Resettlement Program Implementation Impacts on Indigenous Communities' (*Mekong Watch*, 5 November 2015) mekongwatch.org/PDF/LS2_NotesCompensationResettlement.pdf; Submission to UN Special Rapporteur on the situation of human rights in Cambodia Hydropower Dam Development in Cambodia: Lower Sesan 2 and Stung Cheay Areng Hydropower Projects' (n 66) 26.

authors interviewed participants across Cambodia, including those working with the United States Agency for International Development (USAID),[69] the Royal University of Law and Economics,[70] the Documentation Centre of Cambodia,[71] the Cambodia Human Rights Committee,[72] an NGO in Phnom Penh (name preserved to maintain anonymity),[73] and journalists in Chinese-language media.[74] Remarkably, none save one knew of the human rights dimensions of the project, despite their respective expertise in this area. While it is difficult to determine on these bases alone, it may be the case that this topic had been suppressed in the media, which is consistent with the state's recent crackdown on independent news organizations.[75]

Ultimately, 34,000 ha of land were flooded by the dam's construction.[76] While most of this was forest, 7,000 ha were used for farming.[77] The impact of the dam's construction on fish in the Mekong is still being realized, but reduced fishing yields and the projected extinction of regional species indicate that the region's biodiversity is in sharp decline.[78]

The impact of the Lower Sesan II's construction on the livelihoods of displaced communities in Cambodia has been profound – culturally, socially, and economically.[79] Many struggle to maintain their livelihoods on infertile ground far from the river and mourn the loss of sacred areas, including burial grounds and traditional hunting grounds.

3.7 Implications and Outlook

The Lower Sesan II was constructed to gradually improve the lives of Cambodians and may represent a significant step toward the realization of a

---

[69] Interview with Staff Member, USAID Cambodian Office, (Phnom Penh, Cambodia, 20 January 2023).
[70] Interview with Faculty Member, Royal University Law, and Economics (Phnom Penh, Cambodia, 17 January 2023); Interview with a Faculty Member, Royal University Law, and Economics (Phnom Penh, Cambodia, 19 January 2023).
[71] Interview with Upper Management Staff with the Documentation Center of Cambodia (Phnom Penh, Cambodia, 17 January 2023).
[72] Interview with an Attorney with Cambodia Human Rights Committee (online, 20 October 2022).
[73] Interview with Staff Member, An International Human Rights NGO's Cambodian Office (Phnom Penh, Cambodia, 17 January 2023).
[74] Interview with Journalist in Chinese language media (Phnom Penh, Cambodia, 17 January 2023); Interview with Journalist in Chinese language media (Phnom Penh, Cambodia, 18 January 2023).
[75] Human Rights Watch, 'Cambodia: Access to Independent Media Blocked' (2 August 2023) www.hrw.org/news/2023/08/02/cambodia-access-independent-media-blocked.
[76] Jensen-Cormier (n 8) 119.   [77] ibid.
[78] EarthRights International, 'Lower Sesan 2 Dam' https://earthrights.org/what-we-do/mega-projects/lower-sesan-2-dam/.
[79] Chia Chi Hsu, 'Power to the People? Cambodia's Lower Sesan II Dam, Two Years On' (*Southeast Asia Globe*, 23 December 2020) https://southeastasiaglobe.com/lower-sesan-ii-dam/.

collective right to a clean environment. The dam is projected to contribute to meeting rising energy demand in the Mekong region and decreasing the use of nonrenewable energy. In reducing Cambodia's reliance on electricity imports, it also promises to reduce everyday costs and promote accessibility to energy. While civil society organizations suggest that the dam's output is below what was initially projected,[80] it will reduce the complications that arise from the use of fossil fuels and sets a foundation for a regional shift toward renewable energy sources.

However, the lack of preparatory measures taken in advance of construction severely limited the intended environmental benefits. The most significant impacts referenced within the 2008 initial EIA were largely realized and will reduce the biodiversity of the Mekong exponentially over time.[81] Without knowing the full extent of the impact, it is difficult to weigh the harm to the Mekong against the benefits of establishing sources of renewable energy.

Finally, the historical and cultural sites cannot be recovered. Human rights law is predicated on the notion that the enjoyment of one's rights cannot extend to interference with another's. Substantive violations of binding international law, the failure to conduct a regional assessment under the transnational framework, and the rejection of domestic standards resulted in the flooding of sacred forests and burial grounds with great relevance to Indigenous people in Cambodia. It is clear that additional measures are needed to enhance human rights compliance in BRI projects.

4 Conclusion

The Lower Sesan II case is illustrative of the BRI's problematic engagement with applicable human rights instruments. This case and others suggest that Chinese SOEs like CHNG and host countries participating in BRI projects will need to carefully consider their human rights obligations at each level of governance to prevent further violations to human rights laws. To ensure compliance with applicable regulations, significant human rights due diligence should be conducted in advance, particularly with such large-scale projects.

This case offers insight into the short- and long-term impacts that can result from noncompliance with human rights regulations. First, the balancing of human rights – or the suppression of some rights to promote the enjoyment of others – created a problematic approach that minimized the rights of Indigenous peoples and likely reduced the environmental benefits produced by the Lower Sesan II.

These problems were exacerbated when Cambodia refrained from fulfilling or enforcing its human rights obligations. The Cambodian state and CHNG, which as an SOE is held to a higher standard of conduct under the UN Guiding

---

[80] ibid.   [81] Jensen-Cormier (n 8) 119.

Principles on Business and Human Rights,[82] did not engage with local communities, as required by Cambodian law, or consider the submissions of civil rights groups that suggested the dam would cause long-term environmental damage. As a result, significant harm was caused to impacted parties and the project's objectives were undermined. While Cambodia bears responsibility for the failure to ensure the rights of its citizens, both the Cambodian state and CHNG were complicit in ignoring applicable human rights standards.

Second, this case study reveals a significant gap in human rights protections between the bilateral and transnational level. The China-Cambodia BIT does not mention human rights within its text, which is inconsistent with the current model practice of including binding rights protections.[83] Moreover, the instruments that are on point provide significant exceptions that government actions might claim. Coordination at the level that governs the specifics of the relationships between the parties might be productive on human rights matters. Finally, further transparency will be essential in future projects if human rights are to be protected.

5 Discussion Questions and Comments

5.1 For Law School Audiences

1. One of the difficult questions presented by the Lower Sesan II case is how to – and if one indeed should – balance competing human rights interests. Human rights scholars and ethicists agree that some human rights are absolute, including the right to life.[84] The right to life cannot justifiably be leveraged against any other right or value. However, other rights may be subject to a balancing test when pursuing the common interest.[85] For example, privacy rights are frequently suspended in favor of public safety, like when a police officer acquires a warrant to search the home of a suspected criminal. In this case, the history, culture, and livelihoods of several communities were lost to the construction of the Lower Sesan II. Regardless of whether the corporate partners and the state followed ideal construction practices, once approved, the dam was projected to directly impact the cultural rights of nearby Indigenous communities. In contrast, the creation of the Lower Sesan II has generated a new source of clean

---

[82] UNGPS (n 20) at I(A)(4).   [83] Model Bit Agreements (n 36).
[84] The United Nations Human Rights Committee acknowledges that "The right to life is the supreme right from which no derogation is permitted, even in situations of armed conflict and other public emergencies that threaten the life of the nation." UN Human Rights Committee, CCPR General Comment No. 36: Article 6 (The Right to Life) (3 September 2019) UN Doc CCPR/C/GC/36; see also Luminita Dragne and Cristina Teodora Balaceanu, 'The Right to Life: A Fundamental Human Right' (2014) 2 Social Economic Debates.
[85] Francesca Bignami and Giorgio Resta, 'Human Rights Extraterritoriality: The Right to Privacy and National Security Surveillance' in Eyal Benvenisti, Georg Nolte, and Keren Yalin-mor (eds), *Community Interests across International Law* (1st edn, Oxford University Press 2018).

energy that may contribute to ameliorating the devastating impacts of climate change on a global scale. By reducing regional reliance on fossil fuels, the Lower Sesan II serves an important role in pursuing the human right to a clean environment. What considerations should be considered when balancing rights in this case? Should cultural rights be absolute, like the right to life? Does pursuing the common good of reducing global warming outweigh the specific interests of the impacted communities?

2. The legal scholar Ilias Bantekas argues:

> The persistent problem with investment-related human rights is not so much the indifferent or abusive behavior of foreign investors or their home States. It can generally be attributed to two factors: (1) host states' poor domestication and monitoring of their human rights obligations, which to some degree is predicated on the provision of investment guarantees that are detrimental to poor host states; and (2) the absence of a clear developmental plan and objectives [including human rights] in the pursuit of foreign direct investment.[86]

What do you think about this summary in relation to the instant case – were the parties' respective human rights obligations clear enough? And if Cambodia did indeed fail to provide a sufficient development plan in relation to the Lower Sesan II or enforce its rights laws, how much responsibility can be attributed to China's SOE that led this project, CHNG? Does the fact that Chinese representatives were on notice of these rights violations matter?

3. Relevant Cambodian law, international human rights treaties, and other regulations imposed binding human rights standards on the Cambodian government in this case. However, several other instruments that also bound China and CHNG, including the China-Cambodia BIT and China's domestic regulations (e.g., the PRC Administrative Measures for Outbound Investment by State-Owned Enterprises, and PRC Administrative Measures for Overseas Investment), do not include provisions related to human rights. Scholars are engaged in discussions of the merits of incorporating human rights obligations into transnational agreements, which is reflected in the growing consensus on incorporating rights goals within model BIT agreements.[87] Others like Bantekas, however, argue that the current model is proving insufficient in addressing major and ongoing corporate violations of human rights, and that domestic investment laws must evolve to meet these challenges. Would the inclusion of human rights

---

[86] Ilias Bantekas, 'The Human Rights and Developmental Dimension of Investment Laws: From Investment Laws with Human Rights to Development-Oriented Investment Laws' (2021) 31 Florida Journal of International Law 339, 340.

[87] See, e.g., Barnali Choudhury, 'International Investment Law and Noneconomic Issues' (2021) 53 Vanderbilt Journal of Transnational Law 1; Christine Sim, 'Strategies for Addressing Human Rights Violations in Investment Arbitration: Substantive Principles and Procedural Solutions' (2018) 12 Human Rights and International Legal Discourse 153.

standards at the transnational level help to clarify the parties' rights obligations, or should this be left to the realm of each state's legislature? Or, conversely, is the existing international human rights law system sufficient?

5.2 For Policy School Audiences

In this case, local Cambodian NGOs shed light on environmental and social harms brought by the Chinese SOE-led infrastructure project. In the context of nondemocratic states, how can SOEs collaborate internationally to support each other to oppose projects that violate international human rights? How can supranational bodies like the UN provide greater support to such active players in the international system who are upholding international human rights norms and standards?

5.3 For Business School Audiences

How can businesses implement best-practice ethical investment principles in large, international joint ventures like the Lower Sesan II? Discuss.

Case Study 3.3

The Special Economic Zone at Duqm, Oman

A Chinese-Invested Strategic Port

Otari Kakhidze

1 Overview

This case study examines a Chinese-Omani cooperation project in the Special Economic Zone at Duqm, Oman (SEZAD), and illustrates how its significance extends beyond the China–Gulf relationship with broader implications for trade and security in the wider region. It shows how a small fishing village followed the typical Gulf progress narrative of new infrastructure and skylines rising from the desert, and how this vision advanced in conjunction with increasingly Chinese-driven development. The case study demonstrates how a project that began as one of the ports along the Maritime Silk Road (MSR) has gained in importance as being at the intersection of security interests in the region.

With an area of 2,000 km^2 and a coastline of 80 km, the SEZAD is currently the largest special economic zone in the Middle Eastern and North African (MENA) region. It is a strategically located transshipment point for goods moving between Asia, Europe, and Africa and provides a crucial node in facilitating global trade and connectivity. The Sino-Oman (Duqm) Industrial Park is a major industrial park that is being developed within the SEZAD and is expected to attract investment of around US$10 billion. It will focus on a variety of industries including energy, manufacturing, and logistics, with key sectors for investment including agriculture, fishing, oil and gas extraction, the processing of foods, agrifoods, petroleum and nuclear fuel, the manufacture of chemical products, rubber and plastic products, automobiles, and building and construction industries.

This case study first discusses the overall context and considers the investment environment of Oman as well as Oman's relationship with China. It then concentrates on the SEZAD and highlights several aspects that make this case unique. These include the involvement of multilateral funding (namely, the Asian Infrastructure Investment Bank), the involvement of Chinese provinces in the development of an overseas industrial park, and issues for China as it invests in a neutral country, Oman.

2 Introduction

In February 2022, toward the end of the COVID-19 pandemic restrictions, the world witnessed a unique event: European monarchs, the king and queen of the Belgians, inaugurating a port in the Indian Ocean. The Omani Port of Duqm (ميناء الدقم) located in a sparsely populated Governorate of Al Wusta (الوسطى) which literally means "the middle" in Arabic), is poised to play a pivotal role in international trade and shipping today as part of the SEZAD, a Chinese-Gulf cooperative project. This mega project would not have been possible without economic investment from China. The Sino-Arab Wanfang Investment Management Ltd. (中阿万方投资管理有限公司) invested US$10 billion in the project that includes the tripartite urban arrangement of a port, an industrial park, and a residential district. Additional funding was provided by a Western consortium led by the Port of Antwerp, Belgium, with the project aiming to transform an unremarkable fishing village into a major industrial port city.

In the modern era, ports have undergone a transformation from being mere cargo-handling facilities to comprehensive industrial hubs with integrated infrastructure and associated complex contractual and legal frameworks. These state-of-the-art facilities are designed to optimize the process of receiving, storing, handling, and distributing goods in an efficient and timely manner.

While this concept is not new, the Port of Duqm is unique in its multifaceted strategic significance, which goes beyond the typical functions of a modern port. In fact, the largest investment in Duqm has been directed not only to cargo berths and terminals but also to a new city with its own industrial, residential, and tourist areas. Even considering the many Chinese-funded industrial parks across the world, this one is particularly ambitious, a fact which suggests that it is not merely a commercial investment by China but also a strategic decision.

Since the MSR encompasses strategically positioned ports that facilitate trade between Asia, Africa, and Europe, Oman's position at the crossroads of three continents and three seas has ensured its role as a critical link in the MSR for centuries. Historically, the Omani maritime empire also controlled the vast trade routes of the Indian Ocean. In fact, two key ports of the 21st Century MSR, both heavily supported by Chinese investment, Mombasa and Gwadar, marked the original outermost boundaries of maritime Oman before they were transferred to Kenyan and Pakistani governance respectively.[1]

---

[1] The Omani Maritime Empire is split between the Sultanate of Zanzibar, which controlled trade routes to Mombasa and the Sultanate of Oman, and Muscat, which owned the Gwadar port from 1792 until 1958 when Pakistan purchased it. See Beatrice Nicolini, 'Oman's Maritime Activities throughout the Indian Ocean 1650–1856 CE' in Abdulrahman Al Salimi and Eric Staples (eds), *Oman: A Maritime History* (Georg Olms Verlag Hildesheim 2017) ch 6. and Calvin H. Allen, 'Oman's Maritime History since 1856 CE' in Abdulrahman Al Salimi and Eric Staples (eds), *Oman: A Maritime History* (Georg Olms Verlag Hildesheim 2017) ch 7.

Many things have changed since the empire. One thousand miles north of Mombasa, Djibouti port has become a contested ground for "great power" rivalries; the United States and four European countries have set up separate military bases there along with the first overseas Chinese base. Gwadar and nearby ports retain their strategic significance but now as nodes in China's ambitious maritime trade network, the success of which has had varying effects on host countries as made evident, for example, by Sri Lanka's debt crisis. Regardless of such disruptive events (the latest being Hamas's attack on Israel and consequent responses taken by Houthis from Yemen), the Indian Ocean maritime routes remain crucial for global trade, with the Red Sea route alone accounting for around 30% of worldwide container traffic (more than US$1 trillion goods annually).[2] These routes are now coming under additional pressure with problems further north caused by Russian aggression in Ukraine and issues in the terrestrial Middle East as it struggles to find a new peaceful equilibrium.

Such chains of events in the region emphasize the possible role the SEZAD could play for the Gulf Cooperation Council (GCC) and worldwide, first because the terrestrial security issues of the Middle East tend to have a less immediate effect on neutral Oman and second because its coast remains far away from the heavily militarized territorial waters around the Horn of Africa and hotspots within the Red Sea where global trade routes can be disrupted.

3 The Case

3.1 Oman in the GCC

The Sultanate of Oman, a member of the GCC, is a small country with significant strategic importance in the region and to the world at large (for general details, see Table 3.3.1). It is situated at the intersection of three regions (South Asia, West Asia, and East Africa) and three seas (Arabian Sea, Oman Sea, and Indian Ocean). Consequently, Oman controls the Strait of Hormuz, a vital chokepoint for global oil shipments and other commodities. It is also an important link between the Indian subcontinent and the Horn of Africa, and Oman's ports provide a convenient stopover for shipping between these two regions. This strategic location makes Oman an important partner for China, as China seeks to expand its economic and political influence in the region.

In contrast to many of its neighbors, Oman is relatively peaceful and stable, with a long history of independent foreign policy, neutrality, and mediation. As a descendant of a powerful maritime empire, it has maintained close ties with both the Arabian and the Persian sides of the Gulf and these relationships have allowed it to play a crucial role in regional diplomacy, serving as a

---

[2] Robert Perkins and Max Lin 'Shippers Remain Wary of Red Sea Transit as Regional Tensions Rise', S&P Global Commodity Insights, 2024, www.spglobal.com/commodityinsights/en/market-insights/latest-news/oil/010224-shippers-remain-wary-of-red-sea-transit-as-regional-tensions-rise.

Table 3.3.1 Oman facts

Area	309,500 km² (coastline 2,092 km)	Labor force	2.259 million (2021 est.)
Population	3,833,465 (2023 est.)	Foreign labor	About 60% of the labor force are nonnationals
Government type	Absolute monarchy (Sultan Haitham)	Unemployment/ youth unemployment	3.12% (2021 est.) 4.6% (2021 est.)
Legal system	Mixed legal system of Anglo-Saxon law and Islamic law	Exports	US$46.324 billion (2021 est.)
Real GDP purchasing power parity (PPP)	US$155.028 billion (2021 est.)	Export partners	China 46%, India 8%, Japan 6%, South Korea 6% (2019)
Real GDP per capita	US$34,300 (2021 est.)	Imports	US$36.502 billion (2021 est.)
Ratings	Fitch: BB– (2020) S&P: B+ (2020)	Import partners	United Arab Emirates 36%, China 10%, Japan 7%, India 7%

Economic overview: high-income, oil-based economy; large welfare system; growing government debt; citizenship-based labor force growth policy; US free trade agreement; diversifying portfolio; high female labor force participation.

Source: Based on the CIA's 'World Factbook, 2024 Edition' www.cia.gov/the-world-factbook/countries/oman/.

mediator between the GCC and Iran, as well as between the United States and Iran. The country is thus a key player in efforts to maintain stability and promote cooperation in the Gulf region.

Oman has undergone a period of modernization and development over the past five decades under the rule initially of Sultan Qaboos bin Said who transformed the country, diversifying its economic priorities away from oil and exploring new avenues for growth. His successor, Sultan Haitham bin Tariq, the head of state since 2020, has continued this progress by providing a vision document "Oman 2040" focused on five strategic goals: further economic diversification, strong and inclusive private sector growth, sustainable and balanced development, efficient and transparent government institutions, and skilled and competitive Omani human capital.[3]

The future economic policy of Oman places significant importance on free economic zones (FEZs) as an investment instrument to achieve economic

---
[3] The Government of the Sultanate of Oman, 'Oman Vision 2040 | 2040 رؤية عُمان',', www.oman2040.om/assets/books/oman2040-en/index.html#p=19.

diversification and growth, facilitate international trade and exports, help Omani businesses to reach new markets, and create jobs for Omanis. Oman's strategic location and well-developed ports, including the FEZs around them, contribute significantly to the country's trade and economic growth. In 2020, Oman's ports handled a substantial shipping cargo trade volume of US$7,369 million, including 5.2 million TEUs of containers,[4] 18.4 million tons of liquid cargo, and 54 million tons of general cargo. The eight ports of Oman handle an annual average of 5,400 to 6,200 vessels, with Sohar, Salalah, Duqm, and the Port of Sultan Qaboos in Muscat being the most notable. The latter is also currently undergoing a gradual transformation to include a tourist port, enhancing its appeal in the region.

FEZs are special economic zones (SEZs) that offer a variety of incentives to attract foreign investment, including tax breaks, simplified regulations, and easy access to land and labor. However, SEZs and FEZs are not differentiated in Oman at the legislative level, in the Free Zones Law,[5] or in the decree establishing the Public Authority for Special Economic Zones and Free Zones (OPAZ).[6] The OPAZ lists only Duqm as a SEZ together with eight other strategically important entities it oversees including Al Mazunah Free Zone, Salalah Free Zone, and Sohar Free Zone. The terminological differentiation of Duqm's status may suggest greater plans for the SEZAD.

3.2 China–Oman Relationship

The ancient MSR forged strong cultural and trade ties between Oman and China, laying the foundation for a modern relationship that blossomed during Sultan Qaboos bin Said's reign. In 1978, the countries established formal diplomatic relations, recognizing the potential for mutually beneficial cooperation. The Sultanate actively participated in promoting cross-regional communication and interdependence. In addition to its strategic location, Oman is the fourth largest crude oil supplier,[7] reducing its dependence on traditional (coal) energy sources. Oman's neutral foreign policy and shared commitment to the five principles of Chinese Foreign Policy and International Law provide China with a valuable partner in the Gulf region, facilitating dialogue and conflict

---

[4] The twenty-foot equivalent unit (TEU) is a unit of cargo capacity often used for container shipping.
[5] Sultanate of Oman, مرسوم سلطاني رقم ٥٦ / ٢٠٠٢ بإصدار قانون المناطق الحرة [The Law of Free Zones Promulgated by Royal Decree (2002) (OM RD) 56/2002] published in the Official Gazette https://mjla.gov.om/legislation/gazettes/.
[6] Sultanate of Oman, مرسوم سلطاني رقم ١٠٥ / ٢٠٢٠ بإنشاء الهيئة العامة للمناطق الاقتصادية الخاصة والمناطق الحرة وتحديد اختص [The Law Establishing the Public Authority for Special Economic Zones and Free Zones and Defining the Jurisdiction Promulgated by Royal Decree (2020) (OM RD) 105/2020] published in the Official Gazette https://mjla.gov.om/legislation/gazettes/.
[7] 一带一路能源合作网 [Belt and Road Energy Cooperation Network] '中国能源进口量涨跌不一' [China's Energy Imports Are Mixed] (2022) http://obor.nea.gov.cn/detail2/16937.html.

resolution channels.[8] Oman's efforts in maintaining maritime security in the Gulf of Oman and the Arabian Sea align with China's goal of securing safe passage for its commercial vessels.

The trade volume between China and Oman has grown significantly in recent years (see Figure 3.3.1). In 2021, China exported goods worth US$3.13 billion to Oman, while Oman exported goods worth US$23.9 billion to China. In addition, there is a positive trend in cultural exchanges between China and Oman, with a recent increase in Chinese tourists visiting Oman and more Omani students studying in China.

The China–Oman relationship is likely to continue to grow in the years to come. The Belt and Road Initiative (BRI) provides a framework for further cooperation between the two countries, and both sides are committed to deepening their ties.[9] Much of this framework rests on the multilateral relations with the GCC, which have been developing for decades and achieved significant success with regard to the penultimate round of the China-GCC FTA negotiations,[10] the GCC Single Customs Union, as well as the establishment of a number of Sino-Arab platforms for economic cooperation such as the biannual China-Arab States Expo and the China-Arab States Cooperation Forum.[11] These are the main "umbrella" entities for multiple thematic platforms of South-South cooperation,[12] in which Oman has a mandate. In this sense, the creation of the SEZAD has not been just a bilateral effort and strategic partnership between Oman and China but an outcome of significantly wider regional cooperation.[13]

---

[8] The most recent codification of those principles on the national level are to be found in Art 4 of the Law of the People's Republic of China on Foreign Relations Adopted at the third meeting of the Standing Committee of the 14th National People's Congress on 28 June 2023, which states "互相尊重主权和领土完整、互不侵犯、互不干涉内政、平等互利、和平共处的五项原则" [The Five Principles of Mutual Respect for Sovereignty and Territorial Integrity, Mutual Non-aggression, Non-interference in Each Other's Internal Affairs, Equality and Mutual Benefit, and Peaceful Coexistence].

[9] National People's Congress of China, '王毅："一带一路"不是中方"独奏曲"而是各方共同参与的"交响乐"' [Wang Yi: The "Belt and Road Initiative" is Not a "Solo Piece" by China but a "Symphony" in Which All Parties Participate] www.npc.gov.cn/npc/c2/c10134/201905/t20190521_258030.html.

[10] Ministry of Commerce of the PRC FTA Service Network, '中国-海合会自由贸易区' [China-GCC Free Trade Area] http://fta.mofcom.gov.cn/article/chinahaihehui/haihehuinews/202209/49887_1.html.

[11] People's Government of Ningxia Hui Autonomous Region, 中国 – 阿拉伯国家博览会 معرض الصين والدول العربية [China-Arab Sates Expo] www.cas-expo.org.cn/zh/index.html; Ministry of Foreign Affairs of the People's republic of China, 中国 – 阿拉伯国家合作论坛 منتدى التعاون الصيني العربي [China-Arab States Cooperation Forum] www.chinaarabcf.org/chn/.

[12] Ministry of Foreign Affairs of the People's Republic of China, 新时代的中阿合作报告 [Report on China-Arab Cooperation in the New Era] (2022) www.mfa.gov.cn/wjb_673085/zfxxgk_674865/gknrlb/tywj/zcwj/202212/t20221201_10983991.shtml.

[13] Within the Chinese MFA classification of network of partners, Oman is named as a strategic partner (战略伙伴关系), which is different from the partnership (全面战略伙伴关系) level that China holds with Oman's neighbors: UAE and Saudi Arabia. See www.omandaily.om/عمان-اليوم/na/استراتيجية-وشراكة-متجذرة-علاقات-والصين-عمان. The PRC brands cooperate with the Arab states within the South-South Cooperation Framework while also maintaining the longer-term, civilizational perspective on the Sino-Arab relations. In the 2022 December Report on

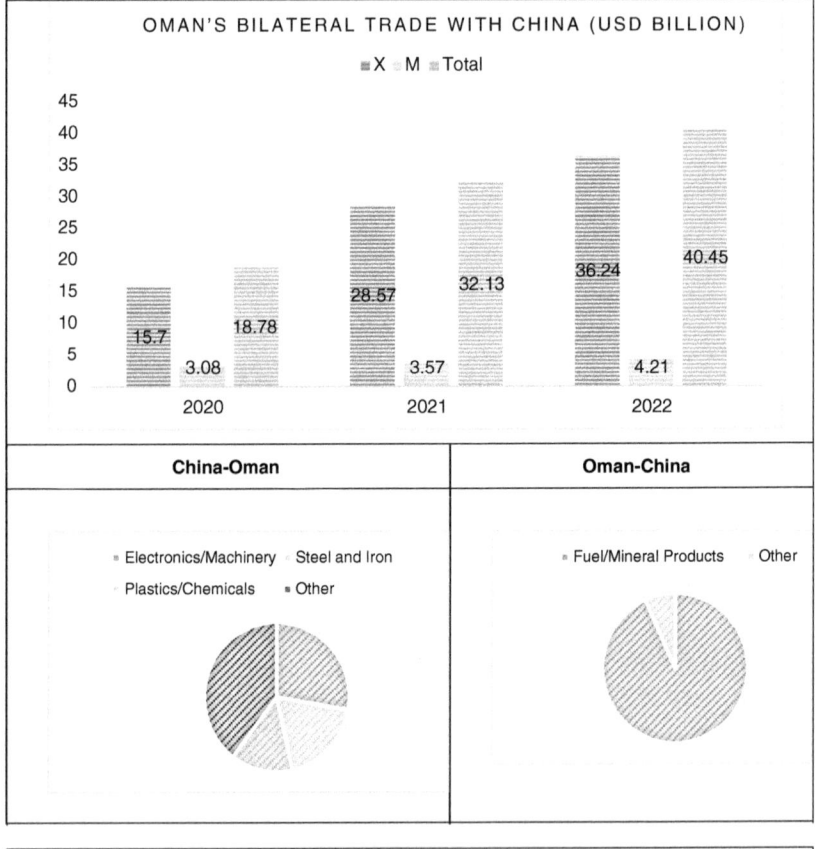

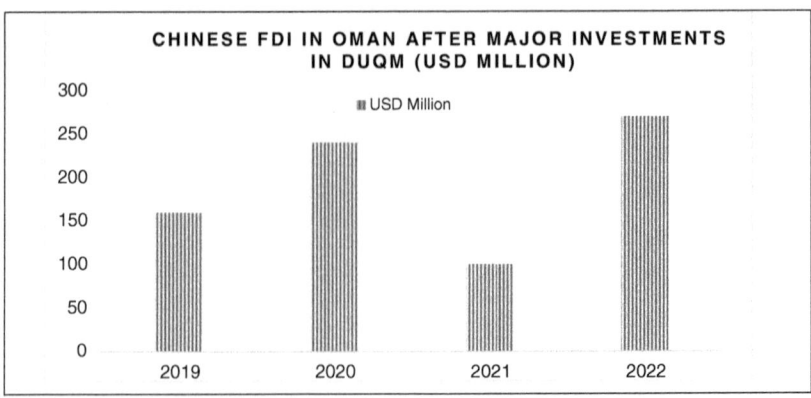

Figure 3.3.1 Oman–PRC trade statistics

Source: Compiled by author. Primarily based on the Chinese Ministry of Commerce data (see 中国商务部非洲西亚司, '双边合作简况' [Ministry of Commerce of the People's Republic of China, 'A Brief Overview of Bilateral Cooperation'] (29 November 2023) http://xyf.mofcom.gov.cn/article/tj/) since the Omani Statistical Office calculates trade volumes in the local currency and differentiates between the oil and non-oil merchandise (see National Centre for Statistics and Information, Statistical Bulletin: Foreign Investment, no.16, 2017–21, February 2023).

3.3 Local Labor and the Investment Environment

The vast majority of the Chinese projects in Duqm are carried out by migrant workers. The total migrant labor force in Oman is estimated to be more than 45% (1.6 million) of the total population in 2023, around 60% of which are migrants from India, Pakistan, and Bangladesh.[14] The construction sector is the largest employer of migrant workers, followed by the manufacturing sector and the services sector.

The situation is similar across Oman, which, like its neighbors, has a foreign worker sponsorship scheme, the *kafala* system.[15] Under this system, in order to obtain a working permit in the country, a foreign worker needs a sponsor (a *kafeel*) who must be a local citizen. This sponsor often ends up controlling the foreign worker's immigration documents, work permit, mobility, and even accommodation. The ethics and fairness of the working relations between the *kafeels* and the blue-collar migrant workers in the Gulf states has been subject to international scrutiny for some time.[16] In recent years, with the latest set of reforms in 2023,[17] the Omani government has implemented a number of progressive changes to the *kafala* system that has made it easier for workers to change jobs and leave the country without requiring their employer's permission.

Apart from the labor reforms, the SEZAD investors also faced the challenge of bringing their own workforce from China as there were already many middle-age male migrant workers in the construction sector in Oman as well as alarming levels of youth unemployment.[18] It must be noted that along with the high number of migrant laborers, the Omani government is currently reviewing the quotas for the minimum number of local workers in the private sector. The goal is to achieve a gradual and sustainable increase in the so-called Omanization (تعمينال) of the private sector labor force. Although benchmarks vary according to industry, the overall categories include the following goals by 2025: professional and

---

China-Arab States Cooperation in the New Era, the MFA of China refers to historical maritime and trade ties between the Arabian Sea and Chinese ports in the dynastic times while President Xi listed inter-civilizational dialogue as one of the eight major initiatives on China-Arab practical cooperation during the historical visit in Riyadh. See The State Council of the People's Republic of China, 习近平在首届中国—阿拉伯国家峰会上提出中阿务实合作"八大共同行动" [Xi Jinping Proposed "Eight Major Common Actions" for China-Arab Practical Cooperation at the First China-Arab Summit] www.gov.cn/xinwen/2022-12/10/content_5731138.htm.

[14] UN Department of Economic and Social Affairs – Population Division, and UNICEF, 'Migration Profiles, Oman – Common Set of Indicators' (2014) https://esa.un.org/miggmgprofiles/indicators/files/Oman.xlsx.

[15] International Labour Organization, 'Labour Migration in the Arab States', www.ilo.org/beirut/areasofwork/labour-migration/WCMS_514910/lang–en/index.htm.

[16] Migrant Forum in Asia Secretariat, 'Policy Brief No. 2: Reform of the Kafala (Sponsorship) System' www.ilo.org/dyn/migpractice/docs/132/PB2.pdf.

[17] Sultanate of Oman, مرسوم سلطاني رقم ٥٣ / ٢٠٢٣ بإصدار قانون العمل [Labour Law Promulgated by Royal Decree (2023) (OM RD) 53/2023] published in the Official Gazette.

[18] World Bank, 'Oman Economic Update' (April 2019) www.worldbank.org/en/country/gcc/publication/oman-economic-update-april-2019.

technical occupations, 80%; administration and clerical occupations, 60%; service occupations, 50%; trade and sales occupations, 40%; production and related occupations, 30%. Such sensitivity toward the local labor force might have a negative effect on Oman's attractiveness for foreign investment, although in the case of the SEZAD, it seems this sensitivity has avoided problems, mostly due to the government's public diplomacy efforts. However, such labor law restrictions could pose additional barriers in the future for Chinese companies hoping to hire local employees in Duqm. Owing to the remote location of the area (more than 500 km from major urban centers), there are not many Omanis willing to relocate to Duqm.

Similar to its Gulf neighbors, Oman used to have restrictive investment laws that imposed on foreign investors a minimum cap for investment volume of around US$500,000 per investor as well as restricted single corporate shareholder incorporation. In addition, laws required foreign investors to partner with an Omani company and limited the number of shares that could be owned by foreign representatives. Owing to the liberalization of foreign direct investment (FDI) legislation, the Commercial Companies Law (2019) allowed single shareholder incorporation,[19] and was followed by the new Foreign Capital Investment Law (2019),[20] which allowed simplified procedures for setting up wholly foreign-owned companies that permitted 100% share ownership in most types of business.

In addition to the more liberalized foreign investment rules that operate at the national level, the SEZAD offers specific incentives to investors such as no minimum registered capital and full foreign ownership, tax exemptions for thirty years, full repatriation of capital and profit, as well as free import or reexport duties. Even though land use is limited to fifty years, the duration can be renewed. The Sino-Oman Industrial Park is therefore at the heart of an advantageous free zone offering attractive incentives for foreign capital. The park has also received permission to build its own water and power plants, and products processed in the zone are regarded as local products for export. One-stop service centers provide businesses with the services they need, including registration, licensing, visas, and residence permits for expatriates. Such reforms are expected to work in favor of Chinese investors in Duqm, especially as they have pledged to invest in the SEZ to help attract additional FDI from across the globe.

3.4 Major Chinese Investors in Duqm

The Sino-Arab Wanfang Investment Management Ltd. is one of the major investors in the SEZAD. It is a Chinese company that was founded in 2015, has

---

[19] Sultanate of Oman, مرسوم سلطاني رقم ١٨ / ٢٠١٩ بإصدار قانون الشركات التجارية [Commercial Companies Law Promulgated by Royal Decree (2019) (OM RD) 18/2019] published in the Official Gazette.
[20] Sultanate of Oman, مرسوم سلطاني رقم ٥٠ / ٢٠١٩ بإصدار قانون استثمار رأس المال الأجنبي [The Foreign Capital Investment Law Promulgated by Royal Decree (2019) (OM RD) 50/2019] published in the Official Gazette.

a registered capital of RMB 200 million, and is headquartered in the Ningxia Autonomous Region. It has a focus on investment and management in the Middle East region. Company subsidiaries were established under the leadership and with the support of the Ningxia Hui Autonomous Region (NHAR) Government, a provincial-level jurisdiction within the PRC, and include Ningxia Shunyi Assets Management Ltd., Ningxia Water Investment Group Co. Ltd., Ningxia Construction Investment Group, Ningxia Residence Group Co. Ltd., Yinchuan Yushun Oilfield Services Technologies Co. Ltd., Yinchuan Fangda Electric Engineering Company, and the Ningxia Small and Medium Sized Enterprises (SME) Association.[21]

In 2016, the Oman Wanfang LLC was formed as a joint venture company by the Sino-Arab Wanfang Investment Management Company and the SEZAD with the sole aim of developing and operating the Sino-Oman (Duqm) Industrial Park. The cooperation agreement between Oman Wanfang LLC and the SEZAD was signed on 23 May 2016 by Yahya Al-Jabri, chairperson of the SEZAD, and Ali Shah, chairperson of Oman Wanfang LLC.[22] As part of the comprehensive agreement for land lease development cooperation, Oman Wanfang was granted 1,172 ha of land for the next fifty years for the development of the Industrial Park. This park is divided into three sections: a heavy industrial area of 809 ha, a light industrial complex of 353 ha, and a five-star hotel and tourist area occupying 10 ha.

The total investment for the development of the industrial park is estimated to be US$10.7 billion, which is funded by Chinese companies and financed by Chinese banks. At initiation in 2016, ten projects worth more than US$3 billion had been signed by Oman Wanfang LLC and its investors from China. These included:

- A building materials market.
- A methanol and methanol-to-olefin project.
- A power station.
- A seawater desalination and bromine extraction plant.
- A high-mobility SUV project.
- A solar equipment manufacturing base.
- A plant for the manufacture of oil country tubular goods.
- A plant for the manufacture of nonmetal composite pipes used in oil fields.
- A plant for the manufacture of steel thread frame reinforced polyethylene pipes and their parts.
- A five-star hotel.

[21] The official names of those companies are 宁夏顺亿资产管理有限公司, 宁夏水务投资集团有限公司, 宁夏建工集团有限公司, 宁夏住宅建设发展(集团)有限公司, 银川玉顺油田服务科技股份有限公司, 银川方达电子系统工程有限公司, 宁夏中小企业协会 respectively.
[22] Special Economic Zone Authority at Duqm, A Quarterly Magazine, '$10.7 Billion in Investments in the Sino-Oman Industrial City' (Issue 5, July 2016) 10 https://duqm.gov.om/upload/publications/en_SEZAD_Quarterly_Magazine_Issue_5.pdf.

In addition to the direct investments made by Chinese companies there was also notable support extended by a multilateral body, the Asian Infrastructure Investment Bank (AIIB).

3.5 AIIB Support

The AIIB, with headquarters in Beijing, has emerged as an alternative development finance institution. Given its focus on the Asian region as well as close ties with the GCC, in September 2023 the Bank established its first overseas office in Oman's neighbor, the United Arab Emirates.[23] Even though the AIIB was established as a Chinese initiative, the PRC currently holds only 27% of its voting shares; the rest are owned by its member countries, with Oman being one of the founding members. Having a wide portfolio, the AIIB has already funded development projects in thirty-six of its member countries, including Oman, which was one of the first high-income countries supported by the AIIB.

The AIIB contributed a US$265 million sovereign-backed long-term loan.[24] Such an amount might look relatively modest in comparison to the Chinese private capital invested in Duqm. Yet, considering the timing and destination of the AIIB contribution, its loan was essential for securing the Duqm Port Loan and launching the SEZAD. In fact, the loan proved instrumental during the early days when the SEZ focused on the port and refinery and project work involved building port-related infrastructure such as access roads, terminal buildings, and operational zone facilities.[25] The project was successfully completed by the end of 2023,[26] and the AIIB assessed the degree of the project readiness positively: "reflected by the high quality of client staff and consultants" the project was implemented with a "high degree of transparency on construction arrangements."[27] The stated indicators of the long-term loan are directly linked to the operational capacity and profitability of the Duqm port during a ten-year monitoring period from the date of completion.

It must be noted that the conditions of the contract were based on the construction laws of Oman as the host country,[28] and that an Environmental

---

[23] Asian Infrastructure Investment Bank, 'AIIB Inaugurates Overseas Office in Abu Dhabi' (20 September 2023) www.aiib.org/en/news-events/news/2023/AIIB-Inaugurates-Overseas-Office-in-Abu-Dhabi.html.

[24] Twenty-five-year term, including a grace period of five years, at the AIIB's standard interest rate for sovereign-backed loans.

[25] Asian Infrastructure Investment Bank, 'Sultanate of Oman Duqm Port Commercial Terminal and Operational Zone Development Project' (PD 0013-OMN, 2016) www.aiib.org/en/projects/approved/2016/_download/duqm-port-commercial/document/20161213051938915.pdf#page7.

[26] Asian Infrastructure Investment Bank, 'Project Completion Note Sultanate of Oman: Duqm Port Commercial Terminal and Operational Zone Development Project' (3 November 2023) www.aiib.org/en/projects/details/2016/approved/_download/Oman/AIIB-PCN_L000013-Oman-Duqm-Port-Project.pdf.

[27] ibid.

[28] Sultanate of Oman, ۱۹۹۹، الطبعة الرابعة، سلطنة عمان العقد الموحد لإنشاء المباني والأعمال المدنية، الطبعة الرابعة [Standard Documents for Building and Civil Engineering Works (Fourth Arabic Edition), September 1999].

Assessment was conducted as required by the Omani authorities. The project also complied with the AIIB environmental and social safeguards, health and safety requirements, and the Construction Environmental Management Plan. The Environment and Social Policy low-risk category was assigned to the project as it was claimed to be implemented on reclaimed land, without land acquisition, resettlement,[29] or marine works. The SEZAD team received training from international procurement and financial management specialists on tendering, auditing, and best financial practices. All contractor variation orders were subject to approval by the SEZAD's implementation unit.

Thus, the SEZAD has become a model project supported via different institutional layers, including international ones in the form of the multilateral financial institution AIIB as well as by private sector companies from the PRC. Interestingly, there is another layer of stakeholders that might be overlooked – at the regional level within the PRC – as Chinese companies that have invested in the SEZAD often have clear regional affiliations. In summary, it could be said that the SEZAD is an example of input from multilateral, national (e.g., government negotiations), regional (e.g., companies from Ningxia), and private sector levels.

3.6 Choice of Ningxia: Winning the Hearts and Minds of the Local Population

It may be surprising that the NHAR, one of the poorest inland areas of China, is playing an active role in the construction of the SEZAD given that it is landlocked in the middle of China. Ningxia has, in recent years, garnered a new life as the Chinese national government has branded it as the gateway to the Arab world and the successor to the historic Silk Road toward the Arabian Sea.[30] Ningxia is relevant not just because of its location but also because of its demographics. It is home to one of the ethnoreligious minorities in China, the Chinese Muslim or Hui people (回族). Their ethnic and linguistic ties to the Muslim world have been a significant factor in enabling investments along the Arabian coast.

---

[29] The claim that there was no resettlement could be an overstatement and requires a detailed examination of the Environment and Social Policy methodology. The Bedouin lifestyle involves seasonal migratory patterns between the coastal and desert areas that might be overlooked in analysis. Such projects as the SEZAD, as elsewhere in the Gulf, make a sedentary lifestyle for coastal and desert communities inevitable and usually include provision of residential spaces. Duqm fishing village is recorded to have less than 5,000 people, and as evident from the recent (and so far, only) detailed area study, humans were present there as early as neolithic times; there is also a picturesque natural rock formation in the hinterland of the current SEZ that should be considered in the environmental and tourism efforts in the context of the new Duqm. See [مريم بنت سعيد البرطمانية' ادقم عراقة الارض وجسور المستقبل] Maryam bint Saeed Al-Bartmaniyah, Advance the Earth's Legacy and Bridges to the Future (February 2019)].

[30] Matthew S. Erie, *China and Islam: The Prophet, the Party, and Law* (Cambridge University Press 2017) ch 6.

The NHAR government has organized the biannual China-Arab States Expo since 2013 in Yinchuan, cosponsored by the Ministry of Commerce and the China Council for the Promotion of International Trade (which serves as a bridge in promoting trade and investment between China and Arab states). The Expo has also been an opportunity to select appropriate partnerships for international industrial capacity development from the Arab countries, showcasing common investment projects along the BRI, including the Sino-Oman Industrial Park.[31]

The people-to-people exchanges associated with the Duqm development are not limited to high-level diplomatic exchanges but extend to people working within the SEZ. The core pattern is inbound migration of the host country population to China for cultural and educational exchanges as well as Chinese initiatives to support the development of training and professional development centers locally. It was announced that the Duqm project would help build the city, contributing not only to the development of Oman's economic diversification but also to local employment including upgrading the professional skills of young Omani workers. This decision could be seen as both benefiting the local economy and enabling Chinese investors to meet the compulsory Omanization requirement while maintaining a skilled workforce in the Industrial Park.

An initiative to send 1,000 Omani students to China on Wanfang scholarships began in 2018 and funds students to train at the Ningxia Polytechnic in Yinchuan. Courses relate to petrochemical engineering, construction materials, computer software, technology, renewable energy, petroleum equipment, and economic management – thus following the economic profile of the Duqm Industrial Park by developing training courses specifically related to SEZAD skills requirements.[32]

The choice of the NHAR with its historical ties with the Muslim world serves as an apparatus of soft power. Supporting cultural and educational professional training and taking account of the employment perspectives in a predominantly young population could be interpreted as supporting the positive image of China in Oman. Oman Wanfang LLC has further undertaken to build a school for children with special needs and facilitate community greening initiatives, such as planting trees, recycling waste, and using renewable energy

---

[31] According to the Expo website, the previous five sessions of the Expo have attracted 24 Chinese and foreign dignitaries, 318 Chinese and foreign ministerial-level officials and more than 6,000 domestic and foreign enterprises from 112 countries and regions. A total of 1,213 cooperation projects have been signed in areas including agriculture, new technology, energy and chemicals, bio-pharmacy, equipment manufacturing, infrastructure, 'Internet plus healthcare', and tourism.

[32] [Oman جريدة عمان, "عُمان والصين, علاقات متجذرة وشراكة استراتيجية" سعادة سفيرة جمهورية الصين الشعبية لدى سلطنة عمان Newspaper, 'Oman and China… deep-rooted relations and strategic partnership' Her Excellency the Ambassador of the People's Republic of China to the Sultanate of Oman] www.omandaily.om/عمان-اليوم/na/عمان-استراتيجية-وشراكة-متجذرة-علاقات-والصين-عمان. (6 July 2023)

sources. Such projects aim to establish a strong and sustainable partnership with the Omani government and people and are examples of very effective public diplomacy that rests on the shared values between two countries, in this case predominately religious values.[33]

3.7 "One Province One Country" and Overseas Industrial Parks

The fact that all the major Chinese investors are from the NHAR appears to follow the noteworthy "one province one country" (一省一国) model. This is not an officially stated slogan of the Chinese government, yet it has been frequently used in the development context, especially with respect to the pandemic.[34] However, the slogan, and more importantly, the concept it signifies, had been used in the context of Chinese development before the pandemic, including by one of the investors in the SEZAD.[35] The matching of sovereign states with Chinese provincial and prefectural administrative units is a significant development in China's industrial transfer policy, and, in the case of the SEZAD, the NHAR is not just transferring capital and technology to the Middle East but also transferring its own domestic institutions and business expertise to inform the setting up of the Industrial Park.

The timeline for selecting such cooperative ventures can be explored using the SEZAD as an example.

- Selecting cooperative countries for overseas park construction:
  - Ningxia SME Association and Ningxia Expo Bureau organized multiple visits of Chinese private sector representatives to Arab countries.
  - Choice of Oman for the Sino-Arab Industrial Park; visits to potential locations in Muscat, Salala, and Duqm. Select the latter for the construction.
- Strengthening the organization and leadership of industrial park construction:
  - Formation of the Sino-Arab Industrial Park construction coordination and promotion working group.
    - The working group promoted mechanisms involving representatives of the:
      - Ningxia NDRC (the National Development and Reform Commission) (for formulation of the overall plan for the park);

---

[33] For public diplomacy, see Hamed Al-Hasni 'The Role of China's Public Diplomacy in Promoting the Belt and Road Initiative in Oman through Communication' (2019) 17 Global Media Journal 32.

[34] 一省包一国 had been used to refer to the pandemic aid packages sent from individual Chinese provinces to specific countries; independent from the pandemic context, there are other provinces with similar connections to the other parts of the world, such as Ningxia to the Arabian Gulf (e.g., Xinjiang and Central Asian countries).

[35] 解孟林, '立足"一省一国"模式推进宁夏国际产能合作'(2016) 中国经贸导刊 [Xie Menglin, 'Promoting Ningxia's International Production Capacity Cooperation Based on the "One Province, One Country" Model' (2016) China Economic and Trade Guide] 3, 21–22 https://d.wanfangdata.com.cn/periodical/zgjmdk201603011. In this short article, the Head of the Ningxia SME Association lists several steps on how the Ningxia investors chose Oman and the designated SEZ for their investment.

- the Information Commission, the Department of Commerce, the Expo Bureau (for supporting its promotion);
    - the Department of Finance (to study Omani financial regulation and policies);
    - the Foreign Affairs Office (working with Omani partners and learning FDI regulations); and
    - the Ningxia Branch of the National Development Bank of China, the Ningxia Branch of the Bank of China (access to finance for overseas investments).
- Planning of the industrial park:
  - Ningxia DRC commissions the Foreign Economic Cooperation Department of the China International Engineering Consulting Corporation (CIECC) to prepare the master plan of the Sino-Arab Industrial Park in Duqm.
  - The CIECC Master Plan aims to:
    - guide the infrastructure construction;
    - attract investments from all over the world;
    - plan industrial fields;
    - lay out major projects; and
    - drive enterprises from Ningxia and regions to go global.[36]
- Determining the areas and priorities for industrial park construction:
  - Cooperation agreement signed between the Ningxia Government and Oman on the industrial park approving the proposed layout of the park as well as the industries to promote given the resource allocation in the region, access to markets, and advantages of the Chinese manufacturing industry, promoting China's international production capacity cooperation.[37]
- Selecting enterprises:
  - Only at this stage does Ningxia invite and select those private companies that are going to be primary investors in the industrial park as well as enterprises from other Chinese provinces that invest in individual projects.
- Formulating work programs for the construction of industrial parks:
  - This stage includes initiating the construction projects in accordance with the master plan.

Such a process for international capacity development, and in particular the role of subnational or province-level actors, is a significant departure from the traditional approach to foreign investment, which has often been characterized by a top-down approach from international institutions. It is a novel approach,

---

[36] Other provinces and countries come into picture at this stage; prior to this it is solely the responsibility of the Ningxia province.
[37] 中国政府网,'李克强：用中国装备和国际产能合作结缘世界推动形成优进优出开放型经济新格局', 2015年4月3日 [Chinese Government Network, 'Li Keqiang: Use Chinese Equipment and International Production Capacity Cooperation to Connect with the World and Promote the Formation of a New Open Economic Pattern That Optimizes Entry and Exit' (3 April 2015)] www.gov.cn/govweb/guowuyuan/2015-04/03/content_2842768.htm.

specific to China, and the interplay between the provincial entities and enterprises that took place in case of the SEZAD could be generalized to planning and policy approaches used for the other thirty-nine Chinese Overseas Industrial Parks (COIPs),[38] as the majority of them have strong provincial affiliations. By pairing its domestic administrative units with foreign countries, China is taking a more proactive approach to its foreign investment strategy, moving away from Western-led international institutions such as the World Bank and the International Monetary Fund (IMF) and adapting its approach to align more with multilateral development banks such as the AIIB. This gives China more control over the process of industrial transfer and allows it to tailor the process to the specific needs of the target country. Linking state investment funds and state offshore industrial associations with local government administrative units ensures that the capital and technology transferred to, in this case, the Middle East is used in a way that is beneficial to both China and the host country.

In terms of the normative or regulatory framework for this type of foreign investment and international development, there is no specific law that supports Chinese provincial enterprises seeking international cooperation and investments in a similar manner to the law that supports foreign firms investing in China's provinces.[39] The main guiding legal text is the "Guiding Opinions of the State Council on Promoting International Cooperation in Production Capacity and Equipment Manufacturing,"[40] which includes four principles:

- Expanding the scope and scale of cooperation and promoting the export of high-quality production capacity and equipment.
- Improving the policy support system and creating a favorable environment for cooperation.

---

[38] The Sino-Oman Industrial Park in Duqm, as a major development project, has been listed as one of the twenty overseas key parks of the National Development and Reform Commission of China, one of the sixteen key parks of the Ministry of Commerce of China as well as "20+20 key park" of the China Council for the Promotion of International Trade. COIPs are a form of economic cooperation between China and its partner countries, aiming to promote industrial development, trade, and investment. However, not all COIPs are the same in terms of their design, operation, and outcomes. One of the key differences is the degree of internationalization, which refers to the extent to which the COIPs attract and accommodate non-Chinese firms and stakeholders.

[39] For example, the Catalogue of Industries for Guiding Foreign Investment classifies outbound investment projects into encouraged, restricted, and prohibited categories and provides preferential policies for the encouraged projects, such as tax incentives, foreign exchange support, and insurance services. See 发展改革委 商务部,'鼓励外商投资产业目录（2022年版）' [National Development and Reform Commission and Ministry of Commerce, 'Catalogue of Industries Encouraging Foreign Investment' (October 2022)] www.gov.cn/zhengceku/2022-10/28/content_5722417.htm.

[40] 国务院,'国务院关于推进国际产能和装备制造合作的指导意见', 国发〔2015〕30号 (2015年05月16日) [State Council, 'Guiding Opinions of the State Council on Promoting International Cooperation in Production Capacity and Equipment Manufacturing', Guofa 2015 No. 30 (16 May 2015)] www.gov.cn/zhengce/content/2015-05/16/content_9771.htm.

- Strengthening the coordination and cooperation mechanism and enhancing the overall effectiveness of cooperation.
- Promoting green development and fulfilling social responsibilities.

Those four principles can be illustrated using the SEZAD case since it is an example of the use of Chinese equipment and international production capacity in an internationalized investment environment and the attempt to promote new patterns of an open economy with optimizing export flows, while also promoting green development.

3.8 The Security Dimension

In addition to its strategic location, Duqm has a number of other qualities that make it a notable location for trade and investment. First, the port has a deepwater harbor that can accommodate large ships, and China is particularly interested in Oman's expanding road networks and railway system.[41] These developments will connect the new Sohar Port and Free Zone to the existing Omani and GCC transportation corridors that extend into the UAE and Saudi Arabia. This will give Oman a competitive advantage over other established logistical and transportation hubs in the region.

Second, the SEZAD is characterized by a diverse portfolio of primary industries within the industrial zone, whether they concern petrochemicals, natural gas processing, oil refining, building materials, chemicals, or the halal food industry. Even those industrial plants that are not Chinese-owned might still serve Chinese economic security interests; it is very important to trace the movement of intermediary goods as well as determining the markets for the final products. Looking at the China–Oman trade statistics, since most Omani petrochemicals and crude oil are exported to the PRC, plants such as oil refineries should still be considered strategically important for China even though Chinese investors might not have any stake in the actual plant. It is likely that once the industrial park is fully operational, it might serve as an international platform for meeting China's growing demand for the energy products from the Gulf. Thus, the multimodal connectivity that makes the SEZAD work must be considered as significant within the overall industrial manufacturing enterprise.

Third and perhaps most prominently, Duqm's strategic location also has implications for regional security. The port is situated relatively near important geopolitical hotspots, such as Yemen, where Oman is mediating the ongoing

---

[41] The land transport connectivity of Duqm to other Arabian cities had been primarily managed by the GCC framework. Though the SEZAD railroad access was a priority for the distant future even a decade ago (see GCC Secretariat, '2013,' التعاون مجلس دول حديد سكة مشروع عمل سير تقدم, [Presenting the workflow of the GCC railway project, 2013] www.gcc-sg.org/ar-sa/CooperationAndAchievements/Projects/Railway/Documents/%20سير%20عمل%20مشروع%20سكة%20حديد%20دول%20مجلس%20التعاون.pdf). The Duqm link to the Sohar line as well as to Riyadh non-passenger lines is already considered part of the GCC Railway Project.

conflict between the Saudi-backed coalition and Houthis, as well as the Horn of Africa. This has drawn attention to its potential military and security significance. The development of the port could have implications for the balance of power in the region, and it could also potentially be used as a base for military operations.

In 2017, just a year after signing the Agreement between Oman Wanfang and the SEZAD, Duqm became a focus for military cooperation between Oman and its allies. The UK Ministry of Defence, Oman's major economic and security partner, announced the expansion of the UK Joint Logistics Support Base at Duqm by investing an additional US$31 million.[42] In 2018, this was followed by an annex to an existing maritime security memorandum of understanding (MOU) signed between India and Oman,[43] granting special access for the Indian Navy to Duqm port as well as to a dry dock and maintenance facilities. Also in 2018, the United States, which has the highest military naval presence in the Gulf,[44] signed a Framework Agreement with Oman expanding US access to facilities and ports in Salalah and Duq.[45] The agreement gave the US Navy berthing rights at Duqm for logistical and maintenance purposes. The maritime security cooperation between Oman and its Western allies goes beyond just granting access and includes joint naval training and anti-piracy cooperation.

Oman also maintains military cooperation activities with the People's Liberation Army Navy (PLAN), including joint training and coastline security cooperation.[46] The military value of the Duqm port to PLAN, however, should be considered as very low. Even if we assume "dual-use" of the port,[47] it would still be of limited value to PLAN given that it already has a military presence much closer to the Bab-la-Mandab strait (between Yemen on the Arabian Peninsula and Djibouti and Eritrea in the Horn of Africa). PLAN has negligible (if any)

---

[42] UK Ministry of Defence, 'The Defence Secretary Has Announced a Further £23.8 Million Investment in the UK Logistics Hub at Duqm Port' (12 September 2020) www.gov.uk/government/news/defence-secretary-announces-investment-in-strategic-omani-port.

[43] The Economic Diplomacy Division, Ministry of External Affairs of India, 'PM Modi's Oman Trip Brings Several New Agreements' (11 February 2018) https://indbiz.gov.in/pm-modis-oman-trip-brings-several-new-agreements/.

[44] The main US naval base and support facilities in the Gulf are located in Bahrain.

[45] US Embassy in Oman, 'U.S. Statement on the Signing of the Strategic Framework Agreement' (24 March 2019) https://om.usembassy.gov/u-s-statement-on-the-signing-of-the-strategic-framework-agreement/#:~:text=On%20March%2024%2C%202019%2C%20the,ports%20in%20Salalah%20and%20Duqm.

[46] China Military Online Bilingual News, (中国海军第44批护航编队14日结束对阿曼的友好访问，于当地时间上午9时离开阿曼首都马斯喀特) [The 44th Chinese naval escort taskforce concluded its goodwill visit to Oman and left the capital city Muscat on 14 October local time] (16 October 2023) http://eng.chinamil.com.cn/BILINGUAL/News_209203/16259094.html.

[47] Isaac B. Kardon and Wendy Leutert, 'Pier Competitor: China's Power Position in Global Ports' (2022) 46 International Security 9–47 https://doi.org/10.1162/isec_a_00433; arguing that the possibility of "dual-use" of China's overseas ports, meaning for both commercial and military functions, remains largely hypothetical although "ascendance in global maritime trade and transportation creates the latent capacity for it."

operational control over the SEZAD port as it is neither owned nor operated by Chinese companies (in contrast to other ports, e.g., Gwadar or Dar as Salam).

Such a wide range of military partnerships and the utilization of Duqm for military purposes puts Oman in a situation similar to Djibouti, which has a comparable, if more permanent, coexistence of different military powers (although not because of its independent neutrality policy but driven by financial motivation). The resemblance of the SEZAD to Djibouti's Doraleh Port lies not as much in the "dual-use" aspect but in the development pattern, specifically the import of the Shekou model (蛇口综合开发模式) in Djibouti.[48] Shekou, similar to Duqm, a small fishing village in Shenzhen in China's Guangdong province, was transformed into a modern center using the port–zone–city model to develop the port infrastructure, an industrial park, and the adjacent urban zones.

3.9 The Shekou Model

The SEZAD covers a multifaceted and integrated coastal urban-industrial space that is divided into eight separate and interconnected zones grouped into three main areas: port, industrial park, and city. This model envisages the initial development of the port with the subsequent gradual development of the industrial district and finally the residential area.[49] For the SEZAD (Figure 3.3.2):

Maritime:

- Port area: This zone includes a world-class deepwater port for shipping and maritime trade, the first phase of the 2.25 km long terminal with eight commercial berths. Two dry docks are to be installed for ship repair and maintenance, one of the largest facilities in the MENA, each 410 meters long, and a terminal with a total length of 2.8 km.
- Fisheries center: This zone supports Oman's largest 10 m deep fishing port, with two long breakwaters, a 1.3 km fixed berth, and six floating berths. It provides facilities for processing and marketing fish and seafood.

---

[48] Comparisons between Doraleh and Shekou are very common in both Western and Chinese press and academic literature (see Jevans Nyabiage, 'China Merchants Signs US$350 Million Deal for Shekou-Style Revamp of Djibouti Port' (*South China Morning Post*, 5 January 2021) www.scmp.com/news/china/diplomacy/article/3116407/china-merchants-signs-us350-million-deal-shekou-style-revamp) primarily due to the same developer being involved. The resemblance with the Shekou model is not just in the spatial arrangement but also in the development approach based on public–private collaboration in the mixed-use urban spaces to promote economic and social transformation. There are profound differences, however. First and foremost, the stakeholders concerned are not comparable because, in the case of the SEZAD, Chinese investors and the Omani government combined in setting up and hosting the SEZ whereas in the case of Shekou it is just a single country (China).

[49] 高江虹, "蛇口模式 4.0" 落地吉布提, 招商局雁身出海, 21世界经济报道 ["Shekou Model 4.0" launched in Djibouti, China Investment Promotion Bureau goes overseas] (5 July 2017) www.sohu.com/a/154520614_119689.

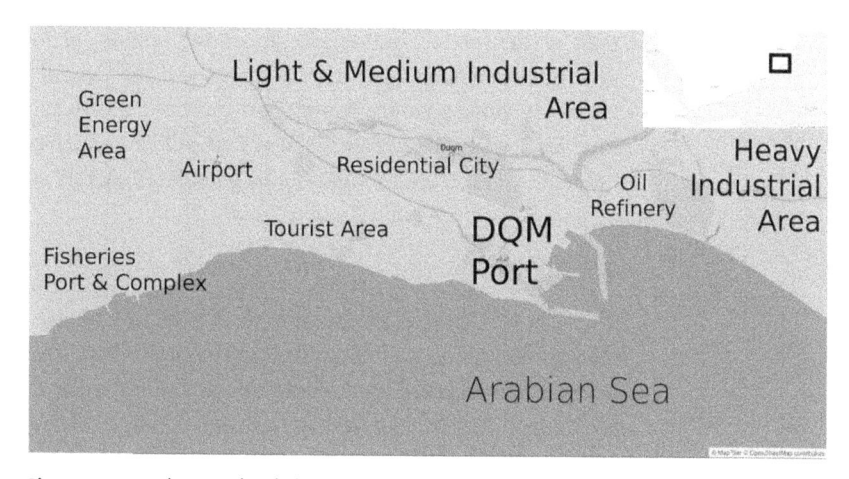

Figure 3.3.2 Implemented and planned zones at the SEZAD

Industrial:

- Industrial zone: This zone is designed to attract investment in a variety of industries, including manufacturing, logistics, and energy.
- Logistics system: This zone provides transportation and storage facilities for goods and materials moving through the park, warehousing facilities, distribution centers, and cargo re-trading services. The airport, currently in operation on a single runway, is expected to be completed by 2024, with an annual design capacity of 500,000 passengers and 50,000 tons of cargo.

City:

- New town: This zone provides housing, schools, and other amenities for the park's employees and residents.
- Central business district: This zone is the commercial heart of the park and is home to banks, offices, and other businesses.
- Tourism and recreation area: This zone offers a variety of tourist attractions, such as beaches, resorts, and golf courses.
- Education and training center: This zone provides training and educational opportunities for the park's workforce.

The main similarity between the Shekou model and the SEZAD is the emphasis on foreign capital and the measures taken to attract it. Duqm stands out as an example of a more internationalized COIP, compared to other COIPs that are mainly oriented toward serving Chinese companies. Even though a large proportion of the project has been funded by Chinese private and development cooperation funds, European and Middle Eastern enterprises are supporting a number of infrastructure projects. For example, the port component is managed via a 50:50 joint venture between the Omani government and the Antwerp Port Group of Belgium (thus the special guests at its inauguration), the dry dock was built by Daewoo Shipbuilding Engineering Company of South Korea and is managed by the Oman Dry Dock Company, and the Omani Investment Authority is the sole manager of the fishing port. Similar patterns prevail beyond the maritime zone, such as a diverse range of stakeholders, which suggests that the development of the SEZAD should not be considered merely as a Chinese project.

4 Conclusion

The case of Duqm is an example of facilitated Chinese investment in a host country located in a globally strategic region of the world. The Chinese have benefited from favorable investment conditions while Oman has maintained its independent foreign and investment policy. Such an approach has manifested itself as a high degree of internationalization in the newly established port city and a potential influx of Western and GCC capital in the area where Chinese investments are concentrated.

As the Duqm port is not yet operational at full capacity, it is not clear at what point the return on investment will be high enough to make statements on the profitability of the project. Apart from the beneficial treatment for Chinese investors and preferential conditions for their investments, there are obvious strategic motivations for the Chinese, which are further enhanced by public diplomacy measures directed toward the local population and host country government.

5 Discussion Questions and Comments

5.1 For Law School Audiences

1. Given that the SEZAD is located in one of the most internationalized of the SEZs that Chinese companies are working in, what does the level of internationalization mean for dispute resolution? Many of the SEZAD contracts use local law, but would foreign investors have sufficient trust in local law for the purpose of resolving their disputes? If not, what are the alternatives? In discussing this question, consider China's push to build Alternative Dispute Resolution both within and outside of China.[50]
2. This case mentions different layers of funding for the development of the SEZ, ranging from provincial to multilateral levels. How do Chinese local administrative structures as well as multilateral strategies influence China's trade and development policy with the Middle East?
3. The case also highlights that the projects had been implemented using the local law and complying with local industry standards. Is this also the case with other Chinese outbound investment projects you are aware of?

---

[50] See Matthew S. Erie, 'The Soft Power of Chinese Law' (2023) 61 Columbia Journal of Transnational Law 1.

5.2 For Policy School Audiences

1. How does regional security shape the construction of the SEZAD? Did the planners of the SEZAD take such concerns into consideration, including what it means to have the industrial park near the highly militarized zone for (a) China, (b) the Omani government, and (c) the wider Gulf region? What are the risks and opportunities for the parties involved given that the Chinese have commercial activities in a port that is used by NATO? What are the possible implications of Chinese trade and development on Oman's security interests?
2. It has been a decade since Xi Jinping proposed the grand goal of the Chinese foreign and development policy, the BRI.[51] How does this case study shed light on the soft power aspects of such initiatives such as the BRI and the relatively newer Global Development Initiative and Global Civilization Initiative?[52] What is the role and value of people-to-people exchanges, common religious/historical backgrounds, and education and training in this process?
3. What light may the SEZAD project shed on China's possible policy choices in the MENA region? China has also played a decisive role in the normalization of the Saudi–Iran relations, which traditionally had been the domain of Omani foreign policy. It has also shown a strong stand on the recently revived conflict in Gaza. Given its interests, what is the possible policy line China could maintain in the regional conflicts of the Middle East? Given that Gulf–China relations have been elevated to the level of comprehensive strategic partnerships, and recognizing that the former relies extensively on US security and geopolitical assistance, what might the hard power projections look like in the greater Indian Ocean region in the case of potential escalation of the relationships between the great powers?

5.3 For Business School Audiences

1. When the SEZAD was first announced, it consisted of just the port and the refinery. It takes confidence by investors to invest at such an early stage of development. Nowadays, geopolitical risks play a crucial role in investment considerations, especially when it comes to the two superpowers, the United States and China, with ongoing technological rivalry and trade wars. What could be the geopolitical considerations for Western companies investing in the SEZAD as well as risks from the perspective of the

---

[51] Encyclopaedia of Chinese Diplomacy in the New Era, '共建"一带一路"' [Jointly build the "Belt and Road"] http://cn.chinadiplomacy.org.cn/2023-07/27/content_86046791.shtml.

[52] Encyclopaedia of Chinese Diplomacy in the New Era, '全球发展倡议' [Global Development Initiative] http://cn.chinadiplomacy.org.cn/2022-09/28/content_78438507.shtml; Encyclopaedia of Chinese Diplomacy in the New Era, '全球文明倡议' [Global Civilization Initiative] http://cn.chinadiplomacy.org.cn/2023-08/04/content_97741364.shtml.

Chinese companies when developing such an internationalized industrial park? To what extent would the Chinese-backed projects and commitments to the SEZAD have encouraged investment from the West and the Gulf region?

2. Duqm has been a major Chinese investment, yet the size of the FDI from China has fallen considerably (from billions to several hundred million US dollars) during the later stages of development. Currently, the focus for the SEZAD has shifted from heavily industrialized production and transportation of minerals toward more green energy and digital initiatives, supported mainly by British, European, and Korean investors. For example, the most sizable investments in the SEZAD in 2023 did not revolve around the Sino-Oman Industrial Park but rather focused on Hydrom,[53] which is coordinating national interest in green hydrogen and aiming to build the world's largest production plant of renewable hydrogen by 2030. What would such a shift mean for China's interests, including, potentially, its hydrocarbon trade? How would the medium-term investment horizon change for those Chinese companies that have been concentrating on the oil and gas production in the SEZAD?

---

[53] Hydrogen Oman, 'About Hydrom' https://hydrom.om/Hydrom.aspx?cms=iQRpheuphYtJ6py XUGiNqiQQw2RhEtKe#about.

Section 4
Labor

Case Study 4.1

Chinese Workers and Forced Labor on the Imperial Pacific Casino Project in Saipan

Aaron Halegua

1 Overview

The case study examines the construction of the Imperial Pacific casino in Saipan, a US commonwealth in the Western Pacific, by Chinese firms employing Chinese workers. The focus is on the serious labor abuses that transpired and the legal and other consequences faced by the companies as a result. The case sheds light on the structure and operations of these Chinese construction projects, including the layers of contracting and subcontracting. It also explores how efforts to maximize speed and minimize costs resulted in numerous violations of local laws and the severe economic and reputational costs that this had for the companies. In addition, the case examines what actions the abused Chinese workers on such projects may take to enforce their rights and address their mistreatment. The case study therefore provides a useful tool to consider the issues involved in hiring and supervising contractors, such as cost, contract provisions, subcontracting, monitoring, and liability. The case also provides a platform to explore what legal, advocacy, and other tools workers and their advocates can use when legal violations and labor abuses occur. Additionally, this case study provides a uniquely detailed account of the events that transpired in Saipan because the author served as a lawyer representing the abused workers in a lawsuit alleging that they were subjected to forced labor. As a result, the case study draws upon court filings from that litigation, as well as construction contracts and subcontracting agreements, documents from local law enforcement agencies, criminal complaints, media reports, and worker interviews.

2 Introduction

In October 2022, seven Chinese construction workers reported that they recovered more than US$6.9 million through a lawsuit against the Imperial Pacific International (IPI) casino in Saipan, part of the US Commonwealth of the Northern Mariana Islands (CNMI) in the Western Pacific, and the two Chinese contractors who employed them to build the casino, subsidiaries of the Chinese firms Metallurgical Corporation of China (MCC) and Suzhou

Gold Mantis (Gold Mantis). The result came after nearly four years of litigation over events that had occurred six years prior. In or around 2016, while in China, the workers had been promised construction jobs in "America" with reasonable hours, high pay, room and board, and good conditions, and therefore paid high recruitment fees for this opportunity to work in Saipan. Instead, upon arrival, they had their passports confiscated, discovered they lacked work visas, worked long hours with no rest days, were not paid, were subjected to verbal threats and physical violence, and faced a worksite less safe than anything they had experienced in China. Each of these seven men also suffered a physical injury on the site, such as a scorched leg, burnt hand, or severed finger. The workers were part of a group of nearly 100 workers who had been directly supervised by Kong Xianghu, an individual with a few registered limited-liability companies, but were provided Gold Mantis T-shirts and hard hats and worked alongside other Gold Mantis workers. A few had also previously been employed by a supervisor working for MCC. The workers lived in dormitories provided by IPI. Between all the various Chinese contractors on the project, there were more than 2,400 Chinese workers with experiences just like those of the seven plaintiffs.

This case study explores the construction of the IPI casino in Saipan by its Chinese contractors, tracing it from the inception of the project until the conclusion of the worker lawsuit. In doing so, the case provides a platform for exploring numerous issues concerning overseas construction projects being carried out by Chinese firms, including relations with local governments; contracting and subcontracting arrangements; compliance with local law; and the criminal, economic, and reputational consequences of noncompliance. The study also provides a window into examining what legal, advocacy, and other tools workers and their advocates can use when legal violations and labor abuses occur.

The case study therefore proceeds in seven sections: the first introduces the political and economic context in Saipan and how the IPI project came about; the second focuses on the structure of the contractor and subcontractor relationships on the project; the third describes IPI's manpower shortage and the illegal recruitment methods used to solve it; the fourth discusses the various labor abuses perpetrated by IPI and its contractors toward the Chinese construction workers; the fifth reports on the various government and private enforcement efforts to remedy these labor abuses, such as criminal punishment, orders to compensate workers, fines, and a forced labor lawsuit; the sixth discusses how the workers themselves and other civil society actors helped to achieve a remedy for the workers; and the seventh explores the broader ramifications of this case on the companies, the CNMI, and US-China relations more generally.

The author served as the lawyer representing the seven workers in their forced labor suit against IPI, MCC, and Gold Mantis. The case study draws upon many of the court filings from that litigation and also the actual construction contracts and subcontracting agreements, documents from local law enforcement agencies, criminal complaints, media reports, and worker interviews.

3 The Case

3.1 Background on Saipan and IPI

The CNMI is a series of islands in the Pacific Ocean, of which the largest and most populated island is Saipan. After World War II, the CNMI was part of the Trust Territory of the Pacific Islands administered by the United States but later formed a political union with the United States in 1976. At that time, there were no quotas or tariffs on goods shipped from the CNMI to the United States. The CNMI also largely retained control over its immigration system and set its own minimum wage. This combination proved very attractive to apparel manufacturers, who could bring in foreign laborers from various parts of Asia, pay them very little, and export the goods to the US market. This allowed for the development of a garment industry that exported US$1 billion in goods each year and employed tens of thousands of factory workers.

However, after the media exposed the horrible labor abuses engaged in by garment employers in the late 1990s, a series of class action lawsuits brought down the industry. In 2009, pursuant to the Consolidated Natural Resources Act of 2008, Congress 'federalized' control over immigration to Saipan, stripping the local government of much of this power.[1] A 2007 law created a schedule for raising the minimum wage in the CNMI to match the federal level by 2018.[2] The US Department of Labor (USDOL) also established a permanent presence on the island. The intention was that such federal oversight over who enters and leaves Saipan, as well as over employers' compliance with federal minimum wage and other laws, would ensure that the abuses experienced in the garment industry would not repeat themselves in Saipan.

Despite these reforms, the CNMI still received special treatment from the federal government in other respects, however. In order to encourage tourism to the islands, a program was created in 2009 that permitted Chinese tourists to be paroled into the CNMI for up to forty-five days without needing to obtain a visa.[3] Between 2013 and 2016, the number of Chinese tourists to CNMI each year grew from 112,570 to 206,538.[4] Around the time that immigration was federalized, Congress also created the CNMI-Only Transitional Worker program

---

[1] *Commonwealth of the Northern Mariana Islands: DHS Implementation of U.S. Immigration Laws*, GAO-19-376T, 27 February 2019.
[2] 'Highlights' *Commonwealth of the Northern Mariana Islands: Implementation of Federal Minimum Wage and Immigration Laws*, May 2017, GAO-17-437.
[3] (n 1) 5, n.19.   [4] (n 2) 65.

(or "CW-1" program) in response to the CNMI's claimed need for foreign workers. While other programs for unskilled guest workers already existed, such as the H-2A and H-2B programs, the CW-1 program allowed workers from a broader list of industries and home countries (such as China) to be legally employed in the CNMI. When first established, the CW-1 program provided a decreasing number of permits each year, as the intention was for this program to be gradually phased out.[5]

After the garment industry more or less dissolved in the mid 2000s, the CNMI never found an economic driver to replace it.[6] But, around 2014, this changed – or so people thought. During this time, the Chinese government was imposing tighter restrictions on the casinos operating in Macau, the only place in China where gambling is legal. It had become increasingly difficult for wealthy Chinese to get their money to Macau, and many of the junket operators and casinos there were losing money or even closing operations. In this context, one of these Macau junket operators approached a group of Saipan government officials about opening a casino on the island.[7]

On 12 August 2014, the CNMI government executed a Casino License Agreement (CLA) that provided IPI the exclusive right to operate a casino with table games in Saipan. The license was for twenty-five years, but IPI then had the option to extend for an additional fifteen years. In exchange, IPI was obligated to invest a minimum of US$2 billion, construct 2,000 new hotel rooms of at least a four-star quality, and pay an annual license fee of US$15 million.[8] The CLA also provided that IPI would seek to have 65% of its workforce comprised of US permanent residents, as opposed to foreign guest workers, and IPI agreed to provide the CNMI Department of Labor (CNMI DOL) with quarterly updates on its progress toward meeting this goal.

IPI is the entity that was registered in the CNMI to operate the casino hotel. But IPI is a wholly owned subsidiary of Imperial Pacific International Holdings (IPIH), a holding company registered in the British Virgin Islands and with offices in Hong Kong. IPIH has been listed on the Hong Kong Stock Exchange since February 2002.[9] The largest shareholder of IPIH was mainland Chinese businesswoman Cui Lijie, although many viewed the project as really driven by her son, Ji Xiaobo. Cui had been listed by *Forbes* magazine as one of Hong Kong's fifty richest people in 2017.[10]

---

[5] (n 1) 5.
[6] Commonwealth of the Northern Mariana Islands: Recent Workforce Trends and Wage Distribution, GAO-22-105271, February 2022, 14.
[7] Daniela Wei and Matthew Campbell, 'Firm Linked to Imperial Pacific Arranged Saipan Lawmakers' Trips' (*Bloomberg*, 27 March 2017) www.bloomberg.com/news/articles/2017-03-28/firm-linked-to-imperial-pacific-arranged-saipan-lawmakers-trips#xj4y7vzkg.
[8] Other sources report that IPI was expected to invest US$3.14 billion in the project. (GAO-19-376T 12, n.30.)
[9] Hong Kong Stock Exchange, Imperial Pacific International Holdings Ltd. (1076) www.hkex.com.hk/Market-Data/Securities-Prices/Equities/Equities-Quote?sym=1076&sc_lang=en.
[10] Forbes, 'Profile: Cui Lijie' www.forbes.com/profile/cui-lijie/?sh=6cbc3f0a3ad0.

3.2 Construction of the Casino Project

On 15 January 2015, IPIH executed an "EPC general contract" (EPC总承包合同) appointing MCC International Engineering Co., Ltd. (MCC International) as the general contractor on the casino resort project in Saipan. MCC International is registered in Hong Kong and is a subsidiary of the Metallurgical Corporation of China, a central state-owned enterprise (SOE) mining conglomerate headquartered in Beijing. MCC International then created its own subsidiary in Saipan, MCC International Saipan Ltd. Co. (MCC Saipan), to operate the casino project.

In December 2015, a "General Construction Contract" (施工总承包合同) was then executed between MCC Saipan and IPI to implement the agreement between the parent companies. (In the course of the forced labor litigation, IPI made public both the original Chinese version of this contract and an English translation.) The first pages of the contract identify the parties and the initial contract price of US$200 million. The remainder of the roughly seventy-six-page contract appears to be a standard form, primarily comprised of boilerplate provisions but including very few details specific to the project. Most of the appendices, which are supposed to be tailored to the project, are left blank. The contract basically puts all obligations for compliance onto MCC. For instance, MCC was obliged to comply with all applicable laws, ensure safety on the site, be responsible for the actions of its subcontractors, hire employees locally, and generally be responsible for complying with all labor laws, including those regarding workers' pay, housing, meals, and transportation.

IPI also engaged numerous other contractors for the project. Although often described as subcontractors of MCC, many of these companies were contracted by IPI directly, not by MCC. For instance, the Suzhou-based construction and design firm Gold Mantis (金螳螂), which is traded on the Shenzhen Stock Exchange, was hired to work on the casino hotel. The firm Nanjing Beilida (倍立达) (Beilida), a privately owned company, was also engaged by IPI. In fact, at least four other Chinese companies, including large firms like Sino Great Wall International Engineering and the Jiangsu Provincial Construction Group, also had contracts related to construction of the casino project.

The contracts between IPI and its contractors took a variety of forms. In contrast to the seventy-six-page contract with MCC, the agreement with Gold Mantis, executed in December 2016, is an eight-page English document with only eighteen sections.[11] Interestingly, while Gold Mantis is referred to as the "Contractor," IPI is called the "Employer/Owner." Nonetheless, the contract

---

[11] It is very possible, however, that IPI had multiple contracts with these entities, many of which were not produced in the litigation. For instance, it may very well be that an agreement exists between IPI and Gold Mantis' parent company in China but that this English-language version is what the companies used to show regulators, and so on. Indeed, the Gold Mantis contract explicitly envisions a supplemental contract fleshing out the details of items like the "cost plus" pricing mechanism. In the case of MCC, in addition to the contract described

provides that Gold Mantis is responsible for the "labor works" of certain classes of workers, but not those subcontractors directly appointed by IPI. IPI was obligated to assist in applying for manager and worker visas as well as dealing with the government policy or legal problems, while Gold Mantis was made responsible for providing sufficient manpower and performing the contract "in accordance with all applicable laws and regulations." The contract set a provisional price of US$6 million and provided that a "cost plus pricing mechanism" will be used, which means that the contractor essentially submits invoices and the developer pays an amount equal to those invoices plus some agreed-upon percentage of that amount as the contractor's profit. It is important to consider what incentives such a pricing structure creates for the contractor.

These contractors often further subcontracted out their work on the casino project. For instance, Gold Mantis worked with an individual, Kong Xianghu, to manage a group of nearly 100 construction workers. Kong operated under at least three different corporate entities. With one of the entities, Gold Mantis executed a two-page contract to provide it with "labor services" on the IPI project for an agreed-upon fee schedule that was not listed in the contract. It stated that "no labor relationship is established" between the parties, and that Kong's entity is "responsible for all safety accidents of its workers." MCC, too, engaged in some similar arrangements, whereby it would engage an individual who was in charge of a group of workers and then make periodic payments to that individual. Beilida, too, had individuals who were in charge of a group of workers, and these individuals would receive a lump sum payment from the company based on the labor performed by their workers, which they were then responsible for distributing to the workers. As discussed further in Section 3.3, a critical issue is the extent to which these "subcontractors" were or were not independent of IPI and the Chinese construction firms.

3.3 Recruitment of Workers

Pursuant to the CLA, IPI was required to open the casino resort by January 2017. From the outset, IPI projected that it would need 2,000 workers to complete construction. (The population of the CNMI was just over 47,000 in 2020, which is a 12.2% decrease from 2010.)[12] There is also a CNMI regulation that requires 30% of any company's workforce to be US permanent residents, as opposed to foreign workers.[13] However, in January 2016, the CNMI DOL said there were only about 1,000 construction workers in the CNMI, meaning there

---

above, several other agreements with slightly different terms were also discovered. It is unclear whether this reflects a strategic plan or just disorganization.

[12] (n 6) 4.
[13] CNMI Administrative Code, Employment Rules and Regulations, § 80-20.1-210, https://cnmilaw.org/pdf/admincode/T80/T80-20.1.pdf.

was an obvious labor shortage. Generally, in order to get US permanent residents from outside the CNMI to come work in Saipan, the employer is required to pay their travel and housing costs as well as a significant wage that is high enough to make this work attractive. Thus, finding US workers to satisfy IPI's need for labor would have been extremely costly.

Instead, IPI petitioned the CNMI DOL to grant an exemption to the 30% rule for its various Chinese contractors. Documents obtained from that agency show that the CNMI DOL approved IPI's subcontractors to bring in more than 6,000 foreign workers. (These foreign workers were still required to have proper authorization to work in the CNMI.) However, getting these workers was not so easy. Whereas the cap on CW-1 workers had never been reached before 2016, all 12,999 CW-1 permits for 2016 had already been issued less than halfway through that year.[14] This was primarily due to the IPI project: for instance, whereas only 1,231 CW-1 workers came from China in 2015, more than 5,000 came from China in both 2016 and 2017.[15] IPI fought to meet its deadline with the workers it had by having them perform construction late into the night and even on Sunday, despite regulations forbidding this practice. Nonetheless, IPI later announced it would need to push back the opening. But IPI still needed more workers to avoid pushing it back even farther.

In order to resolve this manpower shortage, IPI, MCC, and the other contractors then began to bring in workers from China who lacked any work visas. The workers would be paroled into the CNMI as "tourists" but then immediately start working on the construction site. Many of these workers were actually defrauded in China, where recruiters told them that they were going to "America"; that they did not need a visa (or sometimes that one would be provided); and that they would only work six days per week, eight hours per day, and earn a large salary paid regularly. In exchange, the recruiters charged workers a recruitment fee, often around US$6,000 – more than the average annual wage of a Chinese construction worker – and sometimes far more. These "tourist workers" then often worked alongside the other construction workers who had proper visas, sometimes under the same supervisor, and living in the same dormitories.

Later on, when this illegal scheme was uncovered, IPI would claim that this plan to bring in these "tourist workers" – often referred to as *"heigong"* (黑工) – was entirely done by the contractors. The contractors, like MCC and Gold Mantis, argued that they also had hired subcontractors who brought in and supervised these tourist workers. However, evidence later revealed that executives and managers at IPI, MCC, and the other contractors were not only aware of what was happening but actively involved in developing and executing the plan.[16]

---

[14] (n 1) 11.   [15] (n 1) 12.
[16] Superseding Indictment, *United States v. Liwen Wu, Jiamin Xu, and Yan Shi*, US District Court for the Northern Mariana Islands, Docket No. 8 (1 August 2019) www.justice.gov/opa/press-release/file/1300911/download.

3.4 Labor Abuses

In the effort to get this project done quickly and cheaply, IPI and its contractors engaged in a series of practices that violated CNMI and federal laws. Some of these practices seem to be clear imports from how construction sites are run in China, such as paying a daily wage rate, but other policies were not simply what employers were used to doing at home – like confiscating worker passports. In this particular instance, there is much evidence that these companies were not ignorant of the different laws in the CNMI and United States. Instead, they knew the law but nonetheless chose not to comply.

There are numerous illustrations of the contractors' commitment to reducing costs. Documents show that MCC had actually calculated the money that would be saved by hiring Chinese workers and paying a below-minimum wage salary instead of hiring US workers and paying a legal wage. The fact that MCC and other contractors brought in the Chinese workers as tourists rather than go through the expensive and cumbersome process of properly obtaining visas for workers is another example of violating the law to save costs.

The contractors also implemented a management style that included many forced labor-like conditions in an effort to maximize worker productivity and minimize cost. The contractors made workers labor for seven days per week for twelve or more hours per day. The overtime was mandatory. They did not pay workers on time but were always in arrears, meaning a worker could not quit without forfeiting his prior unpaid earnings. The daily wage that the companies promised to pay also violated rules on the minimum wage and overtime. Managers confiscated workers' passports, also making it hard for them to quit, and overtly threatened that if they complained or quit they would be deported to China without receiving their pay. Workers were also housed in a rat-infested dormitory that even lacked a certificate of occupancy. These conditions were remarkably similar across all IPI's many contractors.

IPI, MCC, and the contractors also refused to take proper safety measures. Workers received little or no training and often lacked the proper protective equipment. The fatigue from working so many hours with no rest days also made workers susceptible to getting injured. Indeed, many workers described the condition as worse than anything they had seen in China. An affidavit submitted in court revealed that emergency room doctors at the local hospital documented eighty serious injuries on the casino site just in the year 2016, prompting them to contact the relevant federal agency, the Occupational Safety and Health Administration (OSHA), about the dangerous nature of the worksite. The doctors also reported cases where they recommended that a patient be hospitalized and not transported, like a worker with a broken back, but the Chinese employers sent him back to China nonetheless. The contractor generally did not permit any of the tourist workers to receive medical treatment because they feared it might expose the fact that they were employing undocumented workers.

After performing its inspection in 2016 and 2017, OSHA eventually found twenty-four violations by MCC, Gold Mantis, and Beilida.[17] The citations were for hazards related to inadequate fall protection, unsecured scaffolding, unprotected crane operation areas, and unguarded machines. And, in March 2017, one tourist worker died after falling 24 feet from the casino's scaffolding and breaking his neck.[18] Rather than report all these injuries to OSHA as required by law, IPI and its contractors instead tried to cover them up. It is this incident that prompted the FBI to intervene by raiding the offices of MCC, Beilida, and others, and arresting some of the managers.

3.5 Government and Private Enforcement

The cost-cutting decisions resulted in some serious consequences imposed by various US federal government agencies. First, the FBI and US Department of Justice criminally prosecuted Zhao Yuqing, the MCC project manager, and Qi Xiufang and Guo Wencai, two subcontractors/supervisors for Beilida, for knowingly employing and harboring undocumented workers, resulting in at least three individuals spending time in jail. Court documents show that agents discovered passports of undocumented workers in a drawer at MCC's office and a list of "visa" and "illegal" workers at Beilida's office. Another indictment was later issued against an IPI executive and another MCC manager who coordinated for workers to enter as tourists and devised ways to deceive immigration officials.

The USDOL also investigated the nonpayment and underpayments to the workers. This resulted in MCC, Beilida, and other contractors paying more than US$13.9 million to 2,400 workers, including about US$6,000 per person to reimburse the recruitment fees that were paid in China. Although these companies all claimed that they were not actually the ones recruiting the workers in China or collecting those fees, the USDOL found it proper that they be responsible for repaying them. Even IPI, since it too exercised some control over the workforce, was sued by USDOL and eventually agreed to pay US$3.3 million toward compensating the workers.[19]

As for the health and safety violations, public records show that OSHA's inspection of the site in 2016 that found twenty-four safety violations resulted in fines levied against MCC, Gold Mantis, and Beilida in the combined amount of US$193,750.[20]

---

[17] OSHA, 'Saipan Casino Contractors Face Penalties Following OSHA Investigation' (30 May 2017) www.osha.gov/news/newsreleases/region9/05302017.
[18] Ferdie De La Torre, 'Worker Killed at IPI Construction Site' (*Saipan Tribune*, 23 March 2017) www.saipantribune.com/index.php/worker-killed-ipi-construction-site/.
[19] USDOL, 'U.S. Department of Labor Secures $3.3 Million Judgment against Saipan Casino Developer for Systemic Wage Violations by Contractors' (25 April 2019) www.dol.gov/newsroom/releases/whd/whd20190425-1.
[20] OSHA (n 17).

In addition to this government enforcement, workers also sued IPI and its contractors in the federal court located in the CNMI. In the most noteworthy case, seven Chinese workers filed a complaint in early 2019 alleging that IPI, MCC, and Gold Mantis subjected them to forced labor, which also resulted in the physical injuries they suffered on the construction site. Under the federal Trafficking Victims Protection Reauthorization Act, not only a recruiter or employer but any individual or entity that "knowingly benefited" from the forced labor may be liable to the victims. After the judge found the workers had a plausible claim, MCC and Gold Mantis paid to settle with the seven workers. IPI continued to fight but refused to hand over the WeChat messages, emails, and other evidence requested by the workers, resulting in the court entering a default judgment against the company and setting damages at US$5.9 million. After roughly eighteen months, the workers were then able to collect the full amount of the judgment from the casino.

In each of these proceedings, IPI initially sought to put all the blame for the unpaid wages, unsafe conditions, confiscation of passports, and dismal living conditions onto its contractors, and would point to the language in their agreements making the contractors responsible for all such labor issues. Similarly, the contractors sought to put the blame on their subcontractors, such as individuals like Kong Xianghu, claiming that they were unaware of what those subcontractors were doing. However, the facts failed to support their arguments. IPI had arranged for the workers to live in the same crowded, rat-infested dormitories that lacked a certificate of occupancy, and transported them from the dorms to the worksite each day. IPI's general counsel also denied entry to an OSHA inspector when he first arrived at the construction site. As for the contractors, the workers allegedly employed by the different "subcontractors" often lived in the same dorms, rode the same buses, wore the same company uniforms, and were overseen by the managers. Thus, even if the abused workers were technically supervised by a subcontractor to some degree, these facts made it possible to hold IPI and its contractors liable for the abuses that they suffered.

3.6 Worker and Civil Society Efforts

The Chinese workers themselves also took actions against IPI and its contractors to remedy the abuses they suffered. Some of these efforts worked in conjunction with government enforcement efforts to pressure IPI and its contractors to pay compensation, while others were independent of those efforts.

After the FBI raids in March 2017, many of the company managers fled from Saipan, and the Chinese workers were left stranded and unpaid. Despite previously being terrified to speak out due to their lack of visas and fear of employer retaliation, the workers now began demonstrating in the streets of Saipan demanding that they be compensated for the work that they performed. The workers also insisted that they would not return to China, as both the companies and some government agencies were encouraging them to do, until they had been paid. Not only did the local newspapers and TV stations cover the story but so did major international outlets, like the *New York Times*, which named the contractors and how each one had previously touted their participation in this project as contributing to China's Belt and Road Initiative (BRI). The workers also wrote a public letter to the Chinese Consulate in Los Angeles (which has jurisdiction over Saipan) discussing how they were abused by these Chinese companies and wanted help.

The workers' efforts and the international media coverage then prompted other civil society organizations to get involved. Groups like the National Guestworker Alliance and Hong Kong Confederation of Trade Unions made statements calling on IPI and its contractors to pay the workers. *China Change* released videos profiling the situation, including by documenting the company's efforts to assuage the protesting workers by buying them cigarettes as well as showing the workers who had been injured on the site but received no treatment and no compensation. The videos also called on people to write to the Chinese contractors insisting that the workers be paid. Adding to the reputational costs for the companies, the IPI project was named one of the "Most Controversial Projects of 2017." The labor abuses at the site would become a topic at US congressional hearings on the state of Saipan.[21]

The demonstrations by the workers, their insistence on being paid before returning home, and then the attention from the media and civil society put pressure on IPI and its contractors to resolve the issue. (It also likely put some pressure on the USDOL to ensure that the workers were fairly compensated and to ensure that the money was actually paid.) In addition to the contractors' own interest in preserving their reputation, there have been suggestions that the Chinese government also leaned on the contractors to pay the workers and resolve the case, as it was negatively impacting China's image. In particular, much of the media coverage about the incident noted that the Chinese contractors described their work in Saipan as part of the BRI. Since this is a signature policy of Xi Jinping, allegations of labor abuses on such a project are particularly sensitive for the Chinese government. Accordingly, it is plausible that the government may have pressured the Chinese contractors to resolve the matter and end the stream of negative attention.

Many of these same dynamics were at play after the lawsuit alleging forced labor was filed against IPI, MCC, and Gold Mantis. Numerous international media outlets reported on the case. The litigation was referenced at a US congressional hearing on forced labor perpetrated by Chinese companies. Advocacy efforts were also directed at the investment community and various financial regulators. For instance, Amnesty International argued publicly that IPI's parent company and an MCC subsidiary were not in compliance with

---

[21] S. Hrg. 115-252 – H.R. 339, 'The Northern Marianne Islands Economic Expansion Act' (27 April 2017) www.govinfo.gov/content/pkg/CHRG-115shrg26070/pdf/CHRG-115shrg26070.pdf.

the environmental, social and governance (ESG) disclosure rules of the Hong Kong Stock Exchange on which they were listed. Both MCC and Gold Mantis, unlike IPI, eventually agreed to settle the claims against them in the forced labor suit. This negative attention, along with raising red flags for investors and regulators, may have contributed to the desire of these companies to settle by compensating the workers.

3.7 Aftermath

After the FBI raids, IPI continued its work on the casino-hotel project. It initially hired a contractor that employed US workers, who ended up claiming it was owed money and sued IPI. IPI then hired workers from other countries under the H-2B guest worker program, until USDOL eventually debarred IPI from the program, thus revoking its ability to do so; this forced IPI to rely again on contractors who would bring in the workers. IPI was able to finish construction of the casino and opened it in July 2017; however, to this day, the hotel portion remains unfinished.

The events that transpired on the IPI project had significant implications beyond just that project. Starting in October 2019, the parole program for Chinese tourists was revised so that individuals could only remain in CNMI for fourteen days rather than the forty days previously permitted.[22] Sources suggest that this was driven in large part by the way IPI and its contractors exploited the parole program to bring in workers.

In July 2018, Congress also made changes to the CW program under which many of those construction workers who had visas were working. Although the overall program was extended – it was originally scheduled to phase out in 2018 but was instead extended to phase out in 2030 – no future permits were to be granted to construction workers unless they qualified as long-term workers. Employers would also be required to demonstrate that there were no willing and able US workers in the CNMI before bringing in a CW-1 worker.[23] In addition, employers found to have engaged in human trafficking or serious labor abuses would be barred from the program, which also was largely a result of the abuses on the IPI project.

In short, the massive abuses by IPI, MCC, and Gold Mantis significantly impacted the future of the CNMI's relationship with China, both by making it harder for Chinese tourists to visit and by making it harder for Chinese workers to get permits to be employed on Saipan. It seems logical that this may also lead to a slowing of Chinese investment into the island.

---

[22] US Customs and Border Protection, 'Limit of Parole of Nationals of the People's Republic of China into the Commonwealth of Northern Mariana Islands' (2 October 2019) www.cbp.gov/sites/default/files/assets/documents/2019-Nov/20191002%20PRC%20CNMI%20Parole%20Program.pdf.
[23] (n 1) 6, 7.

4 Conclusion

The story of the IPI casino in Saipan provides a detailed illustration of an overseas Chinese construction project. The case highlights how some firms sought to resolve their need for manpower, deliver fast construction, and minimize costs by adopting practices that largely violated federal and local immigration laws, safety rules, wage and hour laws, trafficking and forced labor laws, and other labor rights protections. However, such practices are not unique to Saipan; instead, they are commonly employed by Chinese firms on projects across the globe.[24] The Saipan case illustrates how failing to adapt these practices to comply with local laws may have extremely high costs to the companies involved as well as the broader relationship between China and that locality.

5 Discussion Questions and Comments

The case of the IPI casino in Saipan identifies several critical issues that arise with large construction and infrastructure projects involving Chinese firms. This section discusses those issues and raises questions that should be considered by all stakeholders, including policymakers in the host country, executives and managers at the construction firms, and worker advocates.

5.1 For Law and Business School Audiences

5.1.1 Subcontracting Arrangements: When and How to Use Them, as Well as Legal Risks and Their Mitigation

An extremely common component of these Chinese construction projects is the extensive use of multiple levels of subcontracting.[25] In Saipan, the developer hired MCC as a general contractor, then engaged other contractors such as Gold Mantis and Beilida, and each of them contracted with supervisors as well as recruiters in China. While there is a business logic to this practice, it is often employed by developers and larger contractors to avoid liability for the labor or other violations taking place. Yet, in Saipan, despite contractual language

---

[24] See, e.g., Aaron Halegua, 'Where Is China's Belt and Road Leading International Labour Rights? An Examination of Worker Abuse by Chinese Construction Firms in Saipan' in Maria Adele Carrai and Jan Wouters (eds), *The Belt and Road Initiative and Global Governance* (Edward Elgar 2020); Ivan Franceschini, 'As Far Apart as Earth and Sky: A Survey of Chinese and Cambodian Construction Workers in Sihanoukville' (2020) 52 Critical Asian Studies 512–529 https://doi.org/10.1080/14672715.2020.1804961; Aaron Halegua and Jerome A. Cohen, 'The Forgotten Victims of China's Belt and Road Initiative' *The Washington Post* (23 April 2019); Fang Lee Cooke, Dan Wang, and Jue Wang, 'State Capitalism in Construction: Staffing Practices and Labour Relations of Chinese Construction Firms in Africa' (2018) 60 Journal of Industrial Relations 77–100; Ching Kwan Lee, *The Specter of Global China: Politics, Labor, and Foreign Investment in Africa* (University of Chicago Press 2017).

[25] See Lee (n 24); Cooke et al. (n 24); Aaron Halegua, 'From Africa to Saipan: What Happens When Chinese Construction Firms "Go Global"?' (2020) 5 Made in China 160–163.

assigning responsibility to the subcontractors, IPI, MCC, and other larger contractors were still held liable for the recruitment, labor, and safety abuses.

The case therefore offers an important lesson to companies about the importance of carefully considering the structure of their subcontracting arrangements. If not managed properly, this may create serious economic and reputational damage to developers and contractors. As a starting point, companies must make themselves familiar with the relevant legal framework. Companies then must decide whether to engage subcontractors or to handle various functions themselves. In what circumstances should companies use or avoid subcontracting arrangements? If subcontractors are hired, how will such arrangements be structured? What mechanisms will be adopted to allow the company to monitor the subcontractors and ensure their compliance with the law? Or will the company take a "hands-off" approach, risking that abuses may occur and intending to then feign ignorance if they are uncovered?

5.2 For Law, Business, and Policy School Audiences

5.2.1 Finding Redress for Labor Exploitation, Including Legal and Extra-Legal Strategies

Even the most careful planning or detailed set of regulatory measures cannot entirely eliminate the risk of noncompliance and abuse. Therefore, it is critical to consider what legal or other avenues are available to raise and remediate grievances. Many Chinese overseas projects lack a well-developed channel for workers (or other stakeholders) to raise complaints about wages, safety, or other conditions. However, when such mechanisms do not exist, or do not resolve the problem, workers and their advocates need to find other means to exert pressure on employers to remedy abuses. The Saipan case offers some important lessons on how this can be achieved. The workers (and then civil society groups) were able to exert pressure on the Chinese companies to remedy the abuses they suffered through a combination of public demonstrations, engaging the media, and appealing to the Chinese government. Some workers successfully used the local legal system to obtain compensation for being subjected to forced labor and for the physical injuries that were never adequately addressed by the construction firms. However, this was only possible due to legal rules that permitted undocumented workers to access the courts, lawyers to charge a contingency fee (i.e., only receive payment if money is collected for the client), and plaintiffs to participate in the legal process even after returning to China. Of course, the ability of media to operate freely and the rules of civil litigation may vary greatly by jurisdiction. Therefore, it is crucial that policymakers consider creating an environment that permits workers to seek redress, and advocates must evaluate how to best navigate that environment in each case. Thinking broadly, when labor exploitation occurs, what avenues are available to raise and remediate grievances? What legal and extra-legal strategies are available to workers and their advocates?

5.3 For Business School Audiences

5.3.1 Managing the Advantages and Disadvantages of Using Foreign Workers

For many large-scale construction or infrastructure projects, particularly in more remote regions, the local population may lack the manpower or skills to perform the job. However, importing a large number of foreign workers also creates risks and challenges. The migrant workers themselves are often extremely vulnerable to severe exploitation. Like in the Saipan case, the workers are transported far away from their homes to an unfamiliar place where they do not speak the language, do not know the law, and are entirely dependent on their employer. If they do not have a proper visa or legal status, their vulnerability is further heightened. So, what are the advantages and risks of using foreign workers? How should the use of foreign workers be managed? What measures should be put in place to minimize the risk of such labor abuses? The influx of foreign workers may also have a significant impact on the host country that must be considered. What will be the effect on the community or environment of this sudden growth in the population, particularly in a place with limited resources? Will the use of foreign workers create resentment among unemployed or underemployed local residents? Serious consideration must be given to these questions before a plan to bring in foreign workers is set in motion.

Case Study 4.2

The Impact of Chinese Investments on the Gold Mining Sector in Kyrgyzstan

Nuraiym Syrgak kyzy and Robin Lee

1 Overview

Gold mines in Kyrgyzstan that are owned and operated by Chinese investors have experienced several problems in recent years, chief among them being labor disputes with local workers. These disputes mark a pattern of dysfunction in one of Kyrgyzstan's most critical industries. They are further significant for a number of additional reasons. First, they shine a light on the realities of doing business in a controversial sector in a developing country. Second, they demonstrate labor issues from the host state side, specifically the difficulties of finding decent work for Kyrgyz laborers, and how certain industries may thereby engage in predatory practices. Third, they show the ineffectiveness of government intervention. This case study will expose readers to the causes of the problem and encourage them to critically assess the responses of various stakeholders to the disputes. It also will assess the extent to which different fields and concepts of governance are either well-established in corporate practice and across industries, a function of supranational governance, or are Chinese-inspired innovations apply to Kyrgyzstan's gold mining sector. These range from corporate social responsibility (CSR) and environmental, social and governance (ESG) to the UN Sustainable Development Goals (SDGs) and the "Green Silk Road."

2 Introduction

2.1 History and Significance

Following independence from the Soviet Union in 1991, Kyrgyzstan's gold mines were initially seen as an opportunity for foreign investors and local actors to work together to develop the country. Since then, however, the gold mining industry has struggled to fulfill its potential and, in general, the view of foreign investors has soured. This is best illustrated in the well-documented case of the Kumtor gold mine, which was once owned and operated by Canadian firms. Located in the east of the country, Kumtor is Kyrgyzstan's largest mine. It accounted for 68% of national gold output in 2022 and is arguably the country's single most significant productive asset.[1] Although a report on Kumtor's contribution to economic growth is no longer available on the mine operator's website, it was reported by commentaries in 2021 and 2022 as accounting for 12% of Kyrgyz GDP and 23% of Kyrgyz industrial output.[2] However, since the start of its operations in 1997, the Kumtor mine has also become the object of scrutiny and criticism because of its river pollution,[3] damage to glaciers,[4] and tax irregularities,[5] as well as corruption scandals that have implicated former Kyrgyz presidents.[6] In 2022, the Kyrgyz authorities unilaterally seized control of the Kumtor mine.[7] This then prompted bankruptcy litigation and international arbitration in the United States, Canada, and Sweden, which culminated in an out-of-court settlement marking the end of Canadian control.[8] Overall, the scandals have tarnished the image of foreign direct investment in Kyrgyzstan, which is now closely associated with corruption, environmental damage, and socioeconomic inequality.[9] However, such scandals have not been exclusive to Kumtor and have grown to pervade a swathe of Kyrgyz gold mines – irrespective of the nationality of the foreign investor. A number of such mines are now operated and owned by Chinese firms. In the region covered by

---

[1] Chris Rickleton, 'Kyrgyzstan's Kumtor Gold Mine and the Fall of a "Great Nomad"' (*Radio Free Europe*, 13 February 2023) www.rferl.org/a/kyrgyzstan-kumtor-gold-mine-great-nomad/32269064.html.

[2] 'Government of the Kyrgyz Republic Announces Global Arrangement Agreement over Kumtor Gold Mine' (*PR Newswire*, 4 April 2022) www.prnewswire.com/news-releases/government-of-the-kyrgyz-republic-announces-global-arrangement-agreement-over-kumtor-gold-mine-301516728.html; Kamila Eshalieva, 'Kumtor: The Gold Mine That Could Make or Break Kyrgyzstan' (*OpenDemocracy*, 22 June 2021) www.opendemocracy.net/en/odr/kumtor-gold-mine-could-make-or-break-kyrgyzstan/; Aru Atibekova, 'Going for Gold: Kyrgyzstan Reaches an Agreement Ending Dispute with Canadian Mining Company' (*Caspian Policy*, 22 April 2022) https://caspianpolicy.com/research/economy/going-for-gold-kyrgyzstan-reaches-an-agreement-ending-dispute-with-canadian-mining-company.

[3] Bruce Pannier, 'At Kyrgyzstan's Kumtor Mine, Not All That Glitters Is Gold' (*Radio Free Europe*, 20 May 2021) www.rferl.org/a/kyrgyzstan-kumtor-gold-mine/31265257.html.

[4] Eshalieva (n 2).

[5] Al Jazeera, 'Kyrgyz Leader Signs Law Threatening Kumtor Gold Mine Takeover' (14 May 2021) www.aljazeera.com/news/2021/5/14/kyrgyzstan-gold-mine.

[6] Radio Free Europe, 'Former Kyrgyz President Akaev Admits "Mistakes" over Kumtor Gold-Mine Project' (9 August 2021) www.rferl.org/a/kyrgyzstan-akaev-kumtor-centerra/31400690.html; Radio Free Europe, 'Corruption Charges against Former Kyrgyz President Dropped' (13 January 2023) www.rferl.org/a/kyrgyzstan-akaev-corruption-charges-dropped/32221902.html.

[7] Reuters, 'Kyrgyzstan in Full Control of Kumtor Gold Mine as Centerra Takes Legal Action' (1 June 2021) www.reuters.com/business/kyrgyzstan-full-control-kumtor-gold-mine-centerra-takes-legal-action-2021-06-01/.

[8] Sullivan & Cromwell, 'S&C Leads Centerra Gold to Successful Resolution of Dispute with Kyrgyz Republic' (12 August 2022) www.sullcrom.com/About/News-and-Events/Highlights/2022/August/SC-Leads-Centerra-Gold-to-Successful-Resolution-of-Dispute-with-Kyrgyz-Republic.

[9] Beril Ocaklı, 'Politics of the Kyrgyz Mining Sector: An Interview with Beril Ocaklı' (*Voices of Central Asia*, 7 May 2021) https://voicesoncentralasia.org/politics-of-the-kyrgyz-mining-sector-an-interview-with-beril-ocakli/.

this case study, Jalal-Abad, eighteen out of twenty-eight gold mines are owned by either a Chinese individual or an organization.[10]

This case study focuses on labor conflicts between Chinese investors and local Kyrgyz workers in the Ishtamberdy and Kichi-Chaarat gold mines. These are both located in Jalal-Abad, which is a mountainous borderland in the west of Kyrgyzstan. Compared to the Kumtor mine, these mines are smaller in scale and output and, therefore, do not have the same economic significance as Kumtor. But focusing on labor disputes in the context of such mines is important as doing so provides a bottom-up view of the potentially adverse social and environmental impact of Chinese investments in the extractives sector. To date, although such investments have not led to the same public fallout as the Canadian-owned Kumtor mine, they are becoming the subject of scrutiny for two reasons. First, CSR and ESG initiatives and responses related to the UN SDGs are being increasingly applied to and adopted by the extractives industry as a whole. Second, this topic provides a lens through which to consider the role of Chinese businesses as a "responsible player" on the global stage and their mandate to shape their investment activities as a means of promulgating a "Green Silk Road."[11]

2.2 Case Study Roadmap

This case study focuses on the "lifespan" of a typical labor dispute between local Kyrgyz workers and Chinese companies, using the Ishtamberdy and Kichi-Chaarat gold mines as examples. Attention is paid to the socioeconomic and legal origins of such a dispute, especially to factors arising prior to and during employment. In addition, it addresses how local and national governments as well as Chinese companies respond to labor strikes and the chosen methods of dispute resolution (e.g., formal litigation or informal settlement). In particular, the case study discusses the Chinese company's mass dismissal of 400 Kyrgyz workers in order to avoid bankruptcy at the Ishtamberdy mine. Laborers there had engaged in long-term disruptive strikes against substandard working conditions and the nontransparent hiring of workers through intermediary organizations. In addition, the case study will also explore the environmental criticisms from local stakeholders that have heightened concerns about worker protests at the Kichi-Chaarat mine, leading management to increase security in and around the facility. Finally, the case study will explain the relevance to the disputes of such factors as corporate culture, labor division, and the promotion

---

[10] Tatyana Kudryavtseva, 'Chinese Interest in Kyrgyz Gold: Companies from China Hold About 30 Licenses' (*24.Kg*, 8 December 2023) https://24.kg/english/281824_Chinese_interest_in_Kyrgyz_gold_Companies_from_China_hold_about_30_licenses/.

[11] Lili Pike, 'Explainer: Will China's New Silk Road Be Green?' (*China Dialogue*, 11 May 2017) https://chinadialogue.net/en/business/9775-explainer-will-china-s-new-silk-road-be-green/; Jacob Mardell, 'BRI at 10: Checking in on the "Green Silk Road"' (*The China Project*, 9 October 2023) https://thechinaproject.com/2023/10/09/bri-at-10-checking-in-on-the-green-silk-road/.

Table 4.2.1 Information on interview respondents

Respondents	Number of interviews	Sociodemographic data
Kichi-Chaarat employees	8	4 men, 4 women, aged 20–63: 3 senior workers (manager, HR, specialists) and 5 junior workers (mine workers, kitchen, laboratory, machinery, etc.)
Ishtamberdy employees	8	4 men, 4 women, aged 22–65: 1 manager, 3 senior workers (HR, engineers), and 5 junior workers (mine workers, kitchen, laboratory, etc.)
Trade unions (national and local level)	2	Both men, 1 at the national level and 1 at the local
Local authorities	3	2 men, 1 woman, from two subdistricts where the two mines are located
Lawyers	1	Male, district-level lawyer, who was involved in the mass firing of employees at Ishtamberdy

and education opportunities for Kyrgyz workers. Hence, this case study will reveal the complexity of local and national conditions encountered by Chinese mine managers and owners in Kyrgyzstan. It will show not just how Chinese investors have responded to these local conditions but also how stakeholders on the Kyrgyz side have reacted, demonstrating how multiple parties contribute to outcomes.

This case study is primarily based on twenty-two in-depth interviews held in November and December 2022 with employees and managers at the Ishtamberdy and Kichi-Chaarat gold mines, as well as with local authorities and representatives of mining trade unions (see Table 4.2.1). The employees of the gold mines were sampled according to age, gender, seniority, management responsibility, and current job status (i.e., whether they are still employed or whether their employment has terminated). Given the general absence of any transparent reporting culture and the sensitivity of critiquing the mining sector, these in-depth interviews were crucial in helping to understand the issue. Some respondents were reluctant to answer and the percentage of refusals to participate in the study was high.

3 The Case

3.1 Background

Kyrgyzstan's economy is dependent on the gold sector, which accounts for 10% of GDP and 39% of exports. In 2021, Kyrgyzstan exported US$908 million in gold, and although this meant that Kyrgyzstan was only the 52nd largest exporter of gold in the world, gold was the primary export from the country.[12] Against this backdrop, foreign investment in gold mining areas has become a battleground for foreign investors, Kyrgyz authorities, the opposition, and local communities. Yet, because of its importance, the mining sector is identified as one of the priority sectors for the economy in strategic government papers concerning national development programs. These include the "National Development Program of the Kyrgyz Republic,"[13] which is in effect until 2026, and the "Concept of Green Economy in the Kyrgyz Republic."[14]

The employment structure in Kyrgyzstan mainly relies on agriculture and farming (18.3%), wholesale and retail trade (15.3%), construction (12.4%), and public services (health, education, etc.). Mining and quarrying employ only 0.7% of the workforce, with 17,900 people working in the industry. Yet this number has doubled since 2016. This increase can be explained by the Kyrgyz president Almazbek Atambaev's active cooperation with China and the issuing of mining licenses to smaller deposits since the start of his term in 2011.

A number of gold deposits have been discovered in the Middle Tian Shan mountains in Jalal-Abad. This region is southwest of the capital, Bishkek, and is a rural, mountainous area that has been traditionally used as summer pastures for local livestock keepers.[15] Jalal-Abad incorporates both the Ishtamberdy and Kichi-Chaarat mines, which are described in turn and in fuller detail below.

First, the Ishtamberdy mine was opened in 2011 as Kyrgyzstan's second foreign-owned mine. However, its operations since then have been intermittent due to license suspensions imposed by the Kyrgyz government in 2013,[16] 2016,[17] 2018,[18] and 2023.[19] Such setbacks have nevertheless not yet resulted in the abandonment of the project, primarily because of the commercial opportunities it presents: Exploration studies indicate that the site contains 140 metric

---

[12] Observatory of Economic Complexity, 'Gold in Kyrgyzstan' https://oec.world/en/profile/bilateral-product/gold/reporter/kgz.

[13] Ministry of Justice of the Kyrgyz Republic, 'National Development Program of the Kyrgyz Republic until 2026' http://cbd.minjust.gov.kg/act/view/ru-ru/430700.

[14] Ministry of Justice of the Kyrgyz Republic, 'Concept of Green Economy in the Kyrgyz Republic "Kyrgyzstan Is a Country of Green Economy"' http://cbd.minjust.gov.kg/act/view/ru-ru/83126?cl=ru-ru.

[15] See Figure 4.2.1.

[16] 24.Kg, 'Ishtamberdy Mine Highlights Kyrgyzstan's Gold Dependency' (11 September 2015) https://24.kg/archive/en/bigtiraj/177018-news24.html/.

[17] 24.Kg, 'Ishtamberdy Deposit Plans to Produce 780 kg of Gold in 2016' (6 April 2016) https://24.kg/archive/en/community/179978-news24.html/.

[18] Akipress, 'Operation of Full Gold Mining Company at Ishtamberdy Gold Mine Suspended' (19 June 2018) https://akipress.com/news:607849:Operation_of_Full_Gold_Mining_company_at_Ishtamberdy_gold_mine_suspended/.

[19] Akipress, 'Full Gold Mining Suspended for 3 Months: Jalal-Abad Region Authorities Discuss Situation' (12 December 2023) https://akipress.com/news:748447:Full_Gold_Mining_suspended_for_3_months__Jalal-Abad_region_authorities_discuss_situation/.

Figure 4.2.1 Tilted view of Ishtamberdy mine

Figure 4.2.2 Aerial view of Ishtamberdy mine

tons of gold.[20] This assessment places the Ishtamberdy mine among the larger of Jalal-Abad mines, whose gold deposits range from 34 tons (in Bozymchak) to 170 tons (in Chaarat). However, when compared to the Kumtor mine in the east, Ishtamberdy's deposit is considered relatively small,[21] containing approximately a quarter of Kumtor's 538-ton deposit.

In terms of its operating capability, as Figures 4.2.1 and 4.2.2 show, the Ishtamberdy mine comprises surface mining works and includes a processing facility;[22] and the stated aim was to mine 300,000 tons of ore per annum and, from that ore, to produce 2 tons of powdered gold concentrate per annum.[23] However,

---

[20] Converted 5 million ounces into metric tons. Accesswire, 'RTG to Acquire 90% Stake in the High Grade Chanach Gold Project in the Kyrgyz Republic' (5 September 2019) www.accesswire.com/558574/rtg-to-acquire-90-stake-in-the-high-grade-chanach-gold-project-in-the-kyrgyz-republic.

[21] Reuters, 'Chinese Miner Launches Gold Plant in Kyrgyzstan' (21 September 2011) www.reuters.com/article/idUSL5E7KL5Y0/.

[22] See Figure 4.2.2.   [23] Reuters (n 21).

it is unclear whether this aim has ever been realized because in 2016, when the mine was expected to start operating in full capacity, Ishtamberdy's chief engineer announced that only 780 kg of gold concentrate would be produced.[24]

In terms of the corporate structure of the Ishtamberdy mine project, the mine asset is owned and operated by Full Gold Mining Limited Liability Company ("Full Gold Mining"). It is a gold mining company and, according to Sayari, has one director and three shareholders. One shareholder is Lingbao Gold Company Limited (靈寶黃金股份有限公司),[25] a Chinese state-owned and Hong Kong-listed corporation that specializes in "mining, processing, smelting and sales of gold and other metallic products."[26] A second shareholder is China Road and Bridge Corporation (中国路桥工程有限责任公司).[27] This may explain why, despite a primary focus on mining, Full Gold Mining appears to have diverse business interests that also include, for example, road building, which have been used to secure the rights to the Ishtamberdy project.

Although detailed corporate information relating to Full Gold Mining and the Ishtamberdy mine is generally inaccessible, online sources indicate that the Chinese company came into control of and assumed the authority to develop the mine in three complementary ways. First, on 16 January 2008, Full Gold Mining secured a twenty-year license from the Kyrgyz government, a necessary prerequisite for any mine development.[28] Second, Full Gold Mining's acquisition was carried out through a multiparty Cooperation Agreement signed by Chinese and Kyrgyz parties from both the government and the private sector. On the Chinese side, signatories included China Development Bank, China Road and Bridge Corporation, and Xinjiang Uyghur Autonomous Region Lin Xi Investment Company, who all appear to have either financed the Ishtamberdy mine or supplied it with goods and services necessary for the mine's operation.

On the Kyrgyz side, signatories included the Kyrgyz Ministry of Transport and Communications and the Kyrgyz State Agency for Geology and Mineral Resources, who played a role in regulating, licensing, and approving the Ishtamberdy project. Third, Full Gold Mining and the Kyrgyz government reached an agreement on "Resources in Exchange for Investment."[29] Under its terms, Full Gold Mining would secure the rights to develop Ishtamberdy on the condition that it improved the local road infrastructure. Consequently, prior

---

[24] Suyunbek Shamshiev, 'Ishtamberdy Deposit Plans to Produce 780 kg of Gold in 2016' (*24.Kg*, 6 April 2016) https://24.kg/archive/en/community/179978-news24.html/.

[25] Bakyt Ibraimov and Jalil Saparov, 'Gold Mining at Heart of Recent Kyrgyz Political Turmoil' (*The Third Pole*, 22 February 2021) www.thethirdpole.net/en/pollution/gold-mining-at-heart-of-recent-kyrgyz-political-turmoil/.

[26] Reuters, 'Lingbao Gold Group Co Ltd' www.reuters.com/markets/companies/3330.HK/.

[27] Sayari, 'Chinese Mining Company Affected by Protests in Kyrgyzstan Has Ties to Major SOE' (12 March 2020) https://sayari.com/resources/chinese-mining-company-affected-by-protests-in-kyrgyzstan-has-ties-to-major-soe/.

[28] ibid.

[29] AidData project pages, 'Project ID: 46364' https://china.aiddata.org/projects/46364/.

to securing Kyrgyz licenses, Full Gold Mining served as the "entity responsible for project implementation" in a project to restore 50 km of the Osh-Sarytash-Irkeshtam Road that was financed by the China Development Bank via a US$38.57 million loan.[30] A peculiar feature of this transaction is that, although the road project was not connected geographically to the Ishtamberdy mine, the China Development Bank loan was to be repaid out of revenues generated by the mine and not the road project.[31] Separately, and following an outcry from villagers, Full Gold Mining also paved the road linking local settlements surrounding the Ishtamberdy mine.[32] These developments suggest a high degree of willingness among prospective Chinese investors (as well as third parties who play a secondary and supportive role, such as banks) to do whatever is necessary to secure the required licenses and agreements with the host country irrespective of the Chinese investor's core business operation.

The second gold mine that this case study explores is the Kichi-Chaarat mine, which lies approximately 70 km to the northeast of the Ishtamberdy mine, separated by the Pikgora mountain. The Kichi-Chaarat mine opened in 2019;[33] and, like Ishtamberdy, operations at the Kichi-Chaarat mine have periodically stalled due to license suspensions. One such suspension occurred in 2022 and applied to Kichi-Chaarat's Suluu-Tegerek deposit.[34] However, unlike Ishtamberdy, the Kichi-Chaarat mine falls into two parts (as it has two deposits) and operates different excavation methods.[35] The mine's Kulu-Tegerek deposit is located up on a mountainside and incorporates a US$220 million underground mine and concentration plant for converting gold, silver, and copper ore into powdered concentrates (Figures 4.2.3 and 4.2.4).[36] According to AidData, "Upon completion, the mine was expected to have an annual processing capacity of about 1.8 million tons, including an annual output of 11,000 tons of copper, 600 kg of gold and 4.6 tons of silver. The annual sales from the mine were expected to be $100 million."[37] Meanwhile, down the mountainside in the Chatkal valley's riverbed lies the Suluu-Tegerek deposit, which incorporates a placer mine.[38] Such mines remove gold deposits from sediment in water, but information on its productive capacity (either projected or actual) is unavailable.

The Kichi-Chaarat mine is owned and operated by Kichi-Chaarat Closed Joint Stock Company ("Kichi-Chaarat"), which is a special purpose organization

---

[30] Ibraimov and Saparov (n 25).   [31] AidData (n 34).   [32] Reuters (n 26).
[33] Kabar, 'Abylgaziev Takes Part in Kichi-Chaarat Concentration Plant's Launch' (15 August 2019) https://en.kabar.kg/news/abylgaziev-takes-part-in-kichi-chaarat-concentration-plants-launch/.
[34] Kyrgyzstan Newsline, 'Kyrgyzstan Suspends 11 Licenses for Right to Use Subsoil in 2022' (26 January 2023) https://newslinekg.com/article/1097928/.
[35] Kabar (n 33).
[36] AidData project pages, 'Project ID: 57683' https://china.aiddata.org/projects/57683/; Julia Kostenko, 'Kichi-Chaarat Concentration Plant Launched in Jalal-Abad Region' (*24.Kg*, 15 August 2019) https://24.kg/english/126525_Kichi-Chaarat_concentration_plant_launched_in_Jalal-Abad_region/.
[37] AidData (n 36).   [38] Kabar (n 33); Ibraimov and Saparov (n 25).

Figure 4.2.3 Aerial view of Kulu-Tegerek deposit at Kichi-Chaarat mine

Figure 4.2.4 Tilted view of Suluu-Tegerek deposit at the Kichi-Chaarat mine

established by Chinese equity investors to oversee the project. As with Full Gold Mining, little corporate information relating to Kichi-Chaarat is available. However, the available information indicates that it was owned by a succession of Canadian and Chinese companies. Specifically, a press release in 2004 indicates that Kichi-Chaarat was acquired by Eurasian Minerals, Inc., a Canadian firm, through a subsidiary called Altyn Minerals LLC.[39] Four years later, a United States Securities and Exchange Commission filing suggests that ownership had changed hands and that, in 2008, Kichi-Chaarat was owned by China Shen Zhou Mining & Resources, Inc. (a publicly listed firm whose shares were traded on what was then known as the American Stock Exchange) through a subsidiary called American Federal Mining Group.[40] Following this, online searches

---

[39] EMX Royalty Group, 'Acquisition of Kuru Tegerek Property in Kyrgyz Republic' (11 June 2004) https://emxroyalty.com/news/2004/acquisition-of-kuru-tegerek-property-in-kyrgyz-republic/.

[40] US Securities and Exchange Commission, 'China Shen Zhou Mining & Resources Announces Approval for Listing on the American Stock Exchange' www.sec.gov/Archives/edgar/data/790024/000102317508000008/chinashenzhounewsrelaese1280.htm.

indicate that Kichi-Chaarat in 2013 was 84% owned by the China National Gold Group Corporation and 16% owned by China CAMC Engineering Hong Kong Company Limited. Furthermore, similarly to Full Gold Mining, Kichi-Chaarat also received support from other Chinese economic actors – in this case, loan financing from both the China Export-Import Bank in 2017 and Skyland (a subsidiary of China Gold International Resources Group Corporation Limited) in 2016.[41] A more recent example of this is illustrated by a company press release by the Shanghai subsidiary of China National Gold, which celebrated its work to quickly provide supplies to Kuru-Tegerek by utilizing a streamlined customs declaration procedure and a combination of trucks and trains:

> On March 3, ten 40-foot containers loaded with RMB 4 million worth of mining machinery and equipment as well as production materials were released at Kashgar and Irkeshtam customs upon sealing inspection and transported to Kuru-Tegerek copper and gold mine in Kyrgyzstan through the Irkeshtam port. This indicated that the speed of the "China-Kyrgyzstan-Uzbekistan" highway and railway intermodal international freight train has been fully accelerated, in which China Gold Trading (Shanghai) was a major participator.[42]

Overall, when considering the role of Chinese investment in the Kyrgyz gold mining sector, it is worth noting that, first, Chinese investors will seek to work in concert with Kyrgyz and Chinese stakeholders from both the private and public sectors not only to agree to the terms of their investments but also to procure the necessary financing and project supplies. Second, Chinese investors will exercise flexibility to fulfill the needs of Kyrgyz stakeholders, even if doing so requires providing business solutions or negotiation concessions that may be novel or unfamiliar. Third, ownership of Kyrgyz mines seems to be particularly dynamic with owners and investors from various nationalities involved at different stages.

3.2 Causes of Tension

Gold mines have occupied a prominent position in Kyrgyzstan's national debates and political life. Over the last twenty years, local protests against foreign-owned mines have become more frequent in line with reducing employment opportunities, rising resource nationalism, and dissatisfaction among the local population who feel deprived from the income generated by the mines.[43] Political unrest has provided an opportunity for local community members to voice their demands to both the companies operating gold mines and state authorities. One example is the unrest that erupted in October 2020 led by local community members against gold mining companies, including those at the

---

[41] AidData (n 36).
[42] China Gold Group, 'China Gold Trading (Shanghai) Further Enhances Its Overseas Service Capability' (22 September 2021) www.chinagoldgroup.com/hjmye/s/2573-7726-40519.html.
[43] Ocakli (n 9).

Chinese-operated mines at Kichi-Chaarat and Ishtamberdy. The protests caused production to halt for several days as the mines were seized by the local population. The local population's grievances against the Chinese-operated mines were fueled by "perceived corruption, the lack of transparency, and discrimination against hiring local residents as well as environmental degradation."[44]

3.3 Opaque Hiring Practices

In late 2022, the Ishtamberdy mine had 585 employees and Kichi-Chaarat employed 129. Typically, Kyrgyz workers occupy various positions, from engineers, geologists and professional positions to regular miners, drivers, repair men, and so on. Women mainly work in the laboratories, kitchens, cleaning departments, and accounting and finance departments. Although our interviews have been unable to ascertain whether these staff numbers comply with Kyrgyz laws decreeing that the foreign labor force in a gold mine may not exceed 10%, recent news reports indicate that Ishtamberdy is compliant: Full Gold Mining, speaking about the Ishtamberdy mine, reported that 91% of workers were local Kyrgyz.[45]

However, in general, Kyrgyz job applicants find it difficult to receive an employment offer from a mining company in Kyrgyzstan. Mining is a well-paid industry so finding positions is intensely competitive. Applicants seeking an edge have paid significant bribes, others have chased job opportunities for years. Seeking employment at Chinese-owned mines is particularly difficult; other foreign companies (i.e., Canadian, British, Turkish, and Kazakh) tend to have a greater degree of accessibility and transparency. They have official websites or social media pages where they announce vacancies. Although the likelihood of Kyrgyz applicants satisfying all the job requirements and being accepted is very low, potential employees at least are informed as to the eligibility criteria and requirements for the position.

3.4 The Human Resources Department as Gatekeeper

Now and then, the Kyrgyz employment websites announce vacancies at the Ishtamberdy and Kichi-Chaarat mines, but most are for positions such as senior specialists or within the mine company's Human Resources department. These departments consist of Kyrgyz employees and play a major role in shaping the employment policy of the Chinese companies. For example, they can shape

---

[44] Saipira Furstenberg and Kemel Toktomushev, 'Understanding Gold Mining and Social Conflicts in Kyrgyzstan' University of Central Asia Institute of Public Policy and Administration Working Paper 63 (2021) 1–22, https://ucentralasia.org/media/ssmbkbyb/uca-ippa-wp63-understanding-gold-mining-and-social-conflicts-in-kyrgyzstan.pdf.

[45] Tatyana Kudryavtseva, 'Gold Reserves in Kyrgyzstan Estimated at 856 Tons' (*24.Kg*, 21 December 2022) https://24.kg/english/254011_Gold_reserves_in_Kyrgyzstan_estimated_at_856_tons/.

Chinese companies' current practice to allocate a quota for its local hires to local authorities, who then try to send their own associates, including relatives or family members (Chinese companies are not alone in adopting this practice). In some cases, positions are given to vulnerable families who have a low income or more children to co-opt those families who might otherwise have a grievance.

As characterized by a number of interview respondents, the Human Resources departments have over time built up power akin to the "mafia" (мафиянын уюгу) by hiring the "convenient" (кытайдын сөзүн сүйлөгөн) workers and firing the "inconvenient," ones, that is, "the ones who speak justice, demand better meals, compensation for night shifts and raise other problems" (акыйкатты сүйлөгөн, тамак-ашты жакшыртуу, түнкү сменага төлөш боюнча жана башка көйгөйдү айткан). As a result, the "convenient" laborers have formed an alliance of like minds and fully obey the instructions of Chinese managers.

The Chinese managers themselves don't participate in the hiring process as this is delegated to local subcontracting companies or locally hired human resources professionals. Due to these informal hiring practices, the process is seen as nontransparent by the local communities. For example, if an agitator is known for initiating demonstrations concerning environmental or other social issues in the villages near the mine, they have a better chance of being accepted for a job as a "silence reward," meaning that they are hired in exchange for their acquiescence. One interviewee recalled: "[Full Gold Mining Company] told me clearly that in exchange for not being an activist and for not mobilizing people to participate in demonstrations against the mine, I would be offered a job (ачык эле айткан, сиз закондошпойсуз, элди үгүттөбөйсүз, ошондо алабыз деген)." Not only does this practice raise ethical questions; it also may risk alienating applicants who have not caused conflict, which, in turn, may precipitate further grievances later on.

3.5 The Utility of Personal Relationships

The easiest and most effective way of being hired in the mining industry is through Kyrgyz acquaintances who already hold senior positions particularly in the Human Resources departments. Alternately, would-be employees need to have influential contacts with Kyrgyz authorities (e.g., such as law enforcement agencies). Of the twenty-two people interviewed, thirteen were hired because they knew someone influential.

Utilizing ties based on a combination of acquaintances, relatives, village neighbors, patrilineal ties, and clan members (тааныш-билиш) is a similar route to employment. For instance, if the senior HR person (Kyrgyz) is from one clan or certain village, most of the employees will be from the same clan or village. Because of the strong affiliation to clans, it is not uncommon for employees from different clans to develop confrontational relationships, which affects operations.

In general, people living close to the mines have a better chance of being accepted, as they are most likely to be affected by the environmental impact of mining activities – such as shoddy maintenance at the Ishtamberdy mine causing the effluent to enter the river, which serves as a water source for nearby villages.[46] People from the affected village would be prioritized for employment. Although regulations on the procedure for licensing subsoil use do not mandate hiring employees from the nearby villages,[47] it is the company's policy to prioritize hiring local people as "compensation."

3.6 Difficulties with Employment Contracts

Mining is one of the sectors that has a low percentage of informal employment in Kyrgyzstan, meaning that almost all workers have a contract. However, at the beginning of the projects, while the Ishtamberdy and Kichi-Chaarat mines were being established, there was a window of time during which many workers may not have had formal written contracts. The main issue with labor contracts is their term and how they are used to remove agitators. According to the Labor Code of Kyrgyzstan, contracts are concluded for a specified period not exceeding five years or for an indefinite term if the position is permanent. If the job is temporary in nature, contracts can run for a fixed term.[48] This mismatch (permanent or temporary) is used by many employers, not only by mining companies, across the sectors. Mining companies tend to offer fixed-term contracts for six months or one year, based on their view that the job is temporary. Interviews revealed that these fixed-term contracts have caused labor violations.

For instance, in Ishtamberdy mine, a one-year contract can be used to remove "inconvenient" workers who openly criticized labor conditions and demand more decent working conditions. Hence, workers could be fired without notice, including without sick leave and mandated holiday pay. Employment contracts have also been terminated for other reasons: After the protests in October 2020, nearly forty people (all men aged fifty-five and higher) were fired in a clear example of age discrimination. Kyrgyz law states that the retirement age for men is sixty-three,[49] but it includes a caveat stating that men working in mining can retire early if they have twenty-five years' work experience.[50] Most of the men fired did not have twenty-five years' experience and on this basis the mass termination of their contracts did not fulfill the caveat.

---

[46] Ibraimov and Saparov (n 25).
[47] Ministry of Justice of the Kyrgyz Republic, 'Regulations on the Procedure for Licensing Subsoil Use' (2018) http://cbd.minjust.gov.kg/act/view/ru-ru/12765.
[48] Ministry of Justice of the Kyrgyz Republic, 'Labor Code of the Kyrgyz Republic' http://cbd.minjust.gov.kg/act/view/ru-ru/1505.
[49] Law of the Kyrgyz Republic dated 21 July 1997 No. 57 State pension social insurance.
[50] Ministry of Justice of the Kyrgyz Republic, 'About State Pension Social Insurance' http://cbd.minjust.gov.kg/act/view/ru-ru/557/340?cl=ru-ru.

3.7 Insufficient Equipment and Unsafe Conditions

The interviews indicated that safety measures adopted by Chinese companies are relatively poor compared to other mines operated by other nationalities. The main reasons are the lack of financing for security measures (e.g., no first aid systems in place) and the incompetence of the responsible employees. The issue of health and safety in the Ishtamberdy and Kichi-Chaarat mines has been further compounded by a lack of cooperation with the Ministry of Emergency Situations in cases of emergencies and accidents. Previously, the companies paid a salary to the officers of the Ministry and, in case of accidents, an official rescue team would help, but this cooperation has stopped.

These issues mean that workers take responsibility for their own safety, for example, by buying special uniforms and equipment themselves when the company's equipment was broken or worn (e.g., including small items such as flashlights). Doing so, however, has unfortunately failed to avert mine accidents. According to interviewees, five persons died in the Ishtamberdy mine in 2022. This included two employees who died of carbon monoxide gas poisoning (and another ten were injured) as the mine did not provide gas masks and mine tunnels were not sealed properly.[51]

Another problem is that all instructions for the machinery is in Chinese. Most local workers cannot read Chinese and this problem is heightened during times of emergency, which are often time critical. The language gap is particularly pronounced by the fact that the Chinese companies do not provide training in the local language.

3.8 Complying with Salary Laws

The latest information on the average salary by sector shows that the mining sector has among the highest-paying jobs, together with manufacturing, information and communication, and the finance and insurance sectors. On average, employees receive about US$400 per month, whereas the average salary, across the largest sectors (agriculture, construction, trade, and public sector), is about US$150–200 per month.[52] However, in Ishtamberdy, the salary of workers is around US$230–250, which is significantly lower than the sector norm. In addition, in violation of local law, night shifts and extra hours are not paid.

According to the Labor Code of Kyrgyzstan, the mine workers' salary should have the following bonuses: high-altitude coefficient (30%), level of danger (30%), and night shifts (50%). Most mines are located above 3,000 m;

---

[51] Business and Human Rights Resources Center, 'Kyrgyzstan: 2 Killed, 10 Injured from Carbon Monoxide Poisoning at Ishtamberdi Gold Mine' (12 October 2022) www.business-humanrights.org/en/latest-news/kyrgyzstan-two-killed-and-ten-injured-from-carbon-monoxide-poisoning-at-ishtamberdi-gold-mine/.

[52] National Statistical Committee of the Kyrgyz Republic, 'Salary by Economic Sectors'.

therefore, mine workers should get at least the high-altitude coefficient. However, such bonuses are rarely granted. The representative of Kyrgyz Geology Trade Union stated:

> When we negotiate with Chinese companies, they say that they do not have the concept of high-altitude coefficient for the salary. They have a fixed salary of 30,000 som.[53] It includes night shift, high-altitude coefficient, and harmfulness. They say they don't have this in China.
>
> We explain to them that all employers working in Kyrgyzstan, regardless of their form of [company] ownership, are subject to the Labor Code of the Kyrgyz Republic. That is, they comply with labor laws.
>
> We have these problems, at the initial stage of interaction, when preparation work is already being carried out. Chinese investors involve lawyers and the lawyers also explain [the requirements] to them. This stage lasts six months or a year; almost all companies have this tendency. Chinese companies are not immediately ready to comply with local labor laws; they need to be explained, convinced, and proven that this must be done. […]
>
> At the beginning, an employment contract is not concluded, only a salary is paid. When the process begins, trade unions are created and people begin to contact the labor inspectorate, [only then] problems are exposed.
>
> And accordingly, [when] a dispute begins, we have several legal companies, Chinese consulting companies, and they explain their rights. The Chinese company leaders contact them, and it becomes clear that our demands are correct.

In summary, although mining salaries are among Kyrgyzstan's highest, there is a sense of injustice among workers in Chinese-owned mines who argue they are not receiving their full entitlement. There is also a view that the process of educating and persuading Chinese investors to pay the full entitlement is long and painstaking.

3.9 Working Conditions

According to the workday calendar approved by the Kyrgyz government,[54] mine workers should work a maximum of thirty-six hours per week. In reality, however, they often work up to fifteen additional hours, which goes unpaid. Sick leave is paid in Kichi-Chaarat, but in Ishtamberdy it depends on the negotiating and persuasive skills of the applicant. If successful, they can receive compensation.

Accommodation and food also need improvement. Accommodation in Ishtamberdy mainly consists of shipping containers, six to eight people in one room, and accommodation conditions for Kyrgyz workers are definitely poorer than those provided for Chinese workers.

---

[53] As of 29 February 2024, 1 Kyrgyz som is equivalent to 0.011 US dollar.
[54] Ministry of Labor and Social Development, 'Production Calendar for 2022' https://mlsp.gov.kg/wp-content/uploads/2021/11/kalendar-2022.pdf.

3.10 Grievances

Since 2010, when Chinese mining companies first began active mineral exploration in Kyrgyzstan, there have been numerous social and environmental conflicts due to mining operations. Participants from the surrounding villages have blocked roads, attacked mine sites, and engaged in other forms of protest. Because of corruption and instability within the political system in Kyrgyzstan, citizens often cannot resort to official channels for redress. Rather, historically, grassroots movements, including demonstrations, have been a more effective means of expressing civil disobedience and protecting social and economic rights. This is particularly so in the context of the mining sector.[55]

Ishtamberdy and Kichi-Chaarat have both seen a number of conflicts related to environmental problems, as expressions of disagreement by the local people to the mining process. This kind of demonstration serves also as a platform where local communities not only expressed grievances but also, and perhaps demonstrating a peculiarity of the Kyrgyz mining industry, expressed their willingness and ability to resume work in the hope that their protests would result in obtaining employment.

3.11 Mine Protests

Since the opening of the Ishtamberdy mine in 2011, at least three instances of service disruption have been documented. First, in 2012, workers called a strike. This led to a 30% pay rise (but less than the 50% being sought).[56] Later, in 2018, nearly 400 workers were dismissed for refusing to accept contracts with lower pay (which was driven by Ishtamberdy mine's poor financial performance). The vice president of Full Gold Mining elaborated:

> Our company has been suffering losses since it began to work. We invested US$200 million in the deposit. At least 958 million som have been spent on the payment of wages. Workers are very expensive, so we decided to change the terms of the contract. We ask for help to survive a difficult period together. The funds invested have not yet paid off. In order not to become bankrupt, we are forced to take such steps.[57]

---

[55] Kemel Toktomushev and Saipira Furstenberg, 'Understanding Gold Mining and Social Conflicts in Kyrgyzstan' (30 June 2021) University of Central Asia – Institute of Public Policy and Administration Working Paper No. 63 http://dx.doi.org/10.2139/ssrn.3896275; Troy Sternberg, 'Conflict and Contestation in Kyrgyz Mining Infrastructure' (2020) 7 The Extractive Industries and Society, 1392–1400 www.sciencedirect.com/science/article/abs/pii/S2214790X20302847.

[56] Aigerim Turgunbaeva, 'Kyrgyzstan Workers Strike for Better Pay at Chinese Mine' (*Eurasianet*, 18 May 2022) https://eurasianet.org/kyrgyzstan-workers-strike-for-better-pay-at-chinese-mine.

[57] Tatiana Kudryavtseva, 'Full Gold Mining Company Explains Dismissal of 400 Workers' (*24. Kg*, 8 January 2018) https://24.kg/english/72735_Full_Gold_Mining_Company_explains_dismissal_of_400_workers/.

The mass dismissal of workers led to villagers from Kizil-Tokoi and Terek-Sair forming a protest and, in turn, a suspension of operations at Ishtamberdy.[58]

In 2020, protestors alleging electoral fraud in the 4 October presidential elections also stormed the premises of Full Gold Mining.[59] This occurred during a period of civil unrest across Kyrgyzstan in which the Kyrgyz White House and Supreme Court were also occupied. The precise motivations for storming the premises are unclear and may have been driven by frustrations beyond the mine itself: government corruption, socioeconomic inequalities, and the presence of foreign-controlled companies in Kyrgyzstan.[60]

Although there are fewer documented instances of unrest at the Kichi-Chaarat mine, the mine has not been insulated against similar incidents and in 2020 "tightened security at its mine, anticipating riots by the locals."[61]

3.12 Inaccessible Justice

Resolving large-scale labor disputes has typically been achieved through negotiations between companies, employees, local and national authorities, and labor unions. Both the government and the companies are interested in not publicizing the disputes and try to resolve conflicts internally.

As for labor disputes initiated by individual workers, litigants officially have recourse to the courts and there are regular court cases. However, most of the local employees have little legal knowledge and thus do not seek recourse in courts. If they are fired or face any labor rights violation, they usually address the local municipality or district level authorities, or simply keep believing the promises of Chinese company representatives.

These issues are further compounded by a number of factors, one of which is that information on court cases is hard to find in the state register,[62] unless you know the full information on the case. This difficulty renders jurisprudence inaccessible and imposes a constraint on litigants and their legal advisors, thereby placing them on the back foot vis-à-vis businesses such as the Ishtamberdy and Kichi-Chaarat mine owners who have their own in-house counsels.

In the meantime, according to Kyrgyz law, a person should address the court with a complaint regarding unfair termination within two months of being fired. The procedure for addressing the complaint is also quite complicated as employees need to have a conclusion from labor inspection. This requirement creates a significant time delay for filing that in the past has impeded a number

---

[58] Akipress, 'Villagers Protest against Full Gold Mining Company Developing Ishtamberdi Mine in Jalal-Abad' (13 June 2018) https://akipress.com/news:607687:Villagers_protest_against_Full_Gold_Mining_company_developing_Ishtamberdi_mine_in_Jalal-Abad/.
[59] Sayari (n 27).   [60] ibid.
[61] Mines and Communities, 'Wave of Protests against Foreign Owned Gold Mines in Kyrgyzstan' (10 July 2020) www.minesandcommunities.org/article.php?a=14399.
[62] Маалыматтык Ресурстар (Information Resources), www.sot.kg.

of suits. For example, interviewees reported losing their age discrimination case(s) because the case(s) expired due to such time delays.

3.13 The Role of Government Agencies

Government agencies and local authorities tend to have insufficient experience and capacity to deal with enforcement issues. For example, corruption is a deep-seated problem, and while some argue that corrupt practices can actually help address certain issues, in general, corruption exacerbates systemic problems. Specific to Chinese investors, local authorities and high-level authorities (e.g., deputies of the Kyrgyz Parliament) have been known to form affiliated companies that win subcontract tenders from the Chinese. Consequently, they may exhibit a protectionist attitude toward Chinese investors even if those investors are violating local environmental and labor rules. This problem creates resentment among local residents who have groups, including on social media, where they share information on, for example, corrupt actions by local government and the nontransparent practices of Chinese investors. These resentments likely resulted in the 2020 election protests.

Local authorities often do not have sufficient human resources to work effectively with Chinese and other foreign investors. In the Chatkal district where several mines, including the Kichi-Chaarat mine, are located, there is only one official responsible for communicating with all mining companies and who seems not to have any background in mining.

In cases of conflict, local employees and communities are known for mobilizing online social media platforms, as well as using demonstrations, to put pressure on national decision makers. The authorities then form national commissions to address the issues, but little seems to be achieved. The president may also be called upon to intervene directly in the matter – even when it may not be entirely appropriate to do so. The effectiveness of such commissions and presidential interventions is therefore questionable.

Chinese companies, in turn, have poor communication strategies and often fail to keep local communities informed. They seem to struggle to understand the value of such communication. Additionally, they are also dependent on organized crime groups that come to "protect" their business. These crime groups work as security officers to watch over local employees. In times of political unrest or acting on information from local employees inside, there have been cases of robbery and theft of gold from the factory. Understandably, the involvement of crime groups against local workers is perceived negatively and there are attempts of local communities to counter this, by organizing their own groups.

Representatives of local authorities mention that Chinese companies are failing to implement communication strategies effectively and engage with the local population. The companies rarely organize public hearings and, as a result, local communities have little interaction with Chinese companies beyond "stealing gold." In parallel, the Chinese companies also have no trust in local communities and authorities. They perceive people approaching their companies as those who came to rob, steal, or ask for funding for charitable causes, develop a business proposition, or ask for resources to fix a public utility in the village. The representatives of Chinese companies who are hired to communicate with the local population often do not have enough experience of working with the public. As a result, they fail to represent the companies positively or to highlight the benefits mines can bring to a region. For example, gold mining can contribute up to 50% of a municipality budget and often supports and improves local infrastructure and facilities.

Fourth, access to company reports is also an issue. Non-Chinese companies publish annual Environmental Impact Assessments (EIAs) and regular reports on their socioeconomic contributions to the local communities on their websites. In contrast, Chinese companies do not even have websites. The results of the interviews show that Chinese companies do support local projects and funding, but there is no strategy or process to make this information available; information is mainly distributed during the local budget hearings once a year.

The labor inspection is implemented by the State Inspection of Labor and Trade Union. The Trade Union has two inspections: a legal inspection and an inspection of safety measures. Since January 2022, the Kyrgyz government abolished inspections of business by the state committee for the support and improving of the investment climate. The Trade Union public inspectors have a right to access enterprises whenever they seek access, and they can exercise both planned and non-planned inspections. Currently they conduct one inspection of Chinese companies annually. Usually, non-planned inspections are carried out when employees report on violations of labor rights – but this is rare in any case.

4 Conclusion

China has significant investment not just in gold mining in Kyrgyzstan but in extractives industries throughout Central Asia. Hence, this case study spotlights issues of broad relevance. Our interviews suggest that Chinese mining companies demonstrate an initial unwillingness to follow local labor legislation at the beginning of their investment projects, and only the efforts of local authorities and trade unions ultimately persuade them to comply, at least in part. Hence, there is a learning curve that Chinese companies undergo.

Owing to language and cultural barriers, Chinese companies delegate the recruitment process to local subcontracting companies and the Human Resource departments consisting of mainly local employees and local authorities. However, this approach opens a way for personal connections and clan-based ties to play a role in hiring. As a result, people with no proper experience are recruited. Such trends can endanger operational processes and put technical safety standards at risk.

Violations of labor rights by Chinese mining companies are prevalent throughout Kyrgyzstan and, in particular, wherever informal employment is prevalent and wherever this can be used to remove undesired workers. Fixed-term contracts are common not only in the mining sector but also in other business sectors. Nevertheless, compared to other mines, Chinese companies pay less attention to occupational safety and providing necessary technical equipment.

Owing to their lack of expertise in communication and public relations, Chinese companies often become the targets of social conflict. In those cases where companies do have a communication strategy, it often depends on employees who lack experience. For example, company websites or social media platforms are not widely used so information is hard to come by. The companies also rarely participate in local meetings or explain how they are contributing to the local economy and fail to take the opportunity of highlighting their positive contributions such as improving local infrastructure. In contrast, some non-Chinese foreign companies are adept at using not only their own media sources but also TV channels and news websites to tell their story and emphasize the value they bring to the country. Unfortunately, when Chinese companies do appear in the media, it is usually in the context of social conflict.

5 Discussion Questions and Comments

5.1 For Law School Audiences

1. The Kyrgyz Labor Code is one source of problems for insufficient protection of workers. What legislative changes would you make to the Labor Code? How would you balance protecting workers' rights with maintaining a competitive commercial environment for foreign investors?
2. Assume the role of a public interest lawyer, instructed by the workers. They have informed you that they wish to pursue a mixture of grassroots actions and alternative dispute resolution methods to secure their rights. Propose what actions (legal and otherwise) the workers should take against (a) the foreign investors; (b) the local government; (c) the national government; and (d) local communities.
3. Assume the role of a general counsel at either the Ishtamberdy or Kichi-Chaarat mine. How might you redraft the company's policies as pertaining to labor relations and management?

5.2 For Policy School Audiences

1. What kinds of policy interventions could Kyrgyz authorities make at the local or national levels to avoid the types of disputes that have occurred at the Ishtamberdy and Kichi-Chaarat mines from developing in the first place?
2. Given that such disputes have in fact arisen, what options are available to Kyrgyz authorities to mitigate the conflicts? Which factors would the authorities consider in trying to resolve the conflicts?

5.3 For Business School Audiences

1. Imagine you are the general manager at either the Ishtamberdy or Kichi-Chaarat mines. What mine-wide measures would you implement that balance the following priorities: (a) increased compliance with local law; (b) enhanced communication and relations between local and foreign employees; and (c) profitability?
2. Language, culture, and customs are perennial issues that create wedges between Chinese mining companies and local Kyrgyz labor. How should Chinese companies refine their approaches to gaining greater proficiency over these issues and what kinds of intermediaries would be helpful to that effect?

Section 5
Finance

Case Study 5.1

Sovereign Debt Restructuring in Zambia
A Chinese Approach

Charles Ho Wang Mak

1 Overview

China, as one of the world's largest creditors, has recently faced numerous defaults on its loans by recipient states, bringing the issue of Chinese debt restructuring to the forefront. This case study unpacks this process, with a particular focus on Zambia, a country emblematic of the broader dynamics at play. The primary aim is to elucidate the mechanisms and negotiations employed by China, a major global creditor, in debt restructuring agreements with low-income countries, with an emphasis on its engagements in Africa.

The case study starts with a deep analysis of the Zambia case, highlighting the negotiation tactics and terms of agreements between Zambia and China. This serves not only as a snapshot of China's dealings with a specific country but also as a springboard for broader discussions. Subsequently, the case study broadens its scope to encompass China's lending dynamics in the African continent. It dissects the patterns, similarities, and disparities in China's lending practices across different African nations, elucidating the motives and implications.

Furthermore, the case study establishes a global context by acknowledging China as the world's largest official creditor. It critically questions China's choice to remain outside the Paris Club and considers China's inclination or aversion toward coordinated debt restructuring.

Relying on primary sources from the Paris Club, World Bank, International Monetary Fund (IMF), and the Chinese and Zambian governments, this case study ensures a robust and credible analysis. While the term "sovereign debt" is used in this case study, it is noteworthy that this terminology is not universally applied in the aforementioned discussions, indicating a divergence in the lexicon across different platforms and analyses.

2 Introduction

In November 2020, Zambia, a landlocked country in south-central Africa, defaulted on its sovereign debts – debts incurred by a government through borrowing from external lenders to finance national projects and programs.

As the first African country to default on its Eurobonds during the COVID-19 pandemic, Zambia has struggled with large debts and a lack of foreign currency, making it difficult to purchase necessary products and repay its debt. China is Zambia's largest sovereign creditor, meaning it is the largest external entity to which Zambia's government owes money, holding almost one-third of the country's total external debt.[1] In addition to being the largest sovereign creditor to Zambia, China is the second largest sovereign creditor in the world after the World Bank.[2]

This case study examines ongoing debt restructuring in China and Zambia, focusing on China's policies, practices, and approaches to debt restructuring in low-income countries. The analysis acknowledges the challenges in sourcing information, given that much of China's debt is considered hidden.[3] Thus, the analysis is based on primary sources from the Paris Club, the World Bank, the IMF, and the governments of China and Zambia, juxtaposing their records with the less transparent aspects of China's lending practices. This case study highlights China's extensive lending activities to numerous countries, thereby establishing its position as the world's largest sovereign creditor. Moreover, this case study will explore how the sovereign debt restructuring between China and debtor countries, including Zambia, lacks a coordinated approach, reflecting China's tendency to negotiate debt agreements bilaterally rather than through multilateral frameworks.

Such a case study is significant because it provides insight into how China can negotiate with its debtors without becoming a permanent member of the Paris Club, an informal group of major creditor countries established in 1956 that have historically coordinated sustainable solutions to payment difficulties faced by debtor countries. The Paris Club plays a crucial role as a forum for debt restructuring negotiations, setting standards for transparency and coordination. However, it is pertinent to acknowledge that in some developing countries the Paris Club is perceived as being a club for former colonial powers. This perception suggests that the Paris Club may not always align with the best interests of recipient countries, a factor that shapes diverse global views on its role. This case study will provide detailed information on whether China is interested in coordinating debt restructuring and why China has not become a permanent member of the Paris Club. It discusses China's approach to sovereign debt restructuring and the implications for countries from the Global South. In doing so, it will also shed light on the broader discourse around

---

[1] Zambia Ministry of Finance, 'Annual Economic Report 2021' (2021) www.mofnp.gov.zm/?wpdmpro=2021-annual-economic-report&wpdmdl=3283&refresh=63c543f9d12441673872377.

[2] World Bank Group, 'International Debt Statistics' (2022) www.worldbank.org/en/programs/debt-statistics/ids#analytical.

[3] Axel Dreher, Andreas Fuchs, Bradley Parks, Austin Strange, and Michael J. Tierney, *Banking on Beijing: The Aims and Impacts of China's Overseas Development Program* (Cambridge University Press 2022) 24–25.

international debt relief and creditor–debtor dynamics. In addition, it will explain China's status as the largest sovereign creditor and the likely impact of its policies on the world economy.

3 The Case

3.1 Background on the Economic and Political Context in Zambia Leading to Debt Restructuring

Zambia has a severe debt crisis, with more than half of its tax income going to debt repayment and a budget deficit of 9.5% of its GDP in 2022.[4] This high level of debt has rendered the government unable to pay its debts and import essential goods, resulting in a foreign currency shortage and a halt in economic growth. Several reasons, including government expenditure, declining commodity prices, and the COVID-19 pandemic, have contributed to Zambia's debt crisis. Although the pandemic has exacerbated the country's debt problems, it did not cause them. In recent years, Zambia has been confronted with a variety of economic issues, including a drop in copper prices (the main export), and these problems have been exacerbated by a lack of economic diversification and bad administration. President Edgar Lungu and his party, the Patriotic Front (PF), are primarily responsible for these difficulties.

Prior to 2011 when the PF came to power, the Zambian economy was enjoying growth and stability. The country's GDP was growing at a constant pace, fueled by the copper mining industry and international investment. In addition, the government had undertaken economic measures that assisted in reducing poverty and improving the living conditions of many Zambians. However, since coming to office in 2011, President Edgar Lungu and the PF have pursued policies and taken actions that have increased the country's debt, including expanding its use of Chinese external finance to support public works.

The IMF has highlighted the growing debt of Zambia and the prospect of debt distress. In 2017, it warned that Zambia's debt levels had become unsustainable, and that the government was in danger of defaulting on its debts.[5] The IMF further noted that the country's debt issue is exacerbated by the government's significant borrowing to fund infrastructure projects.[6]

---

[4] National Assembly of Zambia, '2023 Budget Address by Honourable Dr. Situmbeko Musokotwane, MP, Minister of Finance and National Planning Delivered to the National Assembly' (2022) www.parliament.gov.zm/sites/default/files/documents/articles/2023%20Budget%20Speech.pdf.
[5] International Monetary Fund, 'IMF Executive Board Concludes 2017 Article IV Consultation with Zambia' (2017) www.imf.org/en/News/Articles/2017/10/10/pr17394-imf-executive-board-concludes-2017-article-v-consultation-with-zambia.
[6] ibid.

According to the World Bank, the public external debt owed by the Zambian government is US$24.05 billion,[7] whereas only US$13.04 billion of external debt is reported by the Zambian Ministry of Finance and National Planning.[8] Although there are loans that have been authorized but do not yet appear in official figures, this large difference suggests a lack of transparency about the external debt. The China-Africa Research Initiative at the Johns Hopkins University School of Advanced International Studies has noted that official sources, which include the World Bank and the Zambian government, have not yet provided accurate information on the stock of debt owed by Zambia to Chinese lenders. Based on open sources and interviews, they suggest that the government of Zambia, including its state-owned enterprises, owes Chinese creditors approximately US$6.6 billion as of August 2021. This is nearly double the amount cited by the Zambian government; its Annual Economic Report 2021 disclosed that the country's public external debt stock from China, specifically from the Export-Import Bank of China (Exim Bank) and the China Development Bank, stood at US$3.349 billion in 2021.[9]

Based on the above figures, it is estimated that approximately 30% of Zambia's total loans are attributable to China. Most of these external sovereign debts are owed to China for infrastructure projects, leading to speculation that any debt restructuring with China could involve handing over roads, airports, or even mines.[10] On 22 June 2023, Zambia struck a deal to restructure US$6.3 billion in debt owed to governments abroad, including China.[11] To combat the country's debt crisis, the Zambian finance minister has taken a number of steps, such as suspending certain projects, seeking the advice of debt advisors, and engaging in negotiations with China.

There are possible ripple effects from Zambia's debt default that may affect other countries. It is certain that Zambia's economic growth and development will be hampered by the state's inability to gain future access to international credit markets due to the default. Beyond Zambia, its defaulting on debt might also trigger global financial instability by raising concerns about the ability of other developing countries that have borrowed heavily from China to repay their loans. It might also disrupt countries and sectors that rely on Zambia's economy, such as mining and agriculture. In addition, if Zambia were to default on its debt, it may have a negative impact on international trade and investment.

---

[7] World Bank Group, 'External Debt Stocks, Total (DOD, Current US$) – Zambia' (2022) https://data.worldbank.org/indicator/DT.DOD.DECT.CD?end=2021&locations=ZM&start=1970&view=chart.
[8] Zambia Ministry of Finance (n 1).
[9] Deborah Brautigam and Yinxuan Wang, 'Zambia's Chinese Debt in the Pandemic Era, Briefing Paper, No. 05/2021' China Africa Research Initiative (2021) www.econstor.eu/bitstream/10419/248246/1/sais-cari-bp05.pdf; Zambia Ministry of Finance (n 1).
[10] Zambia Ministry of Finance (n 1).
[11] Zambia Ministry of Finance, 'Zambia Reaches Agreement with Official Creditors on Debt Treatment under the G20 Common Framework' (2023) www.mofnp.gov.zm/?p=7444.

3.2 China's Lending Practices in Africa and Related Concerns

A comprehensive assessment of the debt restructuring process between Zambia and China requires understanding China's lending practices in Africa and their possible influence on states like Zambia. As Zambia is presently facing a debt crisis and has been highly reliant on Chinese lending, it is essential to evaluate how these lending practices affect the difficulties and opportunities African states have in managing debt and supporting economic development. China has extended large-scale loans to Zambia to fund its infrastructure projects as part of its Belt and Road Initiative (BRI), prompting scrutiny in recent years of China's lending practices in Zambia, as well as across Africa. The BRI aspires to construct infrastructure to help promote commerce throughout Asia, Europe, and Africa, with China positioning itself as a significant lender of finance to African countries, such as Zambia, to accomplish this objective.

There are rising concerns over China's general sovereign debt practice, as issues have been raised about the terms of loans, the sustainability of projects, and the potential for debt distress in African countries.[12] Notably, China's sovereign debt practice in Africa has been different from those of conventional lenders. First, Chinese official loans offered by the Chinese government are often not as transparent as those provided via commercial channels. Chinese contracts tend to incorporate atypical confidentiality clauses, which prohibit the sovereign debtors from divulging not only the terms but also the very existence of the indebtedness. Moreover, dispute resolution mechanisms stipulated in these contracts often favor Chinese courts or arbitration institutions, potentially disadvantaging the debtor nations.

Moreover, Chinese financiers endeavor to secure advantageous positions relative to other creditors by employing security arrangements such as financier-managed revenue accounts and commitments to exclude the debt from aggregate restructuring (commonly referred to as "no Paris Club" clauses).[13] Additionally, clauses pertaining to cancellation, acceleration, and stabilization within Chinese contracts grant the lenders the potential to exert influence over the debtors' domestic and international policies.[14] This combination of confidentiality, preferential standing, and policy influence may curtail the sovereign debtor's avenues for crisis management and add layers of complexity to the renegotiation of debt.[15]

---

[12] See Sam Parker and Gabrielle Chefitz, 'Debtbook Diplomacy: China's Strategic Leveraging of Its Newfound Economic Influence and the Consequences for U.S. Foreign Policy' (Harvard Kennedy School Paper, 24 May 2018) www.belfercenter.org/sites/default/files/files/publication/Debtbook%20Diplomacy%20PDF.pdf.

[13] Anna Gelpern, Sebastian Horn, Scott Morris, Brad Parks, and Christoph Trebesch, 'How China Lends: A Rare Look into 100 Debt Contracts with Foreign Governments' Center for Global Development Working Paper 573 (2021) 6.

[14] ibid 37–8. [15] ibid.

Because China is Zambia's largest creditor, and there is a perceived lack of transparency in its financing practices in Africa, allegations of engagement in debt-trap diplomacy arise as seemingly valid concerns. The term "debt-trap diplomacy" refers to the theory that a state, in this case China, provides loans to other states with the purpose of trapping them in a cycle of debt and then using that debt as leverage to obtain control over the states' resources or political decisions. There is a widespread perception among journalists and politicians that Beijing utilizes foreign assistance (including both commercial loans issued by state-owned financial institutions and sovereign credit) to prop up rogue regimes or to control other nations via debt. While this claim has been widely circulated, it is important to critically examine the basis of these allegations.[16] Accessing comprehensive data on China's financial aid programs is challenging, as the information is fragmented across thousands of documents in various languages, making it difficult to draw conclusive insights.

Although China lends money commercially, it does not publish information about its commercial lending operations or disclose information about its assistance programs via international reporting systems like the Organisation for Economic Co-operation and Development's (OECD's) creditor reporting system. In addition, it uses stringent confidentiality rules to keep its lending and financing operations under cover. Even though the Chinese Ministry of Finance publishes statistics on the state's overall foreign aid spending, there is a lack of official information that offers a project-level or country-by-country breakdown of foreign lending. This has prompted concerns over the lack of openness and accountability in the lending procedure and the possibility of corruption. Yet a recent study suggests the evidence basis for examining the aims and impacts of China's sovereign debt practice can be formed by "employing a new set of data collection methods."[17]

For example, using an innovative suite of data gathering techniques, AidData has compiled an invaluable dataset spanning three years.[18] This dataset contains details of 100 Chinese loan contracts involving 24 countries classified as having low to middle incomes and can be used to provide novel insights into the intricacies of China's lending customs. In parallel, AidData, in collaboration with the Center for Global Development in Washington, the Kiel Institute in Germany, and the Peterson Institute for International Economics, undertook a rigorous comparative analysis of Chinese loan contracts and compared them with those furnished by other principal lenders. Through this method, they assessed the legal stipulations in China's loans. By employing

---

[16] The term "debt-trap diplomacy" has gained traction in international discourse, but it requires careful analysis. Past allegations have sometimes been based on anecdotal evidence or studies without robust empirical support. To understand the full dimensions of this issue, there is a need for methodical research that can cut through the complexities and provide a grounded perspective on the motivations and outcomes of China's lending practices.

[17] Dreher et al. (n 3).   [18] See AidData, 'About AidData' (2023) www.aiddata.org/about.

these cutting-edge data collection methodologies and rigorous analytical techniques, Chinese lending practices in the global arena can be better understood.

It is important to note that the conditions of China's loans have benefited developing countries in Africa as they tend to have low interest rates and lengthy payback periods. This has made them appealing to African states, which have traditionally struggled to get financing from other creditors on favorable terms. Also, there are concerns that African states may become overindebted and unable to repay their debts. Indeed, this seems to be the situation in Zambia, highlighting the complexity and risks associated with foreign debts, especially for countries with fragile economies.

China's funding has been motivated by a desire to secure access to African states' natural resources, including oil and minerals. This has prompted fears that African states may grow reliant on China and lose sovereignty over their natural resources. China's financing policies in Africa have been marked by a lack of transparency, preferential loan conditions, and an emphasis on acquiring access to natural resources. However, an analysis of the lending patterns in relation to the locations of onshore deposits of petroleum, gold, gemstones, and diamonds has revealed that, despite the possibility of China's lending practices being motivated by a desire for resources, there is no correlation between these natural resources and the direct outcomes of the loans.[19] This suggests that China's motivations may be multifaceted and not solely driven by resource acquisition. However, it is vital to consider the broader implications and strategic interests that might be at play, even if the loans themselves do not yield immediate gains for China.

Further, it is essential to emphasize that Zambia's debt situation has several causes and cannot be attributed exclusively to China's lending policies. Poor financial management, wasteful politics, and a short-sighted pursuit of money have all contributed to the country's present debt dilemma. Regarding Zambia's development goals, former and current Zambian leaders appear to have a forward-looking development plan centered on infrastructure investment. It is important to note that under the new leadership of the United Party for National Development, the economy is showing resilience. Real GDP growth is now projected to be 4.7% in 2024.[20]

3.3 China's Sovereign Debt Restructuring Practices

Sovereign debt restructuring is defined as a process wherein a sovereign state renegotiates the terms of its debt obligations with creditors to ensure sustainability and manageability. This usually happens when a sovereign state is

---

[19] ibid 170–1.
[20] International Monetary Fund, 'IMF Reaches Staff-Level Agreement with Zambia on the Second Review of the Extended Credit Facility' (2023) www.imf.org/en/News/Articles/2023/11/20/pr23401-zambia-imf-reaches-staff-level-agreement-second-review-of-ecf.

unable to meet its debt obligations or is facing imminent default, and it may involve reducing the principal amount, extending maturity periods, or lowering interest rates. Such a process involves "an exchange of outstanding sovereign debt instruments," which is used by sovereign entities to avoid the risk of debt default of the existing sovereign debt or defer repayment.[21] Guzman, Ocampo, and Stiglitz noted that "the current system for sovereign debt restructuring features a decentralized market-based process in which the sovereign debtor engages in intricate and complicated negotiations with many creditors with different interests"; therefore, it often operates "under the backdrop of conflicting national legal regimes."[22]

With no exception, the current approaches taken by sovereign debtors of China are also decentralized and fragmented. Nonetheless, China has shown a willingness to renegotiate loans, mostly bilaterally, under certain conditions, such as when there is a clear risk of default that may impact its bilateral relations or economic interests. It is crucial to recognize that the differentiation between interest-free and interest-bearing loans is a common financial practice, not unique to China. Interest-free loans often entail less financial burden on the borrower, leading to a more favorable stance toward debt forgiveness by lenders. In contrast, interest-bearing loans, which generate revenue through interest, are usually subject to more stringent negotiations. Within this global context, China's approach to debt management demonstrates a clear preference for leniency toward interest-free loans in terms of debt forgiveness, as opposed to the more complex discussions surrounding interest-bearing loans. Nevertheless, China has earned a reputation for being a skilled negotiator in the realm of debt discussions, particularly for loans that accrue interest.

Since there is no universal international sovereign debt regime for the BRI, there is increasing concern about current approaches to sovereign debt restructuring. China is now establishing a framework to improve the sovereign debt management system, including practical debt sustainability evaluation standards and a standardized sovereign debt restructuring procedure for foreign sovereign debtors.[23] This framework is spearheaded by the Chinese national government, aiming for a more streamlined and systematic approach. It encompasses guidelines for debt sustainability assessments and mechanisms for negotiating restructuring terms. However, the framework is still in early stages and its efficacy remains to be tested.

---

[21] Udaibir S. Das, Michael G. Papaioannou, and Christoph Trebesch, 'Sovereign Debt Restructurings 1950–2010: Literature Survey, Data, and Stylized Facts' IMF Working Paper WP/12/203 (2012) 7.

[22] Martin Guzman, José Antonio Ocampo, and Joseph E Stiglitz, *Too Little, Too Late: The Quest to Resolve Sovereign Debt Crises* (Oxford University Press 2016) 4.

[23] Zhou Chengjun, 'Building the Shanghai Model of Sovereign Debt Restructuring' (构建主权债务重组的上海模式), Speech at the fourth China International Finance Forum, Shanghai (31 July 2021).

As Zambia struggled with high levels of debt, which subsequently led to its default, the government of Zambia sought assistance in managing its debt burden by requesting a suspension of debt payments through the G20 Debt Service Suspension Initiative (DSSI). The primary aim of the DSSI is to address the debt sustainability problems faced by those low and lower-middle income countries during the COVID-19 crisis. Also, the DSSI is "a temporary measure to provide liquidity approved in April 2020."[24] In November 2020, the G20 and the Paris Club countries endorsed the Common Framework for debt treatments beyond the DSSI ("Common Framework"), which seeks to "facilitate timely and orderly debt treatment for DSSI-eligible countries, with broad creditors' participation including the private sector."[25] The Common Framework provides a more structural approach for those DSSI-eligible countries to deal with unsustainable debts. Fundamentally, the Common Framework serves as a set of common rules (i.e., a basis of mutual agreement) for G20 countries (including those non-Paris Club members like China), the Paris Club members, and private creditors to deal with unstainable debts owed by DSSI-eligible countries in a more orderly manner.

On 16 June 2022, a group of sixteen countries established a creditor committee under the Common Framework. This is led by China and France, with South Africa serving as the vice-chair, and met to discuss Zambia's request for debt relief beyond the G20 DSSI (following the guidelines set by the G20 and the Paris Club).[26] Subsequently, the creditor committee held the second meeting under the Common Framework on 18 July 2022. After this meeting, the committee supported Zambia's efforts to secure an IMF upper credit tranche program and encouraged multilateral development banks to provide maximum support to meet the country's long-term financial needs.[27] Such examples of sovereign debt restructuring between China and Zambia indicate that China is willing to work with other sovereign creditors to restructure the debt rather than handle defaults on its own. This could serve as a precedent for other countries, such as Sri Lanka and Pakistan, with significant debts to China.

Instead of being a permanent member of the Paris Club, China continues to participate in the Paris Club's negotiation meetings on an ad hoc basis. Using

---

[24] G20, 'First G20 Africa Advisory Group Meeting under the Italian G20 Presidency' (2021) www.g20.org/first-g20-africa-advisory-group-meeting-under-the-italian-g20-presidency.html.

[25] G20, 'Statement – Extraordinary G20 Finance Ministers and Central Bank Governors' Meeting' (2020) file:///Users/charlesmak/Desktop/english-extraordinary-g20-fmcbg-statement-november-13.pdf.

[26] Paris Club, 'First Meeting of the Creditor Committee for Zambia under the Common Framework for Debt Treatments beyond the DSSI' (Paris Club, 2022) https://clubdeparis.org/en/communications/press-release/1st-meeting-of-the-creditor-committee-for-zambia-under-the-common.

[27] Paris Club, 'Second Meeting of the Creditor Committee for Zambia under the Common Framework for Debt Treatments beyond the DSSI' (Paris Club, 2022) https://clubdeparis.org/en/communications/press-release/2nd-meeting-of-the-creditor-committee-for-zambia-under-the-common.

this approach, it can still affect its debtor countries' decision-making process, including those that sit as permanent members. By joining as an ad hoc member, China does not need to respond to every data-sharing request from other Paris Club permanent members, which is one of the likely reasons why China chooses not to become a permanent member.

The pandemic has to some degree united the interests of different players in the sovereign debt market. Due to the advent of the DSSI and the Common Framework, the distinction between sovereign creditors who are part of the Paris Club and those who do not belong to the current sovereign debt restructuring governing framework has become somewhat blurred. Nonetheless, the existing institutional architecture is inadequate to ensure sustainable debt restructuring and equitable burden-sharing among sovereign debt market players (especially those nontraditional and non-Western countries like China).

3.4 Implications for Zambia and Africa

Zambia's debt crisis and debt restructuring process have significant implications for the country's economy and society. In the short term, Zambia is likely to face economic challenges due to the debt crisis, including a decline in economic growth and a shortage of foreign currency. The Zambian government will also have to implement austerity measures to address the debt crisis, which may impact the population's welfare. In the long term, the debt restructuring process and the terms of the agreement with China will have an important impact on Zambia's economic prospects.

This scenario calls for a detailed understanding of China's financial aid to various African states. China is the major bilateral creditor globally and it was estimated that China provided African states with loans amounting to almost US$160 billion from 2000 to 2020, predominantly via its state-controlled banking institutions.[28] The scrutiny of these lending practices has become more acute as countries like Zambia encounter challenges with loan repayments.

The Chinese government has implemented some measures in an attempt to alleviate the burden of debt, which has included absolving twenty-three interest-free loans extended to seventeen African countries.[29] This action was part of a commitment made by President Xi Jinping during the Forum on China-Africa Cooperation in 2021. In contrast, China exhibits a more rigid

---

[28] BU Global Development Center, 'Chinese Loans to Africa Database' (2023) www.bu.edu/gdp/chinese-loans-to-africa-database/.

[29] Ministry of Foreign Affairs of the People's Republic of China, 'China and Africa: Strengthening Friendship, Solidarity and Cooperation for a New Era of Common Development' (2023) www.fmprc.gov.cn/eng/zxxx_662805/202208/t20220819_10745617.html; Deborah Brautigam, Kevin Acker, and Yufan Huang, 'Debt Relief with Chinese Characteristics', Policy Brief, No. 46/2020, China Africa Research Initiative, School of Advanced International Studies, Johns Hopkins University, Washington, DC (2023) www.sais-cari.org/publications-policy-briefs.

approach concerning the restructuring of debt that constitutes the majority of its loans, particularly those under the BRI. The state typically refrains from divulging the terms of its loans, and its approach to debt relief frequently manifests in the form of extensions in loan maturity or the provision of new loans rather than reductions in the principal amount.

In recent times, there has been a discernible shift in the lending practices of China in Africa. Loans are now disbursed after a meticulous assessment of loan applications and specific schemes. This represents a marked departure from previous practices that largely entailed the allocation of funds for infrastructure. This alteration might signify a more circumspect approach to lending in Africa, which could be attributed to the ongoing crises related to indebtedness. As mentioned, Zambia has reached an agreement to restructure its debt of US$6.3 billion owed to foreign governments, including China. If the debt restructuring is successful and the country can achieve a sustainable debt situation, it will be better positioned to attract investment and promote economic growth. However, if the debt restructuring is not successful and the country is unable to achieve a sustainable debt situation, it may face a prolonged period of economic stagnation.

The debt crisis and debt restructuring process in Zambia also have broader implications for the key challenges that sovereign debt and the decentralized governing framework for sovereign debt restructuring pose to international financial stability. As China is a major lender to many African countries, the experience of Zambia raises questions about the potential risks and benefits of China's lending practices and approach to debt restructuring in Africa. For instance, this case highlights the need for greater transparency and accountability in China's lending practices and the need for international coordination in addressing debt crises in countries from the Global South. Specifically, the lack of clarity in the lending terms emanating from China, encompassing aspects such as interest rates and stipulations regarding collateral, holds the potential to place debtor nations in precarious circumstances that are disadvantageous. This highlights the need for China to embrace an approach that is more transparent and that harmonizes with global norms, as such an approach may engender trust and facilitate collaboration. In addition, current efforts at the international level may provide frameworks that extend beyond the provision of solutions to immediate debt dilemmas and establish economic underpinnings for nations burdened by debt. Such an endeavor warrants a joint initiative involving principal lenders, including China, international fiscal establishments, and the governing bodies of the indebted nations, with the aim of crafting unified strategies that alleviate the strains of debt and catalyze economic stability.

4 Conclusion

The debt crisis and debt restructuring process in Zambia have been complex and ongoing, with significant implications for the country's economy and society. There have also been consequences for other African countries that have received loans from China, and for international financial stability in general. This case study has examined China's policies, practices, and approach to the debt restructuring of countries from the Global South, explicitly focusing on Zambia.

The analysis of the debt crisis in Zambia highlights the country's economic challenges, driven by internal and external factors, including government spending, falling commodity prices, and external factors, such as the COVID-19 pandemic. The high levels of debt, the composition of the debt, and the sustainability of the debt have all been major concerns in the country. The debt restructuring process and the terms of agreements with China will have an ongoing and important impact on Zambia's economic prospects.

In conclusion, this case study highlights the need for greater transparency and accountability in China's lending practices, and international coordination in addressing debt crises in low-income countries. It also highlights the potential implications of China's approach to debt restructuring, not only for Zambia but also for other developing countries and the global economy as a whole.

5 Discussion Questions and Comments

5.1 For Law School Audiences

China's growing economic presence in Africa poses several legal and strategic questions. Its approach to lending in Africa, marked by its distinctive features and strategic implications, warrants critical examination from a legal perspective. The intricacies of China's lending practices, negotiation tactics, and the controversial notion of debt-trap diplomacy are pivotal topics for discussion in the context of international financial law and policy.

Given the above, discuss the following questions:

1. Which salient characteristics define China's lending approaches in Africa, and in what ways do these diverge from conventional Western lending mechanisms?
2. In what manner does China's practices in negotiations with indebted nations deviate from the methodologies deployed by the Paris Club affiliates?
3. Is there an abundance of substantiated evidence buttressing the allegation of "debt-trap diplomacy" pursuant to China's lending practices in Africa, particularly in Zambia?

5.2 For Policy School Audiences

China's burgeoning political influence in Africa illuminates a variety of strategic considerations. Its distinctive lending approach in Africa, marked by its unique characteristics and strategic implications, necessitates a comprehensive policy analysis.

Given the above, discuss the following questions:

1. Which factors underlie Zambia's debt predicament, and what part have Chinese loans played in this context?
2. What are the more long-term ramifications of China's lending practices and debt restructuring strategies for Africa and the additional nations comprising the Global South?
3. It has been argued that the rise of China, which is purportedly bringing about significant shifts in the global power dynamics, is propelled not only by using debt as a geopolitical policy lever but also by the process of lending money – extending credit to countries like Zambia to boost China's influence and strategic interests. According to some observers, "[t]he spread of financialization, the modernization of Zambian space, and the competition for authority over the Zambian state's balance sheet were all enabled by debt. In effect the rise of China was being partially subsidized by the lending of fictitious capital to pay for Chinese goods, services, and even labor."[30] Do the aforementioned facts support the assertion that China engages in debt-trap diplomacy?

5.3 For Business School Audiences

China's growing economic influence in Africa brings to light a range of strategic considerations. Its unique lending approach in Africa, marked by its decision not to accede to permanent membership of the Paris Club, calls for an in-depth analysis from a business standpoint. This choice enables China to function outside the conventional norms pertaining to sovereign debt restructuring, which might accord it augmented latitude in negotiations with debtor countries.

Given the above, discuss the following questions:

1. What plausible rationale could underpin China's resolve not to accede to permanent membership of the Paris Club? How does this choice bear upon its endeavors in debt restructuring?
2. In respect of fulfilling its objectives and preserving its economic and political clout, how efficacious has China's approach to sovereign debt restructuring proven?

---

[30] Joris Gort and Andrew Brooks, 'Africa's Next Debt Crisis: A Relational Comparison of Chinese and Western Lending to Zambia' (2023) 55 Antipode 830, 844.

Case Study 5.2

Exiting International Joint Ventures between Chinese and South African Banks

Thembi Madalane

1 Overview

Sino-African joint ventures (JV) are part of a developing relationship between China and African nations that encompasses a range of sectors and presents opportunities as well as challenges. Chinese investment in Sino-African JVs occurs for reasons such as financial support and strategic partnership to strengthen economic ties with African countries. By engaging in such partnerships, Chinese companies spread their investments across different sectors and regions. However, exiting a Sino-African JV may also be necessary for reasons such as a strategic refocus or business realignment; either Chinese or African parties may wish to exit a JV to focus on areas that are more in line with their changing long-term objectives. However, in the world of JVs, parties often face challenges when attempting to exit a partnership.

ICBC Standard Bank Plc (ICBCS) is a Sino-African JV involving the South African Standard Bank Group ("SB Group") and the Industrial and Commercial Bank of China (ICBC). The JV provided an opportunity for the SB Group to realize proceeds that would release capital to further its growth strategy across South Africa and the rest of the African continent. China's ICBC entered into the JV to elevate its global markets capabilities. In recent years, the SB Group has wished to exit the ICBCS JV but is restricted from doing so by the terms of its Sale and Purchase Agreement with ICBC.

This case study affords insights into some of the challenges of exiting a Sino-African banking JV agreement and explores the multifaceted impacts of Sino-African banking JVs. This knowledge is vital for informed decision-making by policymakers, businesses, and other stakeholders involved in these collaborations. The primary sources used in the case study were shareholder cautionary announcements, the Sale and Purchase Agreement, annual reporting statements, and press releases.

2 Introduction

On 8 November 2013, the Johannesburg Stock Exchange (JSE) released a Stock Exchange News Service announcement that the SB Group was engaged in discussions with ICBC relating to the potential disposal of its controlling stake in the SB Group's London banking operation, Standard Bank Plc (SB Plc).[1] Given SB Group's narrower strategic focus on Africa, it had reached the potential to create considerably more value through growing its franchise and generating incremental revenues from a wider spectrum of opportunities than were currently available to it.

On 29 January 2014, it was announced that Standard Bank London Holdings Limited (SBLH), a wholly owned subsidiary of SB Group, had entered into a Sale and Purchase Agreement with the ICBC.[2] The proposed transaction was to create a Global Markets JV with ICBC, named the ICBC Standard Bank Plc.[3] The Sale and Purchase Agreement was reached through SB Plc, as the primary legal entity used by the Group's London-based Global Markets business ("OA Global Markets Business").[4] The Group's African Global Markets businesses worked closely with the OA Global Markets Business to source and distribute African Global Markets Products.[5]

The JV created a "unique and commercially compelling opportunity for the SB Group and ICBC to partner in Global Markets."[6] It also benefited from the extensive international networks of both ICBC and SB Group, allowing it to serve clients across different regions and time zones.[7]

However, eight years later, it was announced by the SB Group on 11 March 2022 that it was working to exit the JV.[8] The SB Group wished to exit the JV but was blocked by the Sale and Purchase Agreement with ICBC. Specifically, the lock-in provisions specified that SB Group was not entitled to sell its shares in the JV until ICBC exercised its right to buy the shares or until five years following the completion of the Sale and Purchase Agreement.

---

[1] Standard Bank Group Limited (SBGL), SBK 201311080007A Cautionary Announcement – [Standard Bank Group Limited – Cautionary Announcement] (8 November 2013) www.sharedata.co.za/v2/Scripts/News.aspx?c=SBK&x=JSE. See also, SBLG, SBK 201312200021A Cautionary Announcement – [Standard Bank Group Limited – Further cautionary announcement] (20 December 2013) www.sharedata.co.za/v2/Scripts/News.aspx?c=SBK&x=JSE.

[2] SBGL, SBK 201401290020A Cautionary Announcement – [Standard Bank Group Limited – Disposal by Standard] (29 January 2014) www.sharedata.co.za/v2/Scripts/News.aspx?c=SBK&x=JSE. Upon or prior to completion, Standard Bank Group, SBLH, Standard Bank Plc, and ICBC entered into a number of other ancillary agreements, including a shareholders agreement and a services agreement. The shareholders agreement contains, inter alia, provisions regarding governance, funding, and capital arrangements for Standard Bank Plc after Completion.

[3] SBGL, Circular to Standard Bank Group Shareholders, 24 February 2014.

[4] ibid. SB Plc is wholly owned by the SB Group through the intermediate holding company, SBLH.

[5] The OA Global Markets Business includes commodities, fixed income and currencies, credit, and equities trading.

[6] SBGL (n 3).   [7] This is detailed further in the discussion on the objectives of the JV.

[8] SBGL, FY21 Results Presentation Speaker Notes (11 March 2022) https://thevault.exchange/?get_group_doc=18/1647013249-SBG2021AnnualResultsSpeakerNotes.pdf.

The SB Group was also required to hold no less than 20% of its shares in the JV up to seven years following the completion of the Sale and Purchase Agreement.[9] In 2022, the lock-in provisions had expired, and the SB Group communicated its intention to exit the JV. It also started discussions about selling its shares to ICBC.

This case study considers the challenges of the ICBCS Sale and Purchase Agreement in order to gain a granular understanding of the process of exiting a Sino-African banking JV. It analyzes the nature and objectives of a JV between Chinese and African banks and outlines the terms and conditions of the Sale and Purchase Agreement to lay the foundation for an analysis of the triggers to exit a JV. It also explores the impact of changing circumstances on the objectives of the JV and considers whether there is protection against such changing circumstances, as provided in the Sale and Purchase Agreement. In light of the challenges to exiting a JV, the case study explores the importance of negotiating an exit plan in the face of different objectives, as illustrated by the challenges faced by SB Group and ICBC. Whereas the specific exit mechanisms in the lock-in provisions are not unique to the Sino-Africa banking relationship and are found in such agreements globally, in the context of the ICBCS JV this case study shows how such standard mechanisms serve Chinese long-term commercial and geostrategic interest in Africa over short-term gains.

3 The Case

3.1 Background

Corporations and financial institutions in China, the second largest economy and with one of the fastest growing traded currencies in the world, have been expanding rapidly beyond the national borders.[10] Considering that China and Africa in particular are increasingly important contributors to the global economy, a partnership between Chinese and African banks was viewed as unique in the banking sector and reflective of new linkages between emerging market economies.[11] Establishing the platform for a Global Markets partnership between ICBC and SB Group would facilitate the formation of a partnership in Global Markets between the largest banks in China and Africa (see the combined footprint in Figure 5.2.1).[12] Moreover, ICBC had been the SB Group's strategic partner since 2008 (see the ICBC Standard Bank Group structure in Figure 5.2.2).[13] The two groups had cooperated on a wide range of initiatives in Africa and other emerging markets, with a particular focus on growing trade and investment flows between China and Africa.[14]

---

[9] As per lock-in provisions. SBGL (n 3).   [10] SBGL (n 2).   [11] ibid.   [12] ibid.
[13] SBGL (n 3).   [14] ibid.

	SB Countries	ICBC Countries	Combined
Africa	20	0	20
Asia	2	21	23
Rest of World	3	22	25
Total	25	43	68

Figure 5.2.1 Standard Bank and ICBC combined footprint

Figure 5.2.2 ICBC Standard Bank Group structure

3.1.1 Standard Bank Group Limited (SBGL) Growth Strategy

The SB Group, a South African bank with a primary listing on the JSE, can be traced back to the Standard Bank of British South Africa in 1862.[15] It was established as a South African subsidiary of the British overseas bank Standard Bank in London.[16] The original London-based business has gone through many changes, including expansion into China. Subsequently renamed as Standard Bank Group Limited, it has been building and operating a London-based Global Markets business, Standard Bank London Limited, since 1992.[17] It has thereafter served as the hub for the Corporate and Investment Banking (CIB) Division's expansion into emerging markets outside South Africa.[18]

In June 2005, the bank's name in London was changed to Standard Bank Plc,[19] having grown from its African roots to be a significant player in commodity and financial market trading in emerging markets.[20] SB Plc allowed the SB Group to access global capital markets to facilitate growth and development in Africa, as well as to maintain SB Group's position as a significant financial market participant in commodities trading.[21] The London-based business has branches in Dubai, the United Arab Emirates, Hong Kong, Tokyo, Japan, and Singapore. It also has representative offices in several locations such as Shanghai in China.[22] However, in more recent years, only Shanghai in China has remained relevant to the Group's strategy.[23] The other representative

---

[15] SBGL, 'Our Milestones', www.standardbank.com/sbg/standard-bank-group/about-us/who-we-are/milestones. Standard Bank Group has a secondary listing on the A2X Exchange, 11 August 2018.

[16] ibid. The bank was subsequently named the Standard Bank of South Africa, although by then its operations had spread across Africa. In 1962, the South African operations were formed into a subsidiary and the parent company became Standard Bank Limited and then Standard Chartered Bank plc. In 1969, the parent bank merged with the Chartered Bank of India, Australia and China and the combined bank became known as Standard Chartered Bank. In 1969, a South African holding company, Standard Bank Investment Corporation Ltd (SBIC or Stanbic), was established as the holding company of The Standard Bank of South Africa Limited and the bank's other various subsidiary companies (now the Standard Bank Group as the holding company in South Africa). The South African subsidiary became a wholly South African-owned institution for the first time when the parent company sold its remaining shareholding in the South African subsidiary, which subsequently also changed its name to "Standard Bank Group Limited" in 2002. In 1987, Standard Chartered sold its remaining 39% stake in Standard Bank Group. The two banking groups are now under separate ownership. See SBGL, 'Our Milestones' (n 15).

[17] Standard Bank London Limited was the first South African bank to be granted a banking license in Great Britain since the South African debt moratorium of 1985. Standard Bank establishes a representative office in London in 1988. See ibid. Global Markets is a business unit within the Group's Corporate and Investment Banking business. See SBGL (n 2).

[18] SBGL (n 3).

[19] Authorized and regulated by the UK Prudential Regulation Authority and the Financial Conduct Authority.

[20] Standard Bank Plc is a member of, inter alia, the London Bullion Market Association, the London Metal Exchange, the London Platinum and Palladium Market, and the London Stock Exchange Plc.

[21] SBGL (n 2). [22] SBGL (n 3). [23] ibid.

offices have been reported to be in the process of being closed,[24] although the reasons for the closures have not been made publicly available.

Since the global financial crisis started in 2007, SB Plc has experienced significant challenges in adjusting its business model. This was exacerbated by the SB Group's change of strategy from building a Global Emerging Market banking group to focusing primarily on Africa. These challenges included reduced revenue opportunities following the divestiture by the Group of several other businesses in countries outside Africa, among other factors.[25] Eventually, in 2011, the SB Group abandoned its strategy to be a global emerging markets player to concentrate on its investments in Africa. In line with other actions taken to restructure the SB Group's international business and reallocate capital and other resources to deliver on its refined African strategy, the SB Group implemented several initiatives.[26] Substantive action was taken to reduce both the risk profile and the cost base of SB Plc and other operations outside Africa.[27]

3.2 Objectives of the JV

By introducing ICBC as the majority shareholder in the JV, the partners created a new and larger commodity and financial markets platform and expanded the strategic emphasis for the OA Global Markets Business to focus, in particular, on SB Group partnering with China's leading banking group.[28] In combination with the powerful client relationships of ICBC, the JV presented the OA Global Markets Business with promising franchise and revenue growth opportunities, while maintaining the role it performed for SB Group's African business.

As discussed in the background of this case study, the SB Group's strategy was to focus primarily on Africa. The proposed JV with ICBC presented an opportunity to realize proceeds on disposal that would release significant capital for the SB Group from its operations outside Africa, which could then be effectively deployed in furthering the Group's growth strategy in South Africa and across the African continent.[29] Likewise, it would elevate the operations of ICBC.[30]

---

[24] ibid.
[25] Divestiture by the Group of several other businesses, notably from Argentina, Russia, and Turkey, the impact of defaulting exposures dating back to the global financial crisis, and a high and relatively inflexible cost base. SBGL (n 3).
[26] ibid.   [27] ibid.   [28] ibid.
[29] ibid. Also see SBGL (n 2). Some of the consideration received by SBLH were to be used to settle existing liabilities of SBLH. Approximately US$95 million of the consideration received by SBLH on completion would, in terms of the transaction agreements, be used to settle the existing liabilities of SBLH.
[30] The chairman of ICBC stated that, by leveraging SB Plc's global markets business platform, mature business model, and industrial expertise, the transaction would elevate ICBC's global markets capabilities in business development, risk management, operations, and innovation.

3.3 Terms and Conditions of the JV

It was agreed that ICBC would acquire 60% of SB Plc's fully diluted issued share capital from SBLH for cash.[31] SB Group completed the disposal of a 60% controlling interest in SB Plc to ICBC with effect from 1 February 2015 as of the "Closing Date" (see Group structure in Figure 5.2.2).[32] The purchase price was payable by ICBC on the basis of the net asset value of SB Plc, subject to audit verification.[33] Upon completion of the sale and purchase, ICBC would acquire a controlling interest in the Group's London-based Global Markets business, focusing on commodities, fixed income, currencies, credit, and equities products. The SB Group would retain a minority shareholding interest sufficient to maintain the continuity of access to this business for the group's African network and clients.[34]

The completion of the sale and purchase was subject to the implementation of a proposed transaction that was, in turn, itself subject to fulfillment or waiver of the conditions precedent as per the Sale and Purchase Agreement.[35]

Conditions Precedent: The focus of the proposed transaction was the OA Global Markets Business. The implementation of the transaction was subject to the fulfillment (or waiver) of several conditions precedent, such as regulatory approval in multiple jurisdictions.[36] This excluded the Global Markets business within CIB in Africa, which remained with the SB Group after the completion of the Sale and Purchase Agreement.[37]

---

[31] ICBC will acquire fully paid ordinary shares from SBLH, comprising in aggregate 60% of the fully diluted issued share capital of Standard Bank Plc, on an unencumbered basis. See SBGL (n 2).

[32] SBGL, SBK 201502020008A – Completion of disposal to ICBC and voluntary trading statement (2 February 2015).

[33] On completion ("the Closing Date"), the disposal proceeds from the transaction were expected to total less than the illustrative amount contained in the Circular to Shareholders of 24 February 2014, which was based upon Standard Bank Plc's adjusted 30 June 2013 net asset value (US$80 million [the audited consolidated net asset value of the Standard Bank Plc Group at completion of the Sale and Purchase Agreement × 60%]). See SBGL (n 3); SBGL (n 2). It was expected to total approximately US$690 million, US$75 million less than the illustrative amount contained in the Circular to Standard Bank Group Shareholders of 24 February 2014. See also SBGL (n 32).

[34] SBGL (n 1).   [35] The effective date of the proposed transaction was the date of completion.

[36] As set out in the Circular to Standard Bank Group Shareholders, which are only expected to be fulfilled after the third quarter of 2014. That is, approval by the South African Reserve Bank, Standard Bank Group Shareholders (other ICBC) in terms of the JSE Listings Requirements, Chinese Banking Regulatory Commission, State Administration of Foreign Exchange of China, UK's Prudential Regulation Authority, Financial Industry Regulatory Authority and Committee on Foreign Investment in the USA, Monetary Authority of Singapore. See SBGL (n 3). At the General Meeting held on 28 March 2014, both ordinary resolutions in the notice required to authorize the Group to proceed with the proposed transaction were duly passed by the requisite majority of eligible shareholders present or represented by proxy. See SBGL, SBK SBPP 201403280017A Results of General Meeting, 28 March 2014. The successor entities into which the excluded business would be moved will require appropriate regulatory approvals, so that these activities can be continued, as they remain a critical part of the Group's overall competitive positioning in Africa. See SBGL (n 2).

[37] SBGL (n 3).

A series of steps was undertaken to reorganize the SB Plc Group as a condition to completion of the Sale and Purchase Agreement. These steps had to be effected or completed to the reasonable satisfaction of ICBC.[38] The reorganization constituted the SB Group, SB Plc, and relevant subsidiaries and operations in the United States and Singapore as a focused Global Markets platform.[39] In addition to regulatory approval, the SB Group had to remove and close all activities that it currently performed and any previously discontinued activities and legacy assets that did not form part of the OA Global Markets Business. This removal involved SB Plc and its representative offices in any relevant international location.[40] It was intended that SB Plc and its representative offices would be renamed upon completion of the Sale and Purchase Agreement, to reflect the changed ownership of the OA Global Markets Business.[41] A newly established UK entity or other SB Group entities would acquire or take transfer of all of the assets, liabilities, and employees of the businesses excluded from SB Plc, prior to completion of the Sale and Purchase Agreement.[42]

Prior to the proposed transaction, the SB Group also transferred SB Plc Affiliates to SB Plc. So as to retain the Global Markets booking capabilities held by Standard New York Inc., Standard New York Securities Inc. and Standard Americas Inc. provided to SB Plc the shares owned by SBLH in Standard New York Inc.[43] In addition, SB Plc intended to close certain nonstrategic representative offices before completing the Sale and Purchase Agreement.[44]

According to the terms of the Sale and Purchase Agreement, during the reorganization, no "Material Adverse Change" could take effect as of 29 January 2014.[45] This included a reduction in the net asset value (NAV) of the Standard Bank Plc Group of at least US$100 million and/or a decrease in the actual or reasonably projected revenue of the OA Global Markets Business for the twelve-month period commencing 1 January 2014 for an amount of US$50 million or more.[46]

---

[38] SBGL (n 2).   [39] ibid.
[40] These excluded business activities include Investment Banking, Transactional Products and Services, Principal Investment Management, and the Group's London-based Services Unit, which provides key skills and services to the Group (together, the "Excluded Business"). The assets relating to these activities comprised approximately 2% of Standard Bank Plc's total assets at 30 June 2013. Where it is not practicable to transfer specific assets of the excluded business from Standard Bank Plc prior to completion of the Sale and Purchase Agreement, provision has been made for the synthetic, collateralized transfer of all the risk and benefit relating to these assets to other Standard Bank Group entities prior to completion. See SBGL (n 2); SBGL (n 3).
[41] SBGL (n 2).   [42] ibid.
[43] ibid. The shares owned by SBLH are in Standard New York Inc. and indirectly in Standard New York Securities Inc. and Standard Americas Inc.
[44] ibid.   [45] SBGL (n 3).
[46] ibid. Compared with the actual revenue of the OA Global Markets Business for the twelve-month period commencing 1 January 2013.

3.4 The Exit Terms of the JV

There was no prescribed expiration date of the JV term. Rather, the respective rights of ICBC and the SB Group to continue or exit the partnership commenced with the ICBC Call Option, two years after completion of the Sale and Purchase Agreement.

Lock-in provision: The SB Group was not entitled to sell any of its shares in the ICBCS JV until ICBC exercised its Call Option right or until five years following completion of the Sale and Purchase Agreement.[47] Notwithstanding its rights, the SB Group was restricted to hold no less than 20% of the shares in issue, until the seventh anniversary of completion (see Table 5.2.1 on exit mechanism rights and timelines).[48]

3.4.1 Exit Mechanisms

3.4.1.1 ICBC Call Option

Commencing two years following the completion of the Sale and Purchase Agreement, ICBC had the right to exercise a Call Option. For a five-year period from the commencement of the Call Option right, ICBC had the right to acquire a further 20% of the outstanding ordinary shares of SB Plc held by SBLH, in cash.[49] Payable by ICBC, the purchase price for the ICBC Call Option was determined as the higher of "(i) the most recent audited Consolidated NAV of SB Plc attributable to such shareholding, and (ii) the most recent audited consolidated profit before tax of SB Plc, capitalized at a five times multiple, attributable to such shareholding" but subject to a maximum amount of US$500 million.[50]

Table 5.2.1 ICBC Standard Bank Plc exit mechanisms

	Option rights	Counterparty obligations
ICBC Call Option (Exercisable 2–5 yrs. following date of completion of Sale and Purchase Agreement)	Right to purchase furthermore 20% of ICBCS JV	Obligation for SBGL to sell 20% of ICBCS JV: commences when ICBC exercises Call Option (6 months following exercise date of Call Option)
SBGL Put Option (Exercisable 5–7yrs. following date of completion of Sales and Purchase Agreement)	Right to sell 20% of outstanding ordinary shares in ICBCS JV	Obligation for ICBC to buy 20% of outstanding ordinary shares: commences when SBG exercises Put Option

Source: Adapted by author from Circular to Standard Bank Group Shareholders, 24 February 2014.

---

[47] ibid. [48] ibid.
[49] No less than 20% of all the Standard Bank Plc shares then in issue. See SBGL (n 2); SBGL (n 3).
[50] SBGL (n 2).

3.4.1.2 Standard Bank Put Option

In the event that the ICBC Call Option was exercised, SB Group had the right to exercise a Put Option commencing six months after the exercise date of the ICBC Call Option.[51] Valid for a period of five years, the SB Group had the right to dispose of all its residual shares to ICBC, for cash.[52] The price of the shares was determined as being "90% of the most recent audited consolidated NAV of SB Plc attributable to such shareholding" subject to a maximum amount payable by ICBC in respect of the SB Group Put Option of US$600 million.[53]

3.5 Changing Circumstances

Owing to changing circumstances in recent years, the ICBCS JV has faced losses that dragged on the SB Group's earnings.[54] With the exclusion of ICBCS, the SB Group reported revenue growth.[55] The Sale and Purchase Agreement protects against changing circumstances prior to approval of the JV. It provides that prior to the completion of the sale of the controlling stake to ICBC, ICBC will have the right to terminate the Agreement in the event of any change in the circumstances that will, or be reasonably likely to have, a material adverse effect on the business, assets, liabilities, condition (financial or otherwise), and/or results of operation of Standard Bank Plc if it is not remedied.[56] Prior to approval of the JV, an unforeseen matter with potential loss arose relating to SB Plc client exposure at Qingdao Port in China. Certain amendments were agreed to ensure that ICBC did not incur any loss or receive any unintended benefit. Subsequent to approval of the JV, ICBCS incurred a loss as a result of bankruptcy of its client following an explosion at its Philadelphia refinery. Warranties for changes post JV are not provided for in the Sale and Purchase Agreement.

3.5.1 Preapproval of JV

An unforeseen matter arose subsequent to the proposed transaction approval by the requisite majority of shareholders at the General Meeting held on 28 March 2014. In terms of the Sale and Purchase Agreement, the unforeseen matter impacted the disposal of SB Plc.[57] The proposed disposal by SBGL to ICBC of a controlling interest in ICBCS JV was withdrawn.

On 5 June 2014, the SB Group responded to media inquiries regarding stocks of metal held in bonded warehouses in Qingdao Port in China. These sparked suspicions of fraud, specifically concerning the duplication of warehouse receipts to secure funding from banks, thus allowing huge stockpiles of metals. Banks and trading houses conducted investigations on the security of metal holdings in

---

[51] ibid.   [52] ibid. See also SBGL (n 3).   [53] SBGL (n 2).
[54] SBGL (n 8). Also see 'Standard Bank Group Results for the Year Ended 31 December 2021' www.standardbank.com/static_file/Investor%20Relations/Documents/Financial-results/Annual-Results/SBG%202021%20Annual%20Results%20Presentation.pdf.
[55] ibid.   [56] SBGL (n 3).
[57] SBGL, SBK 201412100040A Announcement relating to the disposal by Standard Bank Group to the Industrial and Commercial Bank of China Limited (10 December 2014).

China, which were also complicated by a cascade of financial deals with clients. The SB Group confirmed that it had commenced investigations into potential fraud at the port, with a potential loss arising from the circumstances.[58]

The SB Group commenced legal proceedings to secure its position with respect to the aluminum.[59] The aluminum represented SB Plc's collateral held for a series of commodity financing arrangements, otherwise characterized as repos.[60] The SB Group CIB discontinued operations, including the fair value adjustment on repo positions relating to aluminum financing in China. It recorded a headline loss of RMB 1,032 million.[61] The SB Group continued to pursue various alternatives in order to recover the client exposure in respect of this matter.

Notwithstanding the fact that SB Plc was impacted by the valuation of the client exposure, the changing circumstances were not considered material or in conflict with the terms of the transaction as approved by shareholders.[62] On 10 December 2014, it was announced that SB Group, SBLH, and ICBC agreed to certain amendments to the Sale and Purchase Agreement to ensure that the purchase price correctly reflected the true and eventual net asset impact of the aluminum exposure. The amendment endeavored to ensure that ICBC did not incur any loss or receive any unintended benefit as a result of the relevant client exposure.[63]

3.5.2 Post Approval of JV

3.5.2.1 The US Oil Refinery Deal

In June 2019, ICBCS entered into its first major US trade agreement through a refinery deal with Philadelphia Energy Solutions (PES). The bank brought crude oil to the refinery in order to buy it and then resell refined products. A few days following the deal, the Philadelphia refinery suffered a fire, which resulted in the client filing for Chapter 11 bankruptcy in July 2019.[64]

ICBCS incurred a loss of US$198 million relating to a single client loss arising from this explosion and the subsequent bankruptcy of its client, PES.[65] ICBCS also experienced weak conditions across key markets in the base metals

---

[58] SBGL, SBKP SBK SBPP 201406050020A Voluntary announcement (5 June 2014).

[59] SBGL, SBKP SBK SBPP 201407100005A Update on voluntary announcement regarding stocks of metal held in Qingdao Port in China, 10 July 2014.

[60] SBGL, Interim results announcement and dividend declaration (14 August 2014).   [61] ibid.

[62] SBGL, SBK 201412100040A Announcement relating to the disposal by Standard Bank Group to the Industrial and Commercial Bank of China Limited (10 December 2014).

[63] ibid.

[64] ICBC Standard Bank Plc, Consolidated Annual Report, for the year ended 31 December 2019 https://v.icbc.com.cn/userfiles/Resources/ICBC/haiwai/StandardBank/Download/2020/ConsolidatedAnnualReport.pdf. See also SGBL, Conference Call transcript, Interim Financial Results H1 2019, 8 August 2019 https://thevault.exchange/?get_group_doc=18/1565693035-SBK1H19Transcript.pdf.

[65] Standard Bank Group 2019 Interim Results Summary, https://reporting.standardbank.com/2019-interim-results-summary/. During 2021, ICBCS received a partial net recovery on the loss event of US$8.8 million. See SBGL, Annual Financial Statements for the year ended December 2021 https://reporting.standardbank.com/results-reports/annual-reports/.

Figure 5.2.3 ICBCS annual profit/loss, 2015-2021

business and subdued client activity, causing greater loss to the company.[66] As a result, the performance of the SB Group was below expectations in 2019.[67] Were it not for the explosion, the group's earnings for the year ending December 2019 would have increased.[68]

Although ICBCS's losses weighed heavily on the group's performance (as summarized in Figure 5.2.3), the SB Group Chief Executive Officer (CEO) referred to the ICBCS JV agreement, which restricted the group from selling the shares unless ICBC exercised its Call Option rights.[69] But as "the best outcome for this business ... [was] greater with ICBCS," the SB Group continued support to "get the business to break even."[70]

3.5.2.2 Ukraine and Russia

The ICBCS JV also faced risks related to exposure to entities that were both directly and indirectly impacted by Russia's war in Ukraine.[71] As an emerging markets and commodities business, ICBCS had exposure to such organizations,[72] but at the announcement of the annual financial results for 2022, it was not yet possible for ICBCS to assess the impact of the war on its performance.[73]

---

[66] ICBC Standard Bank Plc (n 5).
[67] STANDARD BANK GROUP LIMITED, Results Announcement for the year ended 31 December 2021.
[68] CEO Sim Tshabalala explained that "Group return on equity was dampened by the loss incurred by ICBCS." See SBGL, FY19 Results Transcript, 5 March 2020 https://thevault.exchange/?get_group_doc=18/1583936228-StandardBankGroupFY19ResultsTranscriptFinal.pdf.
[69] ibid. [70] ibid.
[71] SBGL, Results Announcement for the year ended 31 December 2021 www.sharenet.co.za/v3/sens_display.php?tdate=20220311080000&seq=8&scode=.
[72] ibid.
[73] SBGL, Results Announcement for the year ended 31 December 2021 www.sharenet.co.za/v3/sens_display.php?tdate=20220311080000&seq=8&scode=.

3.6 Exiting the JV

The SB Group has in recent years wished to exit the ICBCS JV and to deploy more capital on the African continent instead.[74] The JV did not align with its evolving strategy and has been described by the SB Group CEO as "off strategy for us and outside our purpose." However, the restrictions placed on the SB Group prevented the sale of its shares or interests in the JV for at least five years or until ICBC exercised its Call Option.

The Group CEO indicated that it was unlikely that ICBC would exercise its Call Option until such time as ICBCS was profitable.[75] In regards to ICBCS, it reported a positive operational performance, contributing to boosting group earnings growth to above those figures recorded at SB activities level.[76] When ICBC's Call Option also expired, the SB Group CEO announced during the annual results presentation on 11 March 2022 that discussions had commenced to exit the ICBCS JV.[77] It was revealed that the bank was trying to convince ICBC to buy its 40% stake in ICBCS,[78] but no time frame was given. The CEO has been quoted in recent years saying: "As a 40% shareholder we have limited influence on the ICBCS. Nor can we [SB Group] simply cut our losses."[79]

4 Conclusion

The ICBCS JV case study sheds light on the nature of Sino-African banking JVs. It demonstrates specific relationships between China and Africa, relating to sources of investment and financing for banks in Africa. The status of the ICBC, as a state-owned enterprise (SOE), underscores the significant role of the Chinese government in the JV. The JV may leverage Chinese government support, which often plays a significant role in facilitating JVs in Africa. This relationship is important to both Chinese and African parties but is not without challenges.

Following changing circumstances, the SB Group wished to exit the ICBCS JV in order to achieve its evolving strategic objectives. The main objective of

---

[74] SBGL (n 68).   [75] ibid.
[76] Standard Bank Group, Pre-Close Call Transcript, 29 November 2021 https://thevault .exchange/?get_group_doc=18/1638202941-20211129StandardBankGroupPreclosecallTranscript .pdf. The improved performance in Liberty combined with the insurance settlement received by ICBCS in January 2022 boosted group earnings growth to above that recorded at a Standard Bank activities level. See SBGL, 1H22 Results presentation Speaker notes, 19 August 2022 https:// thevault.exchange/?get_group_doc=18/1661177760-SBG2022InterimResultsTranscript.pdf. See also SBGL, Pre close call Transcript, 28 November 2022 https://thevault.exchange/?get_group_ doc=18/1669656294-SBKInvestorCall28November2022Transcript.pdf.
[77] The CEO, Sim Tshabalala, reported that: "We [Standard Bank] to engage with ICBC on a path to exit our stake in ICBCS." See SBGL (n 8).
[78] ibid.
[79] Presentation at group's earnings for the year ended 31 December 2019. See SBGL, FY19 Results Transcript (5 March 2020) https://thevault.exchange/?get_group_doc=18/1583936228-Standar dBankGroupFY19ResultsTranscriptFinal.pdf.

the SB Group, to finance its growth strategy in Africa, had been negatively impacted by the financial performance of the JV. However, the main objective for ICBC, leveraging SB Plc to elevate its own capabilities, has remained relevant. This case study illustrates the challenges with respect to exiting a Sino-African JV, especially between parties that seek to achieve different objectives. It explores the terms and conditions of the ICBCS JV as well as the exit triggers and mechanisms of the African and Chinese parties to the JV. It also queries whether protection is offered to the parties of a JV agreement that takes account of evolving circumstances that may impact the interests of those parties and highlights the need to assess whether the parties mutually benefit from a JV or whether a case of asymmetry exists with respect to changing requirements.

Lock-in provisions typically specify a predetermined period during which parties are restricted from exiting a JV. The lock-in provision in the Sale and Purchase Agreement in the ICBCS JV case study restricted the ability to sell shares with the aim of safeguarding the interests of both parties and promoting a long-term commitment to the JV. The inclusion of a lock-in provision depends on the specific circumstances, goals, and preferences of the parties involved in forming the JV. It is not unique to Sino-African JVs but is a common feature in many similar agreements across different industries and sectors. However, the case study describes how the lock-in provisions serve the Chinese long-term perspective with Africa over short-term gains. Due to restrictive provisions in this particular JV, the SB Group did not have the unilateral ability to exit the agreement until the lock-in period had expired. Eventually, on expiry of the contractual restrictions, the SB Group commenced discussions to exit the JV. The outcome is yet to be determined.

5 Discussion Questions and Comments

5.1 For Law School Audiences

1. This case study highlights the opportunity provided by the ICBCS JV for the SB Group to realize proceeds on disposal that would then release significant capital to be deployed in furthering the Group's growth strategy in Africa. This raises questions as to the nature of Sino-African banking JVs and their structure (Figure 5.2.2). How does the Sino-African JV align with the bank's growth strategy in Africa as discussed in the case study? More generally, does the JV capture the relationship of China with Africa, as a source of investment and financing for banks in Africa?
2. The terms and conditions of the ICBCS JV involve various conditions precedent. The case describes a series of steps that were to be undertaken to reorganize the SB Plc Group as a condition for completion of the Sale and Purchase Agreement. Warranties for changes pre approval of the JV are provided for in the Agreement but not warranties against changing circumstances post approval. However, changing circumstances post

approval of the JV also modified the performance of the parties and negatively impacted the financial performance of the JV (Figure 5.2.3). Are changing circumstances prior to approval of the JV significant? Are changing circumstances post approval of the JV pertinent or in conflict with the conditions of the transaction?

3. There is no specific expiration date for the ICBCS JV. The exit mechanisms of the JV, such as the ICBC Call Option and the Standard Bank Put Option listed in Table 5.2.1, are discussed in this study. ICBC had the right to exercise a Call Option. The SB Group only had the right to exercise a Put Option in the event that the ICBC Call Option was exercised. Following completion of the JV, ICBC reported the Option was unlikely to be exercised until ICBCS was profitable. Are there any risks or uncertainties associated with these exit mechanisms? Learning from the case study, how effective are these mechanisms in addressing potential challenges, post approval of the JV? Did mechanisms included in the JV Sale and Purchase Agreement protect the parties involved from changing circumstances?

4. The case study sheds light on the challenges faced by SB Group and the restrictions imposed by the terms of the Sale and Purchase Agreement with ICBC. Due to the restrictive provisions of the Agreement, the SB Group did not have the unilateral ability to exit the JV. The lock-in provision, which restricted the SB Group from selling its shares until ICBC exercised its Call Option or after seven years following completion of the Agreement, raises questions about the flexibility and control of the SB Group over its investment. How does the restrictive provision impact the SB Group's ability to exit the ICBCS JV? How important is it to have a well-defined exit strategy in JV agreements? To what extent does the lock-in provision in the ICBCS JV reflect a balance between short-term gains of SB and Chinese long-term commitment reflected by the strategy of ICBC?

5.2 For Policy School Audiences

1. Foreign direct investment (FDI) can provide both an entry strategy for one organization and access to finance for another. As policies open more sectors to foreign investment, and based on the ICBCS JV, discuss China's use of FDI in the South African bank, SBG. What are the potential benefits of FDI in the economies of the respective parties to the Sino-African banking JV? Discuss the objectives that China aims to achieve through the use of FDI. Is policy formulation significant in defining the economic value of ICBCS JV? Considering the ICBCS JV case, is there value in policies to promote JVs?

2. This case study illustrates that one approach to FDI is through JVs. From the host government's rationale, JV policies protect sovereignty by ensuring that foreign investors are restricted from having control over key decisions in the economy. By that rationale, discuss policy options for exit strategies that further promote host state sovereignty.

3. In terms of outbound foreign direct investment (OFDI), both host state and home state governments regulate such projects. Consider both perspectives. What should be the main criteria for host states in approving FDI projects? How does a host state's relationship with the home state shape such policies? For example, how does the US regulate Chinese FDI versus a country like South Africa? From the home state side, what are the key priorities and how should PRC authorities regulate OFDI? What difference does it make when the JV is based in a third-party state as in this case where ICBC JV is based in the UK? What role should the UK's policies play in such an instance?
4. Many questions may arise when an SOE and a private enterprise enter into a JV. ICBC is a state-owned commercial bank operating for the benefit of citizens. The SB Group is a profit-driven, publicly listed company that is owned by investors. How does the involvement of SOEs, such as ICBC, in JVs like the ICBCS JV reflect broader government policies and objectives, particularly in the context of long-term Sino-African economic relations? What policies may be essential for the success of the ICBCS JV? Is there a need for specific policies aimed at facilitating such FDI initiatives? How can policies "level the playing field" between private and state-owned firms?

5.3 For Business School Audiences

1. What factors should ICBC have considered when deciding to invest in the JV? Analyze the structure of the JV, as illustrated in Figure 5.2.2, and discuss the alignment of the JV structure with the role of Chinese parties in African banks. How does the JV contribute to the SB Group's growth strategy in Africa, and how does it position ICBC in the context of its global markets' capability? In addition to strengthening economic ties, what other assets does ICBC offer that make it an attractive Sino-African banking JV partner?
2. JVs can be a tool for strategic planning such as expanding markets, building capabilities, and aligning goals. The ICBCS JV case describes a series of steps that were to be undertaken to reorganize the SB Plc Group as a condition for completion of the Sale and Purchase Agreement. Explore how the terms and conditions of the ICBCS JV align with the stated objectives of establishing a partnership in global markets. Did the ICBCS JV fit in the wider scheme of the parties' strategic objectives? Did the parties consider a long-term or short-term view of the JV? How can businesses effectively navigate and address asymmetrical interests and objectives between the Chinese and African partners in a JV, as exemplified by the divergent long-term and short-term goals of ICBC and the SB Group in the ICBCS JV, respectively? Assess how changing circumstances post approval align or conflict with the objectives outlined in the case pre approval of the JV. How did the JV contribute to both SB Group's focus on Africa and ICBC's global markets capabilities?

3. Assess the impact of changing circumstances on the performance of the ICBCS JV, both pre and post approval. Consider the conditions precedent and their relevance to the changing circumstances. Are changing circumstances prior to approval significant in the context of JV agreements, and how do they differ from changing circumstances post approval? How do changing circumstances align or conflict with the conditions of the transaction?
4. Evaluate the role and efficacy of the exit mechanisms in addressing potential challenges post approval. Consider the effectiveness of these mechanisms and their associated risks or uncertainties. How do the exit mechanisms in the Sale and Purchase Agreement mitigate risks, especially considering ICBC's reluctance to exercise the Call Option, most likely until the JV is profitable? Are there alternative exit strategies that could have been considered from a business perspective?
5. Analyze the impact of the lock-in provision on the SB Group's ability to exit the JV and its control over the investment. Discuss the trade-offs between the restrictive provision and the SB Group's flexibility. Considering the challenges faced by SB Group due to the lock-in provision, how can businesses entering JV agreements effectively consider and negotiate exit strategies and lock-in provisions?

Section 6
Disputing

Case Study 6.1

Chinese Overseas Investment and Environmental Accountability

A Legal Battle against the Chinese-Financed Coal-Fired Power Plant in Boké, Guinea

Jingjing Zhang and Emily Scherr

1 Overview

In 2014, a Chinese-financed company, Société Minière de Boké (SMB), contracted with the Guinean government and obtained three mining concessions to exploit bauxite reserves in Boké, Guinea.[1] Since then, SMB has had a tumultuous history working in Boké, with local residents complaining of copious amounts of dust being generated, depleted and polluted freshwater sources, and a reduction in farming capacity due to pollution and lack of fresh water. These environmental issues have also led to adverse health impacts within local communities, including respiratory illnesses as a result of excessive dust. However, despite these controversies, SMB's presence in the country has grown. In 2015, SMB began construction of major mining infrastructure, including roads and ports,[2] and in 2020, preparation for the construction of an alumina refinery and a coal-fired power plant in Boké started.

---

[1] As seen on 12 July 2023, SMB lists a Chinese company, Shandong Weiqiao Pioneering Group Company Limited's logo on its website, 'SMB, a Company of the SMB-Winning Consortium' www.smb-guinee.com/en/home/. On its website, Shandong Weiqiao describes itself as "a super large enterprise integrating spinning and weaving, dyeing and finishing, garment, home textile, thermal power, and other industries" (Weiqiao Pioneering, www.weiqiaocy.com/cn/about.html?idd=24). The world's biggest aluminum producer, China Hongqiao Group Ltd., expressed it has devoted itself to promoting the economic development of the places where it has overseas projects in recent years to advocate the economic strategy of China's BRI of the country, China Hongqiao Group Limited, 'Environmental Social and Governance Report 2022' www.hongqiaochina.com/Uploads/File/2023/04/21/3.20230421171705.pdf. The SMB Winning Consortium's operation in Guinea was listed as one of China Hongqiao Group Ltd.'s overseas projects. Both Shandong Weiqiao Pioneering Group Company and China Hongqiao Group Ltd. were founded by the entrepreneur Zhang Shiping, who passed away in 2019. The two companies have been controlled by Zhang Shiping's son, Zhang Bo, and his daughter, Zhang Hongxia, respectively, since then.

[2] Human Rights Watch, 'What Do We Get Out of It? The Human Rights Impact of Bauxite Mining in Guinea' (2018) www.hrw.org/sites/default/files/report_pdf/guinea1018_web2.pdf 112–13.

SMB's operations in Guinea raise important questions about the Chinese leadership's commitment to green and sustainable development in China's overseas projects. The construction of the fossil fuel power plant continued after Chinese President Xi Jinping's public statement in 2021 that "China will vigorously support the green and low-carbon development of energy in developing countries and will no longer build new overseas coal power projects."[3] Civil society organizations have made efforts to force SMB to use a cleaner energy source to power the refinery. Such efforts draw attention to the gap between rhetoric and reality in China's overseas projects.

This case study focuses on how local and international civil society organizations and public interest lawyers use legal instruments to ensure Chinese investors and the Guinean government comply with the laws of Guinea (as the host country of Chinese investments), of China (the home country), and international laws. Specifically, this case study shows how civil society organizations have been able to combat SMB's plan to use coal as an energy source by recourse to a number of legal strategies. More broadly, it demonstrates how non-state actors can use the law to hold Chinese investors accountable for environmental harms inflicted on host states, particularly those in the Global South.

The case study is written by members of an advocacy NGO that is leading actions against SMB for violating relevant laws. While procedures are still pending, the case study provides both the history of the project and a snapshot of current problems.

2 Introduction

2.1 Guinea Country Profile

The target project, the alumina refinery and proposed coal-fired power plant, is located in the Boké prefecture of the Republic of Guinea. Guinea is a West African country located on the Atlantic Ocean and bordered by Sierra Leone, Senegal, Guinea-Bissau, Liberia, Côte d'Ivoire, and Mali. Boké prefecture is located in the northeastern part of the country and is home to more than 480,000 people in ten subprefectures that are composed of twenty-four distinct village communities.[4]

---

[3] Despite this commitment, several Chinese companies, including SMB, have forged ahead with plans to construct coal-fired power plants abroad. Paolo Gonzalez, Jincheng Dai, and Tom Xiaojun Wang, '2 Years Later: China's Ban on Overseas Coal Power Projects and Its Global Climate Impacts' (Centre for Research on Energy and Clean Air, 16 October 2023) https://energyandcleanair.org/publication/2-years-later-chinas-ban-on-overseas-coal-power-projects-and-its-global-climate-impacts/.

[4] Natural Justice, 'Community Audit of Environmental and Social Impacts of the Société Minière de Boké' (February 2023) 17 https://naturaljustice.org/wp-content/uploads/2023/07/community-audit-of-environmental-and-social-impacts-of-the-societe-miniere-de-boke-in-guinea.pdf.

The major exploitable mineral resources in Guinea include bauxite, iron, diamonds, gold, and uranium.[5] Guinea contains a third of all known bauxite reserves in the world and SMB is the largest producer of bauxite in the country.[6] Bauxite is needed to produce aluminum, and China is the world's largest producer of aluminum, thus its access to Guinea's mines is an economic imperative. However, the main economic activities in the region include subsistence agriculture, fishing, salt farming, livestock, and handicrafts – all of which are threatened by bauxite mining activities.[7] Despite Guinea's copious natural resources and bauxite reserves, it is one of the poorest countries in the world.[8]

The country's current predicament reflects a complicated history. Guinea achieved its independence from French West Africa in 1958.[9] After gaining independence, Guinea was ruled by authoritarian leaders, Sékou Touré, Lansana Conté, and Captain Moussa Dadis Camara, for more than fifty years.[10] In 2010, for the first time since gaining its independence from France, Guinea conducted elections to choose its next ruler, President Alpha Condé.[11] A new constitution was passed in 2010 and then again in 2020.[12] These legal reforms had limited effect on the mining industry, which has been central to the country's economy.

Condé expanded the mining sector, particularly the bauxite mining sector, during his time as president and promulgated a new mining code meant to improve mining regulations and increase profits for the government from mining.[13] However, the bauxite mining sector faced some initial setbacks during Condé's first term, including resistance from companies that, as a result of the new regulations, had to pay higher taxes (the 2011 Mining Code was amended in 2013 because of this issue), the Ebola epidemic, and low global prices for bauxite.[14] The bauxite sector boomed after Condé's first term in office after other bauxite-producing countries banned exports and Chinese demand for bauxite increased.[15]

Condé ran for and won a contentious third term in 2020 and remained in power until he was overthrown by a military coup in late 2021.[16] The ruling military junta suspended the 2020 Constitution and instituted a Transitional Charter with Col. Mamady Doumbouya serving as the transitional president.[17] As of 2023, Guinea's ruling military junta has yet to conduct elec-

---

[5] CIA, 'The World Factbook – Guinea' www.cia.gov/the-world-factbook/countries/guinea/#geography.
[6] Natural Justice (n 4) 15.   [7] Natural Justice (n 4) 19.   [8] Human Rights Watch (n 2) 27.
[9] Thomas O'Toole, 'Encyclopedia Britannica – Guinea' www.britannica.com/place/Guinea.
[10] Human Rights Watch, '"We Have Lived in Darkness" A Human Rights Agenda for Guinea's New Government' (May 2011) 1 www.hrw.org/sites/default/files/reports/guinea0511webwcover_1.pdf.
[11] Human Rights Watch (n 2) 26.   [12] O'Toole (n 9).   [13] Human Rights Watch (n 2) 27–8.
[14] Human Rights Watch (n 2) 28.   [15] Human Rights Watch (n 2) 29.
[16] O'Toole (n 9).   [17] O'Toole (n 9).

tions to determine the country's next leader. It is also worth noting that the Natural Resource Governance Institute has consistently given Guinea low scores in the category of rule of law; in 2021, Guinea received a ranking of just 15 out of 100.[18]

2.2 Guinea–China Relations

In the past decade, Guinea and China have deepened their relations. In November 2016, President Condé paid a state visit to China to meet with President Xi Jinping. The two heads of state decided to establish a comprehensive strategic partnership and to take the implementation of the outcomes of the 2015 Johannesburg Summit of the Forum on China-Africa Cooperation (FOCAC) as an opportunity to deepen and expand friendly and mutually beneficial cooperation between the two countries in various fields and create a broader future for China–Guinea relations.

In September 2017, China and Guinea signed the "China-Guinea Resource and Loan Cooperation Framework Agreement" in Xiamen, China.[19] In the agreement, Guinea granted Chinese corporations exploration rights for bauxite, iron, and other mineral resources, while China agreed that Chinese financial institutions would provide the necessary loans for the extraction projects.[20] The agreement notes that over the next twenty years (2017–2036) the amount of money invested in mining projects in Guinea by China would reach US$20 billion.[21] A list of priority projects added as an addendum to the agreement includes bauxite mining projects in Boffa and Boké.[22] Overall, this resource for infrastructure agreement seeks to accelerate China-financed extraction of mineral resources in Guinea.

In September 2021, after the military coup overthrew President Condé from office, Chinese companies remained active in Guinea. However, the Chinese government condemned the coup and urged for the immediate release of President Condé.[23] A spokesperson for the Chinese Foreign Ministry, Mr. Wang Wenbin, stated in a press conference concerning the coup that "[w]e hope relevant parties can exercise calm and restraint, bear in mind the

---

[18] Natural Resource Governance Institute, '2021 Natural Resources Governance Index Guinea' (2021) https://resourcegovernance.org/sites/default/files/documents/2021_resource_governance_index_guinea_mining.pdf.

[19] Research Institute for International Trade and Economic Cooperation, Ministry of Commerce, Economic and Commercial Affairs, Department of the Chinese Embassy in Guinea, Department of Foreign Investment and Economic Cooperation, 'Foreign Investment Cooperation Country (Region) Guide: Guinea' (2021) 4 www.mofcom.gov.cn/dl/gbdqzn/upload/jineiya.pdf.

[20] China-Guinea Resource and Loan Cooperation Framework Agreement (2017).   [21] ibid.
[22] ibid.
[23] Xinhua, 'China Opposes Coup Attempts to Seize Power in Guinea' (*China Daily*, 6 September 2021) www.chinadailyhk.com/article/237059#China-opposes-coup-attempts-to-seize-power-in-Guinea.

fundamental interests of the nation and people, resolve the relevant issue through dialogue and consultation and safeguard peace and stability in Guinea."[24]

2.3 China's Climate and Biodiversity Commitments in the Context of Chinese Laws and Policies on Outbound Direct Investments

China's outbound direct investments regime is designed with the objective of safeguarding state-owned assets and their financial security. The environmental and social impact of offshore projects has not been a core concern of the Chinese government, and as such, there is no legislation with enforcement effect to screen the environmental and social impact of overseas investment projects. In addition, institutionally, the Ministry of Ecology and Environment, the main administrative agency in charge of environmental affairs in China, does not have the mandate to regulate overseas projects.[25]

Recognizing the threat that climate change poses, China has made significant commitments to reduce emissions in its international investments, particularly in developing nations. In 2021, FOCAC published the "Declaration on China-Africa Cooperation on Combating Climate Change."[26] The Declaration states that both China and African countries will advocate for and advance sustainable development and will "promote 'green recovery'" in a post-COVID economy. Further, China commits to promoting low-emission technologies in Africa, including solar and wind-powered energy production. The Declaration also states that China "will not build new coal-fired BRI power projects abroad." China's National Development and Reform Commission (NDRC) has made similar commitments to sustainable development in the Belt and Road Initiative (BRI).[27] Specifically, the NDRC commits China to promoting green energy in its operations abroad linked to the BRI,[28] stating that "[e]nterprises shall be encouraged to promote green and environmental protection standards and best practices for infrastructure." Additionally, the NDRC notes in their opinion that "the full implementation" of China's and participating African countries' commitments under international climate agreements including the Paris

---

[24] ibid.
[25] Matthew S. Erie and Jingjing Zhang, 'A Comparison of Inbound and Outbound Investment Regulatory Regimes in China: Focus on Environmental Protection' in Henry Gao, Damian Raess, and Ka Zeng (eds), *China and the WTO: A Twenty-Year Assessment* (Cambridge University Press 2023) 429–51.
[26] Forum on China-Africa Cooperation, 'Declaration on China-Africa Cooperation on Combating Climate Change' (3 December 2021) www.focac.org/eng/zywx_1/zywj/202201/t20220124_10632445.htm.
[27] Opinions of the National Development and Reform Commission and Other Departments on Promoting Green Development under the Belt and Road Initiative. Document number 408 (2022) of the National Development and Reform Commission www.ndrc.gov.cn/xxgk/zcfb/tz/202203/t20220328_1320629.html
[28] ibid.

Agreement shall be promoted.[29] The NDRC further states that "[t]he construction of overseas coal-fired power projects shall be completely stopped."

China made similar goals for green international development in the notice by the Ministry of Commerce and the Ministry of Ecology and Environment on issuing the "Green Development Guidelines for Overseas Investment and Cooperation."[30] An enumerated goal for Chinese outbound investment stated in the guidelines is to "support outbound investment in clean energy such as solar, wind, nuclear and biomass energy, facilitate the global revolution of energy production and consumption, and build a clean, low-carbon, secure and efficient energy mix." In September 2021, at the 76th UN General Assembly, President Xi Jinping stated, "China will vigorously support the green and low-carbon development of energy in developing countries and will no longer build new overseas coal power projects."[31] Further, China reiterated the goal to not build any new coal power plants abroad in the communication to the UN Framework Convention on Climate Change (UNFCCC) on China's Nationally Determined Contributions.[32]

2.4 Guinean Governmental Structure on Mining, Natural Resource Management, and Environmental Matters

While conducting mining operations in Guinea, SMB not only should abide by the laws and policies of China but is legally bound by the laws of the Republic of Guinea in relation to the environment and human rights. Institutionally, both the Ministère de l'Environnement et du Développement Durable/Ministry of the Environment and Sustainable Development (MEDD) through the Guinean Environmental Assessment Agency (AGEE) and the Ministry of Mines and Geology have oversight of mining projects and the Environmental and Social Impact Assessment (ESIA) process in Guinea.

2.4.1 Ministry of Environment and Sustainable Development and the AGEE

The AGEE coordinates the administrative procedure of the mining projects' ESIAs and audits in Guinea. It approves the terms of reference of all ESIAs submitted by the companies as a first step, receives the ESIA reports, and organizes public audiences with local stakeholders to ensure that the members of

---

[29] Ibid.
[30] The Ministry of Commerce and the Ministry of Ecology and Environment, 'Green Development Guidelines for Overseas Investment and Cooperation' (16 July 2021).
[31] Statement by Xi Jinping, 'Bolstering Confidence and Jointly Overcoming Difficulties to Build a Better World' (translation, 2021) http://english.www.gov.cn/news/topnews/202109/22/content_WS614a9d11c6d0df57f98e0a81.html.
[32] United Nations Framework Convention on Climate Change, 'China's Achievements, New Goals and New Measures for Nationally Determined Contributions' (unofficial translation) 2, 45 https://unfccc.int/sites/default/files/NDC/2022-06/China%E2%80%99s%20Achievements%2C%20New%20Goals%20and%20New%20Measures%20for%20Nationally%20Determined%20Contributions.pdf.

communities who may be affected can participate in the ESIAs and are aware of the conclusions. It is responsible for approving the ESIAs through the Comité Technique d'Analyse Environnementale/Technical Committee for Analysis and Assessment (CTAE). The CTAE is a committee formed by the MEDD and coordinated by the AGEE. The CTAE is composed of members of ministerial departments and civil society representatives.[33]

Additionally, the Comités Préfectoraux de Suivi Environnemental et Social/ Prefectural Committee for Environmental and Social Monitoring (CPSES) was set up by the Ministry in charge of the MEDD to support the AGEE in its mission of monitoring the implementation of the projects' Environmental and Social Management Plans (ESMPs). The CPSES is represented in all prefectures where mining projects occur. It provides close monitoring for certain environmental and social components of mining projects being developed in the territories covered by their activities.

The AGEE carries out the monitoring and audits of the projects' ESMP and delivers, on behalf of the MEDD, the environmental compliance certificate for "Category A projects" (projects that have significant impacts on the environment) and environmental authorization for "Category B projects" (projects that have less effect on the environment).

2.4.2 Ministry of Geology and Mines

The Service National de Coordination des Projets Miniers/National Service for the Coordination of Mining Projects (SNCPM) coordinates the feasibility studies of all mining projects, which consists of evaluating both the technical feasibility and the economic viability of a project. The feasibility report is submitted to the Ministry of Mines and Geology through the SNCPM for the project evaluation and approval. The Direction Nationale des Mines/National Directory of Mines is in charge of monitoring the mining production and all related taxes while the Centre pour la Promotion et du Développement Minier/ Center for the Promotion of Mining Development is responsible for managing the Guinean mining cadastre. The service delivers mining permits and authorizations for research, exploration, and exploitation activities.

2.5 Guinean Environmental Laws and Decrees

The Guinean legal system is highly influenced by its history of French colonization and prescribes a civil law system. The relevant sources of Guinean law that provide the framework for regulating the mining industry include the Guinean Constitution of 2010 and 2020, as well as the Transitional Charter, the

---

[33] Decree D/2014/PRG/SGG, Portant Adoption d'une Directive de Realisation d'une Etude d'Impact Environnemental et Social des Operations Minieres [On the Adoption of a Directive for Carrying out an Environmental and Social Impact Assessment of Mining Operations], (January 2014) art 3.7.

Environmental Code of Guinea 2019 and implementing regulations, and the Mining Code and implementing regulations.

The Constitution of Guinea guarantees the right to a healthy environment along with other environmental protections.[34] Article 16 of the 2010 Constitution states, "[e]very person has the right to a healthy and lasting environment and the duty to defend it."[35] As mentioned, in 2020, a reformed constitution was passed by referendum.[36] The 2020 Constitution contains a similar right to a clean and healthy environment in Article 22, which states in part that "[t]he right to a healthy environment is recognized throughout the territory."[37] After the 2021 coup, the ruling military junta suspended the 2020 Constitution and instituted a Transitional Charter. Because the SMB project began in 2014, all three texts (2010 Constitution, 2020 reformed Constitution, and the Transitional Charter) apply. The Transitional Charter does not contain any explicit protections for the environment.[38]

The Environmental Code of Guinea 2019 sets out a few basic overarching policies when it comes to environmental protection and energy generation. Generally, it promotes environmental sustainability, the consideration of climate issues, and the use of renewable energy. The Code places explicit duties on private companies operating in the extractives sector in Guinea, noting in Article 16 that "[p]rivate enterprises and public and mixed companies carrying out industrial and/or commercial activities shall be required to integrate environmental concerns into their operating, production and responsible management systems, meeting the requirements of sustainable development."[39] Article 9 of the Code notes that development projects in Guinea must take into account the importance of environmental protection and must adhere to several principles of environmental stewardship including, among others, the precautionary principle and the principle of sustainable development.[40]

Procedurally, the Environmental Code specifically requires that projects having an impact on the environment perform an ESIA.[41] Article 142 of the Mining Code also requires that mining companies complete an ESIA as a part of the application for an Authorization or Operation Permit and that the ESIAs

---

[34] In addition to guaranteeing a right to a healthy environment, the 2010 Constitution criminalizes "[t]he transit, the importation, the storage, the dumping on the national territory of toxic waste or pollutants." The 2020 Constitution contains a similar clause. Constitution of the Republic of Guinea, 2010, Art 17; Constitution of the Republic of Guinea, 2020, art 22 www.constituteproject.org/constitution/Guinea_2010.pdf?lang=en.
[35] Constitution of the Republic of Guinea (n 34).   [36] O'Toole (n 9).
[37] Constitution of the Republic of Guinea (n 34).
[38] Transition Charter of the Republic of Guinea, 2021.
[39] Decree No. D/2019/221/PRG/SGG promulgating Law No. L/2019/0034/AN of 04 July 2019 Portant Code de l'environnement de la République de Guinée (2019) art 16. (Environmental Code).
[40] ibid art 9.
[41] ibid art 28 ("Any development or construction project likely to affect the environment is subject to a prior environmental and social impact study").

prepared by companies abide by the Environmental Code and meet "internationally accepted standards."[42]

According to Article 31 of the Environmental Code, "[w]hen the environmental and social impact study is deemed to be satisfactory, the minister in charge of the environment shall issue to the developer a certificate of environmental compliance."[43] Guinean regulations concerning ESIAs require that after the completion of the study period for the ESIA, a report (an environmental and social impact study report, known as REIES) must be submitted to the Ministry in charge of the environment for review by the CTAE.[44] If the REIES is approved by the CTAE, the minister in charge of the environment must issue the environmental authorization or the environmental compliance certificate (*certificat de conformité environnementale*).[45] Article 22 of Order A/2022/MEDD/CAB/SGG of 25 July 2022 on the administrative procedure for environmental assessment states that the environmental compliance certificate, which is granted by the minister of the environment on the recommendation of the CTAE, is valid for one year and is renewable each year.[46]

Additionally, as part of the ESIA process, companies operating in Guinea must produce an ESMP.[47] The ESMP is a document that lays out the procedure for managing, implementing corrective or mitigation measures, monitoring, and following up on the environmental and social risks and impacts in preparation for and during the project that operating companies must adhere to.[48] Each year, the company must submit an ESMP implementation report to the AGEE. This yearly report is a requirement for the renewal of the environmental compliance certificate.

2.5.1 The Use of Guinean Law by Civil Society

The accessibility of the judicial system by civil society organizations or impacted communities remains a challenge to be met in Guinea. Article 24 of the Environmental Code guarantees access to justice to "the State and the local collectivities; any company working in the field of the environment; and any approved association in the field of the environment; any natural person having a sufficient interest to act." Further, Article 19 of the Environmental Code allows for environmental protection organizations to challenge any administrative act that may have a significant impact on the environment. Despite these legal guarantees, in practice, often access to justice is not granted. Specifically, as of the time of this writing, no administrative environmental action has been brought to the Guinean courts.

---

[42] Amended 2011 Mining Code of the Republic of Guinea, art 142 (Mining Code).
[43] Environmental Code (n 39) art 31.   [44] Decree D/2014/PRG/SGG (n 33) art 3.7.   [45] ibid.
[46] Arrete A/2022/MEDD/CAB/SGG Portant Procedure Administrative d'Evaluations Environnementales, art 22.
[47] ibid.   [48] ibid.

2.6 International Treaties and Standards

Both China and Guinea are signatories of the UNFCCC. Article 3 of the UNFCCC states in part that "[t]he Parties should take precautionary measures to anticipate, prevent or minimize the causes of climate change and mitigate its adverse effects."[49] Additionally, the Guinean ESIA regulations note that companies should adhere to national standards when conducting ESIAs, but when national standards are absent, companies should follow international best practices, specifically mentioning the International Finance Corporation (IFC) standards.[50] The IFC standards aim to guide corporations on best practices to ensure that environmental and social rights of affected communities are respected and preserved.

IFC Performance Standard 3 concerns "Resource Efficiency and Pollution Prevention."[51] A key objective of IFC Performance Standard 3 is "[t]o reduce project-related GHG [greenhouse gas] emissions."[52] In relation to GHG emissions, IFC Performance Standard 3 instructs companies to consider less polluting alternatives to energy generation stating, "the client will consider alternatives and implement technically and financially feasible and cost-effective options to reduce project-related GHG emissions during the design and operation of the project."[53] The standard goes on to note that a reasonable project alternative may include "adoption of renewable or low carbon energy sources."

Further, the IFC Performance Standards make reference to the World Bank Group Environmental, Health and Safety Guidelines (EHS Guidelines) and note that the EHS Guidelines are "technical reference documents with general and industry-specific examples of good international industry practice."[54] The IFC Performance Standards note that when the standards of a host country differ from standards presented in the EHS Guidelines, the company should abide by whichever standards are more stringent.[55]

3 The Case

The Société Minière de Boké was founded in 2014 by the SMB Winning Consortium, a consortium of companies including the Shandong Weiqiao/China Hongqiao Group Limited, Winning International Group of Singapore, Yantai Port Group, and United Mining Supply of Guinea.[56] SMB's operations in Guinea include four bauxite mining sites, a railway, two ports, and two mining roads. SMB is the leading producer and exporter of bauxite in Guinea,

---

[49] United Nations, 'United Nations Framework Convention on Climate Change' (1992) 4 https://unfccc.int/resource/docs/convkp/conveng.pdf.
[50] Decree D/2014/PRG/SGG (n 33) s 2.3.2.
[51] International Finance Corporation, 'Performance Standards on Environmental and Social Sustainability' (1 January 2012) www.ifc.org/content/dam/ifc/doc/2010/2012-ifc-performance-standards-en.pdf.
[52] ibid. [53] ibid 7. [54] ibid 6. [55] ibid 7.
[56] China Hongqiao Group Limited, 'Environmental, Social and Governance Report 2021' http://en.hongqiaochina.com/Uploads/File/2022/05/30/E1378-ESG.20220530185231.pdf.

Figure 6.1.1 SMB's operations in Guinea: (a) truck transporting bauxite on an SMB mining road in Boké; (b) trucks kicking up dust on an SMB mining road in Boké; (c) mounds of bauxite at SMB headquarters in Boké; (d) front gate of SMB operations in Boké

responsible for about 40% of bauxite production in 2020 (see Figure 6.1.1).[57] Additionally, SMB is planning on building an alumina refinery; construction was set to begin in 2023 but has been delayed. The refinery will be powered by a captive coal-fired power plant. SMB began the ESIA process in September 2020 for the refinery project. SMB completed the ESIA in February 2021 and the report was validated and given an environmental compliance certificate in April 2021 after a virtual session organized by the validation committee (CTAE). The ESIA conducted by SMB combined both the refinery and the coal plant projects but did not independently assess the impacts of the coal plant. The planned coal plant is a "captive coal plant," meaning that the energy produced from the coal-fired power plant will only be used to power the planned alumina refinery and will not provide any energy to the surrounding communities.

3.1 SMB's Environmental and Social Record in Boké, Guinea

In 2022, a Pan-African environmental NGO, Natural Justice, completed a Community Audit of the Boké area to determine the on-the-ground effects of SMB's mining activities on local communities and their livelihoods. The Community Audit Report notes that the local economic activities impacted by SMB's bauxite mining include agriculture (rice and mahogany), fishing, salt farming, livestock, trade, and handicrafts, and that these forms of subsistence are

---

[57] Natural Justice (n 4) 15.

under threat due to the bauxite mining activities.[58] Generally, the report notes the extreme degradation of the natural environment in Boké.[59] Additionally, according to a report by Human Rights Watch, the required ESIA was not finished and approved before SMB began constructing mining infrastructure such as mining roads and ports.[60] The same pattern of starting the operation before the ESIA was approved can be found at SMB's investors' Simandou iron mine-related infrastructure project, a violation of the Guinean Environmental Code.[61]

One of the main concerns of local communities noted during the community audit is access to safe drinking water. SMB discharges wastewater directly into fields and local waterways, thereby polluting local water sources and making them unsuitable for human domestic use.[62] Uncontrolled and untreated runoff after periods of rain also contributes to pollution of local waterways, turning streams and rivers the deep red color of bauxite.[63] Additionally, local communities complain that many of the boreholes and wells drilled by SMB to compensate for the pollution of streams and rivers are not functional. Of the thirty-one boreholes surveyed for the community audit report, only seven were found to be operational at the time of the audit.[64]

Another key environmental complaint of local communities is the copious amounts of dust generated from heavy machinery used for mining operations, including large trucks that travel through communities and on mining roads (Figure 6.1.1). Individuals from Katougouma complain that passing trucks kick up dust that deteriorates the air quality.[65] Communities also complain that the dust coats their farms and food and has caused respiratory disease among locals.[66] The Community Audit Report also notes that dust kicked up by trucks coats roadside fruit trees and discusses the need for a dust mitigation program.[67] Additionally, community members have complained that their land rights have been violated by SMB. Specifically, in Boké, individuals complain that their customary land rights have been ignored and they have not been provided with adequate compensation.[68]

3.2 Civil Society Actions

Despite Xi Jinping's pledge that China will no longer build coal plants overseas, many Chinese companies have continued with their plans to construct coal-fired power plants.[69] Thus, bottom-up work led by civil society is necessary to ensure companies comply with both the Chinese government's and the host country's laws. A group of Guinean, regional, and international NGOs have been working together to design advocacy strategies to halt the construction of the coal plant

---

[58] Natural Justice (n 4) 19.   [59] Natural Justice (n 4).   [60] Human Rights Watch (n 2) 112–13.
[61] Helen Reid and Joe Bavier, 'EXCLUSIVE: Guinea Rail Builders Blast in Chimp Habitat, No Plan to Protect Apes' (*Reuters*, 17 August 2021) www.reuters.com/world/africa/exclusive-guinea-rail-builders-blast-chimp-habitat-no-plan-protect-apes-2021-08-17/.
[62] Natural Justice (n 4) 37–8.   [63] Natural Justice (n 4) 37.   [64] Natural Justice (n 4) 39.
[65] Natural Justice (n 4) 28.   [66] Natural Justice (n 4) 27.   [67] Natural Justice (n 4) 28, 52.
[68] Natural Justice (n 4) 34.   [69] Gonzalez et al. (n 3).

Figure 6.1.2 CTEA Executive Director, Jingjing Zhang, meeting with the Wawayiré village in the Boké prefecture

in Boké. These NGOs include the Guinean human rights legal nonprofit Les Mêmes Droits pour Tous (MDT), the Association pour le Développement Rural et l'Entraide Mutuelle de Guinée, the US-based environmental legal nonprofit Center for Transnational Environmental Accountability (CTEA, Figure 6.1.2), Natural Justice, and the Ghana-based Advocates for Community Alternatives.

Even though both the validation of the ESIA of the refinery with the coal plant and the environmental compliance certificate were issued to SMB for the planned refinery and coal plant before Chinese President Xi Jinping announced in September 2021 that China would no longer build coal-fired power plants abroad, nonetheless, SMB failed to change its plan of building a captive coal plant to power the alumina refinery to align the project with China's policy direction. The consortium of NGOs decided to take action to stop its plan. The main strategies identified include the following: first, applying pressure to SMB to comply with Chinese and Guinean climate policies and commitments, including by writing letters to the Guinean government and the Chinese Embassy in Conakry, media exposure, and participation in UN human rights mechanisms; and second, taking legal action, including access to information requests, *Compulsoire*,[70] and administrative litigation,[71] in Guinea to challenge the approval process for the coal plant.

---

[70] *Compulsoire* is an old tool from French law and is available in any francophone jurisdiction to obtain permits, contracts, letters, and so on, that were not otherwise publicly available before and during the litigation process.

[71] This administrative environmental litigation will be the first of its kind brought in Guinea by MDT with the help of international partners CTEA and Advocates for Community Alternatives.

According to the news on China's Ministry of Commerce website, other Chinese companies in the Boké and Boffa region, including the State Power Investment Corporation (SPIC), plan to build refineries with captive coal or heavy fuel oil burning plants despite Xi Jinping's policy prohibiting coal plants.[72] The NGO consortium is currently working to expand its advocacy efforts to include all planned coal and heavy fuel oil burning plants.

On 13 June 2022, MDT submitted letters to the Ministry of Environment and Ministry of Geology and Mines urging them to cancel the plan to build a coal-fired power plant and replace it with a cleaner source of energy. Additionally, on 14 June 2022, one of the authors brought the MDT letters, two ESIAs (SMB and SPIC), and a letter calling for stopping the coal plants to the Chinese Embassy in Conakry (the capital of Guinea). These letters were meant to capitalize on China's recent pledge not to build new coal-fired power plants abroad while simultaneously setting up potential administrative litigation if the Guinean government refuses to compel SMB to find a cleaner source of energy for the refinery project. In July 2022, both ministries responded favorably to the letters submitted by MDT with the Ministry of Environment stating that the department "will take all necessary steps to examine the concerns of the communities in the SMB mining area."

In early 2023, MDT and CTEA submitted follow-up letters to both ministries and the Chinese Embassy in Conakry calling for the Guinean government to revoke the environmental compliance certificate and cancel the coal-fired power plant. Additionally, in April 2023, MDT submitted a request to the AGEE asking for a copy of the most recent environmental compliance certificate for SMB's refinery and coal plant project. MDT met with officials from the AGEE and was told that no environmental compliance certificate had been issued to SMB, which was an excuse to avoid disclosing it. If informal processes to obtain the certificate continue to prove unsuccessful, MDT will submit a *Compulsoire* or formal information request seeking the certificate.

Crucially, the *Compulsoire* can be addressed to both the Ministry and the company. The environmental compliance certificate (as discussed in Article 31 of the Guinean Environmental Code) must be renewed each year. The environmental compliance certificate for the SMB's refinery and coal plant ESIA are set to be renewed in May each year. If the certificate is renewed despite obvious deficiencies with the ESIA, as pointed out in MDT's letters to the ministries, then the NGO consortium would bring administrative litigation to challenge the decision to renew in the Guinean courts.

On the international stage, CTEA and Natural Justice coauthored and submitted a shadow report to the UN Committee for Economic, Social, and Cultural Rights during its periodic review of China and highlighted Chinese

---

[72] Ministry of Commerce of the People's Republic of China, 'Summary of Alumina and Steelmaking Projects to be Launched in Guinea in the Coming Years' (2020) www.mofcom.gov.cn/article/i/jyjl/k/202006/20200602972043.shtml.

companies' plans to construct captive coal-fired power plants and made recommendations to the Committee that China has the obligation to oversee Chinese companies operating abroad regarding their human rights impact. As a result of this engagement, the Committee made the following recommendation to China in their concluding observations: "Suspend permissions to construct coal-fired power plants as well as pause ongoing financing construction hereof, including in the State party and abroad," and "[e]nsure that business entities operating in the State party or those domiciled under the State party's jurisdiction and those acting abroad, including their sub-suppliers, as well as institutions that provide financing, are held accountable for economic, social and cultural rights violations, paying particular attention to indigenous and peasants' land rights, environmental impact."[73]

Because of pressures built by the actions above, in July 2023, an SMB manager had orally promised to abandon its plans to build a coal-fired power plant. It was a victory for communities and civil society organizations. However, SMB is now looking to build a heavy fuel oil plant, which comes with more serious health impacts for the local community, and the legal battle and campaign to stop the fossil fuels power plants will be carried on to a new stage.

4 Conclusion

As SMB forges ahead with its plans to construct a coal-fired power plant, civil society organizations are working tirelessly to ensure that SMB respects the environmental and human rights of local communities. China's recent commitment not to build any new coal-fired power plants abroad gives civil society an opportunity to pursue advocacy efforts at the international level and exert pressure on SMB to find a cleaner source of energy for its planned refinery. The planned administrative litigation to challenge the renewal of the environmental compliance certificate for SMB's alumina refinery will be the first of its kind in Guinea and will set the stage for further legal challenges to other companies also planning to construct coal-fired power plants.

5 Discussion Questions and Comments

5.1 For Law School Audiences

Guinea is a country that has had a tumultuous political history and recently experienced a military coup in 2021. The military junta has yet to hold democratic elections to institute a new leader. Additionally, Guinea has suffered from a weak "rule of law." The rule of law is defined by the UN as "a principle of

---

[73] The Committee on Economic, Social and Cultural Rights, 'Concluding Observations on the Third Periodic Report of China, Including Hong Kong SAR, China, and Macao SAR, China' (Document E/C.12/CHN/CO/3, 2023) https://digitallibrary.un.org/record/4007077.

governance in which all persons, institutions and entities, public and private, including the State itself, are accountable to laws that are publicly promulgated, equally enforced and independently adjudicated, and which are consistent with international human rights norms and standards."

While Guinea has several environmental statutes by which international corporations are required to adhere, Guinean institutions have failed to enforce these laws and the Guinean judiciary has proven difficult to access by impacted community members and the organizations representing community concerns. What actions do you propose such organizations take to ensure accountability in a country with a weak rule of law? Do you think mobilizing litigation, including administrative litigation or tort litigation, would be more successful in Guinea? Why or why not? What other legal tools are available? And who are the potential defendants? If formal institutions prove inadequate, what extralegal means may be more effective?

The SMB case may shed light on the disconnect, found elsewhere in China's Belt and Road Initiative, between political rhetoric and the actual conduct of Chinese corporations. What legal avenues are available for affected parties to challenge environmental and human rights violations perpetuated by foreign companies or multinationals? What are SMB's Chinese investors' or its parent company's legal liabilities? Can lawsuits similar to the US's Alien Tort Claims Act be filed in China? What differentiates the legal liabilities of the parent company and its subsidiaries? Will using the corporation's or financiers' grievance mechanisms in China be possible? Are there any climate and biodiversity commitments strong enough to hold Chinese parties accountable to the host country's laws and international law sources? Are current international environmental laws or international human rights laws adequate to provide legal bases and avenues to redress multinationals' wrongdoings on the environment and communities?

5.2 For Policy School Audiences

As discussed in the case study above, SMB began construction of major mining infrastructure before completing the ESIA. The ESIA process is a crucial first step in any development project. Rushed or incomplete ESIA processes can undermine the entire purpose of evaluating the environmental and social impacts of a project. Additionally, SMB's ESIA contained several deficiencies, including lacking a climate assessment, reasonable alternatives, and baseline air quality studies. An Environmental Impact Assessment (EIA) is a planning tool meant to assess environmental risks of a given project so that decision makers can make fully informed decisions regarding the project.[74] If project developers begin construction before completing the ESIA, then decisions are

---

[74] International Institute for Sustainable Development, 'EIA Essentials, EIA: What? Why? When?' www.iisd.org/learning/eia/eia-essentials/what-why-when/.

made without critical environmental and social information that is crucial to ensuring responsible and sustainable development.

Based on the facts in this case study, what policy tools do you think would be the most effective in ensuring that Chinese companies adhere to their ESIA requirements? Additionally, what are some of the dangers to communities when companies begin construction of large development projects without properly conducting environmental assessments?

Under Guinean law, it is the company proposing the project that is required to conduct ESIAs for proposed projects. However, in other countries, such as the United States, it is the government that is required to conduct such studies.[75] What are some of the benefits and/or risks of an EIA law that requires the company to conduct ESIAs? Do you think the purpose of environmental assessment laws would be better served if a company or the government conducted the studies?

---

[75] National Environmental Policy Act, 42 U.S.C. §§4321 et seq. (1969) www.energy.gov/sites/default/files/2023-08/NEPA%20reg%20amend%2006-2023.pdf.

Case Study 6.2

Micron versus UMC and Fujian Jinhua
The Cross-Border Struggle over Integrated Circuits' Trade Secrets

Kai-Shen Huang

1 Overview

This case study examines the dispute between Micron Technology, United Microelectronics Corporation (UMC), and Fujian Jinhua Integrated Circuit Co. Ltd. ("Jinhua") over the alleged theft of Micron's trade secrets in integrated circuits (ICs), specifically dynamic random-access memory (DRAM) chips. This dispute offers a lens through which to analyze China's strategic efforts to strengthen its semiconductor industry by overseas investment. It begins by introducing China's ambitious policy framework aimed at achieving self-reliance in the semiconductor industry, set against the backdrop of geopolitical tensions and the COVID-19 pandemic's impact on global IC supply chains. It then turns to the case adjudicated by Taiwanese courts in 2020, where UMC and Jinhua faced allegations of trade secret misappropriation from Micron. Finally, this study compares the different legal and regulatory approaches of Taiwan and the United States in addressing such disputes, highlighting the challenges in regulating global supply chains amidst evolving geopolitical and economic landscapes. Through exploring both the legal complexities and international responses to Chinese outbound investments in critical technologies, this case study delineates the strategic interplay between China's state-directed industrial goals, international commercial norms, and the pursuit of technological innovation.

2 Introduction

In October 2022, the United States promulgated a series of export controls on China's access to advanced computing chips and semiconductor manufacturing items designed or produced by American companies. Under the new regulations, restrictions on China's reach into the global semiconductor value chain are comprehensive, including high-end artificial intelligence (AI) chips, US-made chip design software, and US-built semiconductor manufacturing equipment and components. These controls illustrate the "stranglehold" or "neck choking" (*kabozi*) challenge that the Chinese authorities have long identified: that Western domination of advanced chip designs and manufacturing can lead to weaponizing its chokepoint positions in the global semiconductor industry to gain leverage over China's economic and national security interests. From the US perspective, however, this set of new regulations may be read as a direct strategic response to China's own peculiar approach to the development of its semiconductor industry, which Americans view as highly aggressive.

China makes no secret of its ambition to become a global leader in the integrated circuits industry. Since the early 2010s, the Chinese government has launched several policy initiatives to do so.[1] Among the most crucial is the State Council's "2020 IC Notice,"[2] which replaces most of the country's previous IC-related policy instructions. Adding muscle to these policy frameworks is the China Integrated Circuit Industry Investment Fund, also known the "Big Fund." Created as a government guidance fund, the fund is designed to assist China in realizing its aim of becoming self-reliant in the semiconductor sector, aligned with the broader objectives of the "Made in China 2025" plan.[3]

While China's drive to develop its semiconductor industry may seem like part of a global trend,[4] the country's circumstances are notably distinct due to geopolitics and the aftereffects of COVID-19. The pandemic exposed vulnerabilities in the international IC supply chain, leading to disruptions and bottlenecks that wreaked havoc across multiple industries. The crisis underscored the perils of depending on a handful of key semiconductor suppliers, especially when they are concentrated in specific geographic regions. This awareness has prompted many countries, including China, to reconsider their reliance on foreign chip suppliers and explore ways to bolster domestic production and research. For China, however, the situation is compounded by additional layers of geopolitical tensions, notably the sanctions imposed by the United States. These sanctions have not only restricted China's access to cutting-edge semiconductor technology but also accelerated its drive for self-sufficiency in IC production. The confluence of geopolitics and pandemic-induced supply chain issues has made China's semiconductor landscape unique, heightening the urgent need for the country to develop a resilient and independent chip industry.

---

[1] See, e.g., the State Council's Notice on Several Policies to Promote the Development of the Integrated Circuit Industry and Software Industry (*Guofa* [2011] No. 4), www.gov.cn/zhengce/content/2011-02/09/content_3378.htm; Guidelines to Promote a National Integrated Circuit Industry (2014).

[2] Notice on Several Policies to Promote the High-Quality Development of the Integrated Circuit Industry and Software Industry in the New Era (*Guofa* [2020] No. 8) www.gov.cn/zhengce/content/2020-08/04/content_5532370.htm.

[3] Made in China 2025 Initiative (*Guofa* [2015] No. 28).

[4] See, e.g., White House, *Building Resilient Supply Chains, Revitalizing American Manufacturing, and Fostering Broad-Based Growth* (2021) www.whitehouse.gov/wp-content/uploads/2021/06/100-day-supply-chain-review-report.pdf; the US government's recent "Creating Helpful Incentives to Produce Semiconductors and Science Act of 2022" (CHIPS Act of 2022), promulgated on 9 August 2022, is a manifestation of the global trend toward securing domestic chip supply chains. The Act provides funding to support US manufacturing, semiconductor R&D, and workforce development, thereby aiming to localize chip production; CHIPS Act of 2022, www.congress.gov/117/plaws/publ167/PLAW-117publ167.pdf.

China's official policy documents thus reveal a pivot toward semiconductor self-reliance that diverges from the current model of global interdependencies. These policies explicitly advocate for a self-sufficient and enclosed semiconductor production system within China, positioning the country as the epicenter of global semiconductor production. This is a striking departure from the highly globalized structure of current IC supply chains and represents an ambitious goal. Contrasting with the approach for deeper global integration, Beijing's leadership perceives the status quo as a national security vulnerability. They prioritize security over efficiency or global cooperation, viewing interdependence as a threat that exposes the country to potential supply chain disruptions, notably from the United States and its allies.

As prescribed in these policy instructions, measures specified or encouraged by the state have been wide-ranging. One key measure is providing a set of tiered tax incentives such as exemptions or reductions in enterprise income tax or value-added tax. IC companies that produce chips with a line width of smaller than 28 nanometers and that have operated for more than fifteen years, for instance, will be exempt from corporate income tax for the first ten years of operation (Article 1.1, 2020 IC Notice). IC companies that have been in operation for less than fifteen years, starting from the year they become profitable, will be exempt from corporate income tax for the first and second years, and for the third to fifth years their corporate income tax will be levied at half of the statutory rate of 25% (Article 1.2, 2020 IC Notice). Other measures include inducement subsidies, concessional loans, mergers and acquisitions (M&As), and talent recruitment.

There is more to the worries about China's ambition in the semiconductor industry than meets the eye. The source of concerns stems primarily from its highly strategic, often strong-armed approach to technological advancement, which is at odds with the liberal ideal of market competition and international commercial norms. To accelerate the self-sufficiency of its chip industry, for example, China's FDI incentive scheme often encourages foreign firms to form joint ventures and share their technology with local partners in exchange for access to the Chinese semiconductor market.[5] This same tactic of technology transfer is also seen in China's overseas investment in the semiconductor industry, particularly through M&As that permit the repatriation of more advanced know-how.[6] However, alongside these more formal and sanctioned strategies, some Chinese companies have been accused of adopting more aggressive, under-the-table tactics such as talent acquisitions and the misappropriation of trade secrets or other forms of intellectual property. Owing to the controversial nature of these practices, they frequently result in legal challenges, criminal

---

[5] See Chris Miller, *Chip War: The Fight for the World's Most Critical Technology* (Simon & Schuster 2022) 255–61 (reporting that IBM, AMD, and Qualcomm each engaged in technology transfer with Chinese entities through joint ventures during the 2010s).

[6] Stephen Ezell, *Moore's Law Under Attack: The Impacts of China's Policies on Global Semiconductor Innovation* (Information Technology & Innovation Foundation 2021) 24–5.

charges, and regulatory crackdowns on Chinese investment in the host state's sensitive areas.

One high-profile example that encapsulates these issues is the criminal case involving trade secrets between Micron, UMC, and Jinhua, which was adjudicated by Taiwanese courts in 2020.

3 The Case

3.1 Court Case: UMC and Jinhua

China's ambition to lead in the semiconductor industry is intrinsically tied to its broader strategic objective of becoming a global powerhouse in AI. Both sectors are interdependent: Semiconductors serve as the foundational technology for AI-enabled applications. Take, for example, DRAMs. These chips are staples in everyday electronic devices like smartphones and computers, but their role has become increasingly important due to the data-intensive nature of modern AI applications. DRAM chips enable quick access to vast amounts of data, a necessity for the real-time processing performed by AI algorithms.

Despite the government's generous funding for the semiconductor industry, Chinese firms have yet to break into the DRAM market. In terms of market share, Samsung and SK Hynix in South Korea continue to dominate the industry, followed by Micron in the United States. This monopolization is largely due to the highly competitive nature of the DRAM industry, which requires not just massive capital investment for manufacturing facilities but also specialized expertise. All these factors make it difficult for latecomers to challenge the dominance of the key players. Nonetheless, this has not stopped some key Chinese companies from trying and Micron was one such target.

Founded in 1978, Micron is a multinational corporation specializing in designing and manufacturing not just DRAM but also other types of memory chips such as NAND flash memory and solid-state drives. Headquartered in Boise, Idaho, in the United States, Micron also operates many production facilities in the Asia-Pacific region. Tsinghua Unigroup's US$23 billion acquisition offer in 2015 was the first attempt to approach Micron.[7] Micron did not think this deal was realistic as it assumed that the US regulator would not approve the transaction due to national security concerns.[8] Hence, the deal did not go forward.

One year later, Micron was targeted by another Chinese company, Jinhua, a Fujian-based DRAM chipmaker. Unlike Tsinghua Unigroup's straightforward

---

[7] Paul Mozur and Quentin Hardy, 'Micron Technology Is Said to Be Takeover Target of Chinese Company' *New York Times* (14 July 2015) https://archive.nytimes.com/www.nytimes.com/2015/07/15/business/international/micron-technology-is-said-to-be-takeover-target-of-chinese-company.html.

[8] Stacey Higginbotham, 'Micron Really Doesn't Seem Interested in Doing a Deal with China's Tsinghua' (*Fortune*, 21 July 2015) https://fortune.com/2015/07/20/micron-really-doesnt-seem-interested-in-doing-a-deal-with-chinas-tsinghua/.

takeover bid, Jinhua took a more circuitous route. Jinhua entered into a licensing agreement with UMC, a major Taiwanese semiconductor manufacturer. UMC had just recruited the president of Micron's Taiwan branch, thereby gaining valuable insights into DRAM production. According to the Taichung District Court,[9] in January 2016 UMC struck a deal with Jinhua that provided UMC with US$700 million in exchange for developing and providing knowledge transfer about DRAM production processes. Up to this point, the deal appeared to be legally sound. However, two years later, in 2018, UMC and three individuals involved in the collaboration – Jianting Ho, Yongming Wang, and Letian Rong – were charged with criminal violations of Taiwan's Trade Secret Law.

In 2020, the Taichung District Court found them guilty of infringing Micron's trade secrets. UMC was ordered to pay a fine of NT$100 million.[10] Ho, Wang, and Rong were sentenced to five years and six months, four years and six months, and six years and six months, respectively.[11] The decision was appealed to the Intellectual Property and Commercial Court (IPCC).[12] In January 2022, the IPCC reversed the district court's decision.[13] UMC's fine was reduced to NT$20 million. Ho's sentence was reduced to one year, whereas Wang's was reduced to only six months. Rong was acquitted of all charges. The IPCC's ruling against UMC is final. The charges against individuals were appealed by prosecutors to Taiwan's Supreme Court. In August 2022, the Supreme Court reversed the decision and remanded the case back to the IPCC for further proceedings. As of September 2023, the criminal charges against Ho, Wang, and Rong are still pending in the IPCC.

According to the information presented in these decisions, the licensing collaboration between UMC and Jinhua raised some questions about potential irregularities, particularly given UMC's area of expertise. UMC is a major semiconductor manufacturer focused primarily on the design and production of logic chips, not memory chips like DRAM. This specialization made the licensing arrangement with Jinhua, a DRAM chipmaker, somewhat unusual and prompted scrutiny.

To further contextualize, in 2015 UMC recruited Stephen Chen, who had previously served as the president of Micron Memory Taiwan Co., Ltd. (hereinafter, "MMT"). Chen was tasked with leading UMC's New Business Development unit, established in January 2016 specifically to finalize a DRAM

---

[9] 106 Zhisu 11 Judgement (Taichung District Court, 12 June 2020) 2–3.
[10] 106 Zhisu 11 Judgement (Taichung District Court, 12 June 2020) 168. [11] ibid.
[12] The IPCC is a specialized court located in New Taipei City, Taiwan. Established initially as the IP Court on 1 July 2008, it was renamed and restructured on 1 July 2021 following its merger with the commercial court system. The IPCC holds jurisdiction over cases related to intellectual property rights and commercial law. This includes first or second instance civil and criminal cases under acts such as the Patent Act, Trademark Act, Copyright Act, and Trade Secrets Act, among others. Post merger, the court's jurisdiction expanded to incorporate commercial cases as specified by the Commercial Case Adjudication Act.
[13] 109 Xingzhishangzhongsu 4 Judgement (IPCC, 27 January 2022) 1–2, 162.

licensing deal with Jinhua. Chen also recruited two former employees from MMT, Ho and Wang, to join UMC's new unit.

Both Ho and Wang had worked at MMT for several years, during which they had gained access to Micron's confidential data and trade secrets related to memory chips. The fact that these individuals, who had access to sensitive Micron information, were now involved in a DRAM deal between UMC and Jinhua raises questions about the true intent behind the licensing arrangement.

Ho was accused of reproducing and using the trade secrets that he had acquired during his employment at MMT. Wang was introduced to UMC by Ho and was offered a salary that was equal to his position at MMT, plus an additional bonus upon signing another employment contract with Jinhua and working in Mainland China. Wang resigned from MMT on 26 April 2016 and started at UMC two days later. However, before leaving MMT, he downloaded and copied the company's trade secrets onto a USB drive and uploaded them to his Google Drive. All these actions took place between 16 April and 23 April 2016 while Wang was still employed at MMT. He then used the data to help UMC develop DRAM products.[14] As the court shows, the licensing collaboration between UMC and Jinhua involved two stages: initially conducting research and development (R&D) in Taiwan and then transferring the technology to Jinhua.[15] In the scenario presented in the court decisions, talent acquisition and trade secret theft were the major measures adopted to achieve the licensing agreement's objectives.

3.2 Regulatory Analysis

Currently, the key legislation that governs China's investment in Taiwan is the Act Governing Relations between Peoples of the Taiwan Area and the Mainland Area (hereinafter, the "Cross-Straits People Relations Act").[16] Pursuant to Article 40-1 of the Act, Mainland Area profit-seeking enterprises, as well as their investments in other territories, are prohibited from conducting any business activities within the Taiwan Area without prior authorization from the competent authorities and the requisite establishment of a local branch or liaison office. Similarly, Article 73 mandates that individuals, juristic persons, organizations, or other institutions from the Mainland Area, along with any companies they invest in within other territories, may not partake in investment activities within the Taiwan Area without explicit permission from the competent authorities.

As the court decisions reveal, the licensing agreement between UMC and Jinhua received regulatory approval from the Investment Commission of the Ministry of Economic Affairs (MOEAIC) in Taiwan,[17] making it legitimate

---

[14] 106 Zhisu 11 Judgement (Taichung District Court, 12 June 2020) 6–7.
[15] 109 Xingzhishangzhongsu 4 Judgement (IPCC, 27 January 2022) 143–4.
[16] In the Act, the term "Mainland Area" refers to Mainland China, which is generally understood to be the territory now controlled by the People's Republic of China.
[17] 106 Zhisu 11 Judgement (Taichung District Court, 12 June 2020) 2.

under current Taiwanese law. However, if Jinhua's objective was merely to develop or acquire expertise related to DRAM production, this collaboration seems inefficient, especially considering that UMC does not specialize in memory chips. This raises the possibility that Jinhua's strategy may have been designed to circumvent Taiwanese laws restricting the recruitment of talent from Taiwan, as prohibited in the Cross-Straits People Relations Act.

Article 34 of the Cross-Straits People Relations Act contains strict restrictions on job recruitment information for positions in Mainland China. According to this article, job positions in Mainland China cannot be advertised in Taiwan without permission. Advertisers or human resources agencies who violate this rule are subject to Article 89, Paragraph 1 of the Act. It stipulates that any person who entrusts to another, is entrusted, or acts on their own to engage in advertisement broadcast or publication, or any other promotion activity in the Taiwan Area for any goods, service, or other item of the Mainland Area other than those prescribed in Paragraph 1 of Article 34, or violates Paragraph 2 of Article 34 or the mandatory or prohibitive provisions of the rules governing the management prescribed in accordance with Paragraph 4 of Article 34, shall be punished with an administrative fine of not less than NT$100,000 and no more than NT$500,000.

In more practical terms, any company registered in Taiwan, foreign company, or foreign company branch office or representative office that is registered or approved to operate in Taiwan, is not allowed to post job advertisements that list Mainland China as the workplace. This means that advertisements for positions in Mainland China cannot be published on job search websites or any other platform, including the company's official website or social media platforms in Taiwan. According to the Regulations for Advertising Goods, Labor and General Services of the Mainland Area in the Taiwan Area, a specific exception exists for posting job advertisements. If a domestic company has received approval from MOEAIC to invest in Mainland China and establish a Taiwan-funded enterprise, it is permitted to list Mainland China as the workplace in job advertisements (Article 6, Paragraph 5).

By entering into a technology transfer agreement with a Taiwan-based chip company like UMC, neither Jinhua nor UMC needed to establish their own R&D capacity in Mainland China. Such a licensing collaboration is not unusual assuming no criminal activities related to trade secret theft are involved. However, as illustrated in a number of court decisions, talent poaching frequently leads to misappropriation of trade secrets and intellectual property in order to facilitate R&D outputs. As Wang himself revealed during the investigation, this behavior is largely motivated by financial gain: "I only have my eyes set on the output, making money, and then retiring."[18]

Under Taiwan's Trade Secret Act, trade secret theft is a serious offense. Promulgated in 1996, the Act initially did not have a criminal clause to regulate

---

[18] 109 Xingzhishangzhongsu 4 Judgement (IPCC, 27 January 2022) 144.

misappropriation of trade secrets. It was not until 2013 that it criminalized such wrongdoing by adopting a dual-track model. Article 13-1 specifies the penalties for committing acts related to trade secret theft, embezzlement, fraud, and unauthorized reproduction, usage, or disclosure, and outlines the fines that may be imposed in addition to imprisonment. Under Article 13-1, the maximum penalty for trade secret misappropriation is five years' imprisonment in addition to a fine of between NT$1 million and NT$10 million.

Article 13-2 adds additional penalties for committing these crimes with the intention of using the trade secret in foreign jurisdictions, including Mainland China, Hong Kong, or Macau, and increases the potential fines that may be imposed for such offenses. Under Article 13-2, the penalty for committing such an offense with the intention of using the trade secret in foreign jurisdictions is imprisonment of between one and ten years, in addition to a fine of between NT$3 million and NT$50 million. The penalties outlined in Article 13-2 are generally considered to be harsher than those in Article 13-1, which may serve as a stronger deterrent against trade secret misappropriation with the intention of using the information in foreign jurisdictions.

The issue at the heart of the UMC-Jinhua case pertains to the potential violation of Article 13-2 of Taiwan's Trade Secret Act by the three individuals in question, namely Ho, Wang, and Rong. The Taichung District Court concluded that they had indeed violated this provision, while the IPCC reversed this decision on appeal, finding that the defendants did not meet the legal standard required for a conviction under Article 13-2. However, the decision was later remanded by Taiwan's Supreme Court, which required the IPCC to consider the following evidence and issues: Wang's confession regarding his knowledge of the UMC-Jinhua licensing collaboration; Ho's statement regarding his employment contract signed with Jinhua during October and November 2016; a witness's statement that UMC planned to arrange for employees involved in the collaboration to open bank accounts in Mainland China with incentive bonuses being wired to their accounts once product development was complete; Wang's communication with his friends where he stated "Conducting R&D in Taiwan and transferring the technology to Mainland"; and UMC's application to MOEAIC for the approval of the UMC-Jinhua licensing collaboration.[19] The Supreme Court indicated that the evidence listed above seemed to suggest that the three individuals had the intention of using Micron's trade secrets in Mainland China.

3.3 International Responses

The UMC-Jinhua licensing collaboration has faced legal challenges not only in Taiwan but also in the United States. In September 2018, the US government indicted UMC and Jinhua for conspiracy to commit economic espionage and

---

[19] 111 Taishang 3655 Judgement (Supreme Court, 17 August 2022) 4–5.

to steal trade secrets from Micron.[20] The following month, the US Department of Commerce added Jinhua to its export restriction list, prohibiting the company from purchasing components, software, and technology goods from US firms.[21] In 2020, UMC pleaded guilty to a single count of criminal trade secret theft and offered to pay a US$60 million fine. In November 2021, the US Department of Justice dismissed other allegations against UMC, including conspiracy to commit economic espionage, and UMC and Micron agreed to a global settlement.[22] Jinhua, on the other hand, denied any wrongdoing related to the allegations. However, the consequences for Jinhua were severe. In the wake of the US export restrictions, Jinhua was forced to cease production of memory chips within a few months, and it did not resume operations until 2022 when it received assistance from Huawei and shifted its focus to manufacturing logic chips.[23]

It is worth noting that the US Department of Justice indicted Jinhua as a major defendant largely due to its technology cooperation agreement with UMC that took place in or around January 2016. The US government's indictment against Jinhua reflects its discourse that China engages in unfair and illegal practices to acquire technology, and as a Chinese state-owned enterprise, Jinhua is particularly vulnerable to such a perception. The statement released by the US Department of Justice implied just that:

> The theft of intellectual property on a continuing basis by nation-state actors is an even more damaging affront to the rule of law. We in the Northern District of California, one of the world's great centers of intellectual property development, will continue to lead the fight to protect U.S. innovation from criminal misappropriation, whether motivated by personal greed or national economic ambition.[24]

Compared to the legal and political backlash in the United States against the UMC-Jinhua licensing collaboration, Taiwan's justice system has taken a more restrained approach. Jinhua has never been considered a defendant in the case and the collaboration was not seen as Jinhua's involvement in a conspiracy to commit economic espionage or steal trade secrets. The court decisions in

---

[20] United States v. UMC et al., CR 18-465 MMC (LHK/SVK 27 September 2018) www.justice.gov/opa/press-release/file/1107251/download.
[21] 83 FR 54519, www.govinfo.gov/content/pkg/FR-2018-10-30/pdf/2018-23693.pdf.
[22] Micron, 'Micron and UMC Announce Global Settlement' (25 November 2021) https://investors.micron.com/news-releases/news-release-details/micron-and-umc-announce-global-settlement.
[23] Cheng Ting-Fang and Shunsuke Tabeta, 'China's Chip Industry Fights to Survive U.S. Tech Crackdown' (*Nikkei Asia*, 30 November 2022) https://asia.nikkei.com/Spotlight/The-Big-Story/China-s-chip-industry-fights-to-survive-U.S.-tech-crackdown.
[24] Office of Public Affairs, US Department of Justice, 'PRC State-Owned Company, Taiwan Company, and Three Individuals Charged with Economic Espionage' (1 November 2018) www.justice.gov/opa/pr/prc-state-owned-company-taiwan-company-and-three-individuals-charged-economic-espionage.

Taiwan have only implicated UMC and its three employees, Ho, Wang, and Rong, in the theft of trade secrets. Jinhua's role in facilitating the theft of Micron's trade secrets was not confirmed in the court decisions.

In February 2024, Jinhua was cleared of charges related to economic espionage and other criminal allegations in the United States.[25] Judge Chesney ruled that the evidence presented by US prosecutors did not sufficiently demonstrate that Jinhua, with state support, had unlawfully acquired confidential information from Micron.[26] Nonetheless, this case, initiated in 2018, has garnered considerable attention, spotlighting concerns over China's pursuit of semiconductor self-sufficiency, which includes acquiring technologies from abroad.[27] Key stakeholders in the global IC supply chain have closely monitored the UMC-Jinhua conflict.

4 Conclusion

Semiconductors have emerged as critical components within contemporary geopolitics, holding significant implications for national security due to their incorporation in both civilian and military applications. Recognizing the strategic imperative of these technologies, China's pursuit of semiconductor development and acquisition is a strategic initiative aimed at enhancing its technological autonomy and may influence the reorientation of the global supply chain to a more China-centric model. This move presents a potential shift from the established supply chain dynamics, traditionally influenced by US-centric alliances.

Taiwan's leading role in manufacturing chips places it at the heart of these geopolitical tensions, particularly considering its political relationship with China. This environment amplifies the sensitivity of semiconductor technology as a point of international contention, where economic ambitions intersect with national security priorities. The UMC-Jinhua case illustrates the challenges in differentiating between sanctioned technological collaboration and the misappropriation of trade secrets. The incident reveals how an endorsed collaboration can potentially lead to unlawful activities, highlighting the importance of thorough oversight in cross-border technological partnerships. While this case involves China, it exemplifies a global concern where informal business engagements require scrutiny to align with the host state's legal and regulatory frameworks.

---

[25] In December 2023, Micron had reached a global settlement agreement with Jinhua, see Debby Wu, 'Micron Settles IP Theft Lawsuit Amid Push to Repair Beijing Ties' (*Bloomberg Law*, 24 December 2023) https://news.bloomberglaw.com/ip-law/micron-settles-ip-theft-lawsuit-amid-push-to-repair-beijing-ties.

[26] Rachel Graf and Robert Burnson, 'Chinese Chipmaker Cleared in US Criminal Trade Secrets Case' (*Bloomberg*, 28 February 2024) www.bloomberg.com/news/articles/2024-02-27/chinese-chipmaker-cleared-in-us-criminal-trade-secrets-case.

[27] See, e.g., Miller (n 5) ch 50.

5 Discussion Questions and Comments

5.1 For Law School Audiences

5.1.1 Law and Politics

The legal dispute involving Micron, UMC, and Jinhua centered on accusations of unauthorized use of Micron's trade secrets. Taiwanese courts primarily assessed the conduct of UMC and certain employees, while the US Department of Justice extended its scrutiny to Jinhua, indicting the company as a major defendant.

The divergent approaches by Taiwanese and US legal systems may stem from their distinct legal frameworks and enforcement priorities. Taiwan's focus on individual and corporate conduct within its jurisdiction aligns with its legal traditions, emphasizing direct involvement and evidence of misappropriation. The United States, conversely, may have broader geopolitical and economic considerations, employing legal instruments as part of its strategic enforcement against perceived threats to its technological leadership.

The indictment of Jinhua by the US government could be interpreted within the larger context of allegations against China's methods of acquiring advanced technology. This framing raises critical legal questions about the international standards of corporate behavior, the enforcement of intellectual property rights, and the nexus between government actions and corporate strategies. The UMC-Jinhua case, initially sanctioned by Taiwanese authorities, now invites scrutiny under the lens of these broader geopolitical conflicts.

1. What legal principles underpin the different approaches taken by Taiwan and the United States, and how do these principles manifest in cross-border enforcement and extraterritorial application of laws?
2. How do these legal actions reflect and impact the regulatory challenges inherent in managing international supply chains, particularly in the high-tech sector?
3. Does the UMC-Jinhua case serve as a microcosm of the broader geopolitical struggle between the world's two largest economies, the United States and China? Why or why not?

5.2 For Policy School Audiences

5.2.1 Economic Espionage and Policymaking

In the UMC case heard by Taiwanese courts, Jinhua was not identified as the primary agent of economic espionage; the focus was rather on UMC and certain employees. The absence of direct evidence in court records tying Jinhua to espionage directives suggests that worries about economic espionage are broader and not necessarily confined to the actions or policies of any one nation.[28] Therefore, it is essential to approach each case on its merits without preconceived notions tied to the national origin of the entities. Many countries are currently challenged with promoting innovation and international cooperation while simultaneously protecting intellectual property rights and ensuring national security. The entanglement of these conflicting goals presents a need for policy considerations beyond the trend of reducing reliance on foreign entities, commonly referred to as "decoupling." Further questions to be discussed include:

1. What legal and regulatory measures can be implemented to impartially address economic espionage, ensuring equal treatment across different national contexts?
2. How might nations tactically support innovation and uphold intellectual property and security without resorting to complete disengagement from international collaboration?
3. What collaborative efforts between the public and private sectors are necessary to mitigate the risks of economic espionage in critical industries like semiconductor manufacturing, without impeding the flow of trade and technological progress?

5.3 For Business School Audiences

5.3.1 Business Strategies and the US-China Tech War

Amid escalating US-China tensions in technology, the outcomes of the UMC-Jinhua case are likely to shape global tech industry practices going forward. US regulatory actions, including the addition of certain Chinese entities to the Entity List and the application of Export Administration Regulations (EAR), have increased scrutiny of international transactions involving sensitive technologies.[29] Consequently, companies worldwide, including those in Taiwan with core technology specializations, are assessing their international partnerships.

In addressing these developments, companies are advised to enhance their strategies for intellectual property protection to align with current international trade regulations. This may include evaluating current alliances, especially those potentially affected by US-China technological disputes and

---

[28] It should be noted that, according to the Center for Strategic and International Studies, from 2000 through March 2023, there were 224 known cases of Chinese espionage targeting the United States. This number of Chinese spying incidents directed at America far exceeds that of any other country over the same period, surpassing even Russian espionage efforts, see 'Survey of Chinese Espionage in the United States Since 2000,' www.csis.org/programs/strategic-technologies-program/archives/survey-chinese-espionage-united-states-2000.

[29] See US Department of Commerce, 'Country Commercial Guides: China – U.S. Export Controls' (7 April 2023) www.trade.gov/country-commercial-guides/china-us-export-controls.

considering engagement with emerging markets for diversification. Key strategic measures could involve:

- strengthening internal protocols to secure intellectual property, aligning them with international best practices, and engaging in regular audits;
- enhancing transparency and communication channels with international partners to foster trust and align business strategies with the global regulatory environment; and
- exploring diversification in customer bases and supply chains, to reduce reliance on a particular market, thereby mitigating risks associated with geopolitical uncertainties.

From a business strategic perspective, consider the following questions for further discussions:

1. In what ways can firms recalibrate their international collaboration models to ensure trust and compliance amidst stringent regulations like the US Entity List and EAR restrictions?
2. What strategic shifts should companies undertake to diversify their market engagement and supply chain dependencies in the face of escalating geopolitical tensions in technology?
3. What specific measures should tech companies adopt to bolster intellectual property protection and foster better communication with international partners to build trust and minimize risks associated with the current US-China frictions over technological supremacy?

Case Study 6.3

The Use of Foreign Investment Treaties in the Protection of Chinese Outbound Investments

Zhongshan Fucheng Industrial Investment Co. Ltd. v. Federal Republic of Nigeria

Ngozi S. Nwoko and Stanley U. Nweke-Eze

1 Overview

Over the years, the economic relationship between China and African states has continued to grow and this is evident in the volume of Chinese investments in Africa.[1] In the wake of these investments, China and African states have signed bilateral investment treaties (BITs), which aim to promote the development of host states and protect foreign investments from one contracting state in the territory of the other contracting state, thereby stimulating foreign investments by reducing political risk. BITs are unique in character in that they provide substantive protections to foreign investors and a basis for claims by an individual or company against a host state on grounds that such substantive protections have been breached by the host state. In order to avoid the need to turn to the national courts in the host state for a judicial remedy, BITs usually contain an arbitration clause submitting disputes to a neutral arbitration tribunal. This case study demonstrates one such instance where, in a first-of-its-kind case, a Chinese investor sued Nigeria, an African host state, for breach of its treaty obligations under the China-Nigeria BIT 2001 ("China-Nigeria BIT"),[2] and throws light on how BITs can be used in the protection of Chinese outbound investments, including in Africa.

---

[1] Although the China-Nigeria Bilateral Investment Treaty, 2001 does not define the word "state," we, however, use the term "state" in this chapter in its traditional sense of a political and sovereign entity that has the following characteristics: a permanent population, a defined territory, an independent government, and the capacity to enter into relations with other states. This definition of the state excludes the political subdivisions of a state or such constituent states in Nigeria as the Ogun State and Lagos State governments. For a discussion of the concept of statehood, see Frederick Tse-shyang Chen, 'The Meaning of States in the Membership Provisions of the United Nations Charter' (2001) 12 Indiana International & Comparative Law Review 25; and James Crawford, 'State' in *Max Planck Encyclopedia of Public International Law* (last updated: January 2011) Oxford Public International Law (http://opil.ouplaw.com).

[2] The China-Nigeria Bilateral Investment Treaty, 27 August 2001, in force 18 February 2010.

2 Introduction

This case study discusses an investment dispute between a Chinese company, Zhongshan Fucheng Industrial Investment Company Limited ("Zhongshan"), and the Federal Republic of Nigeria ("Nigeria") under the China-Nigeria BIT that resulted in an arbitration award dated 26 March 2021 (the "Award").[3] This is the first investment treaty arbitration won by an investor from Mainland China against a sovereign state in Africa. It is also the first arbitration Award ever made against Nigeria in an investment treaty dispute. The place of arbitration was London, United Kingdom, but the arbitration proceedings were held virtually due to COVID-19 travel restrictions. The hearing was conducted under the Arbitration Rules of the United Nations Commission on International Trade Law (UNCITRAL).[4]

This case study sheds light on Chinese corporate behavior, Chinese companies' approaches to mitigating investment risks in international business, their use of the investment treaty arbitration regime,[5] and, ultimately, Chinese investment behavior at large. The case study demonstrates how Chinese companies navigate policy and regulatory challenges in local markets in their host states. The case of *Zhongshan Fucheng Industrial Investment Co. Ltd. v. Federal Republic of Nigeria* is a good example of the use of an investment treaty by a Chinese investor to protect its investment against the unbridled use of power by a sovereign host state, in this case Nigeria. In terms of data and methodology, the case study draws on primary source documents (see Table 6.3.1) and a semi-structured interview with one of the lawyers who indirectly participated in the arbitration proceedings. The interview revealed that this case study should reassure other Chinese companies that recourse to investment treaty arbitration may increase protection for their foreign investment. This case, therefore, serves as a valuable lens through which to examine Chinese investments in Nigeria, and on the African continent at large.

As background to the China–Nigeria investment relationship, China's outbound investments across the world, including in African countries, have continued to grow massively since 2005, now exceeding US$2.3 trillion.[6] In Africa

---

[3] *Zhongshan Fucheng Industrial Investment Co Ltd v Federal Republic of Nigeria* [2021] Final Arbitral Award (UNCITRAL) (David E Neuberger – Presiding Arbitrator; Matthew Gearing – Co-Arbitrator; and Rotimi Oguneso – Co-Arbitrator).

[4] 'UNCITRAL Arbitration Rules, https://uncitral.un.org/en/texts/arbitration/contractualtexts/arbitration. https://perma.cc/PFU4-6QBT.

[5] In this case study, we use the term "regime" to mean a set of principles, norms, rules, and decision-making procedures that govern or relate to an issue area. In this context, the issue area is international investment arbitration. Regimes are sets of governing arrangements that include networks of rules, norms, and procedures that regulate behavior and control its effects. See, for example, Anu Bradford, 'Regime Theory' in *Max Planck Encyclopedia of Public International Law* (Oxford University Press, 2007).

[6] 'China Global Investment Tracker' (*American Enterprise Institute, AEI*) www.aei.org/china-global-investment-tracker/. https://perma.cc/N8M5-V8WW.

Table 6.3.1 List of primary documents

Primary documents

1. Annual flow of foreign direct investments from China to Nigeria between 2011 and 2021
2. Map of Ogun Guangdong Free Trade Zone
3. Agreement between the Government of the People's Republic of China and the Government of the Federal Republic of Nigeria for the Reciprocal Promotion and Protection of Investments (China-Nigeria BIT), 2001
4. Framework Agreement between Zhuhai and Ogun Guangdong Free Trade Zone ("OGFTZ Company") on the Establishment of Fucheng Industrial Park in Ogun Guangdong Free Trade Zone, 2010
5. Joint Venture Agreement between Ogun State, Zhongfu and Zenith Global Merchant Limited for the Development, Management, and Operation of the Ogun Guangdong Free Trade Zone, 2013
6. Framework Agreement between Ogun State, Zhongfu and Zenith Global Merchant Limited, and Xi'an Ogun Construction and Development Limited Company, 2016
7. Final Arbitral Award dated 26 March 2021 in Zhongshan Fucheng Industrial Investment Co. Ltd. v. Federal Republic of Nigeria
8. Order of Seizure of Nigeria's Bombardier Aircraft Issued by the Superior Court of Quebec, Canada, 25 January 2023
9. Entrustment of Equity Management Agreement between Guangdong Xinguang International Group Co., Ltd., and Zhuhai Zhongfu Industrial Group Co., Ltd., 2012
10. Petition Filed by Zhongshan to Recognize and Enforce Foreign Arbitral Award Between *Zhongshan Fucheng Industrial Investment Co. Ltd. v. The Federal Republic of Nigeria* before the United States District Court for the District of Columbia (Case 1:22-cv-00170), Civil Action, 25 January 2022
11. An Order of the United States District Court for the District of Columbia Recognizing the Arbitral Award Between *Zhongshan Fucheng Industrial Investment Co. Ltd., v. Federal Republic of Nigeria* [Civil Action No. 22-170 (BAH)], 26 January 2023

Source: Authors' compilation based on the Award and enforcement proceedings

and Nigeria specifically, Chinese investments are rooted in various institutional and policy frameworks adopted by China and African countries. Since the beginning of the century, Chinese state-owned enterprises and private companies have increasingly invested in Nigeria under China's investment policy framework known as the "Going Out" strategy.[7] The result has been an influx of Chinese businesses into the Nigerian market. Figure 6.3.1 shows the volume of foreign direct investment from China to Nigeria between 2011 and

---

[7] The "Going Out" strategy, which has been subsumed in the Belt and Road Initiative, is a plan of action by China for entering and navigating mainstream global trade and investment and is geared toward developing an expanded and interdependent market for China.

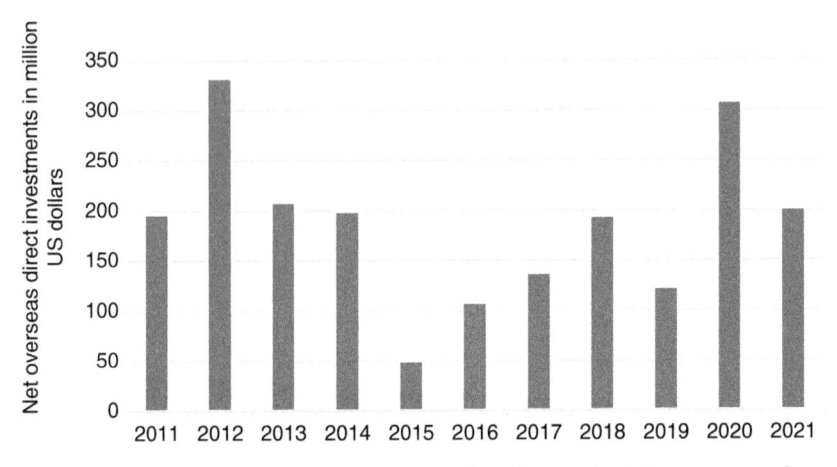

Figure 6.3.1 Annual flow of foreign direct investments from China to Nigeria between 2011 and 2021 (million US$)

2021. As the data shows, about US$201.67 million's worth of direct investments from China were made in Nigeria in 2021. Chinese investment in Nigeria's manufacturing sector can be traced back to as early as the 1960s when private Chinese companies, such as the Lee Group of Companies and Western Metal Products Company, made early strides in Nigeria.[8]

In addition to the "Going Out" strategy, the first Forum on China-Africa Cooperation (FOCAC) Summit was held in Beijing in November 2006 where a new type of strategic partnership between China and African states was declared.[9] The African continent has great potential to attract Chinese investors, particularly given that Africa features natural resources and emerging economies.[10] At the Summit, the Chinese and African governments agreed to establish special economic zones, among other things, to deepen economic and trade relations between China and African states.[11] In fact, the Ogun Guangdong Free Trade Zone (the "Zone"),[12] which is the location of the Chinese investment that

---

[8] Franklin Uzor, 'Lee Group of Companies Partner Jigawa State to Establish 120,000Mt Sugar Company' (Nigerian Investment Promotion Commission, 4 May 2017) www.nipc.gov.ng/2017/05/04/lee-group-companies-establishes-120000mt-sugar-coy-jigawa/. https://perma.cc/P3WZ-V8V2.

[9] 'Beijing Declaration of the Forum on China-Africa Cooperation' (Ministry of Foreign Affairs, the People's Republic of China, 20 September 2006) www.fmprc.gov.cn/zflt/eng/bjzl/t404142.htm.

[10] Virtual interview participant (14 July 2023).   [11] ibid.

[12] Free trade zones (FTZs) were created to attract foreign direct investment, increase foreign exchange earnings, promote technology transfer, and develop export-oriented industries in Nigeria. An FTZ company enjoys numerous incentives such as exemption from all federal, state, and local government taxes, rates, and levies; duty-free importation of capital goods, machinery/components, spare parts, raw materials, and consumable items in the zones; 100% foreign ownership of investments; 100% repatriation of capital, profits, and dividends; waiver of all imports and export licenses; permission to sell 100% of goods into the domestic market; and rent-free land during the first six months of construction (for government-owned zones), among other incentives.

Figure 6.3.2 Map of Ogun Guangdong free trade zone

resulted in the investment arbitration that this case study discusses, was established in 2009 and exemplifies the implementation of one of the declarations of the 2006 FOCAC Summit and the Sino-Nigeria investment partnership. The Zone is located in Ogun State in Southwest Nigeria,[13] and 50 km from Lagos as shown in Figure 6.3.2.[14] The Zone covers an area of 2,000 ha of land owned by the Ogun State government.[15] For Nigeria, the establishment of the Zone is economically significant as the objective is to support the country's plan to diversify its economy away from sole reliance on petroleum. As of September 2023, there are 56 companies operating in the Zone and 600 Chinese employees.[16] The Zone is also seen by Chinese authorities as a necessary component of the Belt and Road Initiative (BRI) adopted by the Chinese government in 2013.

As a general observation, cross-border investments by Chinese companies in emerging markets are sometimes prone to risks, which include adverse or illegitimate actions from the host state. To guard against the attendant risks, China signs investment treaties with foreign states. As of the end of 2023, the Chinese government has 107 BITs with foreign states (including Nigeria) that are in force and 16 BITs that have been signed but are not yet in force.[17] These

---

[13] Ogun State is one of the thirty-six constituent states in Nigeria.
[14] Lagos State is Nigeria's commercial capital. It has the two largest seaports in West Africa, namely the Apapa port and the newly completed Chinese-invested Lekki deep seaport.
[15] It is worth noting that, under Nigerian law, a foreign investor cannot acquire land in Nigeria. The foreign investor will need to partner with a Nigerian entity to establish a company before land can be allocated.
[16] Wang Kang Ceramics Free Trade Zone Company, established in 2011, is the largest ceramic manufacturer in Nigeria and Africa, with a daily production capacity of 120,000 square meters of ceramic tiles. Chinese companies that are operating in the Zone engage in the manufacturing of building materials, ceramics, ironware, furniture, pharmaceuticals, food and beverage processing, electrical products, and computers, among other products. See OGFTZ, 'Ogun Guangdong Free Trade Zone' https://ogftz.org/. https://perma.cc/96HB-EM44.
[17] UNCTAD Investment Policy Hub, 'International Investment Agreements Navigator' https://investmentpolicy.unctad.org/international-investment-agreements/countries/42/china. https://perma.cc/35L3-YHPK.

BITs primarily aim to protect Chinese investors and their investments in the host state, while host states hope that such investments will foster overall socioeconomic development in their country. Therefore, the BITs that China has signed and are in force typically provide substantial protection and guarantees for qualifying Chinese investments abroad. In these BITs, Nigeria, for instance, guarantees Chinese investors that their investments shall be treated in a fair and equitable manner and shall not be expropriated without appropriate compensation. In addition, the BITs, as this case study will demonstrate, allow Chinese investors to institute claims against host states before an arbitral tribunal if their investments are treated in a manner that is contrary to the terms of the relevant BIT, without the need to exclusively rely on the national courts of the host states. In recent times, Chinese business enterprises have demonstrated their willingness to resort to arbitration to resolve investment disputes between them and host states for the protection of their investments abroad. According to the International Centre for Settlement of Investment Disputes (ICSID) case database, as of 10 September 2023, there have been ten ICSID cases filed by Chinese investors as claimants, of which five cases are still in progress.[18]

The case of *Zhongshan Fucheng Industrial Investment Co. Ltd. v. Federal Republic of Nigeria* is an example of an investment treaty claim brought by a Chinese investor against a host state on the basis that Nigeria (through the Ogun State government in Southwest Nigeria and other government agencies in Nigeria) violated the provisions of the China-Nigeria BIT by taking measures that wrongfully affected the Chinese investments. Specifically, the claim concerns the wrongful termination of Joint Venture Agreements (JVAs) for the development and operation of the Fucheng Industrial Park within the Zone.

This case study contributes to the growing literature on Sino-African investment relations and international investment arbitration more generally. It is divided into five broad sections. Following the overview of this chapter discussed in Section 1 above and this introductory part set out in Section 2, in Section 3 we set out the facts of the investment dispute. In this section, we describe the relationship between the parties to the dispute, the issues in dispute between them, and the character of the arbitration and Nigerian court proceedings arising out of the dispute. We further discuss the various strategies adopted by Zhongshan to mitigate the investment risks it faced in Nigeria. In addition, we also discuss Zhongshan's claims against Nigeria in the arbitration proceedings and Nigeria's responses to those claims, before setting out the result of the arbitration proceedings. In Section 4, we provide concluding remarks on the case study, and in Section 5 provide some discussion questions and comments.

---

[18] UNCTAD Investment Policy Hub, 'Investment Dispute Settlement Navigator', https://investmentpolicy.unctad.org/investment-dispute-settlement/country/42/china/investor.

3 The Case

This section sets out a high-level summary of the facts that led to the dispute where Zhongshan (the "Claimant") alleged that the actions of persons and entities attributable to Nigeria under international law deprived Zhongshan of its substantial investments in Nigeria, contrary to the provisions of the China-Nigeria BIT 2001.[19]

3.1 The Relationship between the Parties

The subject of this dispute is the Zone. The Zone was governed by a JVA signed on 28 June 2007 (the "2007 JVA") by the Ogun State government, China-Africa Investment Limited, Guangdong Xinguang International Group, and CCNC Group Limited. Under the provisions of the 2007 JVA, the development of the Zone was to be carried out through the Ogun Guangdong Free Trade Zone Company ("OGFTZ Company"), a subsidiary of the Ogun State government, which was to be jointly owned for ninety-nine years by a consortium of three entities: the Ogun State government, China-Africa Investment Limited, and CCNC Group Limited.[20]

Early in the course of the project, China-Africa Investment Limited (a Chinese business enterprise) experienced financial problems and the development of the Zone was abysmally slow. The financial situation of China-Africa Investment Limited led to another Chinese company, Zhuhai (the parent company of Zhongshan), taking over the development and management of the Zone.[21] On 24 January 2011, the Claimant incorporated its local Nigerian entity, Zhongfu International Investment FZE ("Zhongfu"), to manage its investments in Nigeria on its behalf. Zhongfu was consequently registered as a Free Trade Zone Enterprise in the Zone.[22] On 10 April 2012, the Ogun State government confirmed the appointment of Zhongfu as the manager and operator of the Zone, after terminating the involvement of China-Africa Investment Limited.[23] Consequently, the Ogun State government, Zhongfu, and Zenith Global Merchant Limited ("Zenith") entered into a JVA for the development, management, and operation of the Zone on 28 September 2013 (the "2013 JVA").[24] Under Clause 3 of the 2013 JVA, OGFTZ Company was appointed as the joint venture company, and ownership of OGFTZ Company was divided as follows: 60% to Zhongfu and 20% each to Ogun State and Zenith.[25] Clause 27 of the 2013 JVA also provides that any dispute arising from the 2013 JVA would first be settled by amicable discussions between the parties, failing which either party could refer the dispute to the Singapore International Arbitration Centre for arbitration under the UNCITRAL Arbitration Rules.[26]

---

[19] Paragraph 1 of the Award. [20] Paragraph 4 of the Award. [21] Paragraph 6 of the Award.
[22] Paragraph 10 of the Award. [23] Paragraph 15 of the Award. [24] Paragraph 18 of the Award.
[25] Paragraph 19 of the Award. [26] Paragraph 20 of the Award.

3.2 The Dispute between the Parties

Zhongfu maintained that it has, since 2010, developed and managed the Zone while marketing it to potential occupiers. Specifically, it has improved communication systems, upgraded the roads, erected a perimeter fence, and opened a bank, a supermarket, a hospital, and a hotel to assist potential occupiers in the Zone.[27]

Between April and August 2016 (the "2016 Actions"), Ogun State purported to terminate Zhongfu's appointment as manager of the Zone and attempted to install a new manager immediately. This was, however, preceded by some key events. First, 51% of the shares of China-Africa Investment Limited were acquired by a Chinese company, New South Group (NSG), the notice of which the Chinese Consulate in Nigeria gave to the Ogun State government.[28] Ogun State interpreted this as meaning that Zhongfu's management rights of the Zone would be transferred to NSG.[29] Second, Ogun State reacted by writing to Zhongfu, accusing it of fraud and misrepresentation of facts, demanding that the Zone be handed to Zenith within thirty days.[30] Zhongfu rebuffed Ogun State's claims as erroneous,[31] and Ogun State started taking actions aimed at driving Zhongfu out of Nigeria.

Under direction of the Ogun State government, the police harassed Zhongfu's workers, who were threatened with prosecution and prison sentences in order to get them to vacate the Zone.[32] The chief financial officer (CFO) of the Zone, Mr. Wenxiao Zhao, was arrested, beaten, detained, and starved of food and water for ten days by the police.[33] The CFO's travel document was also seized by the Nigerian Immigration Service (NIS) to prevent him from leaving Nigeria. The CFO was later released on bail and his travel document was returned to him, enabling him to leave Nigeria, albeit hurriedly. Furthermore, the NIS seized the immigration papers of Zhongfu's other expatriate staff so that none of them would be able to work in Nigeria.[34]

Ultimately, Zhongfu's principal officers left Nigeria in October 2016.[35] The departure's proximate cause was the police harassment but there were underlying and aggravating issues as well. Chinese staff struggled with the Nigerian business environment, cultural differences, and the English language. That Zhongshan's investment was located in a community that is somewhat remote

---

[27] Paragraphs 21 and 22 of the Award.
[28] Paragraph 34 of the Award. On 11 March 2016, the Economic and Commercial Section of the Consulate of the PRC in Lagos, Nigeria, sent Diplomatic Note 1601 ("Note 1601") to the Ogun State government stating that it had been officially notified by a PRC authority about the replacement of shareholdings owner of China-Africa Investment Limited to Guangdong New South Group. Note 1601 further stated that this will legally lead to the replacement of the management rights of the OGFTZ company that is now in the hands of Zhongfu to Guangdong New South Group.
[29] Paragraph 33 of the Award.   [30] Paragraph 35 of the Award.
[31] Paragraph 36 of the Award.   [32] Paragraph 39 of the Award.   [33] ibid.
[34] Paragraph 39 of the Award.   [35] Paragraphs 39 and 40 of the Award.

from the center of commerce and in a non-cosmopolitan location may be a plausible explanation for the language and cultural barriers.

What did Zhongfu do to warrant these treatments from Nigeria? As we will show in the following sections, Nigeria accused Zhongfu of misrepresentation and concealment of material facts that, if the Ogun State government had been aware, would have meant it would not have entered into the 2013 JVA. We will discuss how Zhongfu set out to mitigate this challenge.

3.3 Nigeria-Related Court Proceedings Commenced by Zhongfu

Further to the foregoing dispute, Zhongfu commenced an action on 18 August 2016 at the Nigerian Federal High Court in Abuja (the "Zhongfu FHC Action") against the Nigeria Export Processing Zones Authority (NEPZA), the Attorney-General of Ogun State, and Zenith, seeking declaratory and injunctive reliefs that Zhongfu is the manager of the Zone. The Zhongfu FHC Action alleged breaches of Zhongfu's contractual rights as a manager of the Zone and Zhongfu's tenancy rights under the 2010 Framework Agreement.[36] On 9 September 2016, Zhongfu brought another suit at the Ogun State High Court against OGFTZ Company, the Ogun State government, and the Attorney-General of Ogun State, seeking possession of the Zone, injunctive reliefs, damages of US$1,000,797,000, and interest (the "Zhongfu SHC Action"). Zhongfu's claim in the Zhongfu SHC Action was primarily based on its right of possession under the 2010 Framework Agreement.[37]

On the same day, the CFO instituted proceedings at the Nigerian Federal High Court in Abuja against the Nigerian Police Force, the Inspector-General of Police, the Commissioner of Police for the Federal Capital Territory, and others for damages for his mistreatment ("Mr. Zhao Action").[38] All three court actions were discontinued in early 2018 as a result of the refusal of the defendants to comply with the timelines for filing court documents, among other procedures.[39]

In the meantime, and in a bid to enforce its contractual rights, Zhongfu commenced commercial arbitration proceedings against the Ogun State government and Zenith at the Singapore International Arbitration Centre, pursuant to Clause 27 of the 2013 JVA.[40] However, Zenith sought and obtained an anti-arbitration injunction against Zhongfu on 29 March 2017 on the basis that Nigeria, not Singapore, was supposed to be the seat of arbitration and the Zhongfu FHC Action constituted a waiver of Zhongfu's right to arbitrate

---

[36] ibid.
[37] Paragraph 43 of the Award. The only reference to the JVA was in paragraph 5 of the Statement of Claim where Zhongfu averred that its claim was for recovery of possession based on documents preceding 2013 and without prejudice to any claims in other proceedings, arising from agreements between parties to the 2013 JVA.
[38] Paragraph 42 of the Award.
[39] See paragraphs 44 and 45 of the Award respectively.   [40] Paragraph 45 of the Award.

(or rendered the arbitration abusive or oppressive).[41] Zhongfu appealed this order, but the appeal, as noted, was discontinued before the instant investment treaty arbitration was formally commenced by the Claimant (Zhongshan, the parent company of Zhongfu) against Nigeria under the China-Nigeria BIT.[42]

3.4 Zhongshan's Strategies for Mitigation

In terms of their projects in Africa, Chinese investors may be open to negotiation and amicable settlement, as well as the exhaustion of local remedies available in a host state (i.e., including litigation proceedings in domestic courts).[43] Zhongshan employed four strategies for mitigating the investment risk and local challenges it was experiencing in Nigeria. First, and as described in the previous section and in Table 6.3.2, Zhongfu instituted legal actions in the Nigerian courts against (i) the Attorney-General of Ogun State and Zenith for breach of contractual and tenancy rights and (ii) the Ogun State government and the Attorney-General of Ogun State, seeking an order of possession, injunctive reliefs, damages, and interest. In addition, Mr. Zhao, the CFO of the Zone, instituted a legal action in the Nigerian courts against the Nigerian Police Force, the Inspector-General of Police, and the Commissioner of Police for the Federal Capital Territory, Abuja, seeking to protect his fundamental rights.[44] Separate from the legal actions instituted in the Nigerian courts, Zhongfu also commenced commercial arbitration proceedings against the Ogun State government and Zenith under the 2013 JVA.

When it appeared that the Nigerian litigation proceedings and the commercial arbitration proceedings could not move forward, on 21 September 2017 Zhongshan sent a notice of dispute and request for negotiations to Nigeria (the "2017 Notice"), in which it expressed its willingness to discuss the dispute that had arisen as a result of the Ogun State government's purported termination of Zhongfu rights in the Zone and the allegations and counter-allegations by the parties between April and August 2016.[45] This request was made further to Article 9(3) of the China-Nigeria BIT, which provides that if "a dispute cannot be settled within six months after resort to negotiations ... it may be submitted at the request of either Party to an ad hoc tribunal." However, no response was received from Nigeria. Consequently, Zhongshan served a request for arbitration pursuant to Article 9 of the China-Nigeria BIT, which marked the commencement of the investment treaty arbitration that resulted in the Award. The next section sets out the arguments of the parties to the investment treaty arbitration.

---

[41] ibid.
[42] ibid. Under section 54 of Nigeria's Companies and Allied Matters Act, 2004, a foreign company doing business in Nigeria is under obligation to incorporate a local subsidiary.
[43] (n 12).   [44] Paragraph 42 of the Award.   [45] (n 10).

Table 6.3.2 Summary table of cases

	Date	Parties	Court/location	Nature of dispute	Order(s) sought	Outcome
1	18 August 2016	Zhongfu v. Nigeria Export Processing Zone Authority (NEPZA), Attorney-General of Ogun State, and Zenith Global Merchant Limited	Federal High Court, Abuja, Nigeria	Allegations of breaches of Zhongfu's contractual and tenancy rights	A declaration that Zhongfu is the manager of the Zone and a reinstatement of the company's management rights in the Zone	Discontinued
2	9 September 2016	Zhongfu v. OGFTZ Company, Ogun State government, and Attorney-General of Ogun State	Ogun State High Court, Nigeria	Zhongfu's right of possession	Reinstatement of Zhongfu's possession rights of the Zone, injunctive reliefs, damages of US$ 1,000,797,000 billion, and interest	Discontinued
3	9 September 2016	Mr. Wenxiao Zhao v. Nigerian Police Force, the Inspector-General of Police, the Commissioner of Police for the Federal Capital Territory	Federal High Court, Abuja, Nigeria	Physical maltreatment of Mr. Zhao by the Nigerian Police	Damages	Discontinued
4	2017	Zhongfu v. Ogun State government and Zenith	Singapore International Arbitration Centre	Allegations of breach of contract	Payment of restitution	Not concluded (please see the reason in item 5)
5	5 January 2017	Zenith v. Zhongfu	Ogun State High Court, Nigeria	An anti-suit injunction concerning the Singapore arbitration	An order restraining Zhongfu from proceeding with the arbitration in Singapore	A permanent restraining order was granted
6	23 June 2017	Zhongfu v. Zenith	Court of Appeal, Lagos, Nigeria	To set aside the order by the Ogun State High Court	Sought an order to quash the restraining order granted by Ogun State High Court	Discontinued
7	30 August 2018	Zhongshan v. Federal Republic of Nigeria	London, United Kingdom	Breach of Nigeria's obligations under the China-Nigeria BIT	Compensation, interest, and costs	Award issued

3.5 Arbitration

The arbitration tribunal was formally constituted on 5 January 2018 following the appointment of the arbitrators in accordance with Article 9(4) of the China-Nigeria BIT. Zhongshan filed its statement of claim, witnesses' statements, and expert evidence from an accountant on the quantum of compensation.[46] Nigeria responded with its Statement of Defense and witness statements. Through a preliminary application, Nigeria also requested the tribunal to bifurcate (divide) the proceedings and determine the law that should govern the dispute. After Zhongshan's response to the bifurcation of the proceedings and the question of the applicable law, the tribunal declined to bifurcate the proceedings. The tribunal ruled that the applicable law to the dispute was an amalgam of Nigerian law, the provisions of the China-Nigeria BIT, and the generally recognized principles of international law. Notably, Nigeria was uncooperative in the production of any documents requested by Zhongshan and ordered by the tribunal.[47]

3.5.1 Zhongshan's Claims against Nigeria

Zhongshan claimed that Nigeria breached Articles 2, 3, and 4 of the China-Nigeria BIT between April and August 2016 by seizing its assets and depriving it of a substantial investment in the Zone. Specifically, Zhongshan made five interrelated claims against Nigeria. First, Zhongshan claimed that Nigeria breached its obligation of fair and equitable treatment of Chinese investors under Article 3(1) of the China-Nigeria BIT.[48] Second, Zhongshan claimed that Nigeria unreasonably discriminated against it and therefore breached Article 2(3) of the BIT.[49]

Third, it claimed that Nigeria failed to provide the "continuous and full protection and security" afforded by Article 2(2).[50] Fourth, Zhongshan claimed that Nigeria violated its contract with the petitioner and thus breached Article 10(2). Fifth, Zhongshan claimed Nigeria wrongfully expropriated its investments without compensation, in breach of Article 4.[51] Zhongshan claimed US$1,446 million.

Under the China-Nigeria BIT, Chinese businesses in Nigeria are protected from nationalization or expropriation unless the expropriation is in the public interest, the expropriation was done in accordance with domestic legal procedure, and it was done without discrimination.[52] Chinese investors are entitled to fair compensation if their investments are expropriated. Fair compensation is the value of the expropriated investments immediately before the expropriation is proclaimed. The basis or standard of assessment of compensation in this

---

[46] Paragraph 58 of the Award. [47] Paragraph 62 of the Award.
[48] Paragraph 49 of the Award. Article 3(1) of the China-Nigeria BIT provides that "Investments of investors of each Contracting Party shall all the time be accorded fair and equitable treatment in the territory of the other Contracting Party."
[49] Paragraphs 58 and 129 of the Award. By virtue of Article 2(3) of the China-Nigeria BIT, "Subject to its laws and regulations, neither Contracting Party shall take any unreasonable or discriminatory measures against the management, maintenance, use, enjoyment and disposal of the investments by the investors of the other Contracting Party."
[50] Paragraph 48 of the Award. [51] Paragraph 58 of the Award.
[52] China-Nigeria BIT, Article 4(1) and (2).

type of case (a breach of the China-Nigeria investment treaty) is full reparation for Zhongshan's losses. Consequently, Zhongshan relied on Article 9 of the China-Nigeria BIT to ask the arbitration tribunal to order Nigeria to compensate it for the wrongful activities of its government agencies and for the losses it incurred as a result of the breach.

3.5.2 Nigeria's Responses to Zhongshan's Claims

Developing states now pay attention to investment arbitration given the financial implications of losing a legal dispute of that nature. Although Nigeria agreed to and participated in the arbitration, it made some jurisdictional and preliminary objections before the tribunal by arguing that the arbitral tribunal had no jurisdiction over the dispute based on the following grounds. First, Nigeria contended that Zhongshan's claims had to do with the conduct of a constituent state in Nigeria and not the conduct of Nigeria (except the legal actions at Nigeria's federal court) as a sovereign state and therefore there is no valid claim against Nigeria in international law.[53] As we will elaborate in Section 5.1, the tribunal relied on customary international law to attribute the conduct of the Ogun State government, a constituent state in Nigeria, to a sovereign state, Nigeria. Second, Nigeria argued that Zhongshan did not hold an "investment" within the meaning of Article 1(1) of the BIT.[54] Nigeria's argument here is on the basis that Zhongfu, and not Zhongshan, is the investor. As we have noted, Zhongshan invested in Nigeria through its subsidiary, Zhongfu, to comply with the requirements of Nigerian Company Law. Third, Nigeria challenged the jurisdiction of the tribunal to arbitrate the investment dispute on the basis that Zhongshan did not wait for the six-month period referred to in Article 9(3) of the China-Nigeria BIT to expire before it went to arbitration.[55] Fourth, Nigeria asked the tribunal to invoke "the fork-in-the-road" clause contained in Article 9(3) of the China-Nigeria BIT to the effect

---

[53] Paragraph 70 of the Award.
[54] Paragraph 70 of the Award. In the China-Nigeria BIT, the term "investment" means every kind of asset invested by investors of one contracting party in accordance with the laws and regulations of the other contracting party in the territory of the latter, and in particular, though not exclusively, includes (a) movable and immovable property as well as any property rights, such as mortgages, liens, and pledges; (b) shares, debentures, stock, and any other kind of participation in companies; (c) claims to money or to any other performance having an economic value associated with an investment; (d) intellectual property rights, in particular copyrights, patents, trademarks, trade names, technical process, know-how, and goodwill; and (e) business concessions conferred by law or under contract permitted by law, including concessions to search for, cultivate, extract, or exploit natural resources.
[55] Art 9 is the dispute settlement provision of the BIT. Art 9(2) and (3) states:

(2) If the dispute cannot be settled through negotiations within six months, either Party to the dispute shall be entitled to submit the dispute to the competent court of the Contracting Party accepting the investment.
　(3) If a dispute cannot be settled within six months after resort to negotiations as specified in Paragraph 1 of this Article it may be submitted at the request of either Party to an ad hoc arbitral tribunal. The provisions of this Paragraph shall not apply if the investor concerned has resorted to the procedure specified in Paragraph 2 of this Article.

that the tribunal has no jurisdiction because the Nigerian court proceedings operated as a bar to the arbitration.[56] Nigeria argued that the Nigerian court proceedings initiated by Zhongfu amounted to the submission of the "dispute to a competent court" in Nigeria within the meaning of the BIT. Fifth, Nigeria argued that Zhongshan's claim should not be adjudicated in the absence of the People's Republic of China (PRC) government being involved in the arbitration. Lastly, Nigeria posited that as long as Zhongshan was basing its claim on the Nigerian court proceedings and/or the anti-arbitration injunction, it cannot do so because it failed to appeal the court order.[57]

3.6 Result of Arbitration

Drawing on customary international law, the tribunal rejected Nigeria's argument that Zhongshan has no valid claim against Nigeria. The tribunal relied on Articles 1, 4.1, 9.2, and 5, respectively, of the *Responsibility of States for Internationally Wrongful Acts* (2001), adopted by the International Law Commission,[58] to hold that all organs of the Federal Republic of Nigeria, including those that have independent existence under Nigerian law such as the Ogun State government, are to be treated as part of the Federal Republic of Nigeria. The tribunal found that the parties to the 2013 JVA intended that the Ogun State government would strictly observe the terms of the China-Nigeria BIT, which is a strong indication that Ogun State would be subject to the conditions of the BIT. According to the tribunal, investment treaties would be almost meaningless if they did not apply to actions of local, as opposed to national, government. Therefore, it did not matter that Zhongshan's case was primarily based on the actions of the Ogun State government.[59]

On Nigeria's second argument against Zhongshan's claim, the tribunal was not persuaded by Nigeria's argument that Zhongshan had no investment in Nigeria. The tribunal reasoned that Zhongshan invested in Nigeria through a corporate vehicle (subsidiary), Zhongfu, by paying money to acquire the investment and incorporating Zhongfu to undertake the day-to-day responsibilities arising from the investment.[60] The tribunal dismissed Nigeria's third argument that it did not have jurisdiction over the case as Zhongshan did not

---

[56] ibid. A fork-in-the-road clause in an investment treaty excludes, in one way or another, the possibility for an investor to submit the same investment dispute to more than one court or tribunal. An adjudicating body uses either the triple identity test or the fundamental basis test to determine whether the dispute brought before an investor–state arbitral tribunal and the dispute(s) submitted to another court is the same. Markus A Petsche, 'The Fork in the Road Revisited: An Attempt to Overcome the Clash between Formalistic and Pragmatic Approaches' (2019) 18 Washington University Global Studies Law Review 391.
[57] Paragraph 70 of the Award.
[58] Responsibility of States for Internationally Wrongful Acts: Resolution adopted by the General Assembly, New York, 28 January 2002, A/RES/56/83, UNGA.
[59] Paragraphs 72–6 of the Award.   [60] Paragraphs 77–9 of the Award.

wait for the expiration of the six-month period required by the China-Nigeria BIT before filing its arbitration claim. As we noted in Section 3.1, Zhongshan notified Nigeria of its intention to negotiate and settle the dispute through a letter in September 2017, but Nigeria did not respond to the offer. The tribunal, therefore, dismissed Nigeria's argument on the basis that the facts contradicted Nigeria's position as it neither acknowledged the receipt of the 2017 letter nor negotiated with Zhongshan.[61]

Furthermore, the tribunal rejected Nigeria's fork-in-the-road argument because neither Zhongshan nor Nigeria, as a sovereign state, was a party at any of the domestic court proceedings (the parties were, at all times, Zhongfu, NEPZA, the Attorney-General of Ogun State, and Zenith). Nigeria's fork-in-the-road argument also failed because the tribunal distinguished the characters and particularities of the Nigerian proceedings from those of the arbitration. Zhongfu's SHC Action was based on alleged breaches of its contractual and possessory rights under the 2010 Framework Agreement and the 2013 JVA, and Zhongfu's FHC action, on alleged breaches of Nigerian domestic public law, whereas Zhongshan's case in this arbitration is based entirely on the China-Nigeria BIT.

In both the state and federal court actions, Zhongfu, as Table 6.3.2 shows, sought declaratory and injunctive reliefs, whereas in this arbitration Zhongshan sought compensation. The Nigerian court cases are similar to the arbitration only to the extent that Zhongfu also sought damages.[62] Concerning Nigeria's argument that the PRC has to be present before the tribunal to explain the rationale behind Note 1601, the tribunal held that the official representation through Note 1601 from the PRC is irrelevant to Zhongshan's claim as it does not need to rely on the Note to prove the existence of Zhongfu's rights in Nigerian law as a result of entering into the 2010 Framework Agreement and the 2013 JVA, the deprivation of those rights by the statements and actions of various organs of the Nigerian state, and that the deprivation was a breach of Nigeria's obligations under the BIT.[63] The tribunal reasoned that, if Nigeria wanted, it could have called one of the senior employees of the PRC to testify in the arbitration, but it failed to do so. The tribunal also held that the Nigerian court proceedings and anti-suit injunction did not amount to a breach of the China-Nigeria BIT.[64]

In rendering its Award, the tribunal found that the 2016 Actions of Ogun State, NEPZA, and Nigerian Police breached Zhongshan's rights under Articles 2(3), 3(1), and 4 of the China-Nigeria BIT.[65] The reason for this finding is that Zhongfu's interest in the Zone was entitled to continuous protection.[66] The tribunal determined that the 2016 Actions by Nigerian state actors deprived Zhongfu of its rights under the 2010 Framework Agreement and the 2013 JVA.

---

[61] Paragraphs 80–1 of the Award.   [62] Paragraphs 82–91 of the Award.
[63] Paragraphs 92–5 of the Award.   [64] Paragraphs 96–8 of the Award.
[65] Paragraph 198(b) of the Award. [66] Paragraph 126 of the Award.

The tribunal held that the failure of Nigeria's court to restrain the agencies of the host government or to declare their use of state power illegitimate complicated and exacerbated the illegitimacy of the 2016 Actions. The tribunal noted that Zhongfu was doing a good job that had been recognized publicly by the Nigerian Customs Service and in a video by the Economist Intelligence Unit,[67] and what is more, the Zone had begun to generate considerable tax revenue for the Nigerian government.[68] The tribunal ordered Nigeria to pay Zhongshan the amounts as follows:

1. compensation for the expropriation in the sum of US$55.6 million;
2. moral damages in the sum of US$75,000, representing around US$5,000 for each day of Mr. Zhao's mistreatment plus a further sum to reflect the other inappropriate behavior of representatives of Nigeria toward employees and a director of Zhongfu;
3. interest on the aforesaid two sums from 22 July 2016 at the one-month USD LIBOR rate plus 2% for each year, or proportion thereof, such interest to be compounded monthly, until and including the date of the award, in the sum of US$9.4 million;
4. in respect of the Claimant's legal and related costs of the arbitration, the sum of £2,509,789.57;
5. £354,655.17 in respect of the other costs of the arbitration;
6. post-Award interest on the sums specified on all the amounts specified in sub-paragraphs 52(a)–(c) above from the day after the Award until payment. The Award stipulated that this post-Award interest should be calculated at the one month USD LIBOR rate plus 2% for each year, or proportion thereof, such interest to be compounded monthly, until and including the date of payment (and should, for any reason, USD LIBOR cease to be operative while any amount remains outstanding, the interest due shall from that date onward be calculated on the basis of whatever rate is generally considered equivalent to USD LIBOR plus 2%, compounded monthly, until and including the date of payment);[69] and
7. post-Award interest on the sums specified on all the amounts specified in sub-paragraphs 52(d)–(e) above from the day after the Award until payment. The compensation, moral damages, and interests are to be paid in US dollars while the legal fees and costs related to the arbitration are in British pounds.

Investment treaties have a force of law that can affect the economy of a sovereign nation.[70] International investment arbitration students and lawyers need to be pragmatic because of the quantum of award as in this case study.[71] As of the time of writing, Nigeria has not paid the amounts of money

---

[67] A video entitled 'Growth Crossings: Ogun Guangdong Free Trade Zone in Nigeria' The Economist Intelligence Unit (23 April 2016). https://perma.cc/DFJ9-DKD2.
[68] Paragraphs 28 and 127 of the Award. (Up to 160 million Nigerian Naira in the 2016 fiscal year.)
[69] Paragraphs 176–98 of the Award.   [70] (n 10).   [71] (n 10).

awarded against it by the tribunal. A party that received a favorable award in an investment arbitration needs to take procedural steps to enforce the award and reap its benefits. In this connection, on 8 December 2021, Zhongshan filed an enforcement action in an English High Court.

In response, Nigeria challenged Zhongshan's legal action to enforce the Award under the English Arbitration Act,[72] on the basis that the tribunal lacked jurisdiction, but the English court issued an order that recognized the tribunal's Award on 21 December 2021.[73] Nigeria further relied on the UK State Immunity Act of 1978 to plead sovereign immunity from the enforcement of the Award before an English Court of Appeal.[74] However, it was late in filing the application as it had seventy-four days from the date of the English High Court's order to apply to the Court of Appeal to set aside the order. Nigeria, therefore, sought an extension of time to apply and leave (i.e., permission) from the English Court of Appeal to set aside the order of the High Court that ordered the enforcement of the Award.

On 20 July 2023, the Court of Appeal declined to grant the extension and leave primarily on the basis that there was no likelihood that the appeal would be successful. Similarly, Zhongshan has also filed a legal action before the US District Court for the District of Columbia on 26 January 2023 asking the court to recognize the Award and order for its enforcement against Nigeria.[75] Here, Nigeria has unsuccessfully challenged the enforcement of the Award chiefly on the legal basis that the arbitral tribunal did not have jurisdiction to hear the arbitration and that the dispute was not governed by the New York Convention.[76] It is important to explain that, traditionally, the New York Convention governs the enforcement of commercial arbitration awards and does not apply to investor–state arbitration, which is usually governed by the ICSID and other treaties. However, the US courts have regularly confirmed arbitral awards rendered under investor–state arbitration in which sovereign nations have been found to breach treaty, rather than contractual obligations, holding that investment treaty arbitration qualifies as commercial for the purpose of recognition and enforcement under the New York Convention.[77] In furtherance of its efforts to enforce the Award, Zhongshan has begun to seize Nigeria's assets. Zhongshan obtained an order from a Superior Court, sitting in Montreal, Quebec, Canada on 25 January 2023 to seize a Bombardier 6000

---

[72] Arbitration Act 1996 (Chapter 23).
[73] Zhongshan Fucheng Investment Co Ltd v. The Federal Republic of Nigeria [2023] EWCA Civ 867.
[74] ibid.
[75] Zhongshan Fucheng Industrial Investment Co., Ltd v. Federal Republic of Nigeria, 26 January 2023 [Civil Action No. 22-170 (BAH)] (the US District Court).
[76] The United Nations Convention on the Recognition and Enforcement of Foreign Arbitral Awards, New York, 10 June 1958, 330 UNTS 3 New York [the New York Convention].
[77] Zhongshan Fucheng Industrial Investment Co., Ltd v. Federal Republic of Nigeria, 26 January 2023 [Civil Action No. 22-170 (BAH)] (the US District Court).

Jet belonging to Nigeria, all rights of Nigeria in the aircraft, any proceeds from the sale of the aircraft that is payable or belonging to Nigeria, and the aircraft's logbook.[78]

4 Conclusion

As China–Nigeria investment relations continue to grow, this case study demonstrates that international investment disputes are bound to arise from such engagements because of foreign parties, different regulatory regimes, the ownership structure of the investment, issues of state sovereignty, and cultural differences, to mention only a few contentious issues. What is more, investor-state arbitration is becoming a popular mechanism for the settlement of foreign investment disputes, even though the investment arbitration model is currently facing a backlash.[79]

To elaborate, investment arbitrations are widely touted to be faster, guarantee the privacy of the parties, and tend to preserve the investment relations of the disputing parties in comparison with litigation in conventional law courts. However, the arbitration industry has been implicated in perpetuating an investment regime that prioritizes the rights of investors, particularly those from the West, at the expense of democratically elected national governments and sovereign states, especially those in the developing world.[80] There are concerns in the literature that the arbitration sector has built a multimillion-dollar, self-serving industry, dominated by a narrow exclusive elite of law firms and lawyers whose interconnectedness and multiple financial interests raise serious concerns about their commitment to delivering fair and independent judgments.[81] According to Corporate Europe Observatory and the Transnational Institute, the arbitration industry has become big business for arbitrators and lawyers as they profit handsomely from arbitration awards against sovereign states.[82] Critics claim that the neutrality of arbitral institutions is illusory because arbitrators play highly active roles in arbitration proceedings, and many of them have strong personal and commercial ties to transnational companies.[83] According to our interview participant, the China-Nigeria BIT is an old-generation treaty that is due for renegotiation to reflect modern

---

[78] Zhongshan Fucheng Industrial Investment Co. Ltd. v. Federal Republic of Nigeria, 2023 QCCS 791 (CanLII), https://canlii.ca/t/jw78c. https://perma.cc/RM7C-6M6F. [Quebec Superior Court, Commercial Division].

[79] Pia Eberhardt and Cecilia Olivet, 'Profiting from Injustice: How Law Firms, Arbitrators, and Financiers Are Fuelling an Investment Arbitration Boom' Corporate Europe Observatory and the Transnational Institute (27 November 2012) https://corporateeurope.org/en/international-trade/2012/11/profiting-injustice. Malcolm Langford, Daniel Behn, and Ole Kristian Fauchald, 'Backlash and State Strategies in International Investment Law' in Tanja Aalberts and Thomas Gammeltoft-Hansen (eds), *The Changing Practices of International Law: Sovereignty, Law and Politics in a Globalising World* (Cambridge University Press 2018) 70.

[80] Eberhardt and Olivet (n 80). [81] ibid. [82] ibid. [83] ibid.

developments in cross-border investment, and thus its out-of-datedness may reflect some of these larger concerns.

These critiques of the international arbitration system are important and contribute to the ongoing reform of the international arbitration system. In the meantime, this case study demonstrates how non-Western foreign investors can protect their investments under BITs. Regardless of its out-of-datedness, the China-Nigeria BIT (as well as the Nigerian Investment Promotion Commission Act), provides substantive protections for foreign investments. The protections guarantee that every investment (either by Chinese companies in Nigeria or by Nigerian companies in China) will be treated fairly and equitably and the foreign investment will not be expropriated without a fair compensation to the affected party.

5 Discussion Questions and Comments

5.1 For Law School Audiences

The Chinese government has increasingly demonstrated its commitment to the protection of the investments of its nationals in foreign countries as evident in the more than 100 BITs it has signed with other sovereign states. Before the commencement of the investment arbitration that we have discussed in this case study, there were a variety of domestic court cases that were mostly instituted by Zhongfu and Mr. Wenxiao Zhao against the agents of the Nigerian state and substate actors to protect Zhongfu's investment and the company's management from arbitrary expropriation and harassment by the local police. In a jurisdiction such as Nigeria, which is yet to attain judicial independence from the executive arm of government, the reality of obtaining justice through a fair and transparent process may be difficult for a foreign investor, particularly when its economic interests are in direct conflict with those of their host state.

The China-Nigeria BIT played a decisive role in the protection and realization of the investment rights of Zhongshan (from the stage of obtaining a favorable arbitral award to the enforcement stage – seizing the assets of Nigeria in Canada). International investment jurisprudence,[84] customary international law, and the language or wording of the China-Nigeria BIT were crucial in interpreting the treaty both at the tribunal and in the British and American courts where Zhongshan applied for the enforcement of the Award. The interpretation of "investment" in the BIT, the "fork-in-the-road" clause, and the jurisdictional arguments by Nigeria underscore the complex substantive and procedural issues that the tribunal resolved. Crucially, the tribunal drew on customary international law to attribute the conduct of a constituent state (Ogun State government) to a sovereign state (Nigeria). One of the legal implications

---

[84] Paragraphs 130, 131, 134, 136, 143, 144, and 181 of the Award.

of the attribution for the China-Nigeria BIT is that the commitments of the state parties in the BIT are binding upon them, their nationals, constituent states, and state organs in their investment relations with one another. This is notwithstanding the separate legal existence of the constituent states. This case study underscores how Zhongshan (and any other Chinese company) can rely on the provisions of the China-Nigeria BIT to invoke the international investment arbitration regime to hold Nigeria accountable for the unfair and discriminatory treatment of their investment. Further, Zhongshan had to go to a domestic court of signatories to the New York Convention to obtain an order to enforce the arbitral Award against Nigeria. In this connection, Zhongshan has applied to enforce the award in the American, British, and Canadian courts, respectively. Although the process for recovering the other party's assets may take some time, as in this case, Zhongshan has made some progress by seizing Nigeria's aircraft on the orders of a Canadian court.

In light of the above, the following questions may inform a discussion of the legal issues:

1. What are the core objectives of the China-Nigeria BIT and how does the Zhongshan case demonstrate their fulfillment (or not)?
2. Are there any legal or practical difficulties in attributing, as the tribunal did, the conduct of a sub-state actor to a sovereign state with a thirty-six-state structure and a federal capital territory?[85]
3. What types of arbitration are eligible to be recognized and enforced under the New York Convention? What are some of the legal procedures that Zhongshan followed to enforce the Award in the United Kingdom, the United States, and Canada?

5.2 For Policy School Audiences

This case study demonstrates that the arbitrary use of governmental power against a foreign investor is detrimental to national economic development. The two key national economic objectives of establishing the Zone are to promote manufacturing and diversify the Nigerian economy which has been a petro-economy since the 1980s. The Zone had economic prospects as could be seen in the generation of significant tax revenue for the host government and job creation for the local population, but the revenue stream for the government and job prospects appear to be lost due to the sudden departure of Zhongshan and the monetary value of the arbitral award. Further, the Ogun State government justified the harassment, torture, detention, and seizure

---

[85] Under the Nigerian Constitution, 1999 (as amended), the signing of a treaty, establishment of police and other government security services, deportation of persons who are not citizens of Nigeria, and registration of businesses, among other items, are within the exclusive legislative powers of Nigeria's federal government, while such items as trade and commerce fall concurrently under federal and state powers.

of the travel documents of some of Zhongfu's staff by Nigerian police on trumped-up fraud and misrepresentation charges. However, the arbitration proceeding shows that the allegations of fraud and misrepresentation were unfounded.[86]

In this context, consider the following:

1. How can the Nigerian government prioritize its economic development and enable a conducive and transparent business climate? How should the Nigerian government put in place policy processes that would engage in sustainable trade and investment agenda-setting, policy formulation, implementation, and evaluation? What type of policy objectives and reforms can the Nigerian government pursue to improve the business landscape and drive and optimize sustainable development?
2. How can the outcome of the investment arbitration discussed in this case study contribute to policy and legal springboards that may result in responsive and responsible regulation of inbound foreign investments by the Nigerian government?
3. Is there any policy role for the Export-Import Bank of China in terms of financial-related policy support for a Chinese company like Zhongshan?

5.3 For Business School Audiences

Zhongshan's investment in a country such as Nigeria with a weak regulatory system exposed the company and its officers to a variety of risks such as loss of investment without compensation, risk to life, and loss of liberty, among other things. These risks were beyond the company's control and may be difficult to prevent. Zhongshan, however, employed various strategies to respond to and mitigate the risks. The strategies include a request to Nigeria for negotiation and settlement, Chinese diplomatic and consular interventions from Lagos, domestic lawsuits against the organs of the Nigerian federal government and Ogun State government, and investment arbitration in Singapore and the United Kingdom. Every investor's experience in the Nigerian regulatory landscape will differ and may warrant Zhongshan's and other mitigating approaches. The nature of the risks and investment landscape, among other considerations, will inform the company's decision or mitigating strategies.

Based on the foregoing, discuss the following:

1. What can be learned about investment protection from Zhongshan's strategies in Nigeria?
2. Assuming that you are an investment analyst or risk manager in a Chinese company that is planning to invest in Nigeria, what can you identify to

---

[86] Paragraphs 103 to 121 of the Award.

your company officers as the types of risks that could arise in the context of their prospective investment?
3. What are some of the mitigating strategies that you can draw from this case study to advise the company officers on how the company can navigate the risks and local challenges in its Nigerian operations?

Index

Introductory Note

References such as '178–9' indicate (not necessarily continuous) discussion of a topic across a range of pages. Wherever possible in the case of topics with many references, these have either been divided into sub-topics or only the most significant discussions of the topic are listed. Because the entire work is about 'outbound investment', the use of this term (and certain others which occur constantly throughout the *Casebook*) as an entry point has been restricted. Information will be found under the corresponding detailed topics. Cross-references in a form such as 'companies. *See also individual companies*' direct the reader to headings in a particular class (e.g., in this case 'ByteDance') rather than a specific '*individual companies*' entry.

Abuja, 305–6
abused workers, 197, 206
abuses, 199, 206, 208–10
   human rights, 160
   labor, 21, 197, 198–9, 204–5, 207, 208, 211
accidents, 225
accommodation, 179, 226
accountability, 146, 240, 245–6, 282
   environmental. *See* environmental accountability
Act Governing Relations between Peoples of the Taiwan Area and the Mainland Area. *See* Cross-Straits People Relations Act
administrative litigation, 279–82
administrative regulations, 158, 162
administrative units, 185, 187
advisors, 59, 62, 81
   external, 57
   legal, 62, 90
advocacy, 17, 21, 197, 198, 207, 280, 281
Africa, 69–70, 86–7, 239–41, 244–9, 250–4, 260–1, 297–8, 298–300. *See also individual countries*
   China's lending practices, 239–41, 246
African banks, 250, 263
Africa Tech Challenge, 20, 67–87
Africa's Tech Idol project, 78–9

AGEE (Guinean Environmental Assessment Agency), 272–3, 275, 280
Agência Nacional de Energia Elétrica. *See* ANEEL (Agência Nacional de Energia Elétrica)
agriculture, 172, 216, 225, 238, 277
AidData, 219, 240
AIIB (Asian Infrastructure Investment Bank), 172, 182–3, 187
Alibaba/Ant Group, 19, 27–47, 114
   for business school audiences, 47
   fintech ecosystem, 36–9
   initial growth, 29–32
   for law school audiences, 46
   ODI and Alibaba's VIE structure, 35–6
   for policy school audiences, 46
   scandals and tussles with Chinese regulators, 39–42
   VIE-structure and fragmented authoritarian politics, 32–4
Alipay, 30–1, 36, 39, 44, 47
alumina refinery, 182, 193, 258, 267–8, 277, 279, 281
aluminum, 258, 269
ANEEL (Agência Nacional de Energia Elétrica), 92, 96, 98–9
Ant Group. *See* Alibaba/Ant Group
arbitral awards, 299, 313, 316

arbitration, 17–18, 151–2, 302–3, 305–8, 309–13, 316–17
  awards, 298, 314
  investment (treaty), 298, 301, 306, 309, 313–14, 315, 317
  investor-state, 22, 146, 313–14
  proceedings, 298, 302, 314
arbitrators, 308, 314
ASEAN (Association of Southeast Asian Nations), 54, 161–3
Asia, 12, 134, 172, 173, 199, 239. *See also individual countries*
Asian Development Bank, 135, 137, 156
Asian Infrastructure Investment Bank. *See* AIIB (Asian Infrastructure Investment Bank)
assets, 6, 63, 141, 255, 257, 315
Association of Southeast Asian Nations. *See* ASEAN (Association of Southeast Asian Nations)
ATC (Africa Tech Challenge), 67–8, 81–7
  projects, 68, 83
  seasons, 83–5
auctions, 91–2, 95–7, 99–100, 105
audits, 101, 272–3, 278, 296
AVIC (Aviation Industry Corporation) INTL, 67–8, 74–9, 80–6, 87
  headquarters, 78, 80–1, 83
  Kenya office, 69, 78, 81, 85
  shareholding structure, 75
  TVET (Technical, Vocational and Entrepreneurship Training) project. *See* TVET (Technical, Vocational and Entrepreneurship Training) project

baijiu, 50–1, 52–3, 63
  consumption and trends, 52–4
  definition, 50
  production, 50–1
Bank of Chile, 61
bankruptcy, 214, 257–8
banks, 37, 42, 182, 186, 219, 257–8, 260–1. *See also individual banks*
  African, 250, 263
  joint ventures, 248–64
  state-owned, 31, 46
Bantekas, Ilias, 170–1
bauxite, 269–70, 277–8
bauxite, reserves, 267, 269
bauxite mining, 269–70, 276–8
Beihang University, 82, 84

Beilida, 201–2, 205, 209
Belo Monte, 20, 88, 90, 97–9, 101, 104–5, 107, 110–12
Belo Monte, hydroelectric power plant, 98–9
Belo Monte Transmissora de Energia. *See* BMTE (Belo Monte Transmissora de Energia)
Belt and Road Initiative. *See* BRI (Belt and Road Initiative)
Benard, Isalambo S. Shikoli, 78–9, 80
best practices, 112, 171, 271, 276
Biden administration, 113, 122–3, 126
bids, 92, 94, 98–100, 305
bill of attainder, 128–9
biodiversity commitments, 271–2, 282
BITs (bilateral investment treaties), 10, 146, 157–8, 297, 301–2, 308–10, 311, 315–16
  China-Nigeria, 297–8, 303, 306–11, 314–16
BMTE (Belo Monte Transmissora de Energia), 100–2
boards, 6, 55, 59, 89, 95, 97, 101, 198
Boké, 22, 267–83
brands, 30, 52–3, 58
Brazil, 20, 88–112
  arrival of SGCC, 93–7
  Belo Monte hydroelectric power plant, 98–9
  BMTE (Belo Monte Transmissora de Energia), 100–2
  government, 88, 91
  market, 91, 94–5, 104, 108–10, 111–12
  market share by nationality in generation, transmission and distribution sectors, 109
  regulatory framework of electricity market, 91–3, 95
  Rio de Janeiro, 89, 95, 100, 104
BRI (Belt and Road Initiative), 3, 9–10, 68, 133, 154–7, 177, 207, 239, 271, 301
  green, 15
  and human rights obligations, 158–9
  projects, 12, 133, 137, 168
British Virgin Islands (BVI), 94, 200
burial grounds, 166–8
business practices, 57, 112, 158
buyers, 29–30, 36, 57
  international, 27, 29, 35, 45
BVI. *See* British Virgin Islands
ByteDance, 113–14, 117, 119–22, 124–6

Cai Hongxian, 88–91, 95, 97, 101, 104, 106
California, 115, 117, 120, 292
Call Option, 256, 260, 262, 264

Cambodia, 21, 156–71
  domestic legislation and regulations, 162–4, 169
  preparatory measures, 164–5, 168
Canada, 3, 213, 299, 313, 315–16
capital, 2, 12, 16, 17, 135–6, 180, 187, 280
  foreign, 34, 108, 180, 191
case studies. *See individual studies*
casino, 21, 197–211
  construction, 201–2
  hotel, 200–1, 208
Casino License Agreement. *See* CLA (Casino License Agreement)
Cayman Islands, 33, 46, 114
CCCC (China Communication Construction Company Ltd), 138–40
CCP (Chinese Communist Party), 2–3, 6–7, 13, 29, 32, 42–4
  officials, 14, 31
  policies, 7, 44
CCU. *See* Compañía de las Cervecerías Unidas (CCU)
CEA (Central Environmental Authority), 142–3
Central Business District, 48, 137, 191
Central Environmental Authority (CEA), 142–3
centralization, 7–9
CEOs (Chief Executive Officers), 82, 96, 115, 259–60
CFIUS (Committee on Foreign Investment in the United States), 108, 117, 120, 122, 128
  order, 122–3
CFOs (chief financial officers), 304, 305–6
CFPA (China Foundation for Poverty Alleviation), 78
Chief Executive Officers. *See* CEOs (Chief Executive Officers)
chief financial officers. *See* CFOs (chief financial officers)
children, 128, 134, 184, 223
Chile, 20, 48–63, 107
  for business school audiences, 63
  evolution of Chinese FDI, 49
  importance of FTA and appeal of New World wine, 54–6
  for law school audiences, 63
  for policy school audiences, 63
  project roadmap, 60
  transaction, 56–61
  VSPT (Viña San Pedro Tarapacá S.A.), 20, 48, 49–50, 51–2, 58–62, 63
Chile Andes Law Firm, 49, 58

Chile-China FTA (Free Trade Agreement), 48, 50, 54–6, 61, 63
Chile Patagonia Financial Advisors, 58
China. *See also Introductory Note*
  Administrative Measures, 162, 170
  Company Law, 5–6
  Government, 1, 5–6, 7–9, 11, 14–16, 19, 97
  lending practices, 235–6, 239–41, 245–7
  People's Liberation Army Navy, 189
China-Africa Investment Limited, 303–4
China Communication Construction Company Ltd. *See* CCCC (China Communication Construction Company Ltd)
China Development Bank, 9, 136, 219, 238
China Foundation for Poverty Alleviation. *See* CFPA (China Foundation for Poverty Alleviation)
China House, 68, 80–3, 85
China Huaneng Group. *See* CHNG (China Huaneng Group)
China International Engineering Consulting Corporation (CIECC), 186
China Railway Eryuan Engineering Group, 102
China State Power Corporation (CSPC), 93
China–Oman relationships, 176–7
Chinese capital, 2, 4, 12, 16, 17, 136
Chinese Communist Party. *See* CCP (Chinese Communist Party)
Chinese companies, overview, 4–8
Chinese firms, 1–23, 197, 213
Chinese managers, 18, 73, 87, 101, 104, 223
Chinese Overseas Industrial Parks (COIPs), 187, 191
Chinese regulators, 14
  and Alibaba, 39–42, 43, 45
chips, 284, 286–7. *See also* integrated circuits
  memory, 287, 288–90, 292
CHNG (China Huaneng Group), 156–8, 164, 166, 168–70
CIB (Corporate and Investment Banking), 252, 254
CIECC (China International Engineering Consulting Corporation), 186
civil society, 18, 21, 22, 207, 278, 281
  actions, 278–81
  groups, 142, 144, 149, 165, 210
  organizations (CSOs), 69, 87, 166–8, 207, 268, 275, 281
  use of law, 275
CLA (Casino License Agreement), 200, 202
claims, 129, 145–6, 208, 240, 297, 302, 308, 310

Index

class action lawsuits, 199
clean energy, 157, 169, 272
clean environment, 159, 161, 168, 170
climate change, 3, 170, 271, 276
climate commitments, 271–2, 282
CNMI (Commonwealth of the Northern Mariana Islands), 197–200, 202–3, 206, 208
  Department of Labor (DOL), 200, 202–3
coal-fired power plants, 22, 267–83
coal plant, 277, 278–80
COIPs (Chinese Overseas Industrial Parks), 187, 191
collaborative infrastructure initiatives, 111
Colombo Port City. *See* CPC (Colombo Port City)
Colombo Port Expansion Project (CPEP), 137–8
Commerce Clause, 128
commitments, 52, 145, 194, 239, 244, 279, 314–16
  climate and biodiversity, 271–2, 282
Committee for Analysis and Assessment (CTAE), 273, 275, 277
Committee on Foreign Investment in the United States. *See* CFIUS (Committee on Foreign Investment in the United States)
commodities, 174, 252–4
Common Framework, 243–4
common law, 6, 151, 154
Commonwealth of the Northern Mariana Islands. *See* CNMI (Commonwealth of the Northern Mariana Islands)
communication strategies, 229, 231
communities, 20, 148, 163, 165–6, 278, 280–3
Companhia Paulista de Força e Luz. *See* CPFL (Companhia Paulista de Força e Luz)
Compañía de las Cervecerías Unidas (CCU), 59
companies, 4–8, 51–3, 63–8, 87–93, 100–3, 105, 118–20, 204–10, 229–31, 275–6
  American, 115, 119, 125–6, 284
  foreign, 89, 95, 125, 231, 282, 290
  gold mining, 218, 221
  limited by shares, 5
  listed, 6, 58, 74
  OGFTZ, 303, 305, 307
  publicly traded/listed, 59, 105, 263
compensation, 120–2, 146, 148, 166, 206–7, 223–4, 306–8, 311–12
competition, 35, 67, 79–80, 81, 83, 91, 96
  law, 110
competitors, 53, 114
complexities, 27–8, 101, 102, 113, 127, 215, 239–41
compliance, 16–17, 19–20, 65–130, 161–2, 198–9, 201, 207, 210

computers, 29–30, 49, 287
Concession Agreement, 139–43, 146, 147
concessions, 91, 102, 108
conflicts, 22, 130, 227–8, 231, 262, 263–4
Congress, 123, 126, 128, 199, 208
consortium, 94, 96, 98–100, 102, 276, 303
  NGO, 279–80
constituent states, 309, 315–16
constitutions, 134, 146, 150–2, 154, 158, 163, 274
construction, 2, 98–100, 104, 156–8, 163–8, 201–2, 203, 267–8, 282–3
  site, 203–4, 206
  workers, 202–3, 208
consumers, 28, 36–7, 46, 50
  Chinese, 27, 31, 45, 48, 53, 55, 61
contractors, 102, 118, 140, 156, 197–8, 201–8, 209–10
  EPC, 103, 105
contracts, 34, 77–8, 81, 153–4, 201–2, 224, 227
  fixed-term, 224, 231
contractual rights, 136, 146, 305
control, 7, 13–14, 39, 105, 152, 187, 240, 262
Cooper, Sarah, 117
coping strategies, 119–24
corporate behavior, 20, 68, 294, 298
corporate forms, 5–6, 13
corporate governance, 4, 7, 17, 110
corporate income tax, 286
corporate law, 5–6
corporate partners, 158, 164, 169
corporate-political ecosystem, 28, 40, 44
corporate practices, 21, 68, 212
corporate social responsibility. *See* CSR (corporate social responsibility)
corporate structure, 17, 18, 94, 115, 218
corporations, 13, 19, 25–63, 94, 160, 163–4, 166
  Chinese, 8, 18, 19–20, 22–3, 33–4, 133, 163, 282
  foreign, 32–3
corruption, 42, 134, 213, 227, 229, 240
COVID-19 pandemic, 11–12, 83, 185, 236, 237, 244, 246, 285
CPC (Colombo Port City), 20, 133–55
  2014 Concession Agreement, 140–1
  2016 Tripartite Agreement, 146–7
  access to investment-related information, 146–7
  for business school audiences, 154
  Chinese interest in project, 136
  controversies surrounding project, 141–3
  Economic Commission (CPCEC), 149–51, 152–4

establishment of SEZ (special economic zone), 149–53
history of project, 136–40
for law school audiences, 153
litigation before domestic courts, 147–9
for policy school audiences, 154
suspension and resumption of project, 143–5
CPCEC (Colombo Port City Economic Commission), 149–51, 152–4
CPEP (Colombo Port Expansion Project), 137–8
CPFL (Companhia Paulista de Força e Luz), 105–7
Renováveis, 105, 110
credit, 36–9, 254
creditors, 239–43
sovereign, 236–7, 243–4
cross-border investment, 27–8, 301, 315
Cross-Straits People Relations Act, 289–90
CSOs. *See* civil society organization
CSPC (China State Power Corporation), 93
CSR (corporate social responsibility), 67–87
for business school audiences, 87
for law school audiences, 86
overseas, 73–4
for policy school audiences, 86–7
CTAE (Committee for Analysis and Assessment), 273, 275, 277
cultural rights, 169–70, 280
culture, 159, 166, 169, 215, 232
gaps, 57
local, 50, 97
customary international law, 309–10, 315

damages, 3, 165, 206, 213, 305–6, 311
data security, 116, 124
debt, 18, 21, 134, 136, 143, 235–41, 242, 243–7
crisis, 237, 239, 244–6
dilemmas, 241, 245
distress, 237, 239
forgiveness, 242
obligations, 241–2
relief, 243–5
sovereign. *See* sovereign debt restructuring
Debt Service Suspension Initiative. *See* DSSI (Debt Service Suspension Initiative)
debt-trap diplomacy, 246–7
debtor countries, 236, 244, 247
debtors, 236, 239
decent work, 212, 224
demonstrations, 207, 223, 227, 229
developers, 202, 209–10, 275

development, sustainable, 14–15, 16, 161–3, 268, 271–2, 274
diplomacy
debt-trap, 246–7
public, 180, 185, 192
dispute resolution, 10, 141, 153, 155, 192, 214
disputes, 18, 22, 151, 214, 231, 265–318
distributors, 53
diversification, economic, 175, 184, 237
Djibouti, 174, 189–90
domestic courts, 147–9, 306, 316
domestic legislation, 158, 162–4
Doumbouya, Mamady, 269
DRAM (dynamic random-access memory), 284, 287, 288
DSSI (Debt Service Suspension Initiative), 243–4
Duqm
AIIB (Asian Infrastructure Investment Bank), 172, 182–3, 187
local labor and investment environment, 179–80
major Chinese investors, 180–2
and Ningxia, 181, 183–5, 186
port, 173, 182, 189, 192
security dimension, 188–90
special economic zone (SEZ), 172–94
dust, 267, 277–8
dynamic random-access memory. *See* DRAM (dynamic random-access memory)

e-commerce, 27–8, 35–6, 44–5
domestic, 29–32
EAR (Export Administration Regulations), 295
economic development, 5, 153, 239, 317
economic diversification, 175, 184, 237
economic espionage, 291–3, 294–5
economic growth, 35, 40, 43, 176, 213, 237, 238, 244–5
economic interests, 123, 136, 144, 242, 315
economic prospects, 96, 244, 246, 316
economies/economy, 3–4, 7, 11, 14, 30, 32, 69, 116, 262, 301
global, 12, 246, 250
ecosystems, 28, 31, 36, 37–40, 44, 111
education, 76–7, 80, 81, 85, 191, 193, 216
educators, 4, 18, 19
effectiveness, 110, 112, 154, 188, 229, 264
Egypt, 83
EIAs (Environmental Impact Assessments), 102, 137–8, 141–2, 144, 147, 157, 163–4, 282
electricity, 2, 107, 156–7, 164

Eletrobras, 97, 101, 105
Eletronorte, 100–1
emerging markets, 3, 20, 57, 250–2, 259, 296, 301
employees, 215, 223, 225, 228, 291–3, 294
employers, 199, 203–4, 206, 208, 210–11, 224, 226
employment, 18, 21, 214–15, 222, 223–4, 289
   contracts, 224, 226, 289, 291
energy, 75, 126, 163, 164, 272, 277, 280–1
   clean, 157, 169, 272
   renewable, 105, 168, 184, 274
   security, 88, 110–11, 157
enforcement, 44, 120–1, 294, 313, 315
   effect, 15, 271
   government and private, 205–6
engagements, 168, 235, 240, 281, 296, 314
engineering, procurement, and construction. See EPC (engineering, procurement, and construction)
engineers, 82, 140, 215, 222
enterprises, 9, 136, 186–7
entrepreneurs, 3, 30, 34, 82
environment, 15, 148–9, 161, 163–4, 210–11, 271–5, 280
   clean, 159, 161, 168, 170
   healthy, 160, 274
   sustainable, 157, 160–1
environmental accountability, 22, 267–83
   civil society actions, 278–81
   for law school audiences, 281–2
   for policy school audiences, 282–3
   SMB's environmental and social record in Boké, 277–9
Environmental and Social Impact Assessment. See ESIAs (Environmental and Social Impact Assessment)
Environmental and Social Management Plans. See ESMP (Environmental and Social Management Plans)
environmental assessments, 182, 275, 283
environmental compliance certificate, 273, 275, 279–81
Environmental Impact Assessments. See EIAs (Environmental Impact Assessments)
environmental laws, 16, 142, 153
environmental protection, 14–15, 18, 162–3, 164, 274
environmentalists, 142, 145, 146
EPC (engineering, procurement, and construction), 102, 140
   contractors, 103, 105
ESIAs (Environmental and Social Impact Assessment), 272–3, 274–8, 279–80, 282

ESMP (Environmental and Social Management Plans), 273, 275
evidence, 27–8, 55, 62, 203–4, 206, 291, 293–4
executive orders, 113, 116, 118, 120–1, 123, 124–5, 130
exemptions, 154–5, 203, 286
exit mechanisms, 250, 256, 262, 264
exit strategies, 262, 264
Export Administration Regulations (EARs), 295
exporters, 51, 277
exports, 31, 75, 174–6, 180, 199, 215
expropriation, 141, 146, 308, 312, 315
extractives industries, 21–2, 214, 230, 274

families, 121, 136, 166, 223
FDI (foreign direct investment), 5, 56–7, 133–4, 136, 154, 180, 262, 299. See also ODI (overseas direct investment)
   from China to Nigeria, 299, 300
Federal Republic of Nigeria. See Nigeria
fees, 31, 92, 153, 205
   recruitment, 198, 203, 205
FEZs (free economic zones), 175–6
finance, 21, 77, 140, 143, 186, 233–64
financial advisors, 48, 57–8, 62
financial advisors, Chile Patagonia, 58
financial institutions, 8, 250, 270
financial products, 41–2, 45
financial regulation, 19, 28, 186
financial services, 27–8, 36, 45, 47, 74, 153
fintech, 10, 27, 36–9
fish, 88, 157, 164–5, 167
fishing, 159, 166, 172, 269, 278
fixed-term contracts, 224, 231
FOCAC (Forum on China-Africa Cooperation), 244, 270, 271, 300
food, 161, 172, 226, 278, 304
forced labor, 21, 197–211
   for business school audiences, 209–11
   for law school audiences, 209–10
   for policy school audiences, 210
foreign affairs, 124–5, 128
foreign capital, 34, 108, 180, 191
foreign companies, 89, 95, 125, 231, 282, 290
foreign corporations, 32–3
foreign direct investment. See FDI (foreign direct investment)
foreign funding with Chinese management control, 32–4
foreign investment treaties, 22, 297–318
   for business school audiences, 317

for law school audiences, 315–16
for policy school audiences, 316–17
foreign investors, 16, 61, 212–13, 216, 231, 297, 315–16
foreign jurisdictions, 291
foreign markets, 20, 93, 97
foreign ownership, 32, 34, 180
foreign policies, 116, 130, 144, 174–6, 193
foreign workers, 179, 200, 202–3, 211
  advantages and disadvantages of using, 211
Forum on China-Africa Cooperation. *See* FOCAC (Forum on China-Africa Cooperation)
fossil fuels, 14, 157, 168, 170
Framework Agreements, 54, 189, 299, 305, 311
France, 63, 115, 243, 269
fraud, 28, 36, 40, 257–8, 291, 304, 317
  online, 28, 34
free economic zones (FEZs), 175–6
FTAs (Free Trade Agreements), 10, 20, 48, 54–5, 63, 175
  Chile-China, 48, 50, 54–6, 61, 63
Fujian Jinhua, 22, 284
Full Gold Mining, 218–21, 222, 227–8
Furnas, 96, 100–1

G20, 10, 243
garment industry, 199–200
GCC (Gulf Cooperation Council), 174–7, 182
general counsel, 115, 124, 206, 231
geopolitical tensions, 284, 285, 293, 296
  policymaking dilemmas, 129–30
Germany, 3, 10, 115, 240
Ghana, 83
GHG emissions, 276
Gianforte, Greg, 128
global markets, 63, 112, 249–50, 253–5, 263
Global South, 12, 236, 245–7, 268
gold deposits, 216, 219
Gold Mantis, 198, 201–2, 203, 205–6, 207–8
gold mining in Kyrgyzstan, 21, 212–32
  background, 215–21
  case study roadmap, 214–15
  causes of tension, 221
  complying with salary laws, 225–6
  difficulties with employment contracts, 224
  grievances, 227
  history and significance, 212–14
  human resources department as gatekeeper, 222–3
  inaccessible justice, 228–9
  insufficient equipment and unsafe conditions, 225

mine protests, 227–8
opaque hiring practices, 222
role of government agencies, 229–30
utility of personal relationships, 223–4
working conditions, 226
good governance administration, 144–5
goods, 30–1, 172, 174, 199, 218, 237
GOSL (Government of Sri Lanka), 136, 138, 139, 141, 146
governance, 3, 15, 44, 74, 134, 136, 212, 281
  corporate, 4, 7, 17, 110
  good, 16, 137, 144
  sustainable, 14
government agencies, 74, 138, 207, 229–30, 302, 309
Government of Sri Lanka. *See* GOSL (Government of Sri Lanka)
governments, 1–2, 41–2, 44–5, 76–7, 91–2, 123, 133–4, 235–8, 283, 310
  Brazilian, 88, 91
  federal, 122, 128, 199, 317
  Guinean, 267, 279–80
  host, 22, 312, 316
  Kyrgyz, 216, 218, 226, 230
  Nigerian, 312, 317
  Omani, 179, 191–3
  state, 127–8
green BRI, 15
green projects, 15
'Green Silk Road', 212, 214
grievances, 210, 222–3, 227
growth, 4–6, 15, 28, 43, 53, 175–6, 211, 252
  strategy, 248, 252, 261
guarantees, 42–3, 62, 63, 133, 161, 302, 314
Guinea, 22, 267–83
  civil society actions, 278–81
  country profile, 268–70
  environmental laws and decrees, 273–5
  governmental structure on mining, natural resource management, and environmental matters, 272–3
  Guinea–China relations, 270–1
  international treaties and standards, 276
  MEDD (Ministry of the Environment and Sustainable Development), 272–3
  Ministry of Environment and Sustainable Development, 272
  Ministry of Geology and Mines, 272–3, 280
  SMB's environmental and social record, 277
  Transitional Charter, 269, 273–4
  use of law by civil society, 275

Guinean Environmental Assessment Agency. *See* AGEE (Guinean Environmental Assessment Agency)
Gulf Cooperation Council. *See* GCC (Gulf Cooperation Council)
Gulf region, 175–6, 193–4

Haddad, Ramon, 96
health, 183, 205, 216, 225, 276
healthy environment, 160, 274
heart, 140, 180, 183, 291, 293
hearts and minds, 183
high levels of debt, 237, 243, 246
hiring practices, 222
Ho, Jianting, 288–9, 291–3
Hong Kong, 200–1, 252, 291
Hong Kong Stock Exchange, 41, 200, 208
host countries, 67–8, 85, 87, 136, 187, 211, 219
host governments, 22, 312, 316
host states, 3–4, 13–14, 16–17, 18–19, 133, 263, 297–8, 301–2. *See also individual countries*
hotels, 30, 134, 304
housing, 160, 161, 166, 191, 201
Huawei, 1–2, 80, 126, 292
Human Resources departments, 222–3
human rights, 16–17, 20–1, 133, 156–70
    abuses, 160
    and BRI (Belt and Road Initiative), 158–9
    for business school audiences, 171
    domestic legislation and regulations, 162–4, 169
    international human rights law, 157, 159–61, 171, 282
    law, 158, 160, 168
    for law school audiences, 169–71
    obligations, 158, 161, 168–70
    for policy school audiences, 171
    preparatory measures, 164–5, 168
    standards, 158, 161–2, 163, 170
    universal, 14
HVDC (high-voltage direct current), 98–9
hybrid Chinese-international e-commerce platform ecosystem, development, 27–47

ICBC (Industrial and Commercial Bank of China), 74, 248–51, 253–61, 262, 263
    Call Option, 256–7, 262
    exit mechanisms, 256
    Standard Bank Plc (ICBCS), 248, 257–60, 262
    Standard Bank Plc (ICBCS), JVs (joint ventures), 248, 250, 256–7, 259–64

ICCPR (International Covenant on Civil and Political Rights), 159
ICESCR (International Covenant on Economic, Social and Cultural Rights), 159–60
ICs. *See* integrated circuits (ICs)
ICSID (International Centre for Settlement of Investment Disputes), 302, 313
IEEPA (International Emergency Economic Powers Act), 118, 121–2
IFC (International Finance Corporation), 276
    Performance Standards, 276
IMF (International Monetary Fund), 11, 16, 21, 69, 235–6, 237
Imperial Pacific Casino project, Saipan, 21, 197–211
Imperial Pacific International. *See* IPI (Imperial Pacific International)
Imperial Pacific International Holdings. *See* IPIH (Imperial Pacific International Holdings)
imports, 70, 75, 175, 190, 237
inaccessible justice, 228–9
incentives, 7–8, 152–3, 155, 176, 180, 202
incorporation, 13, 95, 293
independence, 70, 102, 269
India, 129, 175, 179, 189
Indian Ocean, 135, 173–4, 193
Indigenous communities, 99, 164–5, 166, 169
Indigenous peoples, 160, 163, 166, 168
Indonesia, 35, 115
Industrial and Commercial Bank of China. *See* ICBC (Industrial and Commercial Bank of China)
industrial parks, 172–3, 181, 184–6, 188–90, 193, 194
infrastructure, 10, 19–20, 77, 131–94, 239, 245, 271
    facilities, 135, 138, 140, 144
    investment, 93, 140, 241
    projects, 20, 191, 209, 211, 238–9
initial public offering. *See* IPO (initial public offering)
injunctions, 1, 120, 122, 305, 306, 311
injuries, 198, 204–6, 210
integrated circuits (ICs), 22, 284–96
integration, 10, 50, 61, 63, 76, 104, 110, 286
intellectual property, 130, 286, 288, 290, 292, 295
intentions, 54, 118, 199–200, 250, 291, 311
interactions, 17, 67–8, 104, 113, 226, 229
international business, 152, 253, 298
international buyers, 27, 29, 35, 45
international cooperation, 110–11, 187, 295

International Covenant on Civil and Political Rights (ICCPR), 159
International Covenant on Economic, Social and Cultural Rights (ICESCR), 159–60
International Emergency Economic Powers Act. *See* IEEPA (International Emergency Economic Powers Act)
International Finance Corporation (IFC), 276
international human rights law, 157, 159–61, 171, 282
international investment agreements, 10
international investment strategies, 4, 8–10
international investments, 94, 237, 271
international investors, 19, 27–8, 33, 35, 47
international law, 126, 133, 166, 168, 176, 268, 308–9
    customary, 309–10, 315
International Monetary Fund. *See* IMF (International Monetary Fund)
international standards, 10, 276, 294
international trade, 29–32, 63, 69, 152, 173, 176, 184, 238
international treaties, 276
internationalization, 86, 95, 114, 192
internet, 29, 30, 32, 35, 118
interview respondents, 215, 223
interviewees, 223, 225, 229
interviews, 70, 156–7, 166, 224–5, 230, 238, 298
    worker, 197, 199
investment (treaty) arbitration, 298, 301, 306, 309, 313–14, 315, 317
investment agreements, 139, 146
    international, 10
investment disputes, 298, 302, 309
investment flows, 11, 250
investment products, 28, 37
investment-related information, access to, 146–7
investment treaties. *See* BITs (bilateral investment treaties); foreign investment treaties
investments, 2–4, 10–13, 37, 135–9, 191–2, 297–8, 302–3, 308–9, 310, 314–17
    cross-border, 27–8, 301, 315
    international, 94, 237, 271
    Nigeria, 303, 310
    US, 117, 118, 127
investor–state arbitration, 22, 146, 313–14
investors, 22, 41–2, 45–6, 154–7, 180–1, 309
    foreign, 16, 61, 212–13, 216, 231, 297, 315–16
    international, 19, 27–8, 33, 35, 47
IPI (Imperial Pacific International), 197–210
    project, 198, 202–3, 207–8

IPIH (Imperial Pacific International Holdings), 200–1
IPO (initial public offering), 28, 33, 35, 41, 45, 47
Ishtamberdy, 214–19, 222, 224–8, 231–2
islands, 199–200, 208

Jack Ma, 29
Jalal-Abad, 214, 216
Japan, 114–15, 175, 252
Japan International Cooperation Agency (JICA), 80
Jiangsu Yanghe Distillery Co. Ltd., 20, 48–63
    as iconic baijiu producer, 50–1
Jinhua, 284, 287–94
Johannesburg Stock Exchange (JSE), 248, 252
joint ventures. *See* JVs (joint ventures)
journalists, 69–70, 167, 240
JSE (Johannesburg Stock Exchange), 248, 252
judicial review, 18, 133, 154
justice, 205, 223, 275, 292, 294
    inaccessible, 228–9
    social, 145
JVs (joint ventures), 22, 35, 191, 248–50, 253, 257–64, 286
    agreements, 261, 262, 264, 299, 302–3, 305–6, 310–11
    for business school audiences, 263–4
    and changing circumstances, 22, 250, 257–9, 260, 262, 264
    exit terms, 256–7
    exiting, 248–64
    for law school audiences, 261–2
    objectives, 253
    for policy school audiences, 262–3
    terms and conditions, 254–5

Kenya, 20, 67–87
    Kenya–China relations, 70–2
    MOEST (Ministry of Education, Science and Technology), 76, 78–83, 85
    NYS (National Youth Service), 76
    Sino-Kenyan relations, 68, 69–70
Kichi-Chaarat, 214–16, 219–22, 224–5, 226–9, 231–2
Kong Xianghu, 198, 202, 206
Kumtor, 212–14, 217
Kyrgyz authorities, 213, 216, 218, 223, 226, 230, 231
Kyrgyz workers, 214–15, 222, 226
Kyrgyzstan. *See* gold mining in Kyrgyzstan

labor, 8, 17, 18, 21, 202–3, 209–10
labor abuses, 21, 197, 198–9, 204–5, 207, 208, 211

labor conflicts, 21, 212–32
    for business school audiences, 232
    for law school audiences, 231
    for policy school audiences, 231
labor disputes, 212–14, 228
labor laws, 16, 153, 201, 226
labor rights, 209, 228, 230
land rights, 160, 278, 281
language(s), 104, 114, 206, 211, 230, 232, 240, 305, 315
Latin America, 12, 18, 20, 88–9, 92, 94. *See also individual countries*
law, 18, 56–8, 94, 125–7, 150, 153, 163, 204, 210–11, 282
    domestic, 139, 161–2
    human rights, 158, 160, 168
    Nigerian, 308, 310, 311
    rule of, 14, 16, 129, 134, 270, 281
law enforcement agencies, 197, 199, 223
lawsuits, 36, 120, 129, 147, 197, 207, 282, 317
    class action, 199
lawyers, 20, 22, 197, 210, 215, 226, 298, 314
Lazada, 35–6
leadership, 85, 113, 149, 181, 185
legal actions, 128, 129, 294, 306, 309, 313
legal advisors, 62, 90
legal authorities, 121, 139
legal disputes, 161, 294, 309
legal risks, 46, 209
legal standards
    regional, 161–2
    transnational, 161–2
legal strategies, 22, 110, 268
legal systems, 17, 175, 273, 294
legislation, 15, 73, 133, 158, 271
    domestic, 158, 162–4
lenders, 239–40, 242, 245
lending, 11, 21, 240, 245, 246–7
    practices, 17, 239–41, 244–5, 246
Li, Tom, 48–9, 52–4, 55, 58, 78–83
liabilities, 6, 159, 197, 209, 255, 257
licenses, 32–4, 94, 95, 200, 218
licensing collaboration, 288–9, 290
listed companies, 6, 58, 74
litigation, 16, 20, 22, 86, 130–3, 147–9, 197–8, 214
    administrative, 279–82
    TikTok, 120–2
    tort, 282
livelihoods, 142, 145, 165, 167, 169, 277
loans, 76, 102, 136, 182, 238–40, 241–2, 244–6
local authorities, 16, 215, 223, 229, 230

local communities, 80, 169, 216, 221, 229–30, 267, 277–8, 281
local courts, 16, 44
local employees, 180, 228, 229, 230
local governments, 44, 91, 149, 187, 198–9, 229
local labor, 3, 179–80
local law, 3, 13, 15–16, 192, 197, 198
local populations, 183, 192, 211, 221–2, 229–30, 316
local public law, 20, 133–55, 311. *See also* CPC (Colombo Port City)
    for business school audiences, 154
    for law school audiences, 153
    for policy school audiences, 154
local residents, 211, 222, 229, 267
local stakeholders, 78, 214, 272
local workers, 21, 179, 212, 225, 229
localization strategies, 18, 20, 88–112
    for business school audiences, 111–12
    for law school audiences, 108–10
    for policy school audiences, 110–11
lock-in provisions, 249–50, 256, 261–2, 264
logistics, 38, 74, 172, 191
losses, 122, 153, 157, 257–9, 260, 309, 317
low-income countries, 22, 235–6, 246
Lower Sesan II, 21, 156–71
    construction, 166–7
    implications and outlook, 167–8

M&A (mergers and acquisitions), 20, 48–63, 97, 286
    failure rate, 56
    industry, 62
    main steps, 59
    strategies, 62
Ma, Jack, 29, 30–1, 44–5
Macau, 200, 291
machines, 77, 86
Mainland Area, 289–90
management, 6, 73, 161, 181, 214, 303
managers, 78, 202, 203–5, 206, 215, 303–5
    Chinese, 18, 73, 87, 101, 104, 223
manufacturing, 172, 191, 225, 284, 287, 316
Maritime Silk Road. *See* MSR (Maritime Silk Road)
market access, 7, 67
market competition, 31, 92, 108, 286
market concentration, 108, 111
market economy, 54, 125
    socialist, 5
market power, 35, 40–1
market shares, 52, 108, 287

markets, 23, 43–4, 87, 89, 91–2, 130–3, 188
  emerging, 3, 20, 57, 250–2, 259, 296, 301
  foreign, 20, 93, 97
mass dismissal, 214, 228
MCC (Metallurgical Corporation of China), 197–8, 198, 201–6, 207–10
MDT (Memes Droits pour Tous), 279–80
mechanisms, 13, 108, 152, 210, 261, 262
  exit, 250, 256, 262, 264
media, 3, 81, 87, 167, 199, 207, 210, 231
  social, 32, 81, 113, 117, 229
Mekong, 161, 164, 165, 167–8
Mekong Agreement, 161, 164
Memes Droits pour Tous. *See* MDT (Memes Droits pour Tous)
Memoranda of Understanding. *See* MOUs (Memoranda of Understanding)
memory chips, 287, 288–90, 292
MENA (Middle Eastern and North African), 172, 190
mergers. *See* M&A (mergers and acquisitions)
Metallurgical Corporation of China. *See* MCC (Metallurgical Corporation of China)
Micron, 22, 284–96
Micron Memory Taiwan Co., Ltd. (MMT), 288–9
Middle Eastern and North African (MENA) region, 172, 190
middle-income countries, 3, 10, 12, 136
migrant workers, 179, 211
mines, 213–14, 219, 221–2, 224–6, 231, 238, 272–3, 280
  Ishtamberdy, 214–19, 222, 224–8, 231–2
  Kichi-Chaarat, 214–16, 222, 224–5, 231–2
  protests, 227–8
mining, 13, 215–18, 222, 224–5, 227, 238, 269, 272–3
  bauxite, 269–70, 276–8
  companies, 222, 224, 229, 274. *See also individual companies*
  gold. *See* gold mining in Kyrgyzstan
  roads, 276–8
Ministry of Commerce. *See* MOFCOM (Ministry of Commerce)
misappropriation of trade secrets, 284, 286, 290–1, 293
mitigation strategies, 306
MMT (Micron Memory Taiwan Co., Ltd.), 288–9
Mnuchin, Steve, 117
mobile phones, 30, 35, 38, 123
MOFCOM (Ministry of Commerce), 8–10, 184, 272

money, 37, 207–8, 210, 236, 240, 270
Montana, 128
MOUs (Memoranda of Understanding), 10, 57, 95, 97, 139, 189
Moutai, 50–3
MSR (Maritime Silk Road), 172, 173, 176
multinational companies/corporations/firms, 47, 87, 110, 112–14, 129–30, 287

Nairobi, 70, 81–2, 85
NARI, 104
National Development and Reform Commission. *See* NDRC (National Development and Reform Commission)
National People's Congress of China. *See* NPCSC (National People's Congress of China)
national security, 115–17, 118–19, 121, 123, 128–9, 143–4
National Youth Service (NYS), 76
nationality, 101, 108, 213, 221, 225
Natural Justice, 277–9, 280
Natural Resource Management, 162–3, 164, 272
natural resources, 10, 241, 269, 300
NDRC (National Development and Reform Commission), 8–10, 185, 271–2
  BRI Center, 15
negative impacts, 27, 32, 45, 145, 161, 165, 238
NEPZA (Nigeria Export Processing Zones Authority), 305, 307, 311
New South Group (NSG), 304
new world wine, 54–6
New York Convention, 313, 316
New York Stock Exchange. *See* NYSE (New York Stock Exchange)
NGOs (nongovernmental organizations), 21, 22, 156, 164, 167, 279
Nigeria, 22, 297–317
  annual FDI flow from China, 299, 300
  court proceedings, 302, 306, 310, 311
  government, 312, 317
  law, 308, 310, 311
  NEPZA (Nigeria Export Processing Zones Authority), 305, 307, 311
  police, 305–6, 311, 317
Ningxia and Duqm, 181, 183–5, 186
NIS (Nigerian Immigration Service), 304
nongovernmental organizations. *See* NGOs (nongovernmental organizations)
NPCSC (National People's Congress of China), 125–6
NSG (New South Group), 304

NYS (National Youth Service), 76
NYSE (New York Stock Exchange), 27, 45, 47, 105, 110

OA Global Markets Business, 249, 253–5
obligations, 158, 160–2, 163, 201, 256, 281
Occupational Safety and Health Administration. *See* OSHA (Occupational Safety and Health Administration)
ODI (overseas direct investment), 2–5, 8–10, 11–12, 14–15, 28, 35, 45–6, 47. *See also* FDI (foreign direct investment)
  effects, 14–16
  main risks and challenges, 57
  and Party-State, 12–14
  trends, 11–12
OECD (Organisation for Economic Co-operation and Development), 240
Ogun Guangdong Free Trade Zone, 298–301
Ogun Guangdong Free Trade Zone Company (OGFTZ Company), 303, 305, 307
Ogun State, 298–301, 302–6, 309–11, 315, 316–17
  government, 303–4
  High Court, 305, 307
oil, 172, 175, 188, 194, 241
oil refinery deal, 258–9
Oman, 21, 107, 172–94. *See also* Duqm
  China–Oman relationships, 176–7
  facts, 175
  GCC (Gulf Cooperation Council), 174–6
  government, 179, 191–3
Oman Wanfang LLC, 181, 184
Omani students, 177, 184
online fraud, 28, 34
'opening and reform', 5
Oracle, 119–20, 125, 128
OSHA (Occupational Safety and Health Administration), 204–5
overseas direct investment. *See* ODI (overseas direct investment)
overseas investments. *See Introductory Note*
overseas projects, 4, 15–17, 73, 271
owners, 17, 215, 221, 228
ownership, 5, 13, 59, 162, 220–1, 226, 303
  foreign, 32, 34, 180
  state, 6, 29

PAA (Project Approving Agency), 138, 142
Pakistan, 107, 129, 179, 243

pandemic, COVID-19, 11–12, 83, 185, 236, 237, 244, 246, 285
parent companies, 7, 81, 201, 282, 303, 306
Paris Club, 235–6, 243–4, 246–7
partnerships, 97, 101, 184, 248, 250, 256, 263
Party-State, 2–3, 4, 6–8, 12–14
  and overseas direct investment, 12–14
passports, 198, 204–6
Patriotic Front. *See* PF (Patriotic Front)
penalties, 45, 128, 291
People's Bank of China (PBOC), 42
People's Liberation Army Navy, 189
People's Republic of China. *See* China
performance, 14, 259, 262, 264
personal relationships, 223–4
PES (Philadelphia Energy Solutions), 258
petitioners, 147–8, 308
petitions, 117, 147–9
petroleum, 2, 172, 241, 301
PF (Patriotic Front), 237
Philadelphia Energy Solutions (PES), 258
Philippines, 35, 94, 107–8
physical injuries, 198, 206, 210
platform firms, 42, 46
platforms, social media, 115, 229, 231, 290
Plena Transmissora, 95, 96
police, 40, 304, 305–6, 311, 317
policies, 3–4, 11–12, 18–19, 46, 93, 262–3
  adjustments, 139, 145–6
policy banks, 9, 21
policymakers, 111, 209–10, 248
political risks, 28, 44, 46, 94, 101, 117, 126, 130
  mitigation, 20
political unrest, 134, 221, 229
politicians, 120, 143, 240
politics, 69, 133, 136, 294
Port City Act, 152–5
ports, 138–9, 172–4, 176, 188–90, 193, 276–8. *See also* CPC (Colombo Port City)
potential risks, 86, 116, 127, 245
poverty, 3
  alleviation, 14, 43–4, 69, 157, 237
power plants, 97, 180
  coal-fired, 267–8, 279–81
  fired, 277, 278
PR. *See* public relations (PR)
preparatory measures, 164–5, 168
prices, 30, 55, 108, 147, 157, 257
private companies/firms, 2, 5, 7–9, 35, 46, 94, 274, 299. *See also individual companies*
private enterprise, 42, 263
private sector, 6, 31, 92, 179, 218, 243

private tech firms, 32–3, 41, 44
products, 29–30, 37, 43–5, 53, 54–5, 78
profitability, 41, 182, 192, 232
profits, 5, 6, 13, 39, 42, 93–4, 180, 269
Project Approving Agency. *See* PAA (Project Approving Agency)
Project Company, 139–41, 144–7
protests, 145, 222, 224, 227–8
provincial councils, 149, 151
PTD (Public Trust Doctrine), 148–9
public auctions, 91–2, 96–7, 105
public diplomacy, 180, 185, 192
public interest, 147, 163, 308
public law, local, 20, 133–55, 311
public offer of shares, 59
public relations (PR), 2, 81–2, 231
Public Trust Doctrine (PTD), 148–9
publicly traded/listed companies, 59, 105, 263

Rajapaksa regime, 135, 143, 149–50
reclamation work, 137, 139–42, 144–5
recruiters, 203, 206, 209
recruitment, 45, 82, 210, 290. *See also* hiring practices
  fees, 198, 203, 205
redress, 210, 227, 282
refineries
  alumina, 182, 193, 267–8, 277, 279, 281
  oil, 258–9
  Philadelphia, 257–8
reforms, 5, 92, 95, 179–80, 199, 315, 317
regional legal standards, 161–2
regulation(s), 8–9, 15, 73, 153–4, 162–4, 170, 202–3
  administrative, 158, 162
  financial, 19, 28, 186
regulators, 17, 18, 20, 40, 42, 45, 61, 208
regulators, Chinese, 14, 39–42, 43, 45
regulatory approval, 254–5, 289
regulatory bodies, 74, 108–10
regulatory environments, 4, 16, 20, 89, 108, 127, 296
regulatory frameworks, 91–3, 95, 108, 111, 187, 293
regulatory measures, 110, 210, 295
renewable energy, 105, 168, 184, 274
representative offices, 75, 252, 255, 290
representatives, 126, 165, 185, 215, 230, 312
residents, local, 211, 222, 229, 267
resilience, 92, 133, 241
resources, 17, 18, 148, 220, 230, 240, 241, 253
  human, 222–3, 229

mineral, 218, 269, 270
natural, 10, 241, 269, 300
respondents, interview, 215, 223
responsibilities, 16, 59, 93, 141, 159, 169–70, 210, 310
restrictions, 1, 34–5, 125–6, 140–1, 262, 298
revenues, 83, 106, 114, 140, 219, 242
Right to Information (RTI) Act, 146
rights, 140, 159, 161, 168–9, 218, 311, 314
  contractual, 136, 146, 305
  cultural, 169–70, 280
  human. *See* human rights
Rio de Janeiro, 89, 95, 100, 104
risks, 36–7, 46, 56–7, 101–2, 193, 210–11, 295–6, 317–18
  investment, 302, 306
  legal, 46, 209
  political, 28, 44, 46, 94, 101, 117, 126, 130
  potential, 86, 116, 127, 245
rivers, 166–7, 224, 278
roads, 74, 238, 267, 304, 309
Rong, Letian, 288, 291–3
Rousseff, Dilma, 88
RTI (Right to Information), 146
Rubio, Marco, 117
rule of law, 14, 16, 129, 134, 270, 281
Russia, 35, 69, 115, 174, 259
Ruto, William, 80, 85

safety, 141, 201, 210, 225, 271
  measures, 159, 204, 225, 230
Saipan, 21, 197–211
  aftermath, 208
  government and private enforcement, 205–6
  labor abuses, 21, 197, 198–9, 204–5, 207, 208, 211
  recruitment of workers, 202–3
  worker and civil society efforts, 206–8
salaries, 120, 225–6, 289
Sale and Purchase Agreement, 248–50, 254–8, 261–2, 263–4
SAMR (State Administration for Market Regulation), 39–41
Santiago Stock Exchange, 48, 52, 58–9
SASAC (State-owned Assets Supervision and Administration Commission), 7, 9, 93
SB Group (South African Standard Bank Group), 248–62, 263–4
  growth strategy, 252–3
  Put Option, 256
SB Plc. *See* Standard Bank Plc

Index

SBLH (Standard Bank London Holdings Limited), 249, 254, 255–6, 258
SCARC (Standing Cabinet Appointed Review Committee), 138–9
scholarships, 78–9, 82, 84, 184
schools, 78, 81, 83, 184, 191
scrutiny, 158, 213–14, 239, 244, 293–4
  public, 142, 144
SDGs (Sustainable Development Goals), 212, 214
security, 3, 10, 113, 172, 214, 257
  data, 116, 124
  national, 115–17, 118–19, 121, 123, 128–9, 143–4
sellers, 30, 31, 36, 57
semiconductor industry, 284–7
services, 43–5, 114–16, 124, 180, 218, 247, 273, 290
  financial, 27–8, 36, 45, 47, 74, 153
SEZAD. *See* Oman
SEZs (special economic zones), 21, 149–50, 152, 172–94, 300
  for business school audiences, 193–4
  CPC (Colombo Port City), 149–50, 152
  Duqm/Oman, 172–94
  for law school audiences, 192
  Oman. *See* Oman
  for policy school audiences, 193
  Shekou model, 190–2
SGBH (State Grid Brazil Holding), 88, 95–7, 100–1, 104
  accessing other stages of production chain, 104–7
  directors, 96, 108
SGBP (State Grid Brazil Power), 105–6
SGCC (State Grid Corporation of China), 88–112
  arrival in Brazil, 93–7
  assets in Brazil, 105
  assets in Brazil via SGBH and CPFL, 107
  global assets, 90
SGID (State Grid International Development Limited), 94, 105
Shanghai, 5, 29, 32, 52, 115, 252
shareholders, 6, 33–4, 52, 59, 102, 141, 218, 257–8
shares, 59–61, 94, 96, 122–3, 249–50, 255–7, 259–60, 261–2
Shekou model, 190–2
Singapore, 35, 114, 116, 252, 255, 276, 305, 317
Sino-African JVs, 248–50, 261, 262
Sino-Arab Wanfang Investment Management Ltd., 173, 180–1
Sino-Kenyan relations, 68, 69–70

SLPA (Sri Lanka Ports Authority), 137–9, 140–3, 144, 146–8
small and medium-sized enterprises. *See* SMEs (small and medium-sized enterprises)
SMB (Société Minière de Boké), 267–9, 272, 274, 276–82
  environmental and social record in Boké, 277–9
SMEs (small and medium-sized enterprises), 28, 31, 35–7, 43, 181
social impacts, 99, 271, 282
social media, 32, 81, 113, 117, 229. *See also* TikTok
  platforms, 115, 229, 231, 290
socialist market economy, 5
Société Minière de Boké. *See* SMB (Société Minière de Boké)
socioeconomic inequalities, 134, 213, 228
sociopolitical contexts, 68, 73
SOEs (state-owned enterprises), 2, 5, 7–8, 20–1, 48–50, 67–8, 85–8, 138. *See also individual enterprises*
  central, 9, 13, 62
South Africa, 69, 243, 248–64
  banking JV and changing circumstances, 22, 250, 257–9, 260, 262, 264
  exit terms of banking JV, 256–7
  Johannesburg Stock Exchange (JSE), 248, 252
  objectives of banking JV, 253
  terms and conditions of banking JV, 254–5
South African Standard Bank Group. *See* SB Group (South African Standard Bank Group)
South China Sea dispute, 94
South-east Asia, 27–8, 35, 45. *See also individual countries*
South Korea, 175, 192, 287
sovereign debt restructuring, 21, 235–47
  for business school audiences, 247
  Chinese practices, 241–4
  implications for Zambia and Africa, 244–5
  for law school audiences, 246
  for policy school audiences, 246–7
sovereign debtors, 239, 242
sovereign states, 153, 185, 241, 298, 309, 311, 314–16
sovereignty, 153, 241, 262
special economic zones. *See* SEZs (special economic zones)
SPIC (State Power Investment Corporation), 280
SPVs (Special Purpose Vehicles), 95, 100

Index

Sri Lanka, 20, 133–55, 174. *See also* CPC (Colombo Port City)
   background to China-funded infrastructure projects, 134–6
   Cabinet of Ministers, 139, 144–5, 150
   Port City Act, 152–5
   Rajapaksa regime, 135, 143, 149–50
   Right to Information (RTI) Act, 146
   UDA (Urban Development Authority), 144, 146
Sri Lanka Ports Authority. *See* SLPA (Sri Lanka Ports Authority)
stability, 94, 175, 237, 271
stakeholders, 67–8, 81, 85, 165–6, 209–10, 212, 215
   local, 78, 214, 272
Standard Bank London Holdings Limited. *See* SBLH (Standard Bank London Holdings Limited)
Standard Bank Plc, 249, 252–8, 261
standards, 3, 62, 91, 236, 275–6, 282
   human rights, 158, 161–2, 163, 170
   IFC Performance, 276
   international, 10, 276, 294
Standing Cabinet Appointed Review Committee. *See* SCARC (Standing Cabinet Appointed Review Committee)
State Administration for Market Regulation. *See* SAMR (State Administration for Market Regulation)
State Council, 5, 7, 8, 285
State Grid Brazil Holding. *See* SGBH (State Grid Brazil Holding)
State Grid Brazil Power. *See* SGBP (State Grid Brazil Power)
State Grid Corporation of China. *See* SGCC (State Grid Corporation of China)
state levels, 123, 127, 129
State-owned Assets Supervision and Administration Commission. *See* SASAC (State-owned Assets Supervision and Administration Commission)
state-owned banks, 31, 46
state ownership, 6, 29
State Power Investment Corporation. *See* SPIC (State Power Investment Corporation)
strategic location, 174–6, 188
strategies, 62, 86, 104–5, 110–12, 253, 306, 317
   communication, 229, 231
   coping, 119–24
   exit, 262, 264
   growth, 248, 252, 261

legal, 22, 110, 268
localization, 18, 20, 88–112
M&A (mergers and acquisitions), 62
mitigation, 306
students, 4, 76–7, 79–80, 82, 83, 123, 177, 184
subcontracting, 21, 105, 197–9, 209–10
subcontractors, 201–3, 205–6, 210
subsidiaries, 75, 94–5, 102–3, 105, 200–1, 220–1, 309
superpowers, 129, 193
supply chains, 2, 284, 285–6, 293, 296
Supreme Courts, 142, 147–51, 228, 288, 291
suspension, 42, 45, 83, 143–5, 219, 243
sustainability, 111, 239, 241, 246
sustainable development, 14–15, 16, 161–3, 268, 271–2, 274
Sustainable Development Goals (SDGs), 212, 214
sustainable governance, 14
Suzhou Gold Mantis. *See* Gold Mantis
synergies, 53, 57, 63, 95

Taiwan, 22–3, 284, 289–90, 291–4, 295
   courts, 284, 287, 294
   MOEAIC (Investment Commission of the Ministry of Economic Affairs), 289–90, 291
Taobao, 27, 30, 39–40, 45
tariffs, 55, 199
taxes, 30, 256, 269, 273
teams, 58, 62, 79, 81, 83, 97, 101
Technical, Vocational and Entrepreneurship Training. *See* TVET (Technical, Vocational and Entrepreneurship Training) project
technology, 82, 88, 184–5, 187, 291–3, 295–6
   firms, 12, 34, 41–2, 44. *See also individual firms*
Tencent, 39, 41, 114–15
TikTok, 20, 113, 115–30
   Americanization, 113, 119–20
   banning, 113, 115–19, 121–2, 126–8
   in Biden era, 122–4
   for business school audiences, 130
   and ByteDance, 114–15
   coping strategies, 119–24
   creators, 121–2
   for law school audiences, 127–9
   litigation, 120–2
   for policy school audiences, 129–30
   reactions from ByteDance and Chinese government, 124–6
   TikTok Global, 119–20
   use on US government devices, 116, 123–4, 128

tourism, 69, 152, 191, 199
tourist workers, 203–5
tourists, 177, 199, 203–4, 205, 208
trade, 3, 54, 74, 126, 130, 172, 180, 277
trade secrets, 22, 284–96
  for business school audiences, 295–6
  law and politics, 294
  for law school audiences, 294
  misappropriation, 284, 286, 290–1, 293
  for policy school audiences, 294
  theft, 289, 290–1, 293
trade unions, 69, 207, 215, 226, 230
trade war, US-China, 1, 3, 12, 22
training, 74, 76–7, 81–2, 83, 183–4, 193, 204, 225
transmission lines, 92, 95–6, 97–100, 104–5
transmission lines, Xingu-Estreito, 88–9, 90, 99–104, 108, 110
transnational legal standards, 161–2
transparency, 146, 158, 166, 236, 240, 245–6
transport, 10, 69, 70, 135, 191, 194, 201, 218
Transportation Security Administration (TSA), 117
treaties. *See* BITs (bilateral investment treaties); foreign investment treaties; international treaties
Trump, Donald, 117–21, 123, 124, 127, 130
Trump administration, 1, 121, 122, 126
trust, 36–9, 40, 149, 229, 245, 296
TSA (Transportation Security Administration), 117
TVET (Technical, Vocational and Entrepreneurship Training) project, 74–7, 80, 83–6
  implementation challenges, 77
  institutions, 77, 79, 81, 85
  Phase I, 76, 77, 86
  Phase II, 76–7, 78

UDA (Urban Development Authority), 144, 146
Uganda, 80, 83
UHVDC (ultra-high-voltage direct current), 88, 100
Ukraine, 69, 174, 259
UMC-Jinhua case, 22, 284, 287–9, 290–5
  court case, 287–9
  international responses, 291–3
  regulatory analysis, 289–91
UNCITRAL (United Nations Commission on International Trade Law), 298
UNDRIP (United Nations Declaration on the Rights of Indigenous Persons), 159–60

UNFCCC (UN Framework Convention on Climate Change), 272, 276
UNGPS (United Nations Guiding Principles on Business and Human Rights), 159–60
United Kingdom, 52, 114, 307, 316–17
United Nations
  Commission on International Trade Law (UNCITRAL), 298
  Declaration on the Rights of Indigenous Persons (UNDRIP), 159–60
  Framework Convention on Climate Change (UNFCCC), 272, 276
  Guiding Principles on Business and Human Rights (UNGPS), 159–60
  Resolution on the Right to a Clean, Healthy and Sustainable Environment, 157, 160
United States, 13, 199, 283–6, 291–4. *See also* Saipan
  Agency for International Development (USAID), 167
  Constitution, 120, 122, 128
  Department of Commerce, 1, 120, 122, 292
  Department of Justice, 292, 294
  Department of Labor (USDOL), 199, 205, 207–8
  government, 113, 116, 118, 122, 124, 291, 294
  market, 113, 115, 199
  Montana, 128
  oil refinery deal, 258–9
  state governments, 127–8
  and TikTok, 113–30
  Trade Representative (USTR), 39
  TSA (Transportation Security Administration), 117
  US-China tech war, 295–6
  US-China trade war, 1, 3, 12, 22
universal human rights. *See* human rights
unsafe conditions, 206, 225
unsolicited proposals, 138–9
Urban Development Authority. *See* UDA (Urban Development Authority)
US investment, 117, 118, 127
USDOL. *See* United States, Department of Labor (USDOL)
users, 28, 36–8, 40, 115, 116, 118, 121, 128
USTR (US Trade Representative), 39

variable interest entities (VIEs), 20, 28, 32–6, 46
videos, 117, 207, 312
Vietnam, 35, 156, 161, 164
villages, 79, 88, 223–4, 230
visas, 94, 180, 199, 203, 205, 206, 208, 211

Index

VSPT (Viña San Pedro Tarapacá S.A.), 20, 48, 49–50, 51–2, 58–62, 63
   directors, 59
   main shareholders, 59

wages, 73, 159, 209, 210, 227
Walmart, 119
Wang, Fred, 52–4
Wang, Yongming, 288
water, 51, 180, 219, 304
   clean, 166
   sources, 165, 224
wealth management products. *See* WMPs (wealth management products)
WeChat, 121, 206
wine, 48–63
wineries, 54, 58, 61, 63
WMPs (wealth management products), 37, 46
women, 29, 134, 215, 222
worker interviews, 197, 199
workers, 73, 198–200, 201–8, 209–11, 214–15, 222–8, 231
   Kyrgyz, 214–15, 222, 226
   migrant, 179, 211
   tourist, 203–5
workforces, 6, 179, 200, 205, 216
working conditions, 214, 224, 226
World Bank, 11, 16, 21, 187, 235–6, 238
Wuliangye, 50–3

Xi Jinping, 7, 32, 193, 207, 244, 268, 270, 272, 279
Xingu-Estreito transmission line, 88–9, 90, 99–104, 108, 110
   design, 103
Xingu-Rio transmission line design, 106

Yanghe, 48–54, 56, 58–61, 63
Yemen, 174, 188–9
Yu'ebao, 37

Zambia, 13, 21, 70, 83, 235–47
   government, 235, 238, 243, 244
   implications of Chinese sovereign debt restructuring practices, 244–5
   PF (Patriotic Front), 237
Zenith, 299, 303–6, 311
Zhongfu. *See* Zhongshan Fucheng Industrial Investment Co. Ltd., dispute between parties
Zhongfu FHC Action, 305
Zhongshan Fucheng Industrial Investment Co. Ltd., 22, 297–317
   arbitration, 308–14
   dispute between parties, 303–5, 306, 307, 309–12, 315
   mitigation strategies, 306
   Nigeria-related court proceedings, 305–6
   relationship between parties, 303
Zimbabwe, 83